Word 97 For Windows® For Dummies®

Cheat Sheet

The Standard Toolbar

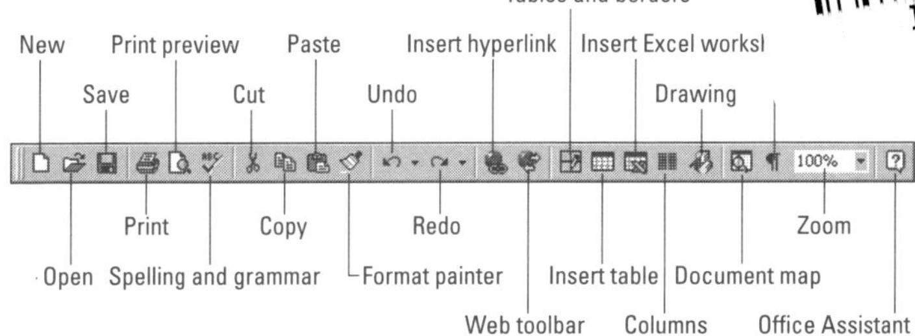

The Formatting Toolbar

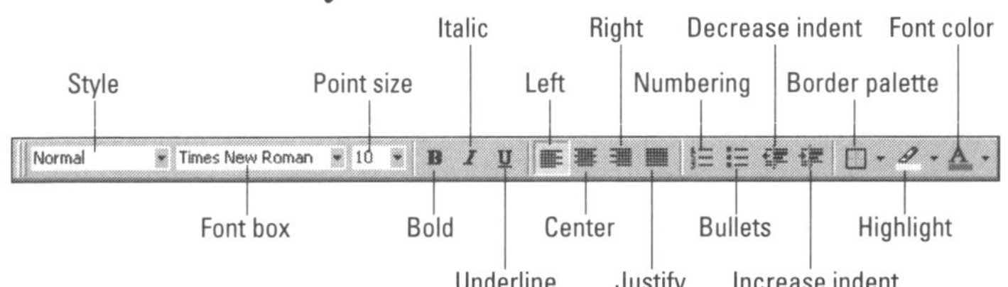

Helpful Tips

- Let the computer do the work! Let Word format your pages and insert page numbers, headers, and footers. Don't ever do that stuff manually on-screen.
- Always save your documents to disk!
- If a document has already been saved to disk, press Ctrl+S to update the document on disk.

Useful Tools

- To proof your document, press the F7 key or Alt, T, S.
- To use the thesaurus, press Shift+F7 or Alt, T, T.
- To print envelopes, press Alt, T, E.

Document Filenames

A document must be saved to disk using a Windows 95 filename. Here are the rules:

- Be brief and descriptive with your filenames.
- The filename can be from 1 to 255 characters long.
- The filename can contain letters and numbers in any combination.
- The filename cannot contain these symbols: \ < > * ? " | ; : /

Getting Around in a Document

↑	Moves toothpick cursor up one line of text
↓	Moves toothpick cursor down one line of text
→	Moves toothpick cursor right to the next character
←	Moves toothpick cursor left to the next character
Ctrl + ↑	Moves toothpick cursor up one paragraph
Ctrl + ↓	Moves toothpick cursor down one paragraph
Ctrl + →	Moves toothpick cursor right one word
Ctrl + ←	Moves toothpick cursor left one word
PgUp	Moves toothpick cursor up one screen
PgDn	Moves toothpick cursor down one screen
End	Moves toothpick cursor to end of current line
Home	Moves toothpick cursor to start of current line
Ctrl+Home	Moves toothpick cursor to top of document
Ctrl+End	Moves toothpick cursor to bottom of document

Word 97 For Windows® For Dummies®

Cheat Sheet

Word 97 for Windows Screen

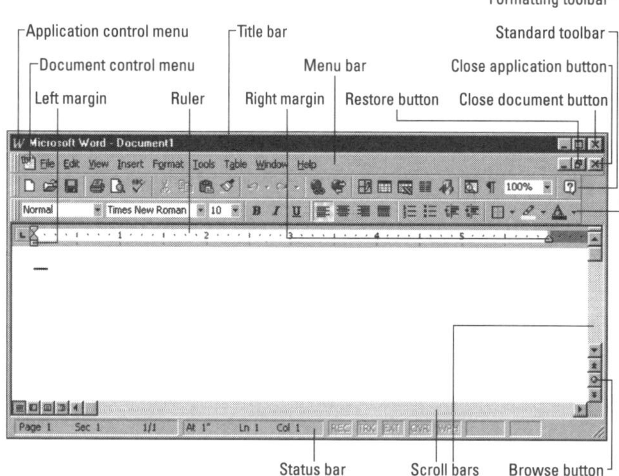

Cheat Sheet $2.95 value. Item 0052-X.

For more information about IDG Books, call 1-800-762-2974.

The Kindergarten Keys

Copy	Ctrl+C
Cut	Ctrl+X
Paste	Ctrl+V
Undo	Ctrl+Z

General Information

To start Word, first start Windows by clicking the Start button, then Programs, and then Microsoft Word.

- Use the Backspace key to back up and erase.
- Use the Delete key to delete a character.
- Press the Enter key to start a new paragraph.
- Press the Tab key to indent or align text.
- F1 is the Help key.
- Press the Escape key to cancel things and make dialog boxes go away.

Ctrl+S means to hold down the Ctrl (Control) key and press the S key. Release both keys. Alt, F, N means to press the Alt key, release it, press the F key, release it, press the N key, and release it.

Choose the Exit command from the File menu when you're ready to quit Word. Follow the instructions on-screen; save your document to disk.

Always quit Word and then quit Windows when you're done working for the day. Don't turn off your computer until you see the message telling you it's safe to do so.

Common Word Formatting Key Commands

Bold	Ctrl+B
Italic	Ctrl+I
Underline	Ctrl+U
Center text	Ctrl+E
Left align	Ctrl+L
Right align	Ctrl+R
Justify	Ctrl+J

Common Word Key Commands

Cancel	Escape
Go back	Shift+F5
Help	F1
Mark block	F8
New document	Ctrl+N
Open	Ctrl+O
Print	Ctrl+P
Quick save	Ctrl+S
Repeat command	F4
Repeat find	Shift+F4

...For Dummies: #1 Computer Book Series for Beginners

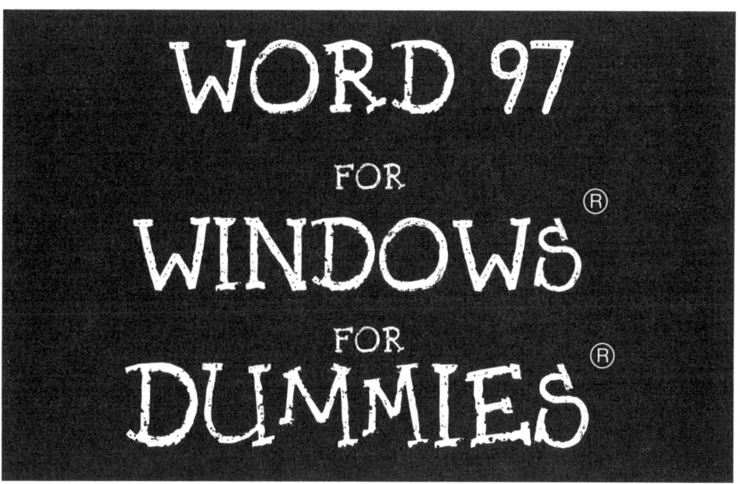

by Dan Gookin

IDG Books Worldwide, Inc.
An International Data Group Company

Foster City, CA ♦ Chicago, IL ♦ Indianapolis, IN ♦ Southlake, TX

Word 97 For Windows® For Dummies®

Published by
IDG Books Worldwide, Inc.
An International Data Group Company
919 E. Hillsdale Blvd.
Suite 400
Foster City, CA 94404
www.idgbooks.com (IDG Books Worldwide Web site)
www.dummies.com (Dummies Press Web site)

Library of Congress Catalog Card No.: 96-79273

ISBN: 0-7645-0052-X

Printed in the United States of America

10 9 8 7 6

1O/QZ/QR/ZX/IN

Distributed in the United States by IDG Books Worldwide, Inc.

Distributed by Macmillan Canada for Canada; by Transworld Publishers Limited in the United Kingdom; by IDG Norge Books for Norway; by IDG Sweden Books for Sweden; by Woodslane Pty. Ltd. for Australia; by Woodslane Enterprises Ltd. for New Zealand; by Longman Singapore Publishers Ltd. for Singapore, Malaysia, Thailand, and Indonesia; by Simron Pty. Ltd. for South Africa; by Toppan Company Ltd. for Japan; by Distribuidora Cuspide for Argentina; by Livraria Cultura for Brazil; by Ediciencia S.A. for Ecuador; by Addison-Wesley Publishing Company for Korea; by Ediciones ZETA S.C.R. Ltda. for Peru; by WS Computer Publishing Corporation, Inc., for the Philippines; by Unalis Corporation for Taiwan; by Contemporanea de Ediciones for Venezuela; by Computer Book & Magazine Store for Puerto Rico; by Express Computer Distributors for the Caribbean and West Indies. Authorized Sales Agent: Anthony Rudkin Associates for the Middle East and North Africa.

For general information on IDG Books Worldwide's books in the U.S., please call our Consumer Customer Service department at 800-762-2974. For reseller information, including discounts and premium sales, please call our Reseller Customer Service department at 800-434-3422.

For information on where to purchase IDG Books Worldwide's books outside the U.S., please contact our International Sales department at 415-655-3200 or fax 415-655-3295.

For information on foreign language translations, please contact our Foreign & Subsidiary Rights department at 415-655-3021 or fax 415-655-3281.

For sales inquiries and special prices for bulk quantities, please contact our Sales department at 415-655-3200 or write to the address above.

For information on using IDG Books Worldwide's books in the classroom or for ordering examination copies, please contact our Educational Sales department at 800-434-2086 or fax 817-251-8174.

For press review copies, author interviews, or other publicity information, please contact our Public Relations department at 415-655-3000 or fax 415-655-3299.

For authorization to photocopy items for corporate, personal, or educational use, please contact Copyright Clearance Center, 222 Rosewood Drive, Danvers, MA 01923, or fax 508-750-4470.

About the Author

Dan Gookin got started with computers back in the post slide rule age of computing: 1982. His first intention was to buy a computer to replace his aged and constantly breaking typewriter. Working as slave labor in a restaurant, however, Gookin was unable to afford the full "word processor" setup and settled on a computer that had a monitor, keyboard, and little else. Soon his writing career was under way with several submissions to (and lots of rejections from) fiction magazines.

The big break came in 1984 when he began writing about computers. Applying his flair for fiction with a self-taught knowledge of computers, Gookin was able to demystify the subject and explain technology in a relaxed and understandable voice. He even dared to add humor, which eventually won him a column in a local computer magazine.

Eventually, Gookin's talents came to roost as he became a ghostwriter at a computer book publishing house. That was followed by an editing position at a San Diego computer magazine, at which time he also regularly participated in a radio talk show about computers. In addition, Gookin kept writing books about computers, some of which became minor best-sellers.

In 1990, Gookin came to IDG Books Worldwide, Inc., with a book proposal. From that initial meeting unfolded an idea for an outrageous book: a long overdue and original idea for the computer book for the rest of us. What became *DOS For Dummies* blossomed into an international bestseller with hundreds and thousands of copies in print and many foreign translations.

Today, Gookin still considers himself a writer and computer "guru" whose job it is to remind everyone that computers are not to be taken too seriously. His approach to computers is light and humorous yet very informative. He knows that the complex beasts are important and can help people become productive and successful. Yet Gookin mixes his knowledge of computers with a unique, dry sense of humor that keeps everyone informed — and awake. His favorite quote is, "Computers are a notoriously dull subject, but that doesn't mean I have to write about them that way."

Gookin's titles for IDG Books include: *DOS For Dummies,* Windows 95 Edition; *PCs For Dummies,* 4th Edition; and the upcoming *Discovering Windows 95.* Gookin holds a degree in Communications from the University of California, San Diego, and lives with his wife and four boys in the rare and gentle woods of Idaho.

ABOUT IDG BOOKS WORLDWIDE

Welcome to the world of IDG Books Worldwide.

IDG Books Worldwide, Inc., is a subsidiary of International Data Group, the world's largest publisher of computer-related information and the leading global provider of information services on information technology. IDG was founded more than 25 years ago and now employs more than 8,500 people worldwide. IDG publishes more than 275 computer publications in over 75 countries (see listing below). More than 60 million people read one or more IDG publications each month.

Launched in 1990, IDG Books Worldwide is today the #1 publisher of best-selling computer books in the United States. We are proud to have received eight awards from the Computer Press Association in recognition of editorial excellence and three from *Computer Currents*' First Annual Readers' Choice Awards. Our best-selling *...For Dummies*® series has more than 30 million copies in print with translations in 30 languages. IDG Books Worldwide, through a joint venture with IDG's Hi-Tech Beijing, became the first U.S. publisher to publish a computer book in the People's Republic of China. In record time, IDG Books Worldwide has become the first choice for millions of readers around the world who want to learn how to better manage their businesses.

Our mission is simple: Every one of our books is designed to bring extra value and skill-building instructions to the reader. Our books are written by experts who understand and care about our readers. The knowledge base of our editorial staff comes from years of experience in publishing, education, and journalism — experience we use to produce books for the '90s. In short, we care about books, so we attract the best people. We devote special attention to details such as audience, interior design, use of icons, and illustrations. And because we use an efficient process of authoring, editing, and desktop publishing our books electronically, we can spend more time ensuring superior content and spend less time on the technicalities of making books.

You can count on our commitment to deliver high-quality books at competitive prices on topics you want to read about. At IDG Books Worldwide, we continue in the IDG tradition of delivering quality for more than 25 years. You'll find no better book on a subject than one from IDG Books Worldwide.

John Kilcullen
CEO
IDG Books Worldwide, Inc.

Steven Berkowitz
President and Publisher
IDG Books Worldwide, Inc.

Eighth Annual Computer Press Awards 1992

Ninth Annual Computer Press Awards 1993

Tenth Annual Computer Press Awards 1994

Eleventh Annual Computer Press Awards 1995

IDG Books Worldwide, Inc., is a subsidiary of International Data Group, the world's largest publisher of computer-related information and the leading global provider of information services on information technology. International Data Group publishes over 275 computer publications in over 75 countries. Sixty million people read one or more International Data Group publications each month. International Data Group's publications include: **ARGENTINA:** Buyer's Guide, Computerworld Argentina, PC World Argentina; **AUSTRALIA:** Australian Macworld, Australian PC World, Australian Reseller News, Computerworld, IT Casebook, Network World, Publish, Webmaster; **AUSTRIA:** Computerwelt Osterreich, Networks Austria, PC Tip Austria; **BANGLADESH:** PC World Bangladesh; **BELARUS:** PC World Belarus; **BELGIUM:** Data News; **BRAZIL:** Annuário de Informática, Computerworld, Connections, Macworld, PC Player, PC World, Publish, Reseller News, Supergamepower; **BULGARIA:** Computerworld Bulgaria, Network World Bulgaria, PC & MacWorld Bulgaria; **CANADA:** CIO Canada, Client/Server World, ComputerWorld Canada, InfoWorld Canada, NetworkWorld Canada, WebWorld; **CHILE:** Computerworld Chile, PC World Chile; **COLOMBIA:** Computerworld Colombia, PC World Colombia; **COSTA RICA:** PC World Centro America; **THE CZECH AND SLOVAK REPUBLICS:** Computerworld Czechoslovakia, Macworld Czech Republic, PC World Czechoslovakia; **DENMARK:** Communications World Danmark, Computerworld Danmark, Macworld Danmark, PC World Danmark, Techworld Denmark; **DOMINICAN REPUBLIC:** PC World Republica Dominicana; **ECUADOR:** PC World Ecuador; **EGYPT:** Computerworld Middle East, PC World Middle East; **EL SALVADOR:** PC World Centro America; **FINLAND:** MikroPC, Tietoverkko, Tietoviikko; **FRANCE:** Distributique, Hebdo, Info PC, Le Monde Informatique, Macworld, Reseaux & Telecoms, WebMaster France; **GERMANY:** Computer Partner, Computerwoche, Computerwoche Extra, Computerwoche FOCUS, Global Online, Macwelt, PC Welt; **GREECE:** Amiga Computing, GamePro Greece, Multimedia World; **GUATEMALA:** PC World Centro America; **HONDURAS:** PC World Centro America; **HONG KONG:** Computerworld Hong Kong, PC World Hong Kong, Publish in Asia; **HUNGARY:** ABCD CD-ROM, Computerworld Szamitastechnika, Internetto online Magazine, PC World Hungary, PC-X Magazin Hungary; **ICELAND:** Tolvuheimur PC World Island; **INDIA:** Information Communications World, Information Systems Computerworld, PC World India, Publish in Asia; **INDONESIA:** InfoKomputer PC World, Komputek Computerworld, Publish in Asia; **IRELAND:** ComputerScope, PC Live!; **ISRAEL:** Macworld Israel, People & Computers/Computerworld; **ITALY:** Computerworld Italia, Macworld Italia, Networking Italia, PC World Italia; **JAPAN:** DTP World, Macworld Japan, Nikkei Personal Computing, OS/2 World Japan, SunWorld Japan, Windows NT World, Windows World Japan; **KENYA:** PC World East African; **KOREA:** Hi-Tech Information, Macworld Korea, PC World Korea; **MACEDONIA:** PC World Macedonia; **MALAYSIA:** Computerworld Malaysia, PC World Malaysia, Publish in Asia; **MALTA:** PC World Malta; **MEXICO:** Computerworld Mexico, PC World Mexico; **MYANMAR:** PC World Myanmar; **NETHERLANDS:** Computer! Totaal, LAN Internetworking Magazine, LAN World Buyers Guide, Macworld Netherlands, Net, WebWereld; **NEW ZEALAND:** Absolute Beginners Guide and Plain & Simple Series, Computer Buyer, Computer Industry Directory, Computerworld New Zealand, MTB, Network World, PC World New Zealand; **NICARAGUA:** PC World Centro America; **NORWAY:** Computerworld Norge, CW Rapport, Datamagasinet, Financial Rapport, Kursguide Norge, Macworld Norge, Multimediaworld Norge, PC World Ekspress Norge, PC World Nettverk, PC World Norge, PC World ProduktGuide Norge; **PAKISTAN:** Computerworld Pakistan; **PANAMA:** PC World Panama; **PEOPLE'S REPUBLIC OF CHINA:** China Computer Users, China Computerworld, China InfoWorld, China Telecom World Weekly, Computer & Communication, Electronic Design China, Electronics Today, Electronics Weekly, Game Software, PC World China, Popular Computer Week, Software Weekly, Software World, Telecom World; **PERU:** Computerworld Peru, PC World Profesional Peru, PC World SoHo Peru; **PHILIPPINES:** Click!, Computerworld Philippines, PC World Philippines, Publish in Asia; **POLAND:** Computerworld Poland, Computerworld Special Report Poland, Cyber, Macworld Poland, Networld Poland, PC World Komputer; **PORTUGAL:** Cerebro/PC World, Computerworld/Correio Informático, Dealer World Portugal, Mac*In/PC*In Portugal, Multimedia World; **PUERTO RICO:** PC World Puerto Rico; **ROMANIA:** Computerworld Romania, PC World Romania, Telecom Romania; **RUSSIA:** Computerworld Russia, Mir PK, Publish, Seti; **SINGAPORE:** Computerworld Singapore, PC World Singapore, Publish in Asia; **SLOVENIA:** Monitor; **SOUTH AFRICA:** Computing SA, Network World SA, Software World SA; **SPAIN:** Communicaciones World España, Computerworld España, Dealer World España, Macworld España, PC World España; **SRI LANKA:** Infolink PC World; **SWEDEN:** CAP&Design, Computer Sweden, Corporate Computing Sweden, Internetworld Sweden, it.branschen, Macworld Sweden, MaxiData Sweden, MikroDatorn, Nätverk & Kommunikation, PC World Sweden, PCaktiv, Windows World Sweden; **SWITZERLAND:** Computerworld Schweiz, Macworld Schweiz, PCtip; **TAIWAN:** Computerworld Taiwan, Macworld Taiwan, NEW ViSiON/Publish, PC World Taiwan, Windows World Taiwan; **THAILAND:** Publish in Asia, Thai Computerworld; **TURKEY:** Computerworld Turkiye, Macworld Turkiye, Network World Turkiye, PC World Turkiye; **UKRAINE:** Computerworld Kiev, Multimedia World Ukraine, PC World Ukraine; **UNITED KINGDOM:** Acorn User UK, Amiga Action UK, Amiga Computing UK, Apple Talk UK, Computing, Macworld, Parents and Computers UK, PC Advisor, PC Home, PSX Pro, The WEB; **UNITED STATES:** Cable in the Classroom, CIO Magazine, Computerworld, DOS World, Federal Computer Week, GamePro Magazine, InfoWorld, I-Way, Macworld, Network World, PC Games, PC World, Publish, Video Event, THE WEB Magazine, and WebMaster; online webzines: JavaWorld, NetscapeWorld, and SunWorld Online; **URUGUAY:** InfoWorld Uruguay; **VENEZUELA:** Computerworld Venezuela, PC World Venezuela; and **VIETNAM:** PC World Vietnam. 3/24/97

Author's Acknowledgments

I would like to thank the French for enjoying past editions of this book so much. I hope this edition doesn't disappoint.

I'd like to acknowledge the contributions made by Ray Werner, who assisted with the original *Word For Windows For Dummies*. I'd also like to thank Lauren Straub, future CBS Evening News anchor, for her help with an earlier edition of this book.

Publisher's Acknowledgments

We're proud of this book; please register your comments through our IDG Books Worldwide Online Registration Form located at: `http://my2cents.dummies.com`.

Some of the people who helped bring this book to market include the following:

Acquisitions, Development, and Editorial

Project Editor: Bill Helling

Assistant Acquisitions Editor: Gareth Hancock

Copy Editor: Susan Diane Smith

Technical Editor: Publication Services, Inc.

Editorial Manager: Mary C. Corder

Editorial Assistant: Chris H. Collins

Production

Project Coordinator: Sherry Gomoll

Layout and Graphics: Cameron Booker, Linda M. Boyer, Maridee V. Ennis, Angela F. Hunckler, Todd Klemme, Jane E. Martin, Anna Rohrer, Brent Savage, Ian A. Smith

Proofreaders: Melissa D. Buddendeck, Joel K. Draper, Nancy L. Reinhardt, Rachel Garvey, Nancy Price, Dwight Ramsey, Robert Springer, Michelle Croninger

Indexer: Sharon Duffy

General and Administrative

IDG Books Worldwide, Inc.: John Kilcullen, CEO; Steven Berkowitz, President and Publisher

IDG Books Technology Publishing: Brenda McLaughlin, Senior Vice President and Group Publisher

Dummies Technology Press and Dummies Editorial: Diane Graves Steele, Vice President and Associate Publisher; Mary Bednarek, Acquisitions and Product Development Director; Kristin A. Cocks, Editorial Director

Dummies Trade Press: Kathleen A. Welton, Vice President and Publisher; Kevin Thornton, Acquisitions Manager; Maureen F. Kelly, Editorial Coordinator

IDG Books Production for Dummies Press: Beth Jenkins, Production Director; Cindy L. Phipps, Manager of Project Coordination, Production Proofreading, and Indexing; Kathie S. Schutte, Supervisor of Page Layout; Shelley Lea, Supervisor of Graphics and Design; Debbie J. Gates, Production Systems Specialist; Robert Springer, Supervisor of Proofreading; Debbie Stailey, Special Projects Coordinator; Tony Augsburger, Supervisor of Reprints and Bluelines; Leslie Popplewell, Media Archive Coordinator

Dummies Packaging and Book Design: Patti Crane, Packaging Specialist; Lance Kayser, Packaging Assistant; Kavish + Kavish, Cover Design

The publisher would like to give special thanks to Patrick J. McGovern, without whom this book would not have been possible.

♦

Contents at a Glance

Cartoons at a Glance

By Rich Tennant • Fax: 508-546-7747 • E-mail: the5wave@tiac.net

"HOW'S THAT FOR FAST SCROLLING?"

page 209

"OK, TECHNICALLY, THIS SHOULD WORK. JUDY, TYPE THE WORD 'GOODYEAR' IN ALL CAPS, BOLDFACE, AT 700-POINT TYPE SIZE."

page 331

"GENTLEMEN, I SAY RATHER THAN FIX THE 'BUGS', WE CHANGE THE DOCUMENTATION AND CALL THEM 'FEATURES'."

page 279

page 245

"THAT'S RIGHT, MS. BINGAMAN, HE'S COLLECTING A ROYALTY FROM EVERYONE ON EARTH, AND THERE'S NOTHING WE CAN DO ABOUT IT."

page 359

The 5th Wave By Rich Tennant

MY GOD! IT'S WORKING! I'M GETTING ITALICS!

page 117

"THAT REMINDS ME—I INSTALLED WORD 97 ON MY 386 LAST WEEK."

page 7

Table of Contents

Introduction

Welcome to *Word 97 For Windows For Dummies,* the 97th book on the 97th version of Word, which is really only about 12 years old. Whatever. This book tells you all the good stuff and none of the boring stuff about Microsoft's latest word processor.

So what is new with Word 97? Nothing, really. Oh, they've souped up a few things and added some bells and whistles. This book shows you what's important, what to ignore, and — most importantly — how to use this word processor to get your thoughts down on paper. But as far as revolutionary changes in computer word processing, Word 97 is nothing big. So there's nothing new to scare you with, which is always my intention.

The truth is that you don't need to know everything about Microsoft Word to use it. Heck, you probably don't *want* to know everything about Microsoft Word. You don't want to know all the command options, all the typographical mumbo-jumbo, or even all those special features that you know are in there but terrify you. No, all you want to know is the single answer to a tiny question. Then you can happily close the book and be on your way. If that's you, you've found your book.

This book informs and entertains. And it has a serious attitude problem. After all, I don't want to teach you to love Microsoft Word. That's sick. Instead, be prepared to encounter some informative, down-to-earth explanations — in English — of how to get the job done by using Microsoft Word. You take your work seriously, but you definitely don't need to take Microsoft Word seriously.

About This Book

This book is not meant to be read from cover to cover. If that were true, the covers would definitely need to be put closer together. Instead, this book is a reference. Each chapter covers a specific topic in Microsoft Word 97. Within a chapter, you find self-contained sections, each of which describes how to do a Microsoft Word 97 task relating to the chapter's topic. Sample sections you encounter in this book include the following:

- Saving your stuff
- Cutting and pasting a block
- Making italicized text
- Creating a hanging indent
- Printing envelopes
- Cobbling tables together
- "Where did my document go?"

There are no keys to memorize, no secret codes, no tricks, no pop-up dioramas, and no wall charts. Instead, each section explains a topic as if it's the first thing you read in this book. Nothing is assumed, and everything is cross-referenced. Technical terms and topics, when they come up, are neatly shoved to the side where you can easily avoid reading them. The idea here isn't for you to learn anything. This book's philosophy is to look it up, figure it out, and get back to work.

How to Use This Book

This book helps you when you're at a loss over what to do in Microsoft Word. I think that this situation happens to everyone way too often. For example, if you press Ctrl + F9, Word displays a {} thing in your text. I have no idea what that means, nor do I want to know. What I do know, however, is that I can press Ctrl + Z to make the annoying thing go away. That's the kind of knowledge you find in this book.

Microsoft Word uses the mouse and menus to get things done, which is what you would expect from Windows. Yet there are times when various *key combinations,* several keys you may press together or in sequence, are required. This book shows you two different kinds of key combinations.

This is a menu shortcut:

Alt,I,S

This shortcut means that you should press and release the Alt key, press and release the I key, and then press and release the S key. Don't type the commas or any period that ends a sentence.

This is a keyboard shortcut:

Ctrl + Shift + P

This shortcut means that you should press and hold Ctrl and Shift together, and then press the P key, and release all three keys.

Any details about what you type are explained in the text. And, if you look down at your keyboard and find ten thumbs — or scissors and cutlery — instead of hands, consider reading Chapter 2, "The Keyboard Is Your Friend," right now.

This book tells you the easiest and best way to perform tasks and offers you alternatives when appropriate. Sometimes it's best to use the mouse — sometimes the keyboard. This book also presents the best keyboard shortcuts and inserts toolbar icons in the margin for those who like to use the toolbar.

Menu commands are listed like this:

File⇨Open

This command means that you open the File menu (with the mouse or the keyboard — it's your choice) and then choose the Open command.

If I describe a message or something you see on-screen, it looks like this:

```
You've just erased all your files!
```

This book never refers you to the Microsoft Word manual or — yech! — to the Windows manual. Even so, it helps if you have a good Windows book as a reference. *PCs For Dummies,* 4th Edition, published by IDG Books Worldwide, Inc., contains lots of supplemental information you'll find useful.

What You're Not to Read

Special technical sections dot this book like late spring mosquito bites. They offer annoyingly endless and technical explanations, descriptions of advanced topics, or alternative commands that you really don't need to know about. Each one of them is flagged with a special icon or enclosed in an electrified, barbed wire and poison ivy box (an idea I stole from the Terwilliker Piano Method books). Reading this stuff is optional.

Foolish Assumptions

Here are my assumptions about you. You use a computer. You use Windows, specifically Windows 95. Microsoft Word 97 is your word processor. Anything else involving the computer or Windows is handled by someone whom I call your *personal guru*. Rely on this person to help you through the rough patches;

wave your guru over or call your guru on the phone. But always be sure to thank your guru. Remember that computer gurus enjoy junk food as nourishment and often accept it as payment. Keep a bowl of M&Ms or a sack of Doritos at the ready for when you need your guru's assistance.

Beyond you, your PC, and the guru, you also should have a computer worthy of running Windows 95. That means that you paid a lot more for it than if you had otherwise stuck with the older version of Windows. You also need a computer mouse. I make no bones about it: Without a mouse, Microsoft Word cannot be done. (By the way, when this book says to click the mouse button, I mean the left button — unless your mouse is set up differently in some way.)

One more thing: I call Microsoft Word 97 by its affectionate short form, *Word*. This name is completely unofficial and even the publisher made me (through the miracle of the Replace command) change Word to "Microsoft Word" in this introduction. Face it, the program is Word. That's what I call it in the main body of this text.

How This Book Is Organized

This book contains seven major parts, each of which is divided into three or more chapters. The chapters themselves have been Ginsu-knifed into smaller, modular sections. You can pick up the book and read any section without necessarily knowing what has already been covered in the rest of the book. Start anywhere.

Here is a breakdown of the parts and what you can find in them:

Part I: Your Basic Word

This is baby Microsoft Word stuff — the bare essentials. Here you discover how to giggle, teethe, crawl, walk, burp, and spit up. Then you can move up to the advanced topics of moving the cursor, editing text, searching and replacing, marking blocks, spell checking, and printing. (A pacifier is optional for this section.)

Part II: Formatting (Or Making Your Prose Look Less Ugly)

Formatting is the art of beating your text into typographical submission. It's not the heady work of creating a document and getting the right words. No, it's "You will be italic!" "Indent, you moron!" and "Gimme a new page *here*." Often, formatting involves a lot of yelling. This part of the book contains chapters that show you how to format characters, lines, paragraphs, pages, and entire documents without raising your voice (too much).

Part III: Working with Documents

Document is a nice, professional-sounding word — much better than *that thing I did with Microsoft Word. Document* is quicker to type. And you sound important if you say that you work on documents instead of admitting the truth that you sit and stare at the screen and play with the mouse. This part of the book tells you how to save and shuffle documents.

Part IV: Working with Graphics

Graphics play a major role in Windows, and Microsoft Word is geared toward having many interesting graphical bits and pieces. This part of the book discusses how graphics can work in your documents, how you can use special little programs that come with Word to create your own graphics, and how you can do some things that previously required a knowledge of desktop publishing (or at least knowing what a Mergenthaller was). The idea here is to make your document look o' so purty.

Part V: Strange Things Living Under the Hood

This part covers some general and miscellaneous topics, items that in previous editions of this book were considered to be too esoteric to be put in chapters on their own. My, how times have changed.

Part VI: Help Me, Mr. Wizard!

One school of thought is that every copy of Microsoft Word should be sold with a baseball bat. I'm a firm believer in baseball-bat therapy for computers. But before you go to such an extreme, consider the soothing words of advice provided in this part of the book.

Part VII: The Part of Tens

How about "The Ten Commandments of Word"? Or consider "Ten Features You Don't Use but Paid For Anyway." Or the handy "Ten Things Worth Remembering." This section is a gold mine of tens.

Icons Used in This Book

This icon alerts you to overly nerdy information and technical discussions of the topic at hand. The information is optional reading, but it may enhance your reputation at cocktail parties if you repeat it.

This icon flags useful, helpful tips or shortcuts.

This icon marks a friendly reminder to do something.

This icon marks a friendly reminder not to do something.

This icon means that you can use Microsoft's new Intellipoint mouse to do something.

Where to Go from Here

You work with Microsoft Word. You know what you hate about it. Why not start by looking up that subject in the table of contents and seeing what this book says about it? Alternatively, you can continue to use Microsoft Word in the Sisyphean manner you're used to: Push that boulder to the top of the hill, and when it starts to roll back on you, whip out this book like a bazooka and blow the rock to smithereens. You'll be back at work and enjoying yourself in no time.

Part I
Your Basic Word

"THAT REMINDS ME – I INSTALLED WORD 97 ON MY 386 LAST WEEK."

In this part . . .

If you know how to use a typewriter, you can probably use a word processor. Oh, don't be scared. You can do it. Human beings, of which you're probably one, can generally figure most things out by themselves. In my years of teaching people how to use word processors, I've seen folks all by themselves devise wondrous solutions for their word-processing puzzles. I've seen people type page numbers. I've seen people double-space lines by using the Enter key. I've even seen people adjust their margins by whacking the spacebar ten times at the start of each line. Each of these personal solutions works, and although these methods aren't exactly wrong, they are just not the best way to get things done.

In this part of the book you read about some of the basic parts of word processing with Microsoft Word, the proper and fast way to do things. After all, it's the computer that's supposed to do the work here.

Chapter 1

The Word Hokey Pokey

In This Chapter

- Starting Word
- Reading the Word screen
- Entering text
- Editing a document on disk
- Printing
- Saving your stuff
- Closing a document
- Moving on
- Exiting Word

Welcome to Chapter 1, the whirlwind tour of Word — just your basic stuff! This is what I call the Word Hokey Pokey. Like the children's song, in this chapter you start Word, look at the screen, put your left hand on the keyboard, print a document out, do the hokey pokey and turn yourself around, quit Word, and get on with your life. That's truly what it's all about.

Rather than gloat about the program or bore you to death with the history of word processing, this chapter slowly unravels the mysteries of Word. It's a top-down tour, taking you from starting the program, to writing something, to printing and saving, and finally to quitting Word. The details come later, though if you want to know them now, I include abundant cross-references for your page-flipping enjoyment.

Here Are the 495 Proven Ways to Start Word

Just kidding! I wouldn't show you all 495 ways Windows gives to start creating something in Word. Other books may list them all for you. This book shows you only two, with the first one being the fastest, bestest, and leastest painful. The second one was added because my editor insists that each section of this book have at least two subheads.

- You need to start your computer and have Windows 95 up and dancing on your screen before you can do anything in Word.
- Refer to my book, *PCs For Dummies*, 4th Edition, from IDG Books Worldwide, Inc., for more information on starting your computer and getting Windows 95 to do the two-step.

The best way to start Word (subhead one)

Here is the way you should start Word if you don't want to go crazy:

1. **Prepare yourself.**

   Physically, are you seated in a comfy chair? Are your hands properly poised over the keyboard — high enough so that your old typing teacher, Mrs. Lattimore, won't whack you with a ruler should your wrists drop a millimeter below your palms? Good.

   Mentally, ponder what you're about to do. "Will I become a computer nerd this way? And how would I look with that pocket protector and cellophane tape around the nose bridge of my glasses? Gosh, I don't even wear glasses! Okay. Deep breath. I will be brave."

2. **Locate the Start button.**

   The Start button is that thing that says Start in the lower-left corner of the screen (see Figure 1-1). Point the mouse at that thing and click the mouse's left button once.

   If you can't see the Start button, press the Ctrl+Esc key combination (the Ctrl and Esc keys together).

3. **Choose Programs⇨Microsoft Word.**

   Point the mouse at the word *Programs* on the Start thing menu. Soon a submenu appears. (You don't have to click the mouse, just point.)

   Look for the line on the Programs submenu that reads *Microsoft Word.* Click the mouse on that line. (Now you have to click.)

Watch in amazement as your computer whizzes and whirs. Before too long, you see a screen that looks like Figure 1-3 (look ahead a few pages). Word is stumbling into town! The whatzits of the screen are discussed in the section, "A Quick, Cursory Glance at the Word Screen."

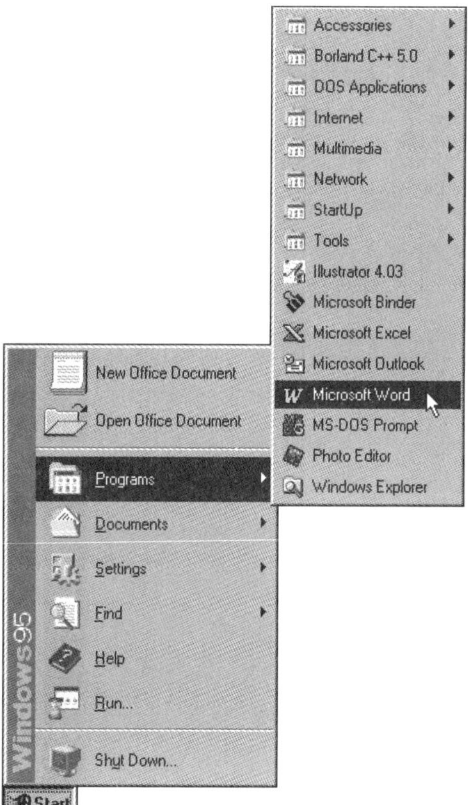

Figure 1-1: Here is where you find Word on the Start thing menu.

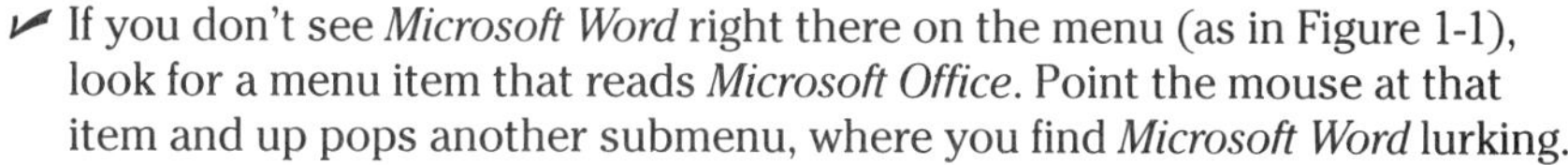

- If you don't see *Microsoft Word* right there on the menu (as in Figure 1-1), look for a menu item that reads *Microsoft Office*. Point the mouse at that item and up pops another submenu, where you find *Microsoft Word* lurking.

- Your computer can be set up to automatically run Word every time you turn it on. Think of the time that would save! If you want your computer set up in this manner, grab someone more knowledgeable than yourself — an individual I call a *computer guru*. Tell your guru to "make my computer always start in Word." If your guru is unavailable, frantically grab other people at random until you find someone bold enough to obey you.

- I prefer to run Word *full screen*, maximizing its window so that nothing else bugs me when I'm writing. To run Word in the full-screen mode, click the box button (the middle one) in the upper-right corner of the window. This button *maximizes* Word to fill the entire screen. If Word is already maximized, two overlapping boxes appear on the button; you don't need to click anything in that case.

The "I want to start a new document" method (subhead two)

If you've installed Microsoft Office on your computer (of which Word is a part), you need not wade through any of the Start thing's menus. Just click the Start button (see Step 2 in the preceding section) and look at the top of the menu for the New Office Document item. Click that item, and you see the New Office Document window (see Figure 1-2).

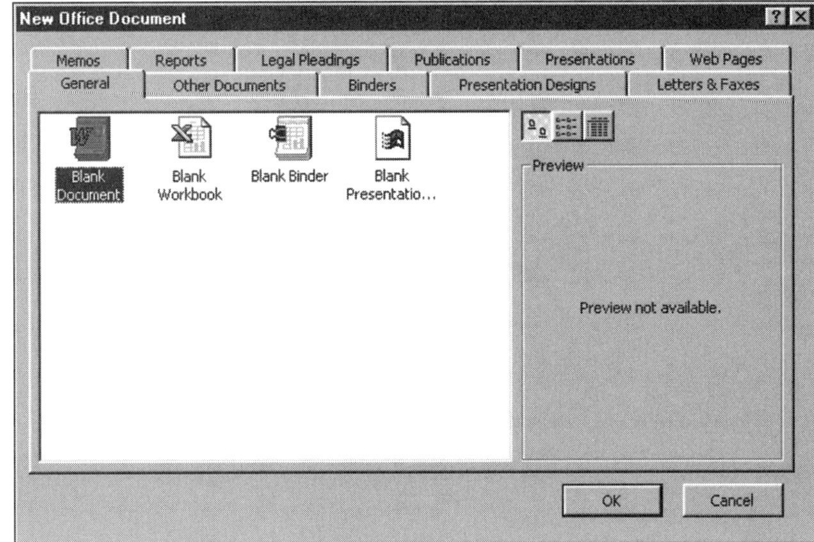

Figure 1-2: The New Office Document window.

Locate the Blank Document icon in the New Office Document Window and double-click it. Click-click. This action starts Word right up with a new document, ready for you to create some snappy bit of text.

Trivial information (bonus subhead)

Each chapter is divided into main heads and subheads. For example, the following section is titled "A Quick, Cursory Glance at the Word Screen," which is a main head. The smaller headings are subheads, which are topics related to the main head.

In Word parlance, a subhead is known as Heading 2. The main heads are Heading 1. Refer to Chapter 15 for the grimy details.

A Quick, Cursory Glance at the Word Screen

After Word starts, you are faced with the electronic version of "The Blank Page," the same idea-crippling concept that induced writer's block in several generations of typewriter users. With Word, the situation is worse; the screen is not only mostly blank, it is surrounded by bells, whistles, switches, and doodads that would be interesting only if they were edible.

Figure 1-3 shows the typical, blank Word screen. A few things are worth noting:

- Several separate strips of stuff: bars, ribbons, rulers, and other horizontal holding bins for horrendous heaps of hogwash. Each strip performs some function or gives you some information. I warn you not to memorize this list: the *title bar,* the *menu bar,* the *Standard toolbar,* the *Formatting toolbar* (also known as the ribbon), and the *ruler* (who thinks he's the king or something). Refer to the nearby, easily avoidable technical information sidebar, "Forbidden information about strip bars," if you want to load your brain with the details of these strips and bars.
- A large empty space. Any text you type and edit appears here. Somewhere in this empty space is the flashing *insertion pointer* — which looks like a blinking toothpick — that tells you where the text you type appears.
- A little square window that contains your animated Assistant — an annoying little helper who's supposed to make using Word easier — or not. I put off discussion of this, uh, *thing,* until Chapter 25. Go there to find out more from the Assistant, or just turn it off.
- The bottom of the Word screen contains the *status bar.* No, this is not a yuppie hang-out. The status bar contains a great deal of information that would impress a bureaucrat but that, frankly, makes my eyes glaze over. The gibberish that is usually there explains where you are in your document. Several word fragments are always followed by numbers (like a tenth-grade algebra problem). Table 1-1 explains what this stuff means.
- Figure 1-3 shows Word in the "Normal" view. If it looks different on your screen, choose View⇨Normal from the menu.
- The final doojobbie on the bottom of your screen is Windows' own taskbar, which is used to hop, skip, and flop between various Windows programs or windows on the screen. Cheerfully ignore this thing while you're using Word.

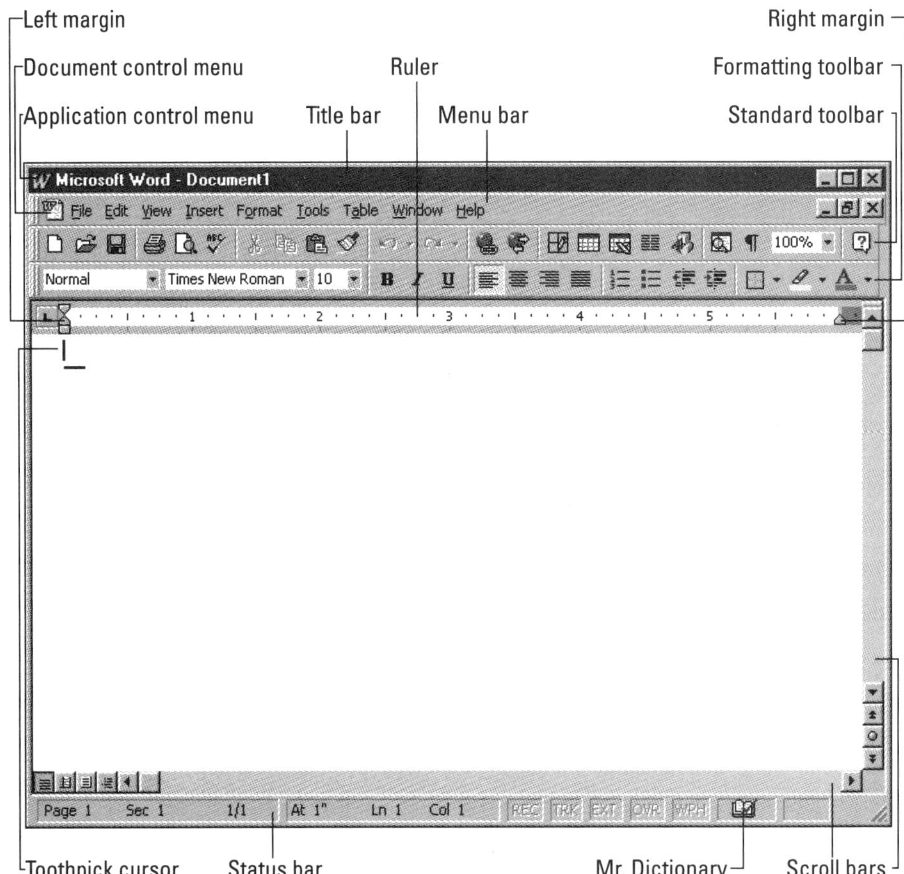

Figure 1-3: Word on the screen.

Table 1-1	**Stuff Lurking on the Status Bar**
Algebra Problem	***What It Means***
`Page` ***xx***	The page you're editing: `1` = the first page, `8` = the eighth page, and so on.
`Sec` ***xx***	The section of the document you're editing (sections are something just about everyone ignores): `1` = the first section, `8` = the eighth, and so on. This number is almost always `1` for section 1.
x/x	The page of the document you're editing appears *over* the total number of pages in the document. So `1/8` means that you're on page one of an eight-page document. (This display is not a math problem; `1/8` does not mean .125 here.)
`At` ***x.xx"***	How far from the top of the document your text is in inches: `At 4.89"` means that the line you are editing is 4.89 inches from the top of the page. Like you would care.

Algebra Problem	*What It Means*
`Ln` ***xx***	What line you're editing: `Ln 5` means that you're working on line 5, the fifth line down where line 1 is the first line on the page.
`Col` ***xx***	What column you are in (columns being those vertical support structures for Greek-style architecture). In Word, the first column starts on the left side of the page, and the `Col` (column) numbers get bigger as you type toward the right side of the page. This number is usually the number of characters and spaces you are over from the left margin.
TLA boxes	These boxes contain various TLAs (three-letter acronyms or abbreviations or what-have-you) — odd things to stick at the bottom of the screen, anyway. They appear dimmed when the option they represent isn't active. Check out the techy sidebar, "What those TLAs mean," for the obscure function each of them may serve.
Mr. Dictionary	This guy looks like a book with a magic pen writing something down. Actually, it's Word's on-the-fly document proofer in action — a truly annoying piece of software engineering you can read about in Chapter 7. (Mr. Dictionary becomes Mr. Printer when you print something in Word.)
Mr. Empty	The last box on the status bar is there to prove to you that Word *really does* save your file to disk. When Word saves something, a wee disk appears in the window. Otherwise you can use this box as a paper clip holder.

- My advice? Ignore the weird numbers on the status bar; concentrate instead on your writing. After all, only the truly disturbed would whip out a ruler and measure a piece of paper in a typewriter as they go along. (The numbers come in handy later to tell you how much stuff you've written or to find your way to a particular spot in a long document. Pretend that they don't exist for now.)
- Four buttons appear in the lower-left corner of your document, just above the status bar. Call them Larry, Moe, Curly, and Outline. They control how you see your document on-screen, a subject dealt with at length in Chapter 30. Please don't mess with them before you read that chapter.
- Any weird stuff you see on-screen (a ¶, for example) is a Word secret symbol. Refer to "Out, Damn Spots!" in Chapter 30 for additional information.
- The exact spot where the text appears is called the *cursor.* It's also called an *insertion pointer* because traditional computer cursors are underlines that slide under what you type. I prefer the term *toothpick cursor* because *insertion pointer* is just too medically geometric for my tastes. Characters you type appear immediately to the left of where the toothpick cursor is flashing, and then the cursor moves forward and waits for the next character.

What those TLAs mean

The status bar contains five boxes with strange letter combinations in them. This list tells you what they mean:

`REC`: Someone, possibly you, is recording a macro. The word `REC` lets you know that you're recording the macro, which is better than repeating, "Okay, I'm recording a macro" over and over in your head. Macros are so obtuse that I am not even covering the subject in this book.

`TRK`: You're telling Word to compare (track) the changes between the document on your screen and any former versions you may have. This feature enables you to see where someone else has made changes — revisions — to your document. See Chapter 27 for some information.

`EXT`: Text is being selected, or blocked off, by using the F8 key — handy thing to know. For more information, see Chapter 6.

`OVR`: Overtype mode is on. Refer to your orthodontist for correction (or look in Chapter 4 for information about deleting text).

`WPH`: For some silly reason, WordPerfect Help is on. As if anyone ever learned all those cryptic WordPerfect commands in the first place. When the letters appear dimmed, the option is off. Black letters mean that the option is on.

Incidentally, you can switch any option on or off by double-clicking its cryptic TLA with your mouse. Better refer to the chapters mentioned above before you mess with such a trick.

- The flat, bold line at the end of your text is the End-of-Text marker. Below this line is a vast, vacuous, void of a place. Nothing exists in the white space below this marker, not even blank pages — only infinite nothingness. The End-of-Text marker is the steel beam that supports your text, holding it from harm's way, in the evil nothingness that exists below your text.
- The *mouse pointer* is different from the toothpick cursor. Normally, it's an arrow pointer-like thing. But if you move the mouse around the writing part of the screen, the pointer changes. Over your text, the pointer becomes what's commonly called an *I-beam.* The I-beam means "I beam the insertion pointer to this spot when I click the mouse."

- You can use the mouse to see what some of the little buttons and things with pictures on them do in Word. Just hover the mouse pointer over the button and voilà! Instant information crystals.
- If you don't actually see the Standard or Formatting toolbars or the ruler, refer to Chapter 30.

Entering Text

Enough looking around!

Forbidden information about strip bars

This section has nothing to do with strip bars. Instead, the topic here is the information you get from those strips of information on the Word screen. Some of them may be visible — others may not show up at all. Chapter 30 discusses turning them on or off.

Title bar: The first strip shows the name of your document. Every window in Windows has a title bar as well as the various buttons and gizmos Windows is famous for: the Control menu, the Maximize and Minimize buttons, the Close button, and the scroll bars you may see on the right and bottom sides of a window. (Please refer to your favorite book on Windows for an explanation of how all this stuff works and what relevance it has.)

Menu bar: The second strip contains a list of menus, each of which disguises a pull-down menu you use to choose the many Word commands at your beck and call.

Standard toolbar: The third strip has lots of buttons you can click to quickly use some of the more common Word commands. This strip may or may not be visible on your screen, depending on how Word is set up. The setup is discussed in Chapter 30.

Formatting toolbar: The fourth strip probably contains the word Normal, on the left side. As with the Standard toolbar, this strip is optional. On the Formatting toolbar, you find the commands that apply styles, type sizes, fonts, attributes (bold, italics, and underline), justification choices (left, center, right, and full), tabs, and other fun formatting frivolity. Again, see Chapter 30 for more information about the toolbars.

Ruler: The fifth strip looks like a ruler. It is. As with the standard toolbar and the Formatting toolbar, your screen may not show the ruler — especially if the country you're in despises monarchy.

To compose text in Word, use your *keyboard* — that typewriter-like thing sitting in front of your computer and below the monitor. Go ahead, type away; let your fingers dance upon the keycaps! What you type appears on-screen, letter for letter — even derogatory stuff about the computer. (Your PC doesn't care, but that doesn't mean that Word lacks feelings.)

New text is inserted right in front of where the toothpick cursor is blinking. For example, you can type this line:

```
We should leave before the roof caves in.
```

If you want to change the sentence, move the toothpick cursor to just before the T in *the*. Type the following text:

```
our upstairs neighbor has another Oreo and
```

The new text is inserted as you type, with any existing text marching off to the right (and even to the next line), happily making room.

You may need to type an extra space after *and* to separate it from the next word.

The whole sentence should now read:

```
We should leave before our upstairs neighbor has another Oreo
and the roof caves in.
```

- You compose text on-screen by typing. Every character key you press on the keyboard produces a character on-screen. This fact holds true for all letter, number, and symbol keys. The other keys, mostly gray on your keyboard, do strange and wonderful things, which the rest of this book tries hard to explain.
- If you make a mistake, press the Backspace key to back up and erase. This key is named Backspace on your keyboard, or it may have a long, left-pointing arrow on it: ←.

- There is no cause for alarm if you see spots — or dots — on-screen when you press the spacebar. These special doohickeys let you "see" spaces on-screen. See Chapter 30 for the lowdown.
- I cover moving the toothpick cursor around the screen in Chapter 3, "Getting Around Your Document."
- The Shift key produces capital letters.

- The Caps Lock key works like the Shift-Lock key on a typewriter. After you press that key, everything you type is in ALL CAPS.
- The Caps Lock light on your keyboard comes on when you're in All Caps mode.
- The number keys on the right side of the keyboard are on the *numeric keypad*. To use those keys, you must press the Num Lock key on your keyboard. If you don't, the keys take on their arrow key function. See Chapter 3, "Getting Around Your Document."

- The Num Lock light on the keyboard comes on when you press the Num Lock key to turn the numeric keypad on. Most PCs start with this feature activated.
- If you're a former typewriter user, please type **1** for the number one (not an I or a little L), and please type **0** for the number zero, not a capital letter O.
- See Chapter 2, "The Keyboard Is Your Friend," for some handy tips on typing and using your keyboard.

- No one needs to learn to type to use a word processor, but you'll do yourself a favor if you learn. My advice is to get a computer program that teaches you to type. Knowing how to type makes a painful experience like Word a wee bit more enjoyable.

Typing away, la la la

Eons ago, a word processor was judged superior if it had the famous *word-wrap* feature. This feature eliminated the need to press the Enter key at the end of each line of text, which is a requirement when you're using a typewriter. Word and all other modern word processors have this feature. If you're unfamiliar with word-wrap, you should get used to putting it to work for you.

With Word, when the text gets precariously close to the right margin, the last word is picked up and placed at the start of the next line. You don't need to press the Enter key, except when you want to end a paragraph.

- Press Enter to create a new paragraph. If you want to split one paragraph into two, move the toothpick cursor to the middle of the paragraph, where you want the second paragraph to start, and press Enter.
- You have to press the Enter key only at the end of a paragraph, not at the end of every line.

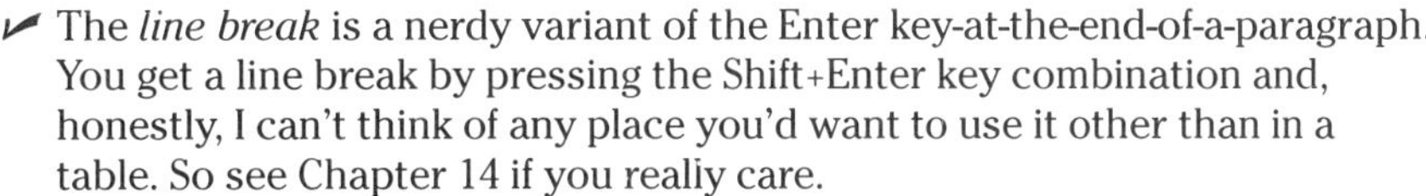

- The *line break* is a nerdy variant of the Enter key-at-the-end-of-a-paragraph. You get a line break by pressing the Shift+Enter key combination and, honestly, I can't think of any place you'd want to use it other than in a table. So see Chapter 14 if you really care.
- Don't be afraid to use your keyboard! Word always offers ample warning before anything serious happens. A handy Undo feature recovers anything you accidentally delete. See Chapter 2, "The Keyboard Is Your Friend."

That annoying line of dots

Occasionally, you see a row of dots stretching from one side of the screen to the other — like a line of ants in military school, marching straight across your screen. Don't spray 'em with bug killer! That thing marks the end of one page and the beginning of another and is called a *page break.* The text you see above the ants, er, dots, is on the preceding page; text below the dots is on the next page.

- You cannot delete the line of dots. C'mon — what good would it even do? Think picnic: You sweep one trail of the little pests away and another trail instantaneously appears. It's insect magic!
- You can see how the line of dots works by looking at the scrambled statistics on the status bar. For example, when the toothpick cursor is above the dots, the status bar says `Page 5` for page 5. When the cursor is below the dots, you see `Page 6` for page 6.
- A row of dots close together — very friendly ants — marks a *hard page break.* The words `Page Break` even appear right in the middle of the line. This row of dots indicates a definite "I want a new page now" command given by the person who created the document. See Chapter 13, "Formatting Pages and Documents."

Editing a Document You've Already Saved to Disk

You use Word to create *documents.* The documents can be printed or saved to disk for later editing or printing. When a document has been saved to disk, it's considered a *file* "on" the disk. (You can still refer to it as a document without any fear of social embarrassment.)

Word offers several ways to load and edit a document already on disk. Because this is Windows, why not use the mouse-menu method?

1. **Choose the File⇨Open command.**

   Using the mouse, click the word File on the menu bar, and a drop-down menu, well, drops down. Click the Open menu command, and the Open dialog box appears, as shown in Figure 1-4. (You can also click the Open tool, pictured to the left.)

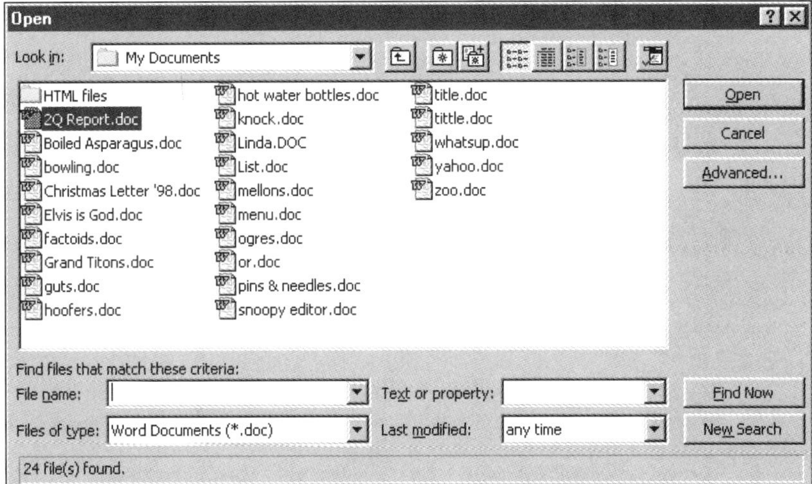

Figure 1-4: The Open dialog box.

2. **Select the name of the document (or file) you want to open and edit.**

   Find the document name in the list and double-click it. You can use the controls in the Open dialog box to whisk yourself around your disk drive and scout out files. Using the Open dialog box is standard Windows stuff. When you find your file, highlight it and Open; or just double-click the filename with the left mouse button.

- If the cat is playing with your mouse, you can open the Open dialog box by pressing Alt,F,O, the menu shortcut, or use the keyboard shortcut Ctrl+O. Then you can use the keyboard to type a filename — although this method is so primitive that you had better lock the door first. No one wants to be seen using a *keyboard* in Windows!
- If you do end up typing the name of the document you want to load, make sure that everything is spelled right; Word is finicky about filename spelling. You can type it in either upper- or lowercase letters; the result is the same. Or you can select the name with the mouse by clicking it. That way, you don't have to worry about spelling.
- The term *editing* means to read, correct, or add to the text you have composed and saved to disk. This process involves using the cursor keys, which I cover in Chapter 2, "The Keyboard Is Your Friend." Also see Chapter 4, "Deleting Text (Or The Art of Un-writing)"; Chapter 5, "Finding and Replacing"; and Chapter 6, "Text Blocks, Engine Blocks, Writers' Blocks."

- If you want to edit a file you recently had open, pull down the File menu and look at the list on the bottom of the menu to see whether the file is listed. Word "remembers" the last few documents you worked on. If you see what you want there, click the file's name to open it.
- When you finish editing a document, you print it, save it back to disk, or do one and then the other. I cover printing later in this chapter, in the section "Getting It Down on Paper (Printing)"; saving a document to disk is covered in the section "Save Your Stuff!"
- Documents you save to disk are given their own, special name. This name — a filename — can be from 1 to 255 characters long and can contain spaces, periods, and all sorts of other hogwash. Honestly, you're better off if you keep your filenames short and to the point. Chapter 20 discusses this in lurid detail.
- Also see Chapter 8 for more information on working the Open dialog box.

Getting It Down on Paper (Printing)

After entering what you feel is the best piece of written work since Hugo wrote *Les Misérables,* you decide that you want to print it. After all, dragging the computer around and showing everyone what your prose looks like on-screen just isn't practical.

To print your document in Word — the document you see on-screen, all of it — do the following:

1. **Make sure that your printer is on and ready to print.**

   Refer to Chapter 9 for additional information about preparing the printer if you need it.

2. **Choose the File➪Print command. (You can also click the Print tool, depicted on the left, on the Standard toolbar.)**

   The Print dialog box opens. This is the place where printing and related activities happen.

3. **Click the OK button with the mouse.**

   Zip, zip, zip. The document comes out of your printer. Or whir, crunch, flap-blap-blap, the document comes out of your laser printer all nice and toasty.

- When you print, the little dictionary on the status bar changes to a wee li'l printer spewing out pages. Out of what you paid for Word, that trick probably cost you $2.56.
- You can also summon the Print dialog box by pressing Alt,F,P or Ctrl+P. This method is more desirable if you have long fingers or do needlepoint or if the mouse is off eating the cheese again.

- You don't need to click the OK button when you click the Print tool on the Standard toolbar; your document instantly prints.
- Chapter 9 provides detailed information about printing , including information about making sure that your printer is ready to print.
- To print only part of your document — a paragraph, page, or block — refer to Chapter 6.

Save Your Stuff!

Word doesn't remember what you did the last time you used the computer. You must forcefully tell it to *save* your stuff! The document on-screen must be saved in a file on disk. To do this, you have to use the Word Save command.

To save a document to disk, choose the File➪Save command, Alt+F, S. (You can also click the Save button on the Standard toolbar, which looks like a wee li'l disk.) This step saves your document to disk. Or if the file hasn't yet been saved, a Save As dialog box appears. In that case, type a name for the file. Click the Save button after you're done.

- If the document you created hasn't yet been saved to disk, you have to give Word a filename to remember it by. The name is how you recognize the file later, when you want to edit or print it again. Type the document's name in the dialog box. If you make a mistake typing, use the Backspace key to back up and erase. Click Save to save the file.

- The fastest way to save a file is to use the keyboard. The Save file key combination is Ctrl+S. Press and hold the Ctrl (Control) key and press the S key. If you can't pick up a basketball with one hand, you can also use the Shift+F12 key combo.

- When you save a document, watch the status bar — it is temporarily replaced with a message that Word is saving your document (or fast saving, for our Frequent Fliers).
- If you entered a forbidden filename, Word tells you about it by displaying an error message. If you're using the Annoying Office Assistant (see Chapter 25), it tells you about the bad filename. Click the OK button and then try again with a new filename (and read the nearby sidebar, "Complicated — but important — information about filenames").
- Save your documents to disk so that you can work on them later! The documents can be reloaded into Word the next time you start it. Refer to the section "Editing a Document You've Already Saved to Disk" earlier in this chapter.
- After the document has been saved to disk, you see its name displayed on the window's title bar. This display is your clue that your document has been saved to disk.

- If you're not in a clever mood, you may decide to name your file with the name of a file already on disk. This decision is a boo-boo because the newer file *overwrites* the other file with the same name already on disk. For example, if you decide to save your new letter by using the LETTER filename and LETTER already exists on disk, the new file overwrites the old one. There is no way to get the original back, so use another, more clever name instead. Word warns you with this message:

  `Do you want to replace the existing` *`whatever`*`?`

  Click the No button. Use another name.
- See Chapter 20, "Managing Files," for more information about filenames and such.

Closing a Document

If you're finished with a document, you can make it vanish from your screen by "closing" it, which is similar to ripping a sheet of paper out of your typewriter — without the satisfying sound it makes.

To close a document, choose the File⇨Close command (Alt,F,C). This step closes the document window and makes it vanish from the screen. Zzzipp! (Although you have to say "Zzipp!" when you do this; Word is strangely mute on the point.)

Complicated — but important — information about filenames

You must name your file according to the Windows loving, yet firm, file-naming rules. This task isn't as tough as memorizing stuff for a DMV test, and it's not as horrid as things were in the ancient days of DOS — but it's darn close:

- A filename can be up to 255 characters long, so just about anything you want to type is okay.

  Even so, try to keep your filenames short and descriptive.

- A filename can include letters, numbers, and spaces and can start with a letter or a number.
- The filename cannot contain any of the following characters:

  \ / : * ? " < > |

- Don't bother typing a three-letter extension — .DOC — on the end of any of your Word files.

Here are some sample filenames:

LETTER: A prim and proper filename, though it lacks passion, like a salad without the garlic. A better and more descriptive example would be the following filename.

LETTER TO MOM: This filename actually describes the type of document and what it's about — without requiring much extra typing.

CHAPTER 1: Another okay filename. Notice how numbers and letters can be mixed — no oil and vinegar here!

941 FORM: A fine, upstanding filename; numbers are okey-dokey.

M*A*S*H: Oops! The forbidden * (asterisk) character has been used. Shame, shame, shame.

I.LOVE.YOU: This example is okay, but it looks stupid. Probably someone who used to work on a mainframe thunk up this one. The alternative, however, is correct and looks much better:

I LOVE YOU: Aw, shucks. I love you, too.

- Why close a document? Because you're done working on it! Maybe you want to work on something else or quit Word after closing. The choices are yours, and they're explained in the next section.
- If you try to close a document before it has been saved, Word displays a warning dialog box. Click the Yes button to save your document. If you want to continue editing, click the Cancel button and get back to work.
- If you are working on one document and you close it, Word looks like it's vacated the premises; toolbars and menus disappear, as do scroll bars and other screen debris. Don't panic; you've just closed a document and Word has little else to do. Word sits patiently and waits for your next command. (See the section "Moving Right Along . . ." for what you can do next.)

- If you're working on other documents, another one appears on-screen in place of the document you just closed. See Chapter 18 for information about working with multiple documents.

Moving Right Along . . .

When the document is closed and Word has gone into comatose mode, you have several options for what to do next. I won't mention the "take a break" or "play with the mouse pointer" options. And if you know how to switch over and play Solitaire for a few eyeball-glazing hours, that's up to you as well. But within Word, you have several options.

First, you can start working on another document on disk. Refer to "Editing a Document You've Already Saved to Disk," earlier in this chapter.

Second, you can start working on a new document. Do this by clicking the "I wanna blank sheet o' paper" button on the Standard toolbar. Or, if you lead a complex life, press the Ctrl+N key combination (or choose the File⇨New command), and click OK in the New dialog box. This action starts you off again with a clean, blank sheet of "electric" paper. Now it's up to the word-processing muse to get you going again.

Third, you can quit Word and do something else in Windows. Refer to the next section.

You don't have to quit Word when you just want to start working on a new document.

Quitting Word When You're All Done

Knowing when to leave is the height of proper etiquette. For example, your three-year-old decides it's too hot in the grocery store and, despite your best parenting efforts, he begins to disrobe. So before he runs down the cereal aisle in the nude, you should discover something else you need to do and leave quickly. It's just proper. Leaving Word is properly accomplished by using the File⇨Exit command. This common Windows command is used to quit all Windows applications and programs.

To politely excuse yourself, get up and leave Word and choose the File menu by clicking it once with the mouse. Then, near the bottom of the list, look for the word Exit. Click that with the mouse. Poof! Word is gone.

- If you haven't yet saved your document, Word asks whether you want to do so before it quits. Again, Word is just being polite. Click Yes to save any unsaved files. This part is important. Then, Word peaceably steps aside and lets you do something else in Windows, possibly something fun. (If the document doesn't yet have a name, Word asks you to think up a name to save your document; refer to "Save Your Stuff!," earlier in this chapter.)

- The File⇨Exit command (Alt,F,X or Alt+F4) is the proper way to exit Word. Do not, under any circumstances, reset or turn off your PC to quit Word. These actions are utterly irresponsible, and you'll go to Computer Etiquette Jail for life if you're ever caught — and that's in Redmond, Washington! You also run the very real risk of scrambling stuff on your disk so well that you won't ever get it back.

- Suppose that you don't want to quit, but instead you just want to get rid of a document and start on a new one. Refer to "Closing a Document," earlier in this chapter. Then refer to "Moving Right Along . . .," for information about starting over with a new document for editing.
- Exiting Word returns you to the Windows Desktop. If you want to turn your machine off, choose the Shutdown command from the Start button's menu; press Ctrl+Esc, U, and then click the Yes button. Only turn off your computer when Windows says that it's safe to do so.
- You can find more information on turning off your computer in *PCs For Dummies,* from the bosom of IDG Books Worldwide, Inc.

Some things that may be bugging you

Word is full of surprises. And if you just upgraded to the latest version, you're probably sitting there right now, scratching your head over why all those surprises were added and what they have to do with *writing* anyway? Allow me to sate your quizzical desires.

One of the most annoying new surprises in Word is the sound. Most of the things you do in Word have sounds attached to them. If your PC is equipped with a sound card, you hear these sounds whenever you save a document, undo something, or perform one of many trivial tasks in Word. If you're eager to turn the sounds off, refer to Chapter 30.

Another thing you may need help with is Word's own Help System. The feature is designed to tell you some specifics about how the program works. Although this book is really your first, best reference, you can use the Help System to find out some details or just to prove to yourself, once again, that the people who concoct computer programs can't write helpful information. To see how the Help System works (or doesn't work), refer to Chapter 25.

Finally, if you're eager to use the new Microsoft Intellipoint mouse with Word, you have to wait until you stumble across an appropriate section in this book. After all, the wheel mouse (which is what I call it) is merely a tool and is not to be worshipped on its own. Primarily, you'll use the Quasimodo of rodents for scrolling your document. You read more about that in Chapter 3.

Chapter 2

The Keyboard Is Your Friend

In This Chapter

- Using the keys on your keyboard
- Pressing the keys
- Knowing when to press the Enter key
- Knowing when to use the spacebar
- Using the Undo and Redo keys
- Using the Kindergarten Keys: Cut, Copy, and Paste
- Using the Help key
- Using the Repeat key

Until they invent a computer you can talk into, everyone will have to settle for using a keyboard to type in a word processor. Yes, the idea sure sounds primitive. You have to use a typewriter keyboard to compose your thoughts in Word just as your ancestors did on noisy typewriters. Word processors offer advantages, of course. But on a basic level, you use the keyboard just like Mark Twain did when he wrote *Tom Sawyer,* the first novel ever created on a typewriter.

If this chapter had a theme, it would be "Be bold!" Yes, even though the keyboard is connected to a computer and not a Smith Corona, it's nothing to be afraid of. For some reason, most people are so timid about using their computer keyboards you'd think there were land mines under the key caps. It just isn't true! Word won't let you do anything sinister by accident; you're always asked a yes/no question before the dangerous-something happens. And then the handy Edit⇨Undo command exists to undo any boo-boos. So fear not the keyboard, gentle reader. The keyboard is your friend.

Hello, Keyboard

Take a look at your keyboard and then at Figure 2-1.

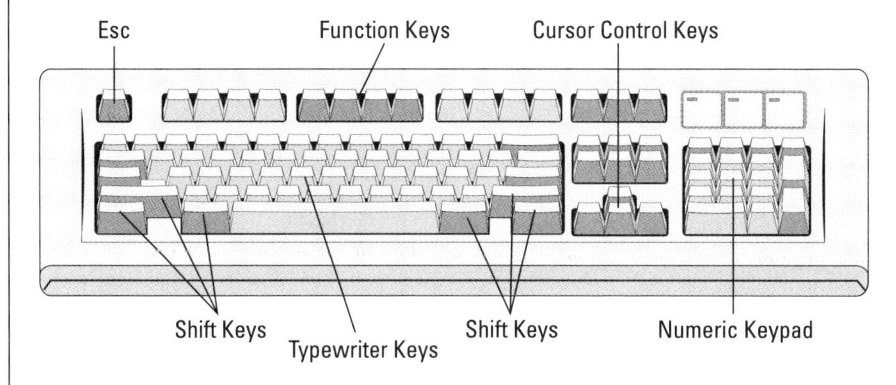

Figure 2-1: Key locations on the keyboard.

See how the keyboard is divided into separate areas, each of which has a special function? You use these keys in Word, either alone or in combination with other keys:

- **Function keys:** Along the top row of the keyboard, labeled F1 through F12. These keys are used alone or in cahoots with the Ctrl, Alt, and Shift keys.
- **Typewriter keys:** Standard *alphanumeric* keys you find on any typewriter: A through Z, 1 through 0, plus symbols and other exotic characters.
- **Cursor keys:** Arrow keys that move the toothpick cursor around the screen. Also lumped in are the Home, End, PgUp or Page Up, PgDn or Page Down, Insert, and Delete keys. Oh, and the big plus and minus keys on the keypad are counted as well.
- **Don key:** A domesticated ass. Like a little, stupid horse.
- **Numeric keypad:** These keys toggle (meaning that they can't make up their minds) between cursor keys and numbers. The split personality is evident on each key cap, which displays two symbols. The Num Lock key and its corresponding light are on if the numeric keypad (1, 2, 3) is active. If the cursor keys (arrows, Home) are active, Num Lock is off.
- **Shift keys:** These keys don't do anything by themselves. Instead, the Shift, Ctrl, and Alt keys work in combination with other keys.

These two individual keys are worth noting:

- **Enter:** Marked with the word Enter and sometimes a cryptic, curved arrow-thing: ⮐. You use the Enter key to end a paragraph of text.

- **Escape:** The Escape key may be labeled Esc on your keyboard. This key is handy to use in Word, but its location may vary. Sometimes Escape is next to the Backspace key. Find its location on your keyboard.
  - Be thankful: A piano has 88 keys, black and white, with no labels. It takes years to master. A computer, by comparison, is easy.
  - Antique PC keyboards have a layout that is different from the currently popular, 101-key enhanced PC keyboard. Some older models have the function keys to the side of the keyboard; some are lacking the separate cursor keys. They all work the same under Word, but this book assumes that you have the 101-key keyboard. (Go ahead and count 'em; there are 101 keys.)
  - Laptop keyboards are all goofed up. Primarily, they lack the numeric keypad. This is okay, but you'll miss the gray plus and minus keys, which can be used for some special formatting commands, divulged in Chapter 10.

Depressing the Keys

When I say to "depress the Enter key," you should look at your keyboard, stare the Enter key square in the eye and say, aloud, "You, you funny-looking key. You're worthless. All the other keys hate you. My right pinky hates you. You're despised! You should leave the keyboard right now and hide in shame, you worthless key, you!" There, now the Enter key is quite depressed.

Seriously, you don't "depress" any key on your keyboard. You *press* keys. Press them down, and then release them. Actually, any swift tapping motion will do. And the better keyboards pleasingly click for you, making your typing as noisy as it would be on an old manual Olympia.

Aside from regular typing, you need to use various key combinations to tell Word how to carry out certain commands. For example:

Ctrl+P

Or if you can lift a basketball with one hand, you can try:

Ctrl+Shift+F12

Both keyboard shortcuts open the Print dialog box — which isn't really important right now. Instead, what that key combination tells you is to press and hold the Ctrl and the Shift key and then press the F12 key. Release all three keys. Or press and hold the Ctrl key while you press P, and then release both keys.

These key combinations appear all the time. Always press and hold the first key (or keys) and then press the last key. Press and release.

- This method works just like pressing Shift+F to get a capital F. It's the same thing, but with the odd Ctrl (Control) and Alt (Alternate) keys.
- Yeah, you have to really reach to get some of those key combinations.
- You don't need to press hard. If you're having trouble working a keyboard shortcut, pressing harder doesn't make the computer think, "Oh, Lordy, she's pressing really hard now. I think she means it. Wake up, wake up!" A light touch is all that's required.

- Remember to release the keys: Press and hold the Ctrl key, press P, and then release both keys. If you don't know which one to release first, release the second key and then the Shift key (Shift, Ctrl, Alt) last.
- Click the Cancel button if you accidentally open the Print dialog box. See Chapter 9 for more information.
- You can also use menu-key shortcuts, which aren't the same as function-key combinations. For example, Alt,F,P chooses the File⇨Print command, the same as Ctrl+Shift+F12. However, Alt,F,P is a menu shortcut, not a function-key combination. Notice that commas separate the keys instead of + signs adding them together. The commas mean that you press and release each of the keys alone. For example, to print by using the menu-key shortcut, press and release Alt, press and release F, and then press and release P. Of course, Ctrl+P is still the easier keyboard option.

When to Press That Enter Key

On an electric typewriter, you press the Return key.

With a word processor, you press the Enter key.

On an electric typewriter, you press the Return key at the end of each line.

With a word processor, you press the Enter key only when you reach the end of a paragraph.

So even though there is no Return key on your computer's keyboard, don't pretend the Enter key works the same way. For example, type the following text. Just type it all and don't bother pressing the Enter key, nope, not at all:

```
"But," J.B. protested, "I followed your instructions to the
letter. I turned off the car's engine and switched off the
headlights. I then rolled silently through the checkpoint's
```

```
out-most lanes while they were busy with other traffic.
You guys never said anything about doing it at night!"
```

You'll notice that the text *wraps,* putting the last part of the text on the next line. And, unlike a typewriter, there is no audible *ding* when you hit the right margin; you don't have to press Enter at the end of the line.

Your word processor *word-wraps* any words hanging over the right margin and moves them down to the next line on the page. Therefore, you have to press Enter only at the end of a paragraph, even a short paragraph that is just a line of text by itself.

- Some people end a paragraph with two presses of the Enter key; others use only one press.
- If you want to indent the next paragraph, press the Tab key after pressing Enter. This technique works just like it does on a typewriter.
- If you want to double-space a paragraph, you have to use a special line-formatting command, covered in Chapter 11, "Formatting Sentences and Paragraphs." You do not use the Enter key to double-space lines.
- If you press the Enter key in the middle of an existing paragraph, Word inserts a new paragraph. The rest of your text is moved to the beginning of the next line. This works like any other key inserted in your text. The difference is that you insert an Enter character, which creates two paragraphs where you had one before.
- You can delete the Enter character by using the Backspace or Delete keys. Removing Enter joins two paragraphs together or, if you press Enter more than once, cleans up any extra blank lines.
- If you make any typos or spelling mistakes in Word, you see them underlined with a wavy red line. That's Word's annoying real-time spell checker in action. Turn to Chapter 7 to discover the secret way to turn it off.

- Your computer has an Enter key because it descends from a calculator background; most calculators (the expensive ones) sport an Enter key. Electric typewriters, on the other hand, used the Return key. Of course, they're obsolete today. (And I won't mention anything about the Macintosh computer having a Return key in the same breath as an electric typewriter. Nope. No way!)

When to Whack the Spacebar

A major vice committed by many Word users is mistakenly using the spacebar rather than the Tab key. Allow me to clear the air on this one.

Use the spacebar to insert space characters, such as between words or between sentences.

Use the Tab key to indent, align columns of information, or organize what you see on-screen.

The spacebar produces the "space character" on the screen. This character separates words and sentences, so the stuff you write doesn't look like Latin on Roman architecture. You know:

EREHAYISETYAYNOTHERAYAEMPLETAY

You should press the spacebar only once between each word or sentence, although some former touch typists (myself included) put two spaces between two sentences. That's fine, but one space is the norm for word processing.

The Tab key, on the other hand, indents text to an exact position. When you print, everything is lined up nice and neat. This organization doesn't happen with the space characters, which tend to bunch up and get confused, making your text look ugly and causing yourself undue embarrassment.

- Use the Tab key to indent; use the spacebar only when you're putting spaces between words and paragraphs. I'm serious: Do not use the spacebar to indent or line up your text. Your stuff will look tack, tack, tacky if you do.
- In fact, I'll make up a new rule right now: Any time you're tempted to use more than two spaces in a row, use a Tab instead. The word-processing gods will bless you.
- The Romans couldn't put spaces between words on buildings because the Chislers Union didn't know how to charge for it.
- To set the tab stops in Word, see Chapter 12, "Setting Tabs and Margins."

Erase Your Mistakes with Undo Haste

Be bold! Why not? Word has a handy Undo command. The Undo command remembers the last several things you added or deleted and quite easily unravels any mistakes you made. Furthermore, there's a Redo command, which is essentially Undo-Undo, though that's a double-negative, and it hurts my brain to think about it.

"Now mark me how I will undo myself." — *Richard II,* William Shakespeare

The blessed Undo command

To undelete any text you just accidentally zapped, do any of the following:

Press Ctrl+Z.

Choose Edit⇨Undo with the mouse.

Press Alt,E,U.

Click the Undo tool on the toolbar.

These are all methods of grasping for the Undo command, though the quickest way to undo something is to press the Ctrl+Z key combination.

- When you choose Edit⇨Undo, the last action you did is undone; if you choose Edit⇨Undo again, you undo whatever you did before that.
- Yeah, you can keep using the Undo command until you're back in bed sleeping in the morning.
- As if!
- The Undo item in the Edit menu changes to pertain to whatever needs undoing: Undo Bold, Undo Typing, Undo Boo-boo, and so on.
- If you're annoyed by the sound the Undo command makes (and I ponder how strange that seems . . . but anyway), refer to Chapter 30 to discover how to turn the darn sound off.
- To undo an Undo, choose Redo. See the section "Redo, or Take Two" a couple of sections from now.
- Yabba-dabba-do.
- The handy Undo command is used in almost all Windows applications.

Undoing stuff you did a while back

Because the Undo command remembers several things you just did, you can select any one of them individually for undoing. You do this by clicking the down-arrow next to the Undo button on the standard toolbar. There you find a brief and terse list of actions (up to 99 of them) Word remembers and can undo. Select any one of them for undoing, but keep in mind that they're out of sequence. To undo everything up to a point, select the action that you want as well as everything above it. Or just keep whacking Ctrl+Z until something looks familiar to you.

Can't Undo? Here's why . . .

Sometimes it eats you alive that Word can't undo an action. On the menu bar, you even see the message `Can't Undo`. What gives?

Essentially, whatever action you just did, Word can't undo it. This result can be true for a number of reasons: There is nothing to undo; not enough memory is available to undo; Word can't undo because what you did was too complex; Word just forgot; Word hates you; and so on.

I know that it's frustrating, but everyone has to live with it.

Redo, or Take Two

If you undo something and — whoops! — you didn't mean to, you must use the Redo command to set things back. To undelete any text you just accidentally zapped, do any of the following:

Press Ctrl+Y.

Choose Edit⇨Redo with the mouse.

Press Alt,E,R.

Click the Redo tool on the toolbar.

How would this work? Well, pretend that Earl stops by your office to bug you and sits his big old butt on your keyboard. He chats for a while and then leaves. You notice that his butt did some typing you don't like. So you use the Undo keyboard shortcut a few times:

Ctrl+Z

Ctrl+Z

Ctrl+Z

But — whoops! — you pressed one Ctrl+Z too many. In that case, use the Edit⇨Redo command (or Ctrl+Y) to yank back the stuff you just undid.

- Honestly, no one uses the Redo command that much. If you do, you'll find it can be very frustrating.
- Like the Undo command, the Redo command has a button on the Standard toolbar. Next to the button is a down-arrow, which you can click to review the last few things you just undid. Or re-did. Or katydid. Oy.
- If there's nothing to redo, the Redo command becomes the Repeat command. See the section "The Repeat Key," just a few paragraphs away in this chapter.

The Kindergarten Keys: Cut, Copy, and Paste

Chapter 6 covers cutting, copying, and pasting text. Three of the keys you use to perform those feats are covered here, however, because by the time you get to Chapter 6, this stuff won't make any sense. The three keys are shown in this list:

Cut	Ctrl+X
Copy	Ctrl+C
Paste	Ctrl+V

Now, I can understand Copy as Ctrl+C. *C* is Copy. And Cut is Ctrl+X. Sorta like X-ing something out, the text disappears from your document right there. But Paste — well, he is a little more complicated.

Paste is Ctrl+V. V for what? Vomit? How about the word *weld* with a German accent? Veld? Does that make sense? Whatever. But what does make a modicum of sense is that these keys — X, C, and V — are all nestled close together on your keyboard (see Figure 2-2). Even the Z key, for Ctrl+Z Undo, is right there. I bet Mr. Qwerty never assumed that the day he designed the keyboard layout in 1870-something.

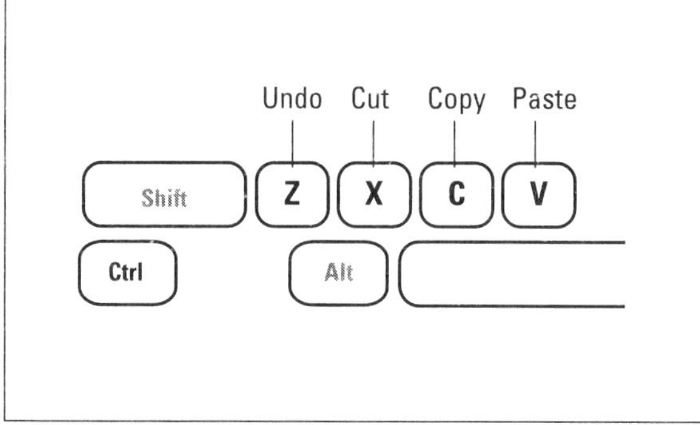

Figure 2-2: How the kindergarten keys line up.

- The Cut, Copy, and Paste (and Undo) keys are all related to commands living in the Edit menu.
- After you get the hang of them, you'll use these keys often to save time.
- Kindergarten is one of only a handful of German words used in English. You'd think there'd be more, but there aren't. (Now French words . . . Oo, la-la!)

The Help Key

No key on your keyboard is labeled *Help*. PCs just aren't that nice. The closest you come to a help key is the F1 key — which is the Windows Help key, by the way.

Don't expect much by pressing the F1 key. It's true that a little man (or thing) may actually appear, ready to help you, but he's only pretending. Refer to Chapter 32 for that and other information on getting help with Word.

The Repeat Key

Here's a good one: The F4 key in Word is known as the Repeat key, and it can be a real time-saver. If you press a Word command, cursor key, or character, and then press the F4 key, that command, cursor key, or character is repeated. (You can also choose the Edit⇨Repeat Typing command or press Ctrl+Y.)

For example, type the following lines in Word:

```
Knock, knock.
Who's there?
Madame.
Madame who?
```

Now press the F4 key. Word repeats the last few things you typed, which includes the hours of entertainment from these lines plus anything else you typed before them.

- Ctrl+Y, the Redo keyboard shortcut, also acts as the Repeat keyboard shortcut — but only when there's nothing to redo (meaning nothing left to undo-undo). For certain, F4 is the repeat key.
- A practical use of the Repeat key is creating forms. Type a bunch of underlines on-screen — your form's blank lines — and then press Enter. Press the F4 key a few times, and the page is soon filled with blank lines.

- F4 not only echoes text, this key is also especially useful when you issue the same command over and over, like when you are doing a find-and-replace, inserting the date, inserting special characters, or extensively formatting a document.
- If you use the F4 key along with the Shift key, as in Shift+F4, Word repeats your last Find or Go To command (see Chapter 5, "Finding and Replacing").
- The F4 key isn't your only access to the Repeat command. It also lives on the Edit menu, although it may be listed as Repeat Typing, Repeat Formatting, or any of a number of Repeat *blank* options.

Chapter 3

Getting Around Your Document

In This Chapter

- Using the arrow keys
- Using Ctrl with the arrow keys
- Moving around your document
- Using the Go To command
- Scrolling through your document
- Going back
- Using the highly useful Bookmark command

When you scribble on a pad of paper, it's hard to lose your place. And in the old typewriter days, a page of paper was only so big. But with Word at the dawn of the 21st century, your documents can be downright humongous. Unfortunately, only a small part of that humongousness appears on your computer screen at a time. To get from one place to another you need to do more than just press the arrow keys. You need to find out about Word's navigation keys and other special commands you can use to get around your document.

Your Basic Arrow Keys

The most common way to move about in your document is to press the arrow keys, which are called the *cursor-control keys* because they control the toothpick cursor on-screen.

On your keyboard, you can find the cursor-control keys on the numeric keypad, and they are duplicated between the keypad and the typewriter keys. The location of these cursor-control keys is shown in Figure 3-1. This duplication enables you to activate the numeric keypad by pressing the Num Lock key and still have access to a set of cursor-control keys.

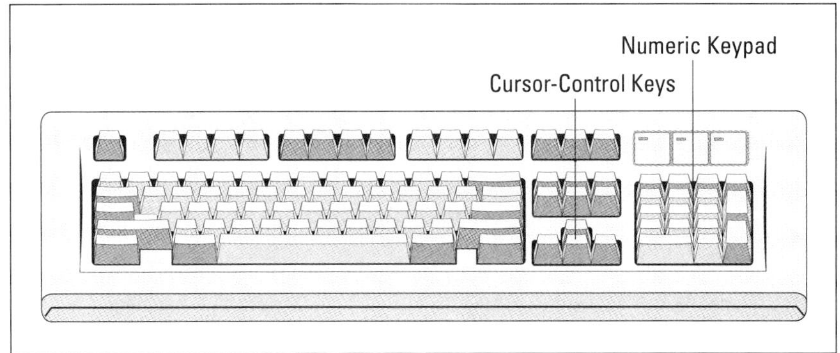

Figure 3-1: Cursor-control key locations.

The four basic cursor-control keys are the up-, down-, right-, and left-arrow keys. On the numeric keypad, they are on the 8, 2, 6, and 4 keys:

↑	Moves the cursor up to the preceding line of text
↓	Moves the cursor down to the next line of text
→	Moves the cursor right to the next character
←	Moves the cursor left to the preceding character

- The cursor-control keys on the numeric keypad and the separate cursor-control keys work in the same way; you can use either set. But keep your eye on that Num Lock light! It must be off for the keypad cursor-control keys to work.

- The mouse provides a quick and easy way to move the toothpick cursor: First spy a new location for the cursor on-screen. Then move the mouse pointer to where you want the cursor to be and click the left mouse button. The cursor is instantly relocated.
- If the cursor is on the top line of the document window (the top line of text) and you press the up-arrow key, the document scrolls to reveal the preceding line of text, if there is one. If not, the computer beeps at you, and the cursor stays in place and blinks with that special look it reserves for the recently deceased.
- When the cursor is on the last line of the screen and you press the down-arrow key, the document scrolls up to reveal the next line of text, if there is one.
- If the cursor has no where to go, Word bleeps at you. Annoyed? Turn to Chapter 30 to find out how to turn the sound off.
- Moving the cursor does not erase characters.

Using Ctrl with the Arrow Keys

If you press and hold the Ctrl (Control) key and then press an arrow key, the toothpick cursor jumps more than one character. This is cursor afterburner mode (rumor has it that this is the *only* cursor mode Arnold Schwarzenegger uses).

Ctrl+↑	Moves the cursor up one paragraph
Ctrl+↓	Moves the cursor down to the next paragraph
Ctrl+→	Moves the cursor right one word
Ctrl+←	Moves the cursor left one word

Press and hold the Ctrl key and then press an arrow key. Release both keys. You don't have to press hard; use the Ctrl key the same as you would the Shift key.

- Ctrl+← and Ctrl+→ always move the cursor to the first letter of a word.
- Ctrl+↑ and Ctrl+↓ always move the cursor to the beginning of a paragraph.
- If you press Ctrl and click the mouse, you highlight, or *select,* a sentence in your document. Click again (without the Ctrl key) to move the cursor or to unhighlight the sentence (see Chapter 6 for information about selecting blocks).

Moving by Great Leaps and Bounds

You could just use the simple cursor keys and, Lordy, it would take you weeks to get around a long document. Besides that, you'd have to poke your finger at the keys and risk contracting Woodpecker Pointy Finger Syndrome. Instead, heed the advice in the following sections for moving around your document in great leaps and bounds.

Moving up and down one screenful of text

No need to adjust your chair here. The screen does not show you the entire document — usually not even a whole page (unless you're working on another 23rd Psalm-on-a-postage-stamp project). To see the next or preceding screen, press the PgUp and PgDn keys. These keys move you or your document (I can't tell which) around by the screenful.

Not-so-moving information about moving the cursor

As you move the cursor around, look at the status bar on the bottom of your screen. It gives you some valuable information about your location within a document:

```
Page 2 Sec 1 2/6 At 2.5" Ln 6
   Col 42
```

The status bar shows which page you are on, which section you are in, your position with regard to the total number of pages in your document, how far down the document you are in inches, the slope of your biorhythm, and the number of past lives. Nah, those Microsoft techies aren't that progressive. Actually, the Ln and Col values tell you which line (from line 1 at the top of the page) and column (from the left margin) the cursor is on — useless stuff, but informative.

PgUp: Moves the cursor up one screen. Or if you're at the tippy-top of your document, this key moves you to the top of the screen.

PgDn: Moves the cursor down one screen or to the end of the document, if you happen to be there.

It's funny how PgUp and PgDn, where Pg is rumored to be short for *page,* moves you up and down a *screen* at a time. You'll get used to this illogic, if you're not already.

Moving to the top or bottom of the current screen

Sometimes you want to zip to the top or bottom of the current screen. This task is easy to do:

Ctrl+Alt+PgUp	Moves the cursor to the top of the current screen
Ctrl+Alt+PgDn	Moves the cursor to the bottom of the current screen

Moving to the end of a line

To get to the end of a line of text, press the End key.

- To move to the end of a paragraph, press Ctrl+↓ and then ←. Pressing Ctrl+↓ actually moves to the beginning of the *next* paragraph. Pressing the ← key moves you back to the end of the current paragraph.
- Moving to the beginning of a line is accomplished with the Home key, which is covered . . . well, here it is.

Moving to the beginning of a line

To get to the beginning of a line of text, press the Home key.

- There's no key like Home.
- To move to the beginning of a paragraph, press Ctrl+↑.

Moving up and down one page at a time

You knew that there had to be a way to move up and down by page. Whereas the obvious PgUp and PgDn keys move you up or down a *screen* at a time, moving around a page at a time requires the able assistance of the Ctrl key:

Ctrl+PgUp	Moves the cursor to the beginning of the current page
Ctrl+PgDn	Moves the cursor to the beginning of the next page

A page is actually a printed page of text, which you can see on-screen by a line of dots marching from left to right. The Pg thing to the left of the status bar (on the bottom of the screen) also tells you which page you're looking at.

Moving to the end of a document

If you use the Ctrl key with the End key, as in Ctrl+End, you're whisked to the end of your document.

You can use this keyboard shortcut to get a feel for how big your document is. Press Ctrl+End and then look at the numbers on the status bar. You can see which page you are on, how far down the page you are, which line you are on, and which column you are in. Feel satisfied. Feel accomplished. Take a moment to gloat.

Ctrl+End is an easy key combination to mistakenly press. It throws you — literally — to the end of your document. If you do this and feel that you have boo-booed, press Shift+F5, the Go Back keyboard shortcut, to return from whence you came (that is, back to your previous edit). Also see "Going Back," later in this chapter.

Moving to the beginning of a document

To go to the beginning — nay, the tippy-top — of a document, press the Ctrl key and the Home key: Ctrl+Home.

Going to with the Go To Command

The Ctrl+Home and Ctrl+End key combinations let you fly to the beginning and end of a document, but what if you want to go off somewhere in the middle? Then the Go To command is what you need.

Go To, as in the Shakespearean "Getteth thee outta hereth," enables you to go directly to just about wherever in the document you want to be. Go To is like the Find command (which looks for text), but instead the Go To command lets you find a specific page number, line, or what-have-you in your document.

To use the Go To command, choose the Edit⇨Go To command (or press Alt,E, G), and the Go To tab of the Find and Replace dialog box appeareth before thine eyes (see Figure 3-2).

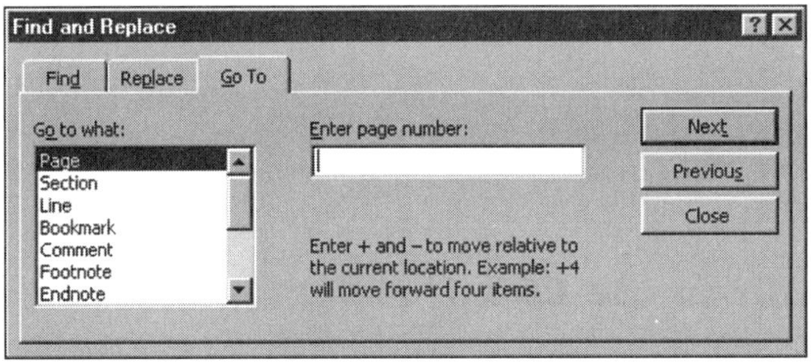

Figure 3-2: The Go To part of the Find and Replace dialog box.

You can type a number of things in the Go To tab of the Find and Replace dialog box. The most effective use is typing a page number; Word instantly beams you to the top of that page. For example, type **14** in the box and press Enter, and you go to page 14.

- You can also press the F5 key to open the Go To tab of the Find and Replace dialog box.
- Heck, you can also press the Ctrl+G keyboard shortcut. (Makes more sense than F5, anyway.)
- If you click twice on the page number on the status bar (muttering "Change, you idiot. Change, change," while you do this helps), the Go To dialog box appears like a genie out of a lamp.
- To be even more specific in your Go To commands, see "Using the Highly Useful Bookmark Command," later in this chapter.

The Go to what part of the Find and Replace dialog box enables you to select a specific whatzit in your document in order to relocate yourself. You find an ugly assortment of items in there, most of which pertain to advanced Word formatting. But if you are inserting graphics or footnotes or using the useful Bookmarks, you can select them from the list, type the proper number or name in the box, press Enter, and you're there. Needless to say, this feature is only for the truly bold.

Scrolling Around

If you love your mouse — and you do hold it a great deal — you can use the power of Windows to help you traverse your documents in two ways. First, you can use the scroll bars that adorn the right and bottom sides of the Word main window. Second, you can use the wheel mouse to help you zoom around, scrolling through your document like it was some ancient text instead of fuzzy black dots on a computer screen.

Sailing with the vertical scroll bar

Though your document window may sport two scroll bars, horizontal and vertical jobbies, you'll probably need the vertical scroll bar to the right of your document most often. This bar looks like a one-lane highway, but it is really used like an elevator shaft (see Figure 3-3).

- To scroll your document up one line of text, click the mouse on the up scroll arrow at the top of the scroll bar.
- To scroll down one line of text, click the mouse on the down scroll arrow at the bottom of the scroll bar.
- In the middle of the scroll bar is a scroll box or elevator button. This box gives you an idea of which part of your document you're looking at; if the box is at the top of the scroll bar, you're near the top of your document, and vice versa.
- The size of the elevator button also tells you how much of your document you can see in the Word window as opposed to the document's true size. So a very large elevator button, like an elevator for giraffes, means that you can see most of your document at once. A thin, bread-slice of an elevator button means that your document is huge and you only see a relative sliver of it at a time.
- To see the preceding screen of text, click the scroll bar just above the elevator button.
- To see the next screen of text, click the scroll bar just below the elevator button.

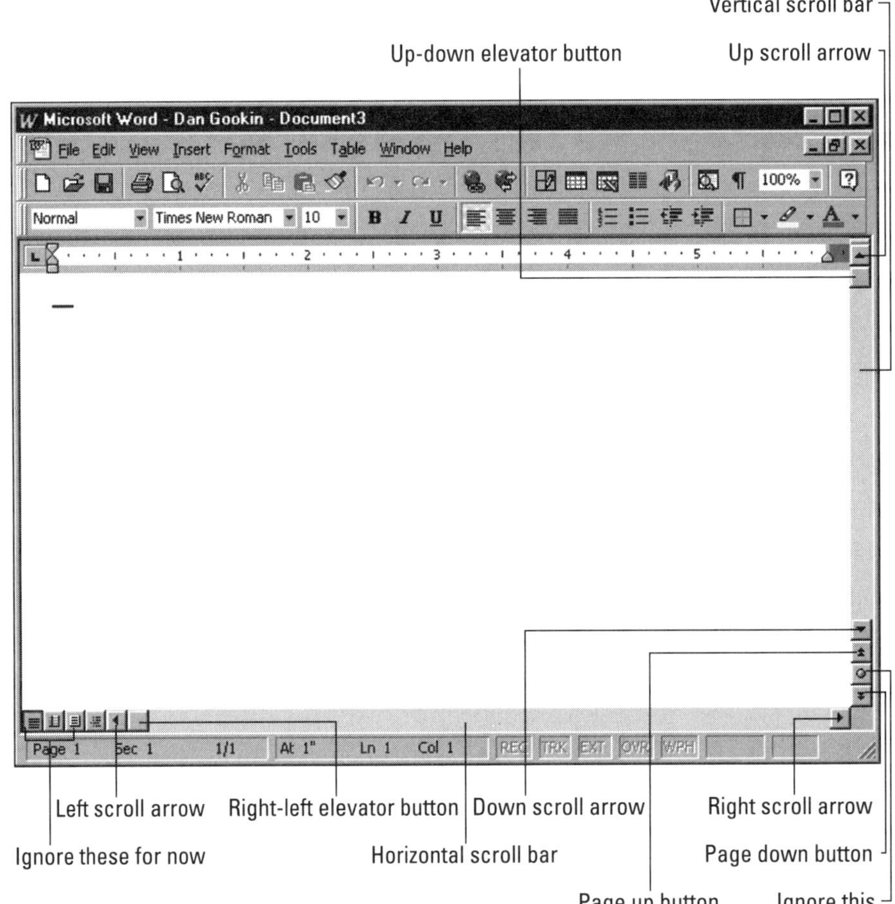

Figure 3-3: The scroll bars on the Word screen.

- Use the Page Up or Page Down buttons (at the bottom of the scroll bar) to move to the top of the preceding or next page.

- Don't click the dot button between the Page Up and Page Down buttons. That is, unless you've read the section, "Abusing the scroll bar" just a few paragraphs from here.
- The scroll bar is not where Greek philosophers went to get drunk. Well, okay, maybe they had a *few drinks* there.

Dragging the elevator button

To move to a specific position in the document, use the mouse to *drag* the elevator button up or down. The elevator button's position indicates which portion of the document you want to see.

As a bonus for having the latest version of Word, when you drag the elevator button around you see a tiny pop-up bubble that tells you approximately which page you'll be looking at when you release the mouse button (see Figure 3-4).

Figure 3-4: Working a scroll bar.

If you've used the Word built-in heading styles, you'll also see the titles of various sections in your document as you scroll the elevator button around. Refer to Chapter 15 for more information on using those heading styles.

Abusing the scroll bar

Lurking at the bottom of the vertical scroll bar you find three buttons (below the final down button that you find on traditional scroll bars). These are the *browse* buttons, which allow you to scroll through your document in leaps and bounds of various sizes.

Normally, the browse buttons let you jump back or ahead in your document a page at time. However, by clicking the round button in the middle, you can see a palette of icons, each representing a different thing in your document that the browse buttons will jump to, either ahead or behind of what you see on the screen.

Figure 3-5 shows what you see when the round button is clicked. You can see what each of the various pictures represents by pointing (not clicking) the mouse at it.

Normally the first item, Browse by Page, is selected. I would say 99 percent of the time this is the option you want. In other words, you can safely leave this sucker alone.

The rest of these options are typically used by people who really know what they're doing. If you're just starting out, refer back here later.

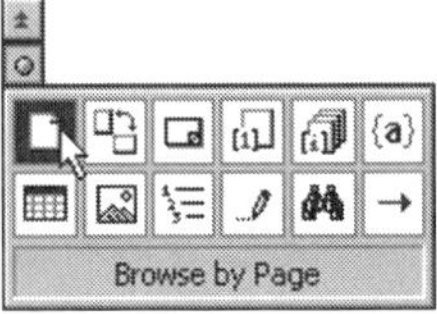

Figure 3-5: Various ways to use the browse buttons.

If you're using heading styles (as described in Chapter 15), you can click the Browse by Heading icon; click the tiny 1-2-3 picture. Clicking the up or down browse button then takes you to the preceding or next heading in your document.

The tiny pencil icon allows you to use the browse buttons to visit the various places you've been editing in your document. (My editor would love that one.) Click the up or down browse button to visit the spots where you've just made some changes.

When you click the binoculars, the Find and Replace dialog box appears. After entering some text to find (Chapter 5 tells you how to work things), you can use the browse buttons to locate that bit of text in your document over and over again.

Using the horizontal scroll bar

Normally, you won't use the horizontal scroll bar. Only if you set your document's margins real wide will this bar come in handy. See Chapter 12 for information on setting margins and such.

Scrolling with the wheel mouse

The wheel mouse is my name for the new Microsoft Intellipoint mouse. This mouse has a third button — a wheel actually — between the two normal mouse buttons. You can click the wheel button, or you can use your index finger to roll it back and forth. Or you don't really have to use it at all, so don't feel left out if you don't have a wheel mouse.

When you're editing, you can roll the wheel up (away from you) to scroll up in your document. Roll the wheel toward you to scroll down through your document.

If you drag the mouse's wheel button (press and hold the wheel button down, and then move the mouse away from or toward you), you can *pan scroll* your document. The further you drag the mouse down (toward you) the faster your document scrolls down, likewise for dragging the mouse up.

Going Back

They say that once you commit, there's no going back. That is, unless you're running for office or using Word. If you go anywhere you don't want to be, press Shift+F5, and Word carries you back to where you started.

The Shift+F5 keyboard shortcut works only in Word; you can't try this command in real life.

If you keep pressing Shift+F5, you return to where you were before; if you press it again, you're back to where you were before that. This keyboard shortcut works about three times before it starts repeating itself.

Using the Highly Useful Bookmark Command

Have you ever done this: You're working away on great stuff, but occasionally you need to zip off elsewhere in your document? So you try to fold down the edge of the screen — *dog-ear* it, if you will — to remember where you were? I do it all the time. Fortunately, Word has a command that helps save wear and tear on your monitor. It's the highly useful Bookmark command.

Setting a bookmark

To mark your place in your document, set a bookmark. Follow these steps:

1. **Put the toothpick cursor where you want to place a bookmark.**
2. **Choose the Insert⇨Bookmark command (or if you have three hands, try Ctrl+Shift+F5).**

   The Bookmark dialog box opens, as shown in Figure 3-6.
3. **Type a name for the bookmark.**

   Be clever! The name reminds you of where you are in your document. So if you're writing a chronicle of one of our country's great politicians, the bookmark name *convict* would be appropriate.

   By the way, bookmark names cannot contain spaces. And it's for the best — no sense in getting carried away.
4. **Press Enter or click the Add button with the mouse.**

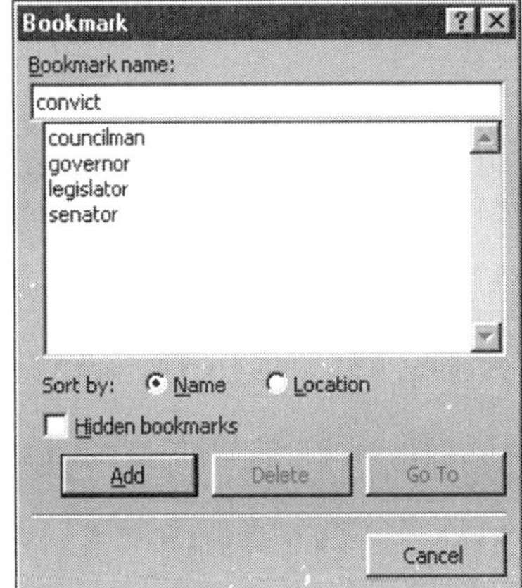

Figure 3-6: The Bookmark dialog box.

Finding a bookmark and moving to that spot in your document

To return to a bookmark, use the Go To command, as covered in "Going to with the Go To Command," earlier in this chapter. These steps keep you from turning the page and losing your train of thought:

1. **Press the F5 key.**

   The Find and Replace dialog box splats across your screen.

2. **Highlight Bookmark in the Go to what list.**

   Bookmark is the fourth item down.

   The Enter page number box changes to read Enter bookmark name. Your most recent bookmark appears in that space.

   If you don't see your bookmark, click the down-arrow and you see a long list of bookmarks in your document. Click the one you want by using the mouse.

3. **Click the Go To button.**

   You're there!

4. **Click the Close button to get rid of the Find and Replace dialog box and return to editing your document.**

Chapter 4

Deleting Text (Or The Art of Un-writing)

In This Chapter

- Using Insert and Overtype modes
- Using your basic delete keys: Backspace and Delete
- Deleting a word
- Deleting a line of text
- Deleting paragraphs
- Deleting odd shapes with blocks
- Undeleting

There is writing and then there is un-writing. You'll probably be writing most of the time, jabbing your fingers at the keyboard in a desperate attempt to make something sensible appear on the screen. Oh, you don't have to worry about spelling because the computer helps you with that. But the *concepts,* that's something only you can muster from your brain. So if you don't like what you see, you can easily un-write it. That's because, unlike the archaic typewriter with its correction ribbons, erasable bond or White Out, your word processor lets you effortlessly blow away unneeded text. Deleting is easy to do, even if you don't like editing your own stuff. And if you're editing someone else's stuff then, golly, blasting away unwanted text is almost as much fun as playing Doom.

Insert and Overtype Modes

Normally, new text you type is inserted just before the blinking toothpick cursor. New text pushes any existing text to the right and down as you type. This is *Insert mode.* Insert mode wouldn't be necessary if there wasn't an *Overtype mode.* In Overtype mode, all the text you type overwrites any existing text on-screen.

There is no reason to type in Overtype mode. Insert mode is fine by itself; you can use the various commands in this chapter to delete text at your whim. But if you really need to activate Overtype mode, double-click the letters OVR on the status bar. This action darkens the letters and throws you into Overtype mode. To return to normal, double-click the OVR again.

- In the olden days, people used the Insert key to switch between Insert and Overtype modes. I don't know why Microsoft changed the setup.

- In Overtype mode, new text gobbles up text already on the screen. If you see this weirdness happen, double-click the OVR thing on the Status bar to stop it, and then use the Ctrl+Z keyboard shortcut to yank back any deleted text.
- The new characters you type in Insert mode appear right in front of the flashing toothpick cursor. Then the cursor moves to the right, awaiting the next character you type.

- The OVR in the status bar indicates that you are in Overtype mode. Any new text you type overwrites existing text. I point this out because a stray elbow can press the Insert key and put you in that mode when you don't want it. This is a good reason not to type with your elbows. But if you are typing along and suddenly notice that part of your text seems to be missing, check your status bar to see whether you're in Overtype mode.
- Leaving Word in Insert mode all the time is a safe bet. If you want to overwrite something, just type the new text and then delete the old.

Your Basic Delete Keys: Backspace and Delete

You can use two keys on the keyboard to delete single characters of text:

- **Backspace key:** Deletes the character to the left of the toothpick cursor
- **Delete key:** Deletes the character to the right of the toothpick cursor

```
Be|fore you meet my folks I should let you know that they're
really into snakes.
```

In the preceding line, the toothpick cursor is "flashing" between the *e* and the *f* in "Before." Pressing the Backspace key deletes the *e* in "Before"; pressing the Delete key deletes the *f*.

- After deleting a character, any text to the right or below the character moves up to fill the void.

- If you're in Overtype mode, the Backspace key still pulls the rest of the text to the right.
- Backspace works like the Backspace key on a typewriter. The difference is that when you press Backspace in Word, the cursor backs up and erases. (The Word equivalent of the typewriter's Backspace key is the left-arrow key.)
- You can press and hold Backspace or Delete to continuously "machine-gun delete" characters. Release the key to stop your wanton destruction.

The Backspace-Blip Phenomenon

Word's childlike reaction to something it doesn't like is the *blip,* a nice and brief beep from your PC's speaker. Sometimes you may hear the blip when you press Backspace to delete. Nothing is deleted; you hear the blip, blip, blip only once for each desperate stab at the Backspace key.

The blipping is Word's way of warning you. What you're trying to do is delete one of the secret, hidden codes littered about the document — codes that change paragraph formatting and other covert stuff. You can't indiscriminately delete this stuff with the Backspace key.

- If you really want to delete the codes, press the ← key and then press the Delete key. No blip.
- Whenever you want to hear the blip, press the End key more than once. Keep holding down the End key to hear Word's equivalent of a raspberry.

- The blip can really scare the pee out of you if you have a sound card and external speakers set up with Windows.
- Don't be surprised by the mystery codes in your document. You put them there as you create and format your text. They're not evil.

- If you want your old formatting back, choose Edit⇨Undo or press Ctrl+Z before you do anything else (or click the Undo tool).

Deleting a Word

Word lets you gobble up entire words at a time by using one of two delete word commands:

- Ctrl+Backspace deletes the word that is in front (to the left) of the cursor.
- Ctrl+Delete deletes the word that is behind (to the right) of the cursor.

To delete a word by using Ctrl+Backspace, position the cursor at the last letter of the word. Press Ctrl+Backspace and the word is gone! The cursor then sits at the end of the preceding word or the beginning of the line (if you deleted the first word in a paragraph).

To delete a word by using Ctrl+Delete, position the cursor at the first letter of the word. Press Ctrl+Delete and the word is gone. The cursor then sits at the beginning of the next word or the end of the line (if you deleted the last word in a paragraph).

- No mere pencil can match Ctrl+Delete or Ctrl+Backspace for sheer speed and terror.
- If the cursor is positioned anywhere in the middle of a word, Ctrl+Backspace deletes everything from where the cursor is to the last letter of the preceding word.
- If the cursor is positioned anywhere in the middle of a word, the Ctrl+Delete command deletes everything from where the cursor is to the first letter of the next word.
- To delete a word, position the mouse pointer on the offending critter and double-click the mouse button. The word is highlighted, and pressing the Delete key erases it.

Deleting a Line of Text

Word has no single command for deleting a line of text from the keyboard. But with the mouse, deleting a line is only a matter of a click and a key press. Follow these steps:

1. **Move the mouse into the left margin of your document.**

   The cursor changes into an arrow pointing northeast rather than northwest. The winds of change are a-blowin'. . . .

2. **Point the mouse pointer arrow at the line of text you want to obliterate.**
3. **Click the left mouse button.**

   The line of text is highlighted, or *selected.*

4. **Press the Delete key to send that line into the void.**

When the mouse cursor is pointing northeast, you can drag it down the left margin and select as many lines of text as you care to. All the lines can then be deleted with one stroke of the Delete key.

Also see Chapter 6 on marking text as a block and then blowing it to Kingdom Come.

Deleting Paragraphs

To mark a complete paragraph for destruction, give it the symbolic kiss on the cheek and click three times (quickly) on any word in the paragraph. This action highlights the paragraph as a block. Now press either the Backspace or Delete key and — presto! — vaporized text!

If you're fond of the northeast-pointing mouse, move the mouse pointer into the left column on the page (where it turns into the northeast pointer) and then double-click it. The paragraph to the right of the mouse cursor is selected and primed for deletion.

Deleting Odd Shapes with Blocks

Word can delete characters, words, and lines all by itself. To delete anything else, you have to mark it as a block of text and then delete the block.

To delete a block of text, follow these steps:

1. **Mark the block.**

   The block can be highlighted by using the mouse; click the mouse at the beginning of the block and then drag to the block's end.

   Using the keyboard, you move the toothpick cursor to the beginning of the block; then press F8 and press the cursor keys to highlight the block.

2. **Press the Delete key to remove all the highlighted text.**

Chapter 6 contains more information about selecting, highlighting, and otherwise playing with blocks.

Undeleting

Deleting text can be traumatic, especially for the timid Word user. But editing is editing, and mistakes happen. If you want some of your freshly deleted text back, you can use the Undo keyboard shortcut, Ctrl+Z, to undelete text. The process usually works like this:

1. **Panic!**

   "Whoops! It took me four hours to concoct the perfectly written paragraph. There is no way I'll ever be that creative again. I may as well jab a letter opener up my thumbnail."

2. **Press Ctrl+Z.**

See? Your thumbnail will thank you.

- Don't forget the Undo command in the Edit menu — first item, by the way. If you can't remember Ctrl+Z or if you find yourself pressing other keys by mistake, just choose Edit⇨Undo *whatever* (or click the Undo tool).

- You can be sloppy with the Undo shortcut because Undo remembers the last several things you just did. But don't get lazy! If you delete text and want it back, press Ctrl+Z without thinking about it.

Chapter 5

Finding and Replacing

In This Chapter

- Finding text
- Finding formatting information
- Finding stuff you can't type in
- Using Find and Replace
- Removing excess spaces
- Deleting the stuff you find

Little Bo Peep has lost her sheep. Too bad she doesn't know about the Word Find command. She could locate her little lost ruminants in a matter of microseconds. Not only that, Bo could use Find and Replace, maybe replacing all her sheep with Chippendale models. It's all really cinchy when you get to know the Find and Replace commands real chummy. Sadly, only words are replaced. If Word could find and replace real things, we'd probably have to look elsewhere for our wool.

Finders Keepers!

Word can locate any bit of text anywhere in your document, from a bombastic oratory down to the tiniest iota of plot. The command used to find text is called, surprisingly enough, the Find command. It dwells in the Edit menu. Follow these steps to use the Find command and locate text lurking in your document:

1. **Think of some text you want to find.**

   For example, "sheep."

2. **Choose the Edit⇨Find command.**

   You see the Find and Replace dialog box, shown in Figure 5-1.

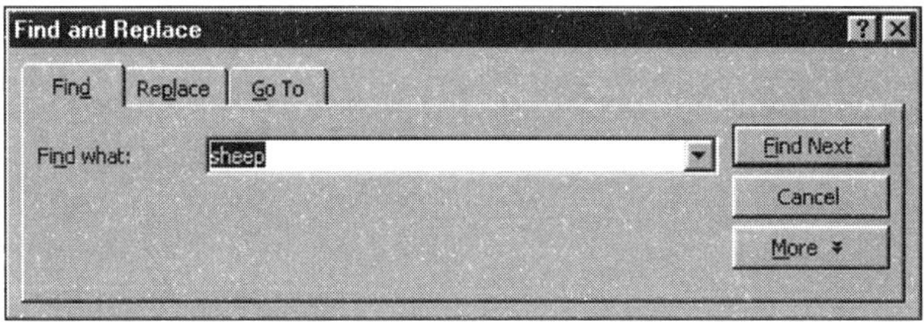

Figure 5-1: The Find and Replace dialog box.

3. **Type the text you want to find.**

   Enter the text into the box titled Find what. For example, **sheep**. Type lowercase letters.

4. **Click the Find Next button to start the search.**

   Or you can press Enter.

If any text is found, it's highlighted on-screen. The Find and Replace dialog box does not go away until you click the Cancel button or press the Escape key. (The dialog box remains so that you can keep searching for more text, if you're so inclined.)

- The quick shortcut key for finding text is to press Ctrl+F (the F stands for Find, in this case).
- Type the text you want to find exactly. Do not end the text with a period unless you want to find the period, too.
- If the text isn't found, you see this message:

  ```
  Word has finished searching the document. The
  search item was not found.
  ```

  Oh, well. Try again and check your typing.

- To find any additional occurrences of the text, click the Find Next button.
- After you close the Find and Replace dialog box, you can use the handy Shift+F4 key to repeat finding the next matching bit of text in your document. This keystroke saves time over using the full-on Find command again.
- You can search for a variety of things by using the Find command: text, spaces, the Enter character, and formatting codes. The section "Finding secret codes," later in this chapter, covers this subject.

Finding or not finding bits and pieces of words

Word finds any matching text in your document. The program can find things so well that it can drive you crazy. Suppose Bo Peep cashes in her sheep for zeppelins and then, on a whim, decides she wants to become a shipping magnet (magnetically attracted to ships). So she searches her document for the word *ship* and, lo, Word shows Bo ships in places she hadn't yet thought of: friend*ship*, court*ship*, relation*ship*, not to mention the *ship*shape *ship*ment of *ship*mates waiting down at the *ship*yard.

To make Word more precise — to locate only a whole *ship*, for example, the type that sails on the ocean blue — click the More button to open up the Find and Replace dialog box (see the section "Finding *More* stuff") and then select the Find whole words only check box. When that box is checked, the Find command logically locates only words and not things nestled in other words.

Finding More stuff

The basic finders-keepers dialog box (refer to Figure 5-1) is okay for quickly finding tidbits of text. But sometimes you may want to find more detailed stuff, or stuff you can't readily type from the keyboard (like a new paragraph). Or you may want to find text that specifically matches "Sheep" instead of plain old "sheep." In those cases, you need to use a more detailed Find and Replace dialog box.

Press Ctrl+F to summon the Find and Replace dialog box, and then click the More button. The Find and Replace dialog box gets taller, with a bunch of options and doodads at the bottom (see Figure 5-2).

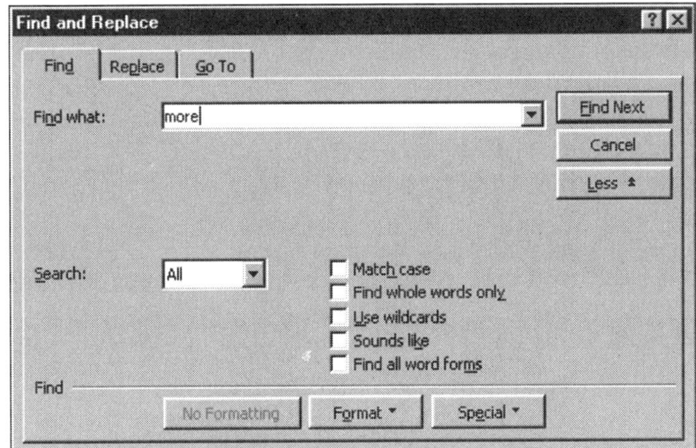

Figure 5-2: The more detailed Find and Replace dialog box.

The following sections tell you why you may want to mess with some of those doodads.

- Two options you may consider using in the expanded, *More* dialog box are Match case and Sounds like.
- When you want to find text that matches uppercase and lowercase text, be sure to select the Match case check box. This box makes the Find command know the difference between Marbles and marbles.
- You may also select the nifty Sounds like option so that Word notifies you of all instances in the document where anything sounding like the text you're looking for occurs. So if Bo Peep loses focus and, for some reason, decides to find any *zeplins*, Word magically locates and matches *zeppelins* (as well as *zeplins*).

Searching up, down, left, and right

Because the Find command is kind of stupid, it always looks for text from the toothpick cursor's location to the end of your document. Once there, the command jumps up back up to the top of the document and keeps on searching — not very efficient.

But if you click the More button (see the preceding section), you can control where and how Word looks for stuff. Locate the Search drop-down box (see Figure 5-2) and click the down-arrow. There you find three options:

Down: Searches from the toothpick cursor to the end of the document

Up: Searches from the toothpick cursor to the beginning of the document

All: Damn the toothpick cursor — searches the *entire* document!

I was just kidding about searching left and right in this section's title. Left is actually "up" or before the toothpick cursor; right is "down" or after the toothpick cursor. And starboard is right and port is left, if you happen to be using Word on a laptop somewhere in the ocean.

Finding secret codes

Laced throughout a document are secret codes and printing instructions. You don't see these codes on-screen, but they affect the way your document looks and prints. Basically, the secret commands — bold, underline, center, and special paragraph formatting — can be searched for just like text can.

To search for a secret code, gallop through these steps:

1. **Choose Edit⇨Find.**

   This summons up the Find and Replace dialog box (refer to Figure 5-1).

2. **Click the More button.**

   This opens up the big Find and Replace dialog box (see the section "Finding *More* stuff").

3. **Click the Format button.**

   A drop-down menu appears with a bunch of menu items on it. Each one asks you whether you want to search by Font, Paragraph, Tabs, Language, Dopey, Sneezy, or Doc. Oops! Wrong seven dwarfs. The other three secret things you can search for are Frame, Style, or Highlight. In real life, however, you'll probably only use the Font and Paragraph items, maybe Style, too.

4. **Choose a special something to search for.**

   Because you probably don't know what's going on, I'll give you an example to trudge through: Select Font; click that item by using your mouse.

5. **Another dialog box opens, one particular to the item you chose in Step 4.**

   If you're following along with the font example, you see the Find Font dialog box, as shown in Figure 5-3. You can find a bunch of character-related stuff with this dialog box.

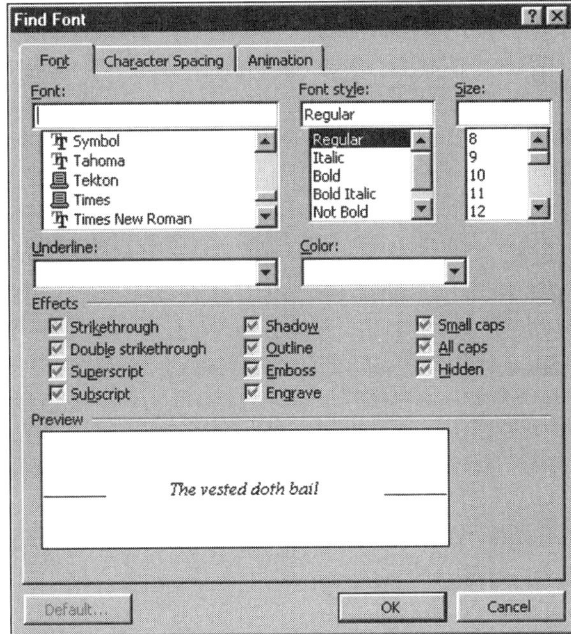

Figure 5-3: One of many specific Find dialog boxes to help you locate weird stuff.

6. **Choose the settings you want to hunt for.**

   For example, if you want to search a document for italicized words in a 9-point Roman font, select each of these attributes from their menus. Or just select Italic if you want to locate any italic text.

7. **Click OK.**

   The specific dialog box closes, and you're returned to the Find and Replace dialog box.

   Notice how the word Format appears below the text box, followed by whichever options you selected? That's your clue that you're now using the Super Find command to look for not only a tidbit of text, but a tidbit that's formatted in a specific manner.

8. **Click the Find Next button to look for your special stuff.**

- Remember that Word not only looks for your specific format but also any text you have typed into the Find what box. So if you want to look for the word *ruminant* in italics, type *ruminant* into the box in addition to selecting the italic font to find.
- You can use this box to look for specific occurrences of a font, such as Courier or Times New Roman, by selecting the font from the selection list. Scroll through the font menu to see what you can choose.
- You can look for a particular size of type (24 point, for example) by selecting it from the Size selection list. See Chapter 10, "Formatting Characters," for information about character formatting.
- You can also search for paragraph formatting by choosing Paragraph rather than Font from the Format menu in the Find and Replace dialog box. See Chapter 11 for information about paragraph formatting.
- You can also search for styles by choosing Style rather than Font from the Find and Replace dialog box. Refer to Chapter 15 for a discussion of styles.
- If you often find yourself slipping back and forth between more than one language (it's tough being fluent in so many different tongues, I'm sure), you can also search for text by the language in which it is written. Word even discriminates between the English used by Aussies, the Brits, and us Yanks. What-what.
- No, no language called "Texan" is known to Word.

Un-screwing up the Find Command

If you use the Find command to look for secret formatting codes (as discussed in the preceding section), you may notice that suddenly the regular Find command seems not to work. For example, you try to find the word "the" and you keep getting that `Word has finished searching the document. The search item was not found` message. Ugh.

No Formatting

The problem is that you were once searching for formatting information, and Word just hasn't forgotten it. To make Word forget, click the No Formatting button. After that, the Find command should work as you expect it to.

Finding stuff you just can't type in

No, this isn't a censorship issue. Some characters you just can't properly type in the Find and Replace dialog box — unprintable, unmentionable stuff. Try typing a Tab character, for example; Press the Tab key and — whoops! — nothing happens. That result is because the Tab character, plus a few others, are special, and you must force-feed them into the Find and Replace dialog box.

To find a special, unprintable character, click the More button to see the expanded Find and Replace dialog box and then click the Special button. You see a pop-up list of various characters Word can search for but that you would have a dickens of a time typing (see Figure 5-4). Click one of them, and a special, funky shorthand representation for that character appears in the Find what box (such as ^t, for Tab). Click the Find Next button to find that character.

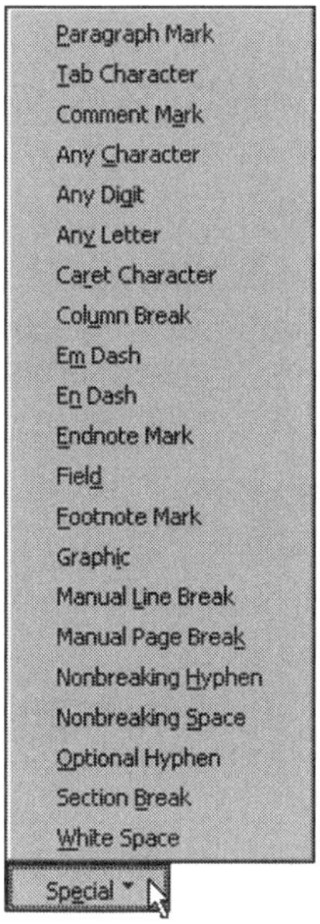

Paragraph Mark
Tab Character
Comment Mark
Any Character
Any Digit
Any Letter
Caret Character
Column Break
Em Dash
En Dash
Endnote Mark
Field
Footnote Mark
Graphic
Manual Line Break
Manual Page Break
Nonbreaking Hyphen
Nonbreaking Space
Optional Hyphen
Section Break
White Space
Special

Figure 5-4: Some special stuff to find.

- The special characters appear in the Find what box in secret code. That code starts with a caret (^) and then a letter of the alphabet. Please don't try to make sense of it.
- The Paragraph Mark special character is the same as the Enter character — what you press to end a paragraph.
- Any Character, Any Digit, and Any Letter represent, well, just about anything. These buttons are used as wildcards for matching lots of stuff.
- The caret (^) is a special character. If you want to search for it, be sure to select Caret Character from the Special button's pop-up list.
- Yes, you can mix and match the special characters with other text you want to find. So if you want to find a Tab character followed by Bo Peep, you use the Special button to insert the Tab Character (^t on the screen), and then you just type in **Bo Peep** using your fingers.

Finding Something and Replacing It with Something Else

Find and replace is the art of finding a bit of text and replacing it with something else. You'll be using this all the time. It's one of those word-processor features that helped put various typewriter companies out of business. For example, you can replace the word *goat* with *caprine* (yet another ungulate since this chapter has been herded that way). Word makes the replacement in a snap, by using the Replace command:

1. **Choose Edit⇨Replace.**

   The Find and Replace dialog box, shown in Figure 5-5, appears on-screen. It's actually a cheap variation on the Find and Replace dialog box — another panel, if you will — which makes sense because finding is a big part of find and replace.

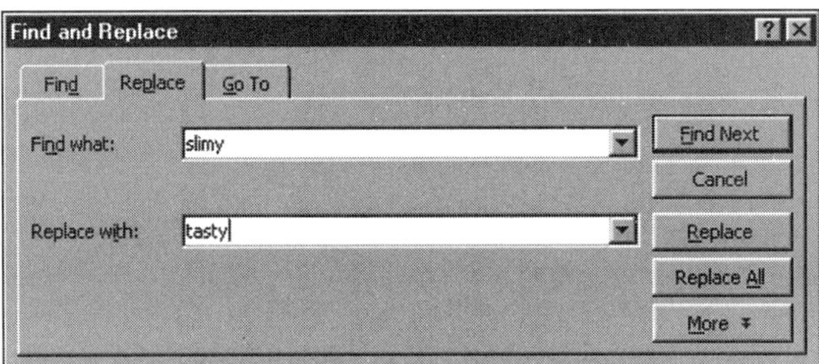

Figure 5-5: The Find and Replace dialog box.

The Find and Replace dialog box also has a More button. If you see the More options, click the Less button to make your screen look like Figure 5-5. Also see the section "Find *More* stuff" earlier in this chapter.

2. **In the Find what box, type the text you want to find.**

   This text is found and replaced with something else. For example, you could type **goat**. Press the Tab key when you're done typing.

3. **In the Replace with box, type the text that you want to use to replace the original text.**

   For example, type **caprine**, which is a fancy-schmancy, duded-up term for a goat.

4. **Ask yourself, "Do I want the chance to change my mind before replacing each bit of found text?"**

   If so, click the Find Next button (this action is usually a good idea). If not, you can click the Replace All button; text is found and replaced automatically, giving you no chance to change your mind.

5. **If you clicked Find Next, Word pauses at each occurrence of the text.**

   The found text is highlighted on-screen just like in the regular Find task. When this highlighting happens, you can click the Replace button to replace it or click Find Next to skip and find the next matching bit of text. Click the Cancel button or press the Escape key when you tire of this process.

When the Replace operation reaches the end of your document, you may see this message:

```
Word has reached the end of the document. Do you want to
continue searching at the beginning?
```

Click the Yes button to continue.

When finding and replacing is all done, you see a message like:

```
Word has completed its search of the document and has made 23
replacements.
```

Of course, the number of replacements depends on what you were searching for.

- You can click the More button in the Find and Replace dialog box to find and replace more than just plain text. Refer to the first part of this chapter for more information on finding and replacing interesting doodads. All the information that applies to the Find command also applies to Find and Replace.

- Always type something in the Replace with box. If not, you systematically delete all the text found in a wanton round of wholesale slaughter. This process is called "Find It and Delete It," and it's covered later in this chapter, in a section by the same name.
- The quick shortcut key combination for the Replace command is Ctrl+H. Uh-huh. H means what? Hunt and replace?
- And as long as I'm complaining: The true name of this command is *Search* and Replace. That's what everyone calls it. I have no idea why Microsoft chose *Find* instead of Search.
- My advice is to click Find Next most of the time. Only if you're replacing something and you're certain (a rare occurrence, at least in my travels) should you click Replace All.

- The Undo command restores your document to its previous condition if you foul up the Replace operation. Refer to Chapter 4 for more information about undoing things.
- A ruminant is an animal with a four-part stomach. An ungulate is an animal that has hoofs.

Zapping Excess Spaces from Your Document

Here's a practical use for the Replace command. Too many Word users litter their documents with excessive spaces. You do it. I do it. Bill Gates does it all the time. The most harmless of all these spaces comes at the end of a line of text, after the period but before you press Enter. Yet the extra spaces serve no purpose. These steps show you how to get rid of them, which is something you should do to all your documents at least once:

1. **Choose the Edit⇨Replace command.**

   Or just press Ctrl+H. Either way, the Find and Replace dialog box appears.

2. **Click the More button to see the bigger Find and Replace dialog box.**

   No need to do this if the Find and Replace dialog box is already huge, sprawling its big ol' belly across your PC's screen.

3. **Click the Special menu.**

   A menu of strange characters appears, including Uncle Cedric dressed in Aunt Ruth's 1934 Atlantic City bathing suit and a pink garter.

4. **Select White Space from the pop-up list.**

   It's the last item in the menu (see Figure 5-4).

5. **Repeat Steps 3 and 4 to select Paragraph Mark from the list.**

   Paragraph Mark is the top item in the menu.

   What you've done is tell the Replace command to look for a space (**^w**) followed by the Enter key (**^p**). The following characters appear in the Find what box:

   ```
   ^w^p
   ```

   These characters represent any extra space (that no one needs) at the end of a paragraph.

6. **Press the Tab key to move to the Replace with box.**

7. **Click the Special button and select Paragraph Mark.**

   So you're replacing **^w^p** with **^p**, which is just getting rid of the ^w — excess spaces. If you didn't put a **^p** in the Replace with box, you would delete all spaces and Enter key combinations from your document, which isn't what this madness is all about.

8. **Click Replace All.**

   Word cleans the excess spaces from your document.

- To replace double spaces between sentences with single spaces, don't use the White Space character (**^w**). A single space and the White Space character are not really the same thing. To rid your document of double spaces, just type two space characters in the Find what box and only one space in the Replace with box. Then try to wean yourself from the double-spacing-after-period habit they taught you in typing class.

- A quick way to transform extra spaces into a Tab character is to search for five spaces in a row and translate them into tabs. In the Find what box, press the spacebar five times (space-space-space-space-space). In the Replace with box, select Tab Character (**^t**) from the pop-up Special button. Those spaces are replaced with tabs, which are much easier to align. See Chapter 12 for more information about using and setting tabs.

Find It and Delete It

If you don't type anything in the Replace with box, the Word Replace command systematically deletes all the Find whats. This process can be a scary thing, so be sure to click Find Next. Otherwise, you may zap parts of your document and, boy, would you be bummed (until you used the Undo command).

Suppose, however, that Bo Peep wanted to get rid of her sheep. Instead, she wants to be a truck driver. These steps show you how to delete the *sheep* from a Word document:

1. **Choose Edit⇨Replace.**

   Or type Ctrl+H (if that ever makes sense to you).

2. **In the Find what box, type the text you want to find.**

   For example, **sheep**. Enter the text exactly. Any previously searched for text appears at the prompt. Edit it or type new text, secret codes, or whatever to search for.

3. **Don't type anything in the Replace with box; leave it blank.**

   Remove any text that may happen to be in the Replace with box.

   You're deleting text here and replacing it with nothing — a bold concept Rod Serling touched upon a few decades back in some *Twilight Zone* episodes.

4. **Click the Replace All button.**

   In moments, your text is gone. Bo Peep's sheep just up and leave. Pop! Pop! Pop!

- If you're timid and clicked the Find Next button instead of Replace All, the process takes a bit longer because you have to squint at the screen and then press the Replace button at each occurrence.
- Someday, you may delete all the Enter characters (new paragraphs) or spaces from your document. Whatta mess! If so, remember the Undo command; Ctrl+Z restores your document to the way it was before.
- If a Find and Replace operation is too memory intensive (meaning that you have a large document or are replacing lots of things), Word may warn you that it won't be able to undo the operation. If so, double-check that you're finding and replacing the right things, and plow forward.
- Let's all wish Miss Peep the best of luck in her new profession.

Chapter 6

Text Blocks, Engine Blocks, Writers' Blocks

In This Chapter

- Marking a block
- Marking a block with the Find command
- Copying and pasting a block
- Cutting and pasting a block
- Pasting a previously cut or copied block
- Pasting a block to the desktop
- Copying a Scrap icon from the desktop
- Deleting a block
- Formatting a block
- Proofing a block
- Using Find and Replace in a block
- Printing a block

I remember hearing from a seasoned old writer in my youth. If I was going to be a writer, he said, I should triple-space everything and type it on thick, 20-pound paper. Then keep some scissors and rubber cement handy to help me rearrange and edit. After all, he boasted, cutting and pasting your text beats typing it over and over again. His advice may have been true at the time, but it's completely moot today. Word lets you cut and paste blocks of text any which where in your document. And you don't have to worry about triple-spacing, typing on 20-pound paper, or even spending $1.29 for the industrial-sized jar of rubber cement.

Roping Off a Chunk of Text as a Block

A block in a word processor is a marvelous thing. You can rope off a section of text — any old odd section, a letter, word, line, paragraph, page, or a rambling polygon — and then treat the text as a unit — a *block.* You can copy the block, move it, delete it, format it, spell check it, use it to keep the defensive line from getting to your quarterback, and on and on. Think of the joy: Years after childhood, Word has made it okay for us to play with blocks again.

Yet, before you can do anything with a block of text, you need to *mark* it. You can mark a block two ways in Word: by using the mouse or by using the keyboard.

Marking a block with your mouse

To mark a block with the mouse, follow these rodent-like steps:

1. **Position the mouse pointer where you want the block to start.**
2. **Hold down the left mouse button and drag the mouse over your text.**

   As you drag, the text becomes highlighted, or *selected,* as shown in Figure 6-1. Drag the mouse from the beginning to the end of the text that you want to mark as a block.

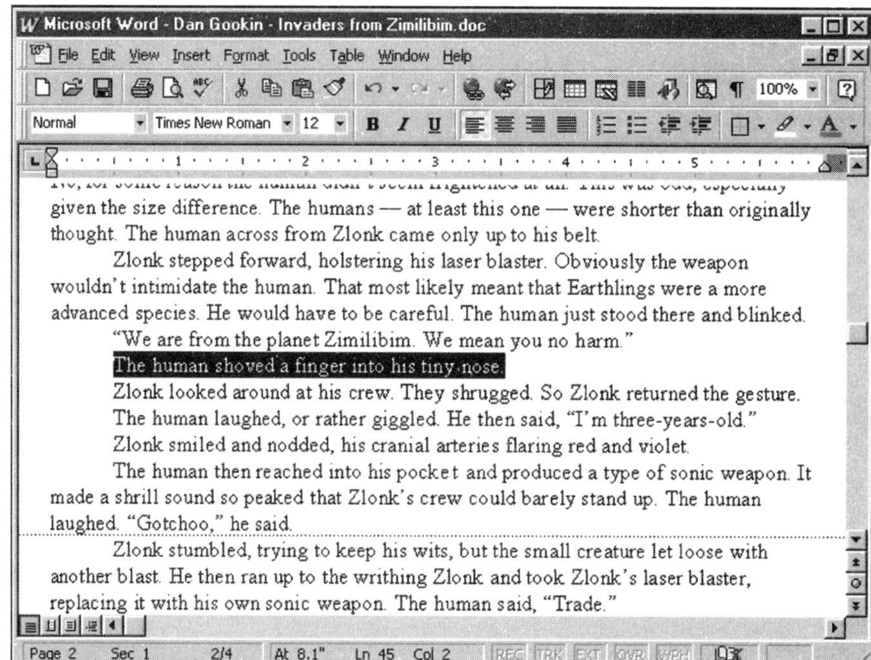

Figure 6-1: A block of text is marked on the screen.

3. **Release the mouse button — stop the dragging — to mark your block's end.**

- If you continue dragging above or below the text that appears on-screen, the screen scrolls up or down.
- To quickly mark a word, position the mouse pointer over that word and double-click.
- To quickly mark a sentence, press and hold the Ctrl key while clicking the mouse.

- To mark a line of text, move the mouse pointer to the left margin. The pointer becomes an arrow that points northeasterly. Click the mouse to highlight one line of text, or drag the mouse to select several lines at a time.
- Word automatically selects whole words when you mark a block by using your mouse. To tell Word not to select whole words, choose Tools⇨Options and in the Edit panel, remove the check mark from the When selecting, automatically select entire word check box. Click the OK button to save your change.
- To mark an entire paragraph, place the insertion pointer anywhere in the paragraph and click three times.

Marking a block with your keyboard

Dragging over the screen with the mouse is great for selecting small portions of text. Marking anything larger than a screenful, however, can get a bit out of hand with the mouse — which tends to think that there's a cat around or something whenever you scroll-drag and move too fast to control. In those instances, it's much better to mark text by using the keyboard. Follow these steps:

1. **Press the F8 key.**

   This is the Start Block command. The F8 key "drops anchor" by marking one end of the block.

2. **Use the cursor navigation keys to move to the other end of the block.**

   Chapter 3 discusses the navigation keys.

Word highlights text from the point where you dropped anchor with F8 to wherever you move the toothpick cursor (refer to Figure 6-1). Text appears in white-on-black. After the block is marked, you're ready to do something with it.

- After you press the F8 key, you see EXT (for Extend Selection) on the status bar. The block-marking mode is active until you type a block or formatting command or press Escape to cancel.

- To quickly mark a word, position the toothpick cursor on the word and press the F8 key twice.
- To quickly mark a sentence, position the toothpick cursor somewhere in the sentence and press the F8 key three times.
- To quickly mark a paragraph, position the toothpick cursor in the paragraph and press the F8 key four times.
- To quickly break your keyboard, press the F8 key 100,000 times.
- To mark your whole do-dang document, press the F8 key five times or press Ctrl+5 (the 5 key on the numeric keypad).

  Actually, pressing Ctrl+A to select *all* of your document as a block is much easier.
- Press the Escape key to cancel the block-drop-and-chop F8 method of marking text. The block is still marked; move the cursor to unhighlight it.
- You can use the mouse *and* the F8 key to get real fancy. Position the cursor at either end of the block you want to mark and press the F8 key. Then position the mouse cursor at the other end of the block and press the left mouse button. Everything from there to there is marked.
- After a block is marked, you're ready to type a block command. You can copy the block, cut it, paste it elsewhere, format the block, print it, spell check it, or do a dozen more interesting things, all covered in this chapter. Refer to the appropriate section later in this chapter for the next step.

- Rather than use the cursor keys to mark a block with the keyboard, you can type a character. Word locates the next occurrence of that character and includes inside the block all the text between it and the beginning of the block. You can do this several times to make the block as large as you want.
- Get used to using the keyboard commands to block your text, and you will be much happier, believe me.

Another keyboardy way: The Shift key

The Shift key used in combination with any of the cursor-movement keys also marks a slab of text on-screen. Refer to Chapter 3 for information about keys that you can use to move around your document. Just press and hold the Shift key with those keys to mark text as you move the cursor. (This method may tie your fingers in knots, so be careful.)

Marking a block with the Find command

Marking a block can get sloppy with the mouse or the cursor-navigation keys — especially if you're pressing the PgUp or PgDn keys to mark large swaths of text. A better way is to use the Find command to locate the end of the block. Do this:

1. **Position the toothpick cursor at the beginning of the block.**

   The cursor must be blinking right before the first character to be included in the block. Be precise.

2. **Press the F8 key.**

   This step turns on the EXT word-fragment message on the status bar. You're in block-marking mode.

3. **Choose Edit⇨Find.**

   You see the Find and Replace dialog box open on-screen. Yes, you're still in block-marking mode, but now you can use the Find command to locate the end of your block.

4. **Type the text that you want to locate, which marks the end of the block.**

   After typing the text, press Enter. Word stretches the block highlight down to that point in the text and includes the found text in the block.

When the cursor is at the end of the block, you're ready to use a block command. Refer to the proper section later in this chapter for additional details.

- Until you type a block command, the block remains highlighted and EXT continues to stare at you from the status bar. Remember to press the Escape key to cancel block-marking mode.
- If text isn't found by using the Find command, you see an appropriate not found error message box displayed — but you're still in block-marking mode. Click the OK button to tell Word what a good little program it is and that you are sorry it was unsuccessful.
- To find the next occurrence of the matching text, you can click the Find Next button in the dialog box. Or . . .
- If you don't see the dialog box on-screen, pressing the Shift+F4 key combination does a Find Next for you.
- Although you're using the Find command to help mark your block, you can still use the cursor-navigation keys. Heck, you can even use the mouse if you press and hold the Shift key first. Blocking is a liberal thing here; you're not limited to using only the cursor or Find command methods to mark a block.
- More details about the Find command are in Chapter 5, in the section "Finders Keepers!"

Marking the whole dang-doodle document

To mark everything, choose the Edit⇨Select All command. The commonly accepted Windows key equivalent for the Select All command is Ctrl+A.

Copying and Pasting a Block

After a block is marked, you can copy and paste that block into another part of your document. The original block remains untouched by this operation. Follow these steps to copy a block of text from one place to another:

1. **Mark the block.**

   Locate the beginning of the block and select text until you've highlighted to the block's end. Detailed instructions about doing this task are offered in the first part of this chapter.

2. **Conjure up Edit⇨Copy.**

   Choose Copy from the Edit menu. Or if you're adept at such things, press Ctrl+C for the Copy shortcut (or click the Copy tool).

   Word places a copy of the marked block in the Windows Clipboard — a storage area for text or graphics that you've cut or copied and are about to paste back into your document.

3. **Move the cursor to the position where you want the block copied.**

   Don't worry if there isn't any room there; Word inserts the block into your text just as though you had typed it there manually.

4. **Choose Edit⇨Paste.**

   Pressing Ctrl+V is the Paste shortcut (or click the Paste tool).

   You now have two copies of the block in your document.

- You can also copy blocked text with the mouse. Position the mouse cursor anywhere in the blocked text, hold down the Ctrl key and the left mouse button while you drag the block to the location where the copy will be placed. The mouse pointer changes to an arrow-with-square-lasso design while you're dragging. Release the mouse button to paste in the block copy.
- After a block has been copied, you can paste it into your document a second time. This subject is covered in "Pasting a Previously Cut or Copied Block," later in this chapter.
- You can also copy or drag a block of text to the Windows desktop for long-term storage. This weird activity is discussed in "Dragging Blocks to the Desktop," later in this chapter.

Fancy linked-copy stuff you'll never use

When you copy and paste a block of text, both the copy and the original contain the same text. From that point on, however, you can edit either the copy or original and they'll be different. This is expected. But a remote instance may occur when you always want the copies to look like the original, even after you've edited the original. To make that happen, you need to make a linked copy, or *shortcut.*

A linked copy is done by dragging a selected block of text with the mouse and holding down *both* the Shift and Ctrl keys. When you release the mouse button, the copied block plops down into your document, but with a gray shading behind it. From that point on, any time you edit the original text, the copy is edited and updated as well. Strange, but Word can do it, and I'd be chastised if I didn't write about this capability somewhere in this book.

You can also perform a linked copy by dragging a block of text with the *right* mouse button instead of the left button. When you release the mouse button, choose Link Here from the pop-up menu.

Oh, this trick only works within a single document. To copy and paste linked text between documents, you need to use the Edit⇨Paste Special command and click the Paste link button, and then choose Word Hyperlink from the list. I know, complex stuff. But that's why it's in this technical sidebar you aren't supposed to read.

Cutting and Pasting a Block

Cutting a block is like deleting it — but nothing is really gone. Instead, as you snip out an article in the newspaper, the cut block can be pasted into your document at another location. This process is technically called a *move;* you move a block of text from one spot to another in your document. (Talk about writing moving text!)

Cutting a block of text works like copying a block. Follow these steps:

1. **Mark the block of text you want to move (cut).**

   Locate the block's start by using the cursor; press the F8 key and press the cursor keys or use the mouse to highlight the block.

2. **Choose the Edit⇨Cut command.**

   You can also press Ctrl+X, the Cut shortcut (or click the Cut tool). Either way, the block disappears. That's okay — it's been stuffed into the Windows Clipboard, an electronic storage place nestled deep in your computer's memory.

3. **Move the toothpick cursor to the position where you want the block pasted.**

   Don't worry if there isn't any room for the block; Word makes room as it inserts the block.

4. **Summon the Edit➪Paste command.**

You can also press Ctrl+V to paste in your block (or click the Paste tool).

- Additional information about marking a block is in the first two sections of this chapter.
- Copying a block works just like moving a block, although the original isn't deleted. Refer to the preceding section, "Copying and Pasting a Block."
- Moving a block is not the same as deleting a block; the block can be recovered only by positioning the cursor and pasting it in with the Ctrl+V key combination.
- The Ctrl+Z Undo shortcut undoes a block move.
- After a block has been cut and moved, you can repaste it into your document a second time. This subject is covered in the next section, "Pasting a Previously Cut or Copied Block."
-  You can also move blocked text by dragging the mouse — although I recommend using this tip only when the move is just a short distance away. (Scrolling the screen while dragging with the mouse can be unwieldy.) Position the mouse cursor anywhere in the blocked text and hold down the left mouse button while you drag the bar-looking cursor to the location where the block is to be moved. This dance step is particularly useful when you are rearranging stuff on a page.

Pasting a Previously Cut or Copied Block

Whenever a block of text is cut or copied, Word remembers it. You can re-yank that block into your document at any time — sort of like repasting text after it's already been pasted in. You use Ctrl+V, the Paste shortcut.

To paste a previously cut block of text, follow these exciting steps:

1. **Position the toothpick cursor in the spot where you want the block of text to be pasted.**

   This step should always be done first. The block appears right at the cursor's position as though you typed it in yourself.

2. **Choose the Edit➪Paste command.**

You also can press Ctrl+V, the Paste shortcut. Ctrl+V equals paste? Uh-huh. (Or click the Paste tool.)

Zap. There it is on your screen.

- If nothing has been copied or cut by using the other block commands, nothing is pasted by this command. Duh.
- Word has a small brain. It remembers only the last cut or copied block. Anything cut or copied before that cannot be pasted again.

Dragging Blocks to the Desktop

Because this is Windows 95 you're dealing with, you can do a few Windows 95-like things with a Windows 95-happy program like Word 97. One of these is taking advantage of the desktop — that background thing upon which Windows icons float.

- If you're following my suggestions, you're using Word at full-screen strength. In that maximized mode you cannot see the desktop. So if you want to see the desktop and take advantage of its cut-and-paste block action, you need to click the Restore button in the upper-right corner of Word's window.
- You may also need to restore or minimize other windows that may also be blocking your view of the desktop.
- If you find all this window rearranging to be a pain, just don't bother with this stuff.

Dragging a block out to the desktop

When you drag a block to the desktop, you're copying it to something called the *Scrap*. That's a little icon that sits on the desktop until you drag it somewhere else — a completely strange Windows 95 concept that no one will ever get used to. But since I started discussing it, here are the steps you take to make it happen:

1. **Mark the block you want to fling onto the desktop.**

   Obey the proper block-marking instructions located near the beginning of this chapter.

2. **Point the mouse at the block.**
3. **Drag the block out of Word's application window and onto the desktop.**

   You see the mouse pointer change. A fuzzy box and plus sign appear, which indicate that you're dragging, copying, and pasting something to the desktop, as shown in Figure 6-2.

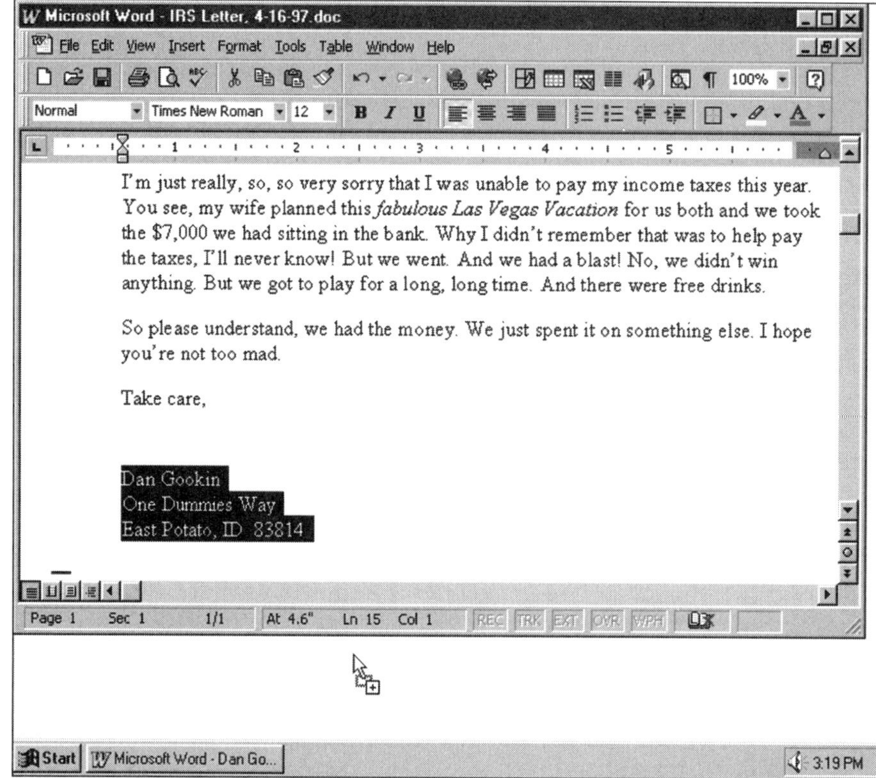

Figure 6-2: A block is dragged out to the desktop.

4. **Release the mouse button.**

   This action ends the drag and places a copy of the block on the desktop.

The pasted block is given the name *Document Scrap,* followed by the first few bits of text in the document. You can change the icon's name to something else using the proper Windows 95 "I wanna change an icon's name" command. Refer to your favorite Windows 95 book for the details.

- This operation can be done a number of times. Unlike copy or cut, where only the last thing you've copied or cut is remembered, you can drag any number of blocks to the desktop for long-term storage.

  As in the figure, the text you want to drag to the desktop should be something you'll be using over and over — your address, for example. Or it can be a block you'll want to repaste into a document several times — typical "use-over" stuff.

- If you want to cut the block, you're out of luck. This technique only *copies* something to the desktop.

- To rename an icon in Windows, click the icon once with the mouse. This step highlights it. Then press the F2 key and type a new name. Be sure to be descriptive about what the Scrap icon contains. Press the Enter key to lock the new name into place.

- Whenever you drag a block, the mouse pointer grows a little fuzzy rectangle. When you drag a block to the desktop, the mouse pointer also grows a little plus sign. And if you drag the block off the screen, it grows teeth and eventually eats you.

Dragging a block in from the desktop

If you're a drag-em-to-the-desktop pro, you'll eventually want to use all those little bits of scrap blocks, pasting them back into your document at some point or another. To do so is really cinchy. Follow these steps:

1. **Locate the spot where you want to paste the block.**

   For example, suppose that you have a scrap block of text on the desktop that contains your name and address to close a letter. If so, you'll want to make sure that part of your document is visible in Word's application window. (You don't need to be fussy with the toothpick cursor here; just ensure that the proper part of your document is visible on the screen.)

2. **Locate the Scrap icon.**

   Scrap icons live on the desktop. If Word's window covers the icon, drag the icon to a spot where it will be visible when you're in Word.

3. **Drag the icon into your text.**

   Drag the icon from the desktop into your document: Point the mouse at the icon. Press and hold the mouse's button (the left button). Roll (drag) the mouse cursor into your document's window. Release the mouse button.

- Be careful where you release the mouse button. Place the toothpick cursor at that exact spot where the block of scrap text will be pasted into your document.
- This operation is a copy-only. The Scrap icon still lives on your desktop after you drag it into a document. The only way to rid yourself of a Scrap icon is to drag it into the Windows Recycle Bin.
- Because the Scrap icon lives (It lives! It lives!), you can use it over and over.
- Not every bit of scrap you drag into Word will be text. Sometimes those Scrap icons contain graphics, spreadsheets, or any of a number of low-life characters. Hopefully, whoever put them there will have properly named them. Hopefully.

- In the same vein, you can drag your Word scraps into other documents as well. It all sounds so handy that it makes you wonder why they call them “scraps.”

Deleting a Block

There are two ways to delete a block: the complex way and the easy way. How about the easy way, eh?

1. **Mark the block.**

   Refer to the first section of this chapter for the best block-marking instructions in any computer book.

2. **Press the Delete key.**

   Thwoop!

- You can also press the Backspace key to delete the block.
- The first section of this chapter covers additional and detailed information about marking a block.

- This time, the block can be recovered by using the Edit⇨Undo command (or the Undo tool). This step is what makes deleting a block different from cutting and pasting a block. When you Undo, however, the block appears in the same position from where it was deleted.
- Chapter 4 covers the vast subject of deleting and destroying text. Turn there to quench your destructive thirsts.

Formatting a Block

When you’ve roped off a section of text as a block, you can format the text and characters as a single unit. Formatting is covered in detail in Part II of this book, “Formatting (Or Making Your Prose Look Less Ugly).” So instead of going over the details, here are the various things you can do to a block for formatting:

- You can make the text bold, underlined (two different flavors), italicized, superscripted, or subscripted by using various Ctrl-key combinations, all of which are detailed in Chapter 10.
- You can change the font for the block’s text, which also is covered in Chapter 10.
- Any formatting changes affect only the text roped off in the block.

- Chapter 10 offers information about changing the text style, bold, underlining, italics, and all that. The same chapter presents information about shifting between uppercase and lowercase.
- Chapter 11 covers information about changing the position of a block — its *justification*.

Proofing a Block

If you want to check your spelling or grammar in a small or irregularly sized part of your document, you can block it off and then use Word's Spelling and Grammar command. This command is much quicker than going through the pains of using the full spell check, and it allows you to check specific parts of your document — words, paragraphs, or pages — without having to sit through a full document proof.

To see whether your English is up to snuff, follow these steps:

1. **Mark the block.**

   Refer to the first section in this chapter.

   The highlighted area marked by the block is the only part of your document that is spell checked.

2. **Select the Tools⇨Spelling and Grammar command.**

   No muss, no waiting — the block is proofed. (You can click the Spelling tool.)

3. **Word compares all words in the block with its internal dictionary and a miniature Miss Higgins, your fourth grade English teacher.**

   If a misspelled or unrecognized word is found, it is highlighted, and you are given a chance to correct or edit it. If any sentence violates one of the weird rules of English, you're told about the violation as well.

   If you tire of this process, click the Cancel button.

4. **After the block has been proofed, Word asks whether, by the way, you want to continue checking the rest of your document. Press N.**

   Or press Y if you really want to see how poor your spelling is outside the block.

- I often use this technique to look up the spelling of a single word I don't trust: Just double-click the word to select it and then click the Spelling tool.
- Word's on-the-fly spell checker has more-or-less made this function unnecessary. However, if you're like me, you'll turn that annoying little sucker off. In that case, spell checking a block makes a lotta sense.

- Chapter 7 covers Word's spell checker in glorious detail. Refer there for additional information about changing or correcting your typos.

Using Find and Replace in a Block

You cannot find text in a marked block, but you can use Word's Replace command. When a block is on, Replace finds and replaces only text in the marked block. The rest of your document is unaffected (unless you tell Word to replace outside the block when it's done).

- A full description of this operation is offered in the Chapter 5 section "Finding Something and Replacing It with Something Else." I'm too lazy to rewrite all that stuff here.
- The Find command cannot be used in a block because the Find command is used to mark the block; see "Marking a block with the Find command," earlier in this chapter.

Printing a Block

Word's Print command enables you to print one page, several pages, or an entire document. If you want to print only a small section of text, you have to mark it as a block and then print it. Refer to Chapter 9 for more information.

Chapter 7

Spelling and Grammer Made Easily

In This Chapter

- Understanding on-the-fly proofing
- Proofing your document all at once
- Adding words to the dictionary
- Using the miraculous AutoCorrect
- Using the thesaurus
- Counting your words

Nothing is wrong with English spelling. It's the pronunciation that's all goofed up. Think about it. If people actually said "Ka-nig-hut" for "knight," anyone could spell. And no more embarrassment would result over ugly words like *weird* and *facetious* that any human can pronounce, but only those who've memorized them can spell.

Fortunately, you don't need to risk any more embarrassment over your spelling. The same goes for your grammar, which is even more bizarre and twisted. Your computer, equipped with Word, can check even the worst English and come up with the proper suggestions. And because computers today are so dern fast, Word can even do it while you type (which is like having someone correct you while you sing, but I get into that annoyance in just a few paragraphs).

Word's Amazing, Annoying, On-the-Fly Document Proofing

On-the-fly document proofing was something that was bound to happen sooner or later. As computers get faster, they're capable of more and more things. Word processors don't really work very fast because they spend a lot of time waiting for you to type. So they sit and spin, wasting much of the computer's power and boring the microprocessor to tears.

"But, ah-ha!" they said at Microsoft one day. "We can use all that extra time floating around inside the computer to correct users' spelling as they type!" Cries of "Amazing! Fantastic! Applaudable!" rose in the room. Then they decided to add grammar checking as well. Cries of "Superior! Overwhelming! Fortuitous!" sounded in the air. Then they declared another stock split, left the room for some cheap food in Building 16, and saddled you and me with quirky, on-the-fly document proofing. The good news is that it's easy to ignore. The bad news is that it takes time to understand how to ignore it.

You misspelled another one. You misspelled another one. You misspelled another one.

Word automatically checks everything you type as you type it. Make a boo-boo, and Word lets you know. The second you press the spacebar or type some punctuation character, Word examines what you typed and immediately flags it as *wrong, wrong, wrong.* It does this by underlining the word using a red zig-zag pattern. See Figure 7-1 for a sampling.

If you're mentally fit, you can go on typing. Otherwise, you should point the mouse at the word and click the right mouse button (a right-click) to get further instructions.

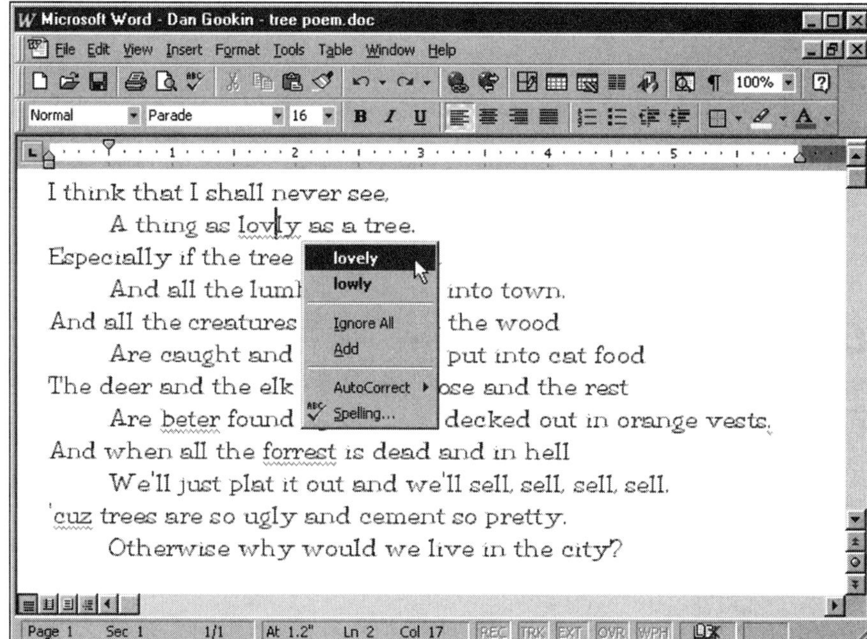

Figure 7-1: Word rubs it in that you cannot spell worth a dam.

You can select a new spelling word from those listed (see Figure 7-1), or you can click Ignore All so that Word won't bug you when you type that word again.

- Right-click a red-underlined word to see possible correct spellings.
- Word flags as wrong anything it doesn't recognize. This includes the five million-or-so words not represented in Word's electronic dictionary. Among them will probably be your name, street name, city name, and favorite ice cream flavor.
- Words underlined in green are being flagged as misused by Word's grammar checker. See the next section.
- Personally, I'd rather concentrate on my writing than worry about misspelled words as I'm composing my thoughts. If you're like me, you can turn this function off. See "Turning the bloody thing off" later in this chapter.

Checking your grammar on the fly

Like the spell checker, grammar checking is done on the fly. The difference is that your ugly misuse of the English tongue is underlined in wavy green instead of red (see Figure 7-2). So before you scrunch up your face and become concerned with red-green color blindness, keep in mind that a green-underlined word is most likely spelled correctly, it just doesn't fit in with the rest of the sentence (at least, according to the Word grammarmiesters).

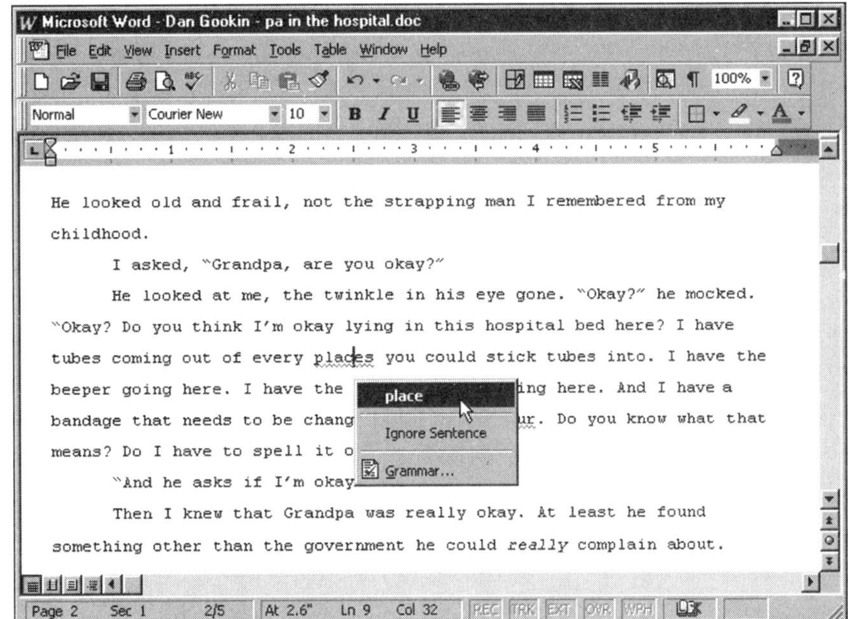

Figure 7-2: A horribly misused word is flagged.

To see what's amiss with your grammar mistakes, point your mouse at the green-underlined word and click the right mouse button. A pop-up menu appears with alternative words or a description of which English rule you violated. Choose the new word or sentence construction from the list. That word or sentence replaces the offending sentence in your document.

And if you think the grammar checker is full of bunk, choose Ignore Sentence from the pop-up menu.

- You must point the mouse at the word or phrase underlined in green, and then right-click to see the pop-up menu of suggestions.
- You don't need to take the grammar checking as seriously as spelling. In fact, the grammar checker is kind of dumb; I tried a number of English fouls on it — prepositions at the end of a sentence, missing verbs, mismatched tenses — and it couldn't detect any of them. (I suppose that I was too subtle.)

- If you're in the dark about something, the grammar checker *helps*. Sometimes its suggestions are off. For example, it may suggest "had" instead of "have." But if you think that you made the right choice, consider checking the rest of the sentence. Chances are you may have an unwanted "s" at the end of some word.
- If you detest on-the-fly grammar checking, you can turn it off. Follow the steps in the next section "Turning the bloody thing off."

Turning the bloody thing off

If you find the on-the-fly document proofing as annoying as I do, be thankful that you can turn it off. Follow these blessed steps:

1. **Choose Tools⇨Options.**

   The Options dialog box appears on the screen.

2. **Click the Spelling & Grammar tab.**

   Clicking this tab brings the Spelling & Grammar panel forward for your viewing pleasure.

3. **Remove the check mark from the Check spelling as you type item.**

   Just press Alt+P or click the box by Check spelling as you type to remove the check mark. This action disables Word's annoying habit of ringing out misspelled words on the screen.

4. **Remove the check mark from the Check grammar as you type item.**

   Press Alt+H or click the box by Check grammar as you type. This step removes the check mark and frees you from the burden of on-the-fly grammar checking.

5. Click the OK button.

Clicking OK closes the Options dialog box and makes your settings known to Word and mankind.

- You can always switch automatic document proofing back on by going through the preceding steps again and putting the check mark back into the box.
- With spelling and grammar checking disabled, you need to use the Spell tool to discover how badly you've abused English. See the next section.

Proofing Your Document All At Once

As someone who is more interested in getting the words down first as opposed to getting them down *properly,* I prefer to do my spell and grammar checks after I'm done writing. To check my work, I use Word's Spelling and Grammar command, which takes care of everything that could possibly go wrong with English all at once.

Even if you prefer to spell check on-the-fly, running the spell checker after you're done writing (and just before you print) is always a good idea. This operation is good for picking up those misspelled words you invariably miss. Face it: The computer knows English spelling better than you do.

To proof your entire document, choose the Tools⇨Spelling and Grammar command. You can also click the Spell tool or press F7, the Spelling and Grammar shortcut.

Word scans your document for offenses to English that would debun your seventh-grade English teacher's hair. When a boo-boo is encountered, the proper dialog box is displayed on the screen. You see either a spelling or a grammar dialog box; both look similar (see Figures 7-3 and 7-4).

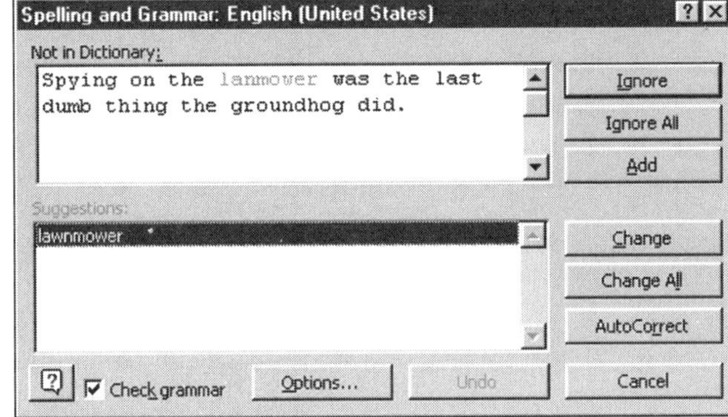

Figure 7-3: A misspelled word is caught.

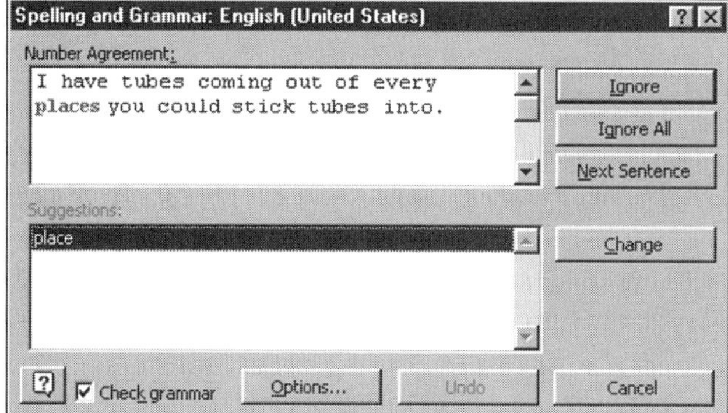

Figure 7-4: Grammar trouble.

Instructions on how to handle each of these are given in the check mark list that follows the next paragraph. Basically, if you find a suggestion or correction that appeals to you, click the Change button. Otherwise, click the Ignore button until the entire operation is over.

Word continues checking your document until it says it's all done. Or, if you started checking in the middle somewhere, Word asks if you want to continue checking at the start of the document; click OK.

- If the correction you want isn't in the list at the bottom of the dialog box, you can make up your own. Just edit the text that appears in the top part of the dialog box, making the change you feel is necessary. Then click the Change button. Word continues checking your sentence and the rest of your document.
- If you encounter a misspelled word that's repeated often in your document, click the Change All button.
- If the misspelled word is really a word, consider adding it to Word's dictionary. See the section "Adding Words to the Dictionary" later in this chapter.
- If the Add button appears dimmed, see "What? The Add Button Is Dimmed!" later in this chapter.
- If you don't want to be bothered with the same mistake over and over, click the Ignore All button.
- Select Change All if you want to change every instance of a misspelled word to whatever is in the Change box. If you have the annoying habit of typing *breif* rather than *brief,* for example, you can click Change All so that Word automatically makes the substitution without bothering you every time.

- If you find yourself making a large number of consistent mistakes — *teh* for *the, fi* for *if; alright* for *all right* — take advantage of Word's AutoCorrect tool. Refer to "The Miraculous AutoCorrect Thing," later in this chapter.

- Undo undoes your corrections, most of the time. This option is great for those sleepy nighttime checks when you quickly select the wrong replacement word and aren't sure. Just click Undo and check out the last word again. (Undo may not work all the time; don't count on it.)
- The Word dictionary is not a substitute for a real dictionary. Only in a real dictionary can you look up the meaning of a word, which tells you whether you're using the proper word in the proper context. No computer writer works with an electronic dictionary alone; a good, thick *Webster's* is usually sitting within arm's reach.
- If two identical words are found in a row, Word highlights them as a `Repeated Word`. Error, error! Click the Ignore button to tell Word to forget about the double word or click the Delete button to blow the second word away.
- My, but this is a long list of check marks.
- The Spelling and Grammar command also locates words with weird capitalization. For example, `gONer`. You're given an opportunity to correct the word to proper capitalization just as though it were misspelled.

- The word *spell* here refers to creating words by using the accepted pattern of letters. Spelling has nothing to do with magic. Many people assume that a spell check instantly makes their document better. Wrong! You have to read what you write and then edit, look, and read again. Spell checking doesn't fix things other than finding rotten words and offering suggested replacements.

Adding Words to the Dictionary

Some common words don't appear in the dictionary — my last name, for example. Perhaps your last name is as unique as mine or maybe your first name, city, business name, and so on, are all spelled correctly yet are unknown to Word. This means that every time you spell check your document, it will come up with alternative suggestions for those words. You have two options for avoiding this tautological conundrum:

The first, and most stupid option, is to press the Ignore button after the spell checker finds the word. Word then ignores that word during the spell check. But next time you spell check, you have to do the same thing. Dumb, dumb, dumb.

The second, and wiser, option is to Add said word to your custom dictionary. This dictionary is a list of words Word keeps and skips every time you spell check because you've told the program that they're all okay.

You can add words to the dictionary in one of two ways, depending on how you check your document.

If you're using on-the-fly checking, right-click the mouse on the word and choose Add from the pop-up menu. Otherwise, click the Add button in the Spelling and Grammar dialog box.

Either way, the word is stuffed into the custom dictionary, and you never have to mess with it again.

- When a word is in the custom dictionary, Word knows and recognizes the term as it does the words that come in the real dictionary — the one your fourth-grade English teacher wrote.
- Be careful when you decide to add a word to the custom dictionary, because un-adding a word from the dictionary isn't easy. This task is something you may want to do after you commit a flub and inadvertently put a seriously misspelled word in the dictionary. (I once added "fo" to the dictionary and spent three weeks in the Word penalty box.) You can get the word out again. The sidebar "No need to bother with this trivial drivel about the custom dictionary" covers this process.

What? The Add Button Is Dimmed!

The Add button is dimmed because you haven't set up a custom dictionary. To do so, follow these steps:

1. **Fire up the Options for the Speller.**

   If you're in the Spelling dialog box, click the Options button. Otherwise, choose the Tools⇨Options command and then click the words *Spelling and Grammar* located on one of the tabs in the top of the Options dialog box.

2. **Click the Dictionaries button to create your own dictionary.**

   The Custom Dictionaries dialog box is displayed.

   The first item in the list of custom dictionaries should be CUSTOM DIC. That's the one you want.

3. **Click the box by CUSTOM DIC.**

   Clicking puts a check mark in that box, telling Word that you want to use it as your own, personal, custom dictionary.

4. **Click the OK button in the Custom Dictionaries dialog box.**

   It goes away.

5. **Click the OK button in the Options dialog box.**

   Poof!

   You can now use the Add button in the Spelling dialog box to stick words into your own personal dictionary.

The Miraculous AutoCorrect Thing

One of the handy things Word can do is correct your foul spelling as you type. No, this process isn't the same as on-the-fly spell checking. Word isn't out to waggle its finger at you. Instead, this time Word actually *corrects* your boo-boos, sometimes so fast you don't even see it.

Word's AutoCorrect feature is amazing stuff. You type *teh,* and Word quickly and quietly corrects the spelling. So if you know how to spell a word but find out that your fingers just don't have a clue, AutoCorrect comes to your rescue.

Activating AutoCorrect

To ensure that AutoCorrect is on, Choose Tools⇨AutoCorrect (or press Alt,T,A). The AutoCorrect dialog box is displayed, as shown in Figure 7-5.

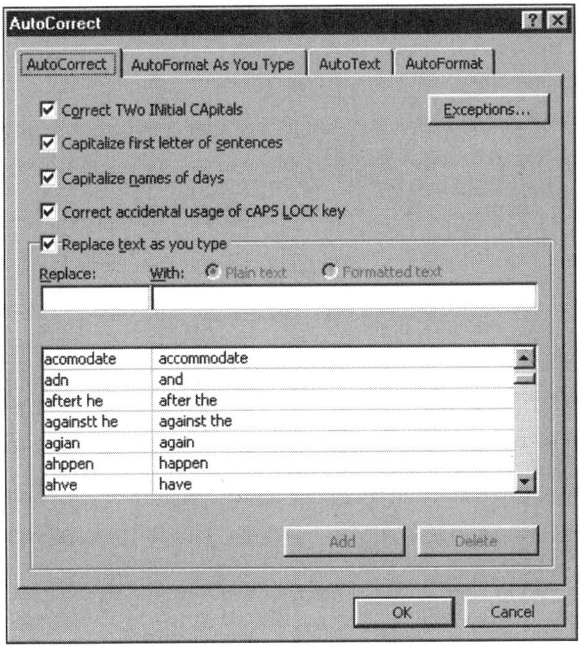

Figure 7-5: The AutoCorrect dialog box.

About midway down the left side of the box, you see the Replace text as you type item with a wee box by it. If the box is empty, click it (or press Alt+T). That sticks a check mark in the box, which means that AutoCorrect is on and ready to work while you type.

No need to bother with this trivial drivel about the custom dictionary

The custom dictionary is a text document on disk. It contains, in alphabetical order, all the words you added. And as a special bonus, you can edit the list and remove any deleterious words you may have added.

To remove nasty words, follow Steps 1 and 2 in "What? The Add Button Is Dimmed!" Then click the dictionary you want to edit (if more than one exists) to highlight it. Then click the Edit button. This action opens the dictionary as a document in Word, where you can go about your business removing any mistakes you've made. (You may see a warning about on-the-fly spell checking being disabled. It only makes sense.)

For example, suppose that you accidentally stuck "fo" in the dictionary. Only by editing the CUSTOM.DIC file can you get "fo" out of there.

Save the CUSTOM.DIC file after you're done. The custom dictionary is saved to disk just as any other Word document is. See Chapter 20 for more information on saving stuff in Word.

Click the OK button to close the AutoCorrect dialog box.

AutoCorrect's main role in life is to automatically replace words that you commonly goof. The feature also has four other functions, each of which is listed at the top of the AutoCorrect dialog box. These functions are described in the following check mark items. To activate or deactivate any item, click it with the mouse. A check mark in an item's box means that it's on and working.

- The Correct TWo INitial CApitals item directs Word to correct this common typing *faux pas* by switching the second capitalized letter back to lowercase.
- The Capitalize first letter of sentences item controls whether Word automatically capitalizes the first letter in a sentence when you forget to. e. e. cummings should leave this item unchecked.
- The Capitalize names of days item capitalizes Monday, Tuesday, and so on, as they should be capitalized. Of course, if you weren't asleep in class that day in the fourth grade, you'd remember this tiny bit of English trivia.
- The Correct accidental usage of cAPS LOCK key item fixes a minor, yet annoying problem: If you unwittingly type with the Caps Lock key on, your text looks very bizarre. Checking this item tells Word to fix it automatically. I suppose this option is primarily intended for those who don't look at the screen as they type.

Adding words to AutoCorrect's repertoire

The bullies at Microsoft have already inserted a few common typos into AutoCorrect's brain. These common mistakes are listed at the bottom of the AutoCorrect dialog box, in a scrolling list. The dojobbie on the left is the way you often spell something. The whatzis on the right is what Word replaces it with.

From Figure 7-5, you can see the common adn-and combination; type **adn** in Word, and it automatically is corrected to *and*. (It's those three-letter words that get you.)

To add a new item to the list, follow these steps:

1. **Choose the Tools⇨AutoCorrect command.**

   Use your mouse or press Alt,T,A. The AutoCorrect dialog box appears.

2. **Focus in on the Replace box, where you type a common goof.**

   Click the mouse in the Replace box or press Alt+R on your keyboard.

3. **Type the word you often goof.**

   Don't worry if you can't think of words to add; adding words to AutoCorrect's repertoire when you check your spelling is also possible. See the next section for information.

4. **Press the Tab key.**

   This step moves you over to the With box, where you type the proper way the word goes.

5. **Type the proper way the word goes.**

6. **Click the Add button after you're done.**

7. **To add more AutoCorrect words, repeat Steps 2 through 6.**

   Or click the OK button after you're done.

- You can remove words from AutoCorrect that you don't want repaired automatically. Just highlight the word in the list and click the Delete button. Poof! It's gone.

- You may notice the (r) thing in AutoCorrect's word list. That (r) is an abbreviation for a special symbol AutoCorrect automagically inserts into your document. To specify a special symbol, type that character in the With box. For example, to assign the em dash (a longer dash than a hyphen) to two -- (double hyphen) characters, type two hyphens in the Replace box and press Ctrl+Alt+– (the minus key on the keyboard's numeric key pad) in the With box. (See the Chapter 26 section, "Inserting Oddball and Special Characters," for more information about such characters.)

- You can also add graphical characters to AutoCorrect. You see an arrow and happy face in the list at the bottom of the AutoCorrect dialog box.
- Being cruel with AutoCorrect is entirely possible. For example, inserting a meanie like **thier** for **their** would drive some people nuts. Remember, AutoCorrect is subtle. If you type looking at the keyboard rather than the screen, you never know what it's up to.

Adding to AutoCorrect when you check your spelling

An easier way to get words into AutoCorrect's list is to click the AutoCorrect option when you check your spelling.

When you check on-the-fly spelling, choose the AutoCorrect item from the pop-up menu (refer to Figure 7-1). That displays a submenu with the correct spellings.

In the Spelling and Grammar dialog box, you can use the AutoCorrect button to add a word and its correction to AutoCorrect's list. Just pluck the correct word from the list of suggestions and click the AutoCorrect button.

Be careful when adding words to AutoCorrect. When you do, you're sticking both the misspelled word and its replacement into AutoCorrect's list. Make sure that you have the proper replacement word highlighted *before* you add it.

A Li'l Bit o' Help from Word's Thesaurus

If you think that I'm smart enough to use all the big words in this chapter, you're grievously mistaken. Witness *grievously.* That's just another word for *badly.* Behold! It's Word's thesaurus in action. An amazing tool, astounding utensil, or marvelous implement. You get the idea. The thesaurus helps look up synonyms or other words that have the same meaning but carry more weight or offer more precision.

Here's how to instantly become a master of big, clunky words in English:

1. **Hover the cursor on a simple word, such as big.**

   Adjectives are best for the thesaurus, although the Word Statistical Department tells me that the thesaurus contains more than 120,000 words.

2. **Do the Thesaurus command.**

   Choose Tools➪Language➪Thesaurus or press the Thesaurus shortcut, Shift + F7. Instantly, the Thesaurus dialog box opens (see Figure 7-6). Word displays several alternatives for the word. They're grouped into categories by meanings on the left and synonyms on the right.

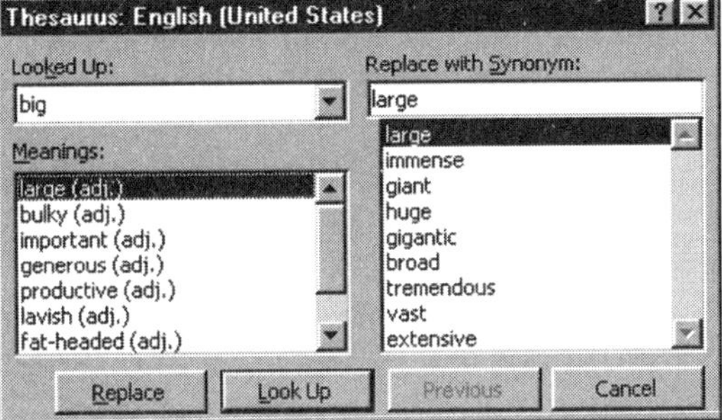

Figure 7-6: The thesaurus displays other terms for big.

3. **To replace the word in your document, highlight your choice and click the Replace button.**

   After selecting a word, you return to your document. If you don't find a word, click the Cancel button to return to your document.

- A thesaurus is not a colossal, prehistoric beast.
- If one of the words in the left column is close but not exactly what you want, select it and click the Look Up button. The new word's synonyms appear in the right column.
- If the word that you select has no synonym, the thesaurus displays an alphabetical list of words. Type a new, similar word or click the Cancel button to get back to your document.
- After inserting a new word, you may have to do a bit of editing: Add "ed" or "ing" to the word or maybe replace "a" with "an" in front of it. A bit of editing is usually required whenever you replace one word with another.

Pulling a Word Count

One of the silliest writing assignments you probably ever got in school was the "I want you to write a five-page dissertation on why ketchup isn't green" type of project — five pages! Are they nuts? Didn't Strunk and White stress brevity and clarity of thought over ghastly verbiage? I mean, if you can't offer a lucid argument in a single seven-word sentence, why do it? But I digress.

Then there are those of us who get paid by the word. "Dan, write a 1,000-word article on Windows Registration Editor." I need to know when to stop writing. Also, curiosity generally gets the best of any writer, and you want to get a good feel for how many words you have in your document. To do that, choose the Tools➪Word Count command.

The Word Count dialog box displays a summary of your document's pages, words, characters, paragraphs, and lines. Figure 7-7 shows the stats for this document (before my editor got his blue ink-stained hands on it). How impressive. Okay. Click the Close button to get back to work.

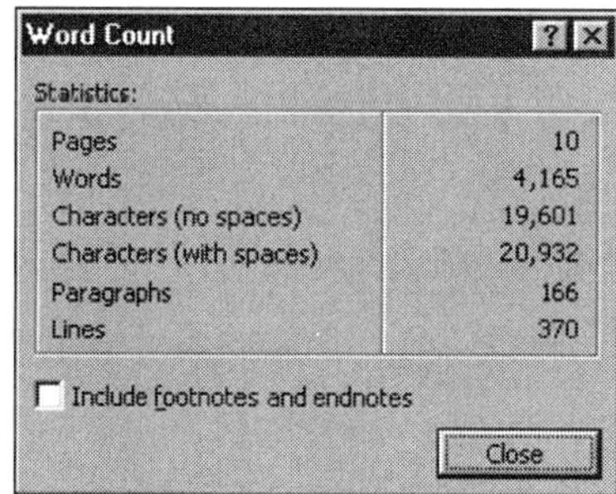

Figure 7-7: Gonna count me up some words.

The Word Count command is far more accurate than a page count. Pages can be fudged. Larger fonts and narrower margins have saved many a student from the perils of turning in a paper that's too short.

Chapter 8

Saving Your Stuff

In This Chapter

- Saving a document to disk (the first time)
- Saving a document to disk (after that)
- Saving a document to disk and quitting
- Saving and starting again with a clean slate
- Opening a document on disk
- Inserting one document into another document

Your computer doesn't have disk drives just because it needed another pretty light on the console. No, the disk drives are there for the same reason people have closets and garages; they exist to store our junk. Of course, what constitutes *junk* is different for everyone. My neighbor's garage, for example, has nothing but junk in it, cement floor to unfinished ceiling. My garage, on the other hand, well I *need* all those old magazines and clothes from 40 pounds ago.

The point to all this (if there is one) is that you need a place to store your documents after you create them. You can't just leave things on the screen forever. Save even silly stuff to disk. After all, you may want to turn the computer off once in a while. Or maybe the power company in your area will randomly do that for you. In that case, you definitely want to save right away and often. This chapter shows you how.

Saving a Document to Disk (The First Time)

There's no need to save your document to disk only when you're done with it. In fact, saving should be done almost immediately — as soon as you have a few sentences or paragraphs. Save! Save! Save!

To save a document that hasn't already been saved to disk, follow the steps listed below. If you've already saved the file, skip to the next section.

1. **Summon the Save command.**

   Just click the Save button on the toolbar. Other ways to save (if you have the time): Choose File⇨Save; press Alt, F, S; press the Ctrl+S shortcut; or use the F12 key. (Ugh.) No matter how you do it, the Save As dialog box enlightens you with its presence, as shown in Figure 8-1.

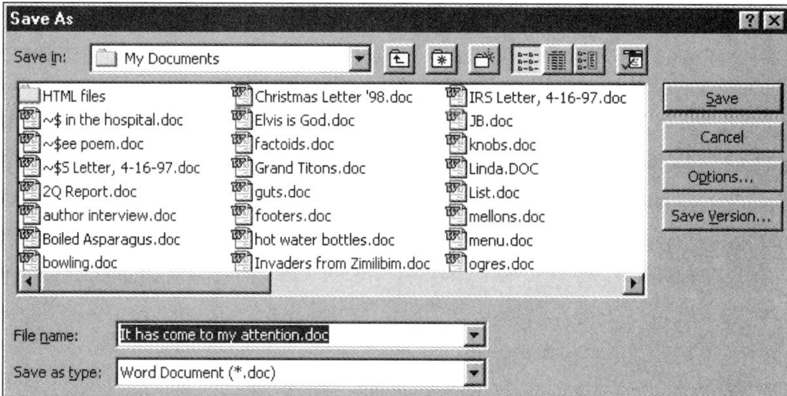

Figure 8-1: The Save As dialog box.

   If you don't see the Save As dialog box, you've already saved your document once. You've merely saved it again. That's okay. See the very next section.

2. **Type a name for your document.**

   You can name your document anything, using letters, numbers, a smattering of symbols, spaces, and other whatnot. Though the filename can be tediously long, my advice is to keep it short, simple, and descriptive (which rules out most lawyers from effectively naming files).

   You'll notice in the Save As dialog box that Word automatically gives your document a name that equals the first few words of text. Oftentimes, this name is more than adequate (unless you start everything with "It has come to my attention . . .").

3. **Click Save.**

   If everything goes right, your disk drive churns for a few seconds and eventually your filename appears in the title bar. Your file has been saved.

   If a problem arises, you'll likely see one of two error messages:

```
Do you want to replace the existing WHATEVER.DOC?
```

There already is a file on disk with that name. Press N for No, skip back up to Step 2, and type another name. If you press Y, your file replaces the other file on disk, which is probably not what you want.

```
Word cannot give a document the same name as an open
document.
```

This message means that you tried to save a file to disk using the name of another document you're working on. Just try again using a different name.

Another problem you may encounter happens when you type an incorrect filename. Yeah, even though you're allowed to type in just about anything for a filename, some characters just drive Windows mad. If so, you get some kind of error message about it. Click the OK button and try again with another filename.

- Always save your document, even after you've typed only a few lines of text.
- You should also organize your files by storing them in their own special folders on your disk. I cover this subject in Chapter 20 in the section "Making a Place for Your Work."

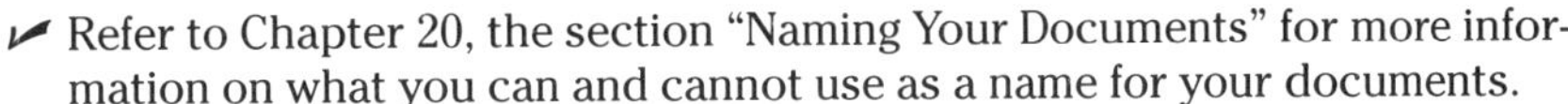

- Refer to Chapter 20, the section "Naming Your Documents" for more information on what you can and cannot use as a name for your documents.

Saving a document to disk (after that)

The instructions in this section assume that you already saved your file to disk once. So why save your file again (and again)? Because saving is smart! You should save your file to disk every so often — usually after you write something brilliant or so complex that you don't want to retype it again. (If you haven't yet saved your document to disk, refer to the preceding section.)

Saving your document to disk a second time updates the file on disk. This procedure is painless and quick:

1. **Choose File⇨Save or press the Ctrl+S shortcut.**

   You see the status bar change oh-so quickly as the document is saved. (You can also click the Save button.)

2. **Continue working.**

   I recommend going back and repeating this step every so often as you continue to toss words down on the page.

- Save! Save! Save!
- Save your document to disk every three minutes or so, or any time after you write something clever.
- If you are working on a network, execute the Save command between each keystroke.
- If you already saved your file to disk, its name appears in the title bar. If the title bar does not display the name (it says `document` or something equally boring), refer to the preceding section for saving instructions.
- Word can be trained to automatically save your document every so often. See Chapter 34 for the how-to.

Saving a document to disk and quitting

You're done for the day. Your fingers are sore, your eyes glaze over, "I don't want to type no more!" Everywhere you look, you see a mouse pointer. You blink and rub your eyes and stretch out your back. Ah, it's Miller time. But before you slap your buddies on the back and walk into the sunset in a beer commercial, you need to save your document and quit for the day:

1. **Exit.**

   Choose File⇨Exit or press Alt+F4. You see a box that asks

   ```
   Do you want to save the changes you made to whatever?
   Yes No Cancel
   ```

2. **Press Y to save your document.**

   The document is saved and Word closes — quit, kaput.

- If a second document remains in Word and changes have been made to the document since it was last saved, you see the same message again. Press Y to save that document.
- If you haven't yet given your document a name, you can do so after pressing Y to save it. Refer to the instructions for "Saving a Document to Disk (The First Time)," earlier in this chapter.
- After you quit Word, you find yourself back in Windows. There you can start another program or exit Windows and sell your PC and join the French Foreign Legion.

- Always quit Word properly. Never turn off your PC or reset when Word or Windows is still on-screen. Only turn off your PC when Windows tells you that it's safe to do so.

Saving and starting over with a clean slate

When you want to save a document, remove it from the screen, start over with a clean slate, and choose the File⇨Close command. This action keeps you in Word, ready for more word-processing action.

- The shortcut key for the File⇨Close command is Ctrl+W.

- You can also start afresh in Word and work on a new document by clicking the New button on the Standard toolbar.
- You can also choose the File⇨New command or press Ctrl+N on the keyboard, but then you see the ugly New dialog box — an extra step. Just click OK to start a new document. See Chapter 16 for more information on the New dialog box.
- If you haven't yet saved your document to disk, refer to "Saving a Document to Disk (The First Time)," earlier in this chapter. Always save your document right after you start writing something (and approximately every 2.3 seconds after that).

- There is no reason to quit Word and start it again to begin working with a blank slate.

Opening a Document on Disk

When you first start Word, or after closing one document and starting again with a clean slate, you have the option of retrieving a previously saved document from disk into Word for editing. After all, if you can save stuff to disk, you need some way to get it back again.

To grab a file from disk — to *open* it — follow these steps:

1. **Summon the Open command.**

   Choose File⇨Open, press Ctrl+O (the Open shortcut), or click the Open button in the Standard toolbar. You see the Open dialog box, as shown in Figure 8-2.

2. **Click the document's icon with the mouse pointer.**

   Just click once. You may need to use the scroll bar at the bottom of the file list to see more files to the right.

   Clicking the file *selects* it, making it appear highlighted in the file list.

3. **Click the Open button.**

   Word opens the file, carefully lifting it from your disk drive and slapping it down on the screen where you can edit it, print it, read it, or just look at it in glowing admiration.

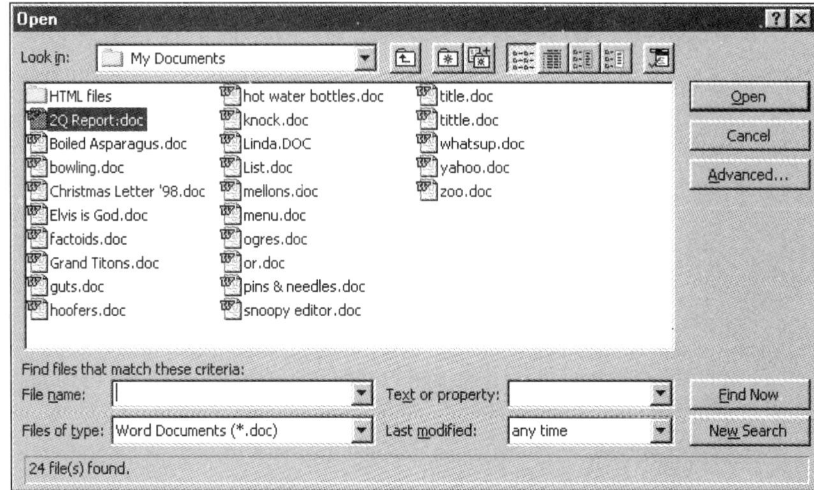

Figure 8-2: The Open dialog box.

- Opening a document does not erase it from your disk drive.
- After editing the document, remember to save it occasionally. See "Saving a document to disk (after that)" earlier in this chapter. (Since you've opened a document already on disk, you don't need to save it for the first time again.)
- However, if you want to save an edited document to disk with a new name, use the File➪Save As command. Then you can refer to the section "Saving a Document to Disk (The First Time)" earlier in this chapter.

- If you're not sure what's in a document, click the Preview button in the Open dialog box. That adds a window to the dialog box where you can sneak-peek a look at what's in a document before you open it.
- You can use the gizmos in the Open dialog box to browse through various disks and folders on your PC to look for documents you may have stored elsewhere. Read through Chapter 20, which touches upon the subject lightly.
- If you can't find your document, refer to Chapter 32, the section titled "I Lost My Files!"
- If you load a file written by another word processor, you may see a dialog box asking whether it's okay to convert the file to Word-speak. Answer Yes. Refer to Chapter 19 for more information on alien word-processor documents.

Inserting One Document into Another

This sounds peculiar, like something only a disk drive utility could do, but inserting one document into another is not that complex. Sometimes you want to load one document into another. For example, you may have your biography, résumé, or curriculum vitae in a file on disk, and you want to add that information to the end of a letter begging for a job. If so, or in any other circumstances that I can't think of right now, follow these steps:

1. **Position the toothpick cursor where you want the other document's text to appear.**

   The text will be inserted just as if you typed the whole thing right there with your little, stubby fingers.

2. **Choose Insert⇨File.**

   Or press Alt, I, L. A dialog box similar to the Open dialog box appears. This box works the same way (see the section "Opening a Document on Disk" earlier in this chapter).

3. **Pluck the icon representing the document you want to paste.**

   Click the document's icon using the mouse.

   You can also use the gadgets and gizmos in the dialog box to locate a file in another folder or on another disk drive or even on someone else's computer on the network. Such power.

4. **Click the Open button.**

   The document appears, or rather is inserted, right where the toothpick cursor is. All the formatting, text, and everything else looks the same as when you last saved that document to disk, though now it sits in the belly of another document.

- The resulting, combined document still has the same name as the first document.
- You can retrieve any number of documents on disk into your document, one at a time. There is no limit.
- These steps allow you to grab a block of text saved into one document and stick the text into another document. This process is often called *boilerplating,* where a commonly used piece of text is slapped into several documents. This process is also the way sleazy romance novels are written.
- See Chapter 6 for information on copying Scrap icons from the Windows Desktop into your document.
- Biography. Résumé. Curriculum vitae. The more important you think that you are, the more foreign the language used to describe what you've done.

Chapter 9

The Printer, the Paper, the Document Maker

In This Chapter

- Preparing to print
- Previewing your document before printing
- Printing a whole document
- Printing a specific page
- Printing a block
- Printing several documents
- Printing several copies of a single document
- Printing envelopes
- Printing labels

You sure didn't need a printer if you were "word processing" on a typewriter; writing and printing happened at the same time. The process works the same way with a pencil, too. Obviously you're being silly by using a computer with word-processing software and a printer. Look at the cost! Then again, look at the fine output from a printer. And if you tame Word, that output is close to perfection — no dollops of White Out, no eraser smudges.

Of course, making everything turn out so splendidly requires that you get your printer to work. And no single device in your entire computer system deserves a good flogging like the printer. After you mess with your printer for a while, you discover that it's a stubborn little guy, rarely cooperative and hard to tame. This chapter should give you some tips for using your printer with Word, hopefully making what it prints look exactly like you imagined.

Do This before You Print!

Before printing, you must make sure that your printer is ready to print. This involves more than flipping on its power switch.

Start by making sure that your printer is plugged in and properly connected to your computer. A cable connects the computer and your printer. The cable should be firmly plugged in at both ends. (This cable needs to be checked only if you're having printer problems.)

Also, make sure that your printer has a decent ribbon. Old, frayed ribbons produce faint text and are bad for the printing mechanism. You may spend more later in repair bills if you're trying to save a few bucks now by using a ribbon longer than recommended. Laser printers should have a good toner cartridge installed. If the laser printer's toner low message appears or a toner low light is on, replace the toner at once.

Your printer must contain paper to print on. The paper can feed from the back, come out of a paper tray, or manually feed one sheet at a time. However your printer eats paper, make sure that you have it set up properly before you print.

Finally, your printer must be *online* or *selected* before you can print anything. Somewhere on your printer is a button labeled Online or Select and, usually, a corresponding light or display. Press that button to turn on the option (and the light). Although your printer is plugged in, the power switch is on, and the machine is doing its warm-up stretching exercises, the printer doesn't print unless it's online or selected.

- Before you can print, your printer must be plugged into the wall, plugged into your computer, turned on, full of paper, and online or selected. (Most printers are in the online or selected mode when you turn them on.)

- Never plug a printer cable into a printer or computer that is on and running. Always turn your printer and computer off whenever you plug anything into them. If not, you may damage the internal electronic components.
- If you're printing to a network printer — and the thought makes me shudder — someone else is in charge of the printer. The network printer should be set up and ready to print. If not, someone to whom you can complain is usually handy.
- The printer you use affects the way Word displays and prints your document, so before you do a lot of formatting, check to be sure that you have the correct printer selected. Refer to the section "Choosing Another Printer (If You Have More Than One to Choose From)" in Chapter 31.

- Chapter 31 covers some additional information about setting up, or *installing,* your printer for use with Word. That chapter also contains troubleshooting information and a detailed anatomical guide to popular printers that tells you where to shoot the printer for a quick death or a lingering, slow, and painful one.

Preview Your Printing

Printing something 1,000 times to get it right sure doesn't make Mr. Bunny feel good. Not that I have anything against slaughtering trees. I own a few myself. It's a cash crop! But that's not an excuse to waste paper. Instead, you can take the more environmentally conscious route — and save yourself time as well — by employing Word's fancy Print Preview command. That command lets you see what your document will look like printed before you print it.

To sneak a preview of how your printed document will look, choose File⇨Print Preview or click the handy Print Preview button on the Standard toolbar. That action switches Word's display to a rather standoffish look at your document, as shown in Figure 9-1.

Take note of how your text looks on the page. Look at the margins. If you're using footnotes, headers, or footers, look how they lay out. The idea here is to spot something dreadfully wrong *before* you print.

When you're done gawking, click the Close button to return to your document.

Or if everything looks hunky and dory, click the little printer tool and your document is instantly printed.

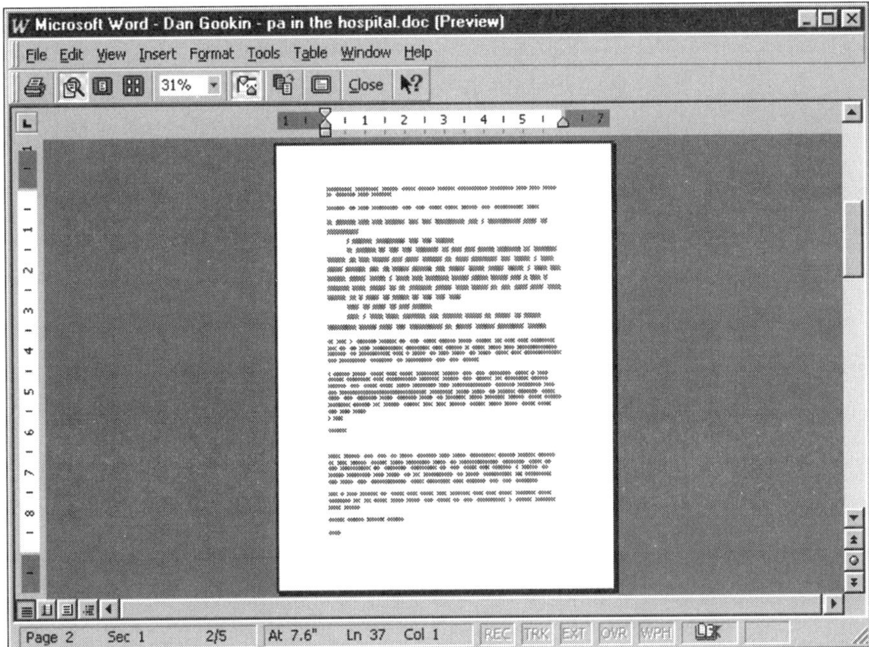

Figure 9-1: A document is pre-viewed before printing, saving countless trees.

- Use the scroll bars to see more of your document.
- You can use the wheel in your wheel mouse to scroll through your document in Print Preview mode. One click of the wheel equals one page up or down in your document.
- If your mouse is wheel-less, you can use the Page Up and Page Down buttons to peruse various pages of your document.

- The mouse pointer changes to a magnifying glass in Print Preview mode. Click the mouse on any part of your document to zoom in for a closer look. Click the mouse again to zoom back out.
- You can, kind of, sort of, edit in Print Preview mode. Even so, I don't recommend it. Instead, if you want to edit, click the Close button to return to proper editing mode.
- I don't really use Print Preview much. However, if I'm really formatting something heavily — with footnotes, strange columns, and stuff like that — Print Preview can be a godsend.

Printing a Whole Document

If you think that your work is worthy enough to be enshrined on a sheet of paper, follow these steps. To print your entire document, from top to bottom, gavel to gavel, head to toe, from *once upon a time* to *happily every after*

1. **Make sure that the printer is *online* and ready to print.**

   What's that noise? Is Grandma juicing again? No, the printer is humming its merry tune.

2. **Save your document.**

   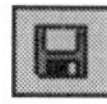

   Ha! Surprised you. Saving before you print is always a good idea. Click the little Save tool for a quickie save, and if you need any extra help, refer to Chapter 8 on saving your stuff to disk.

3. **Print your document.**

   The quickest way to do this is to click the Print tool.

4. **The printer warms up and starts to print.**

   Printing may take some time — really. A long time. Fortunately, Word lets you continue working while it prints in the *background*. To ensure that Word works this way, refer to the techy sidebar, "Printing and getting on with your life."

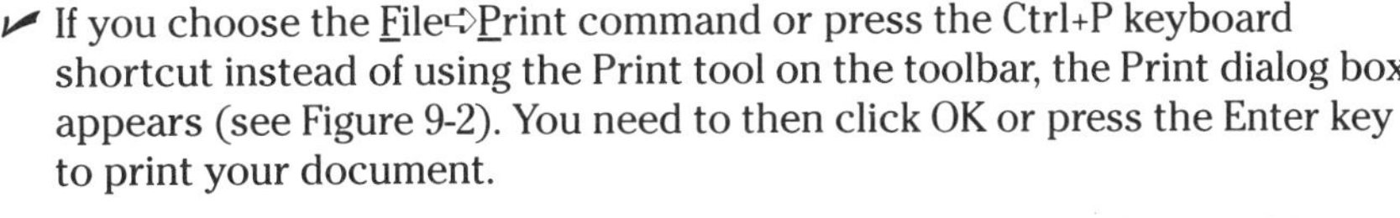

- If you choose the File⇨Print command or press the Ctrl+P keyboard shortcut instead of using the Print tool on the toolbar, the Print dialog box appears (see Figure 9-2). You need to then click OK or press the Enter key to print your document.

- If nothing prints, don't hit the Print command again! There's probably nothing awry; the computer is still thinking or sending (downloading) fonts to the printer. If you don't get an error message, everything will probably print, eventually.
- If you have a manual-feed printer, the printer itself begs for paper. Your printer says, "Beep, feed me!" You must stand by, line up paper, and then shove it into the printer's gaping maw until your document is done printing. Refer to "Printing Envelopes," later in this chapter, to figure this one out.

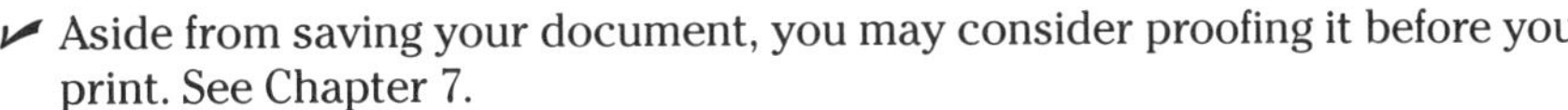

- Aside from saving your document, you may consider proofing it before you print. See Chapter 7.
- Do you have printer problems? See Chapter 31.
- Also see Chapter 31 if you print something and then want to change your mind. (Good luck!)
- Windows actually does the printing. Word simply acts as a messenger. Because of this fact, you see Windows' li'l printer guy appear by the current time on the taskbar whenever something is printing in Word. This display isn't very important.

Printing and getting on with your life

Word has the capability to print while you do something else. If this capability isn't coddled to life, you may have to wait a dreadfully long time while your document prints. To ensure that the background printing option is on, click the Options button in the Print dialog box (press Ctrl+P and then Alt+O to get at the Options button). A special dialog box appears.

In the upper part of the dialog box, you find the Printing Options corral. The top item in the right column is Background Printing. Make sure that it has a check mark in the little box. If not, click the box or press Alt+B. Click the OK button to close that dialog box, and then click the Close button to banish the Print dialog box. Now you're all set with background printing.

Printing a Specific Page

Follow these steps to print only one page of your document:

1. **Make sure that your printer is turned on and eager to print something.**
2. **Move the toothpick cursor so that it's sitting somewhere in the page you want to print.**

   Check the Page counter in the lower-left corner of the screen (on the status bar) to ensure that you're at the page that you want to print.
3. **Choose the File⇨Print command or press Ctrl+P.**

   Do not use the print tool here, because it prints your entire document without question. Only by choosing the Print command from the File menu or pressing the Ctrl+P shortcut will you see the glorious Print dialog box, as depicted in Figure 9-2.

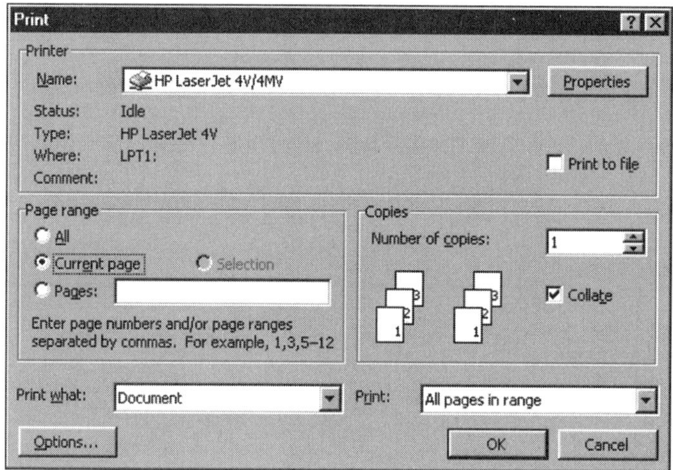

Figure 9-2: The Print dialog box.

4. **Select Current page.**

   Click Current page in the Page range area in the Print dialog box.
5. **Click OK.**
6. **You return to your document when that sole page is printed on your printer.**

   The page should have a header, footer, all formatting — and even a page number — just as though you had the complete document, but only that page prints.

Printing a Range of Pages

Word enables you to print a single page, a range of pages, or even some hodge-podge combination of random pages from within your document. To print a range or group of pages, follow these steps:

1. **Make sure that the printer is online, happy, and ready to print.**
2. **Conjure up the File⇨Print command.**

   You need to use the Printer dialog box here, so choose File⇨Print from the menu or press the Ctrl+P keyboard shortcut. Do not click the Print tool on the toolbar.
3. **Click the Pages button in the Page range area of the Print dialog box.**

   Click Pages with the mouse. This action puts a dot in that radio button and puts a blinking toothpick cursor into the text box by the word Pages.
4. **Type the page numbers and range of page numbers.**

   To print pages 3 through 5, type **3-5**. To print pages 1 through 7, type **1-7**.
5. **Click OK.**

   Click the OK button or press the Enter key. The pages you specified — and only those pages — are printed.

You can get very specific with the page ranges. For example, to print page 3, pages 5 through 9, pages 15 through 17, and page 19 (boy, that coffee went everywhere, didn't it?), you type **3**, **5-9**, **15-17**, **19**.

Printing a Block

After a block of text is marked on-screen, you can beg the Print command to print only that block. Refer to "Printing a Block" in Chapter 6 for the down-and-dirty details.

1. **Make sure that your printer is on and ready to print.**
2. **Mark the block of text that you want to print.**
3. **Choose the File⇨Print command.**

   You can also press Ctrl+P or qualify for the Finger Gymnastics event at the next Olympics and press Ctrl+Shift+F12. Do not click the Print tool on the toolbar!

4. **Tickle the button by the word Selection.**

   Press the Alt+S key or click the button by the word Selection with your mouse. (Selection is located in the Page range area of the Print dialog box.) This step tells Word that you want to print only your highlighted block.

5. **Click the OK button.**

In a few moments, you see the hard copy sputtering out of your printer. The page selection prints in the same position and with the same headers and footers (if any) as it would had you printed the entire document.

- The Print tool on the Standard toolbar is used only to print the entire document, not your selected block. Use Ctrl+P to print your block instead.
- The Selection item in the Print dialog box is available only when you have a block selected.

Printing Several Documents

You may think that the best way to print several documents at a time is to load them one at a time and print them one at a time. A better way exists, however, and it's hidden in the Open dialog box, the same one you use to open any old document on disk. You can use this trick to select documents on disk and do a "gang print." This process is rumored to be easier than loading each file into Word, printing it, putting the file away, and then loading another file. You be the judge.

To print several files at a time, follow these steps:

1. **Make sure that the printer is on, selected, and rarin' to print.**
2. **Choose File⇨Open.**

   Or you can press Ctrl+O or click the Open tool. Either way, the Open dialog box appears in all its glory.

3. **Select the documents you want to print.**

   To select a document, Ctrl-click it with the mouse: Press and hold the Ctrl key and click the file. This highlights that document.

   Keep Ctrl-clicking documents until you've highlighted all those you want to print.

4. **Click the Commands and Settings button at the top of the Open dialog box.**

   A list of commands appears in a pop-up menu (see Figure 9-3). The one you want is the third one down, Print.

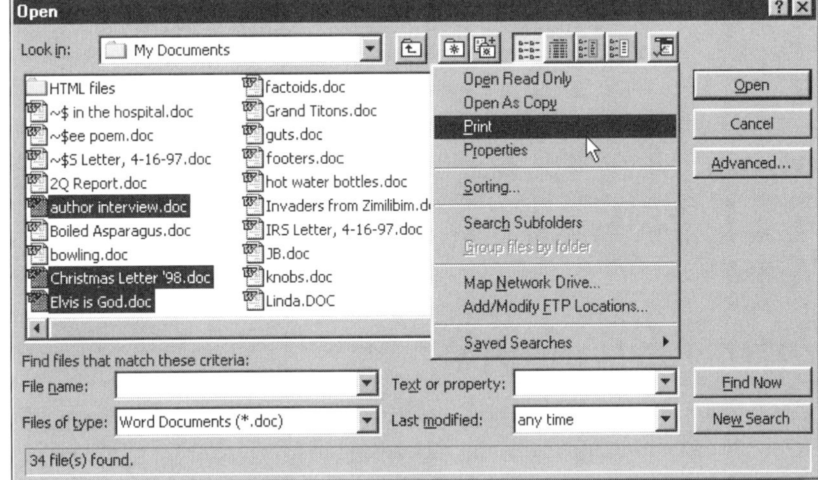

Figure 9-3: Choosing the Print command in the Open dialog box.

5. **Click the Print command with the mouse.**

   Word happily prints all the documents that you selected.

- When you print a gang of documents, they just all print. No Print dialog box or no warning asks you if the printer has enough paper or if you're really spiritually prepared to print all those documents at once.
- See Chapter 8 for more information on the Open dialog box.
- This method is perhaps the most obtuse way of printing multiple files that I've ever encountered in any word processor.
- Yes, as with printing a single document, printing multiple documents takes a while.

Printing More Than One Copy of Something

Every year I concoct a family Christmas letter and bring joy to the hearts of dozens of friends and relatives by sending them a copy. Rather than drive off to Kinko's and pay the exorbitant fee of two cents per copy, I instead opt to do my own printing and direct Word to have the printer spew out the several dozen copies I need. This approach is real cinchy, providing you have enough paper, and you know which part of the Print dialog box to tweak.

Although you may not have dozens of Christmas letters to zip off, you may occasionally want more than one copy of a document. To make extra copies, locate the Copies area in the Print dialog box next time you visit (refer to

Figure 9-2). In the Number of copies box, type the number of copies you want Word to spew out. For three copies of a memo, type **3**. Then print as you normally would by clicking the OK button. It's that easy.

Under normal circumstances, Word prints each copy of the document one after the other. This process is known as "collating." However, if you're printing seven copies of something and you want Word to print seven page 1s and then seven page 2s (and so on), click the little box by the word Collate to *remove* the check mark. (Normally you leave the check mark there.)

Printing Envelopes

Yes, Word can print envelopes. Yes, envelopes can even be a snap. A special Word command is specifically designed for this purpose. (Alas, Word does not print the stamp as well. And if it could, it may as well print money.)

To print an envelope, follow these steps:

1. **Make sure that the printer is oh-so-eager to print something.**
2. **Choose the Tools⇨Envelopes and Labels command.**

   This step opens the Envelopes and Labels dialog box, shown in Figure 9-4. If an address had been selected in your document or if Word has somehow magically located the address near the toothpick cursor, it appears in the Delivery address box.

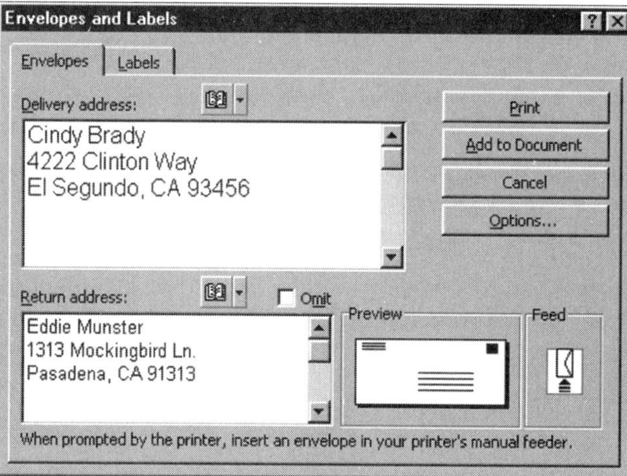

Figure 9-4: The Envelopes and Labels dialog box, please.

If Word didn't automatically fill in the address, type it now.

3. **Stick an envelope in your printer.**

   I mention this step because most printers must be spoon-fed envelopes one at a time. (Mine works like this.) In some fancy-schmancy offices, printers may have *envelope feeders.* Well, la-de-da.

   By the way, you can double-click the Feed part of the Envelopes panel to tell Word how the envelope will arrive through the printer. This result really depends on how your printer sucks in envelopes. Mine has a special slot for them that takes 'em face up in the middle.

4. **Click the Print button.**

   Your printer may beep or otherwise prompt you to insert the envelope or it may just print it right then and there.

- Check the envelope to make sure that you didn't address the backside or put the address on upside down — as so often happens to me. This last step is important because you can just repeat the above steps to reprint your envelope if you goof.

- Place the envelope in your laser printer's manual-feed slot-thing. The envelope goes in face up with the top side to your left. Draw a picture of this or print the preceding two sentences on a piece of paper and tape it to the top of your laser printer for future reference.
- On a dot-matrix printer, the envelope goes into the feeder upside-down and faces away from you. Wedging the envelope in there a bit to make sure that the printer grabs it helps. Or you may have a newfangled printer that has a special envelope slot. And if you do, well, la-de-da.
- Printing envelopes on a dot-matrix printer is a study in frustration. They usually look like something that a four-year-old did in preschool, all smeared up and not legible. You may be able to reduce the amount of smear by increasing the distance between the paper and the roller; you have to experiment.
- If you don't want the return address to print, check the Omit box in the upper-right part of the Return address space in the dialog box. I do this routinely because my printer munges the top part of the envelope and the return address never prints right.
- If you print many envelopes, you can add a new envelope button to Word's Standard toolbar. See the section "Adding an Envelope Button to the Standard Toolbar" in Chapter 34.

Printing Labels

Labels are those gummy things that you can peel and chew just like gum! Seriously, they stick to envelopes. Because my handwriting is so darn lousy, I print labels with my return address on them and stick those on my bills and whatnot. I do it as a favor to the overworked men and women of the U.S. Postal Service.

To print labels, you choose the same command as you do when you want to print envelopes — same command, different panel. Before you mess with this process, I recommend that you go out and buy some Avery sticky labels for your computer. I use Avery laser labels in my laser printer. Stock number 5160 is ideal for return address and mailing labels.

Here are the instructions for printing labels in Word:

1. **Choose Tools➪Envelopes and Labels.**
2. **Make sure that the Labels panel is in front.**

   Click the word Labels with your mouse or press Alt+L. What you see on your screen should look like Figure 9-5.

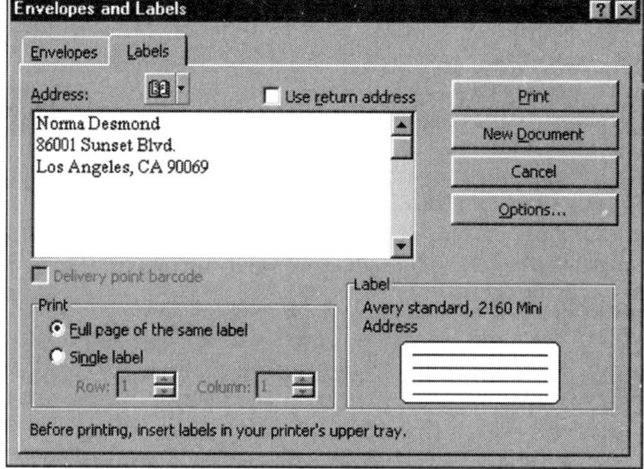

Figure 9-5: The Labels side of the Envelopes and Labels dialog box.

3. **Choose the type of label you're printing on.**

   You need to make sure that Word knows which set of labels you're printing on. The Avery standard number is displayed in the lower-right part of the Labels panel. Match that up with the labels you're using.

To change the type of labels, for example, to Avery Standard 5160 address labels, click the Options button. Choose Avery standard from the Label products drop-down list. Then locate the number in the Product number list. Click OK.

4. **Type what you want printed on the label in the Address box.**

   Click the mouse in the Address box and type the label you want to print. Keep in mind that you only have so many lines for each label, and that each label is only so wide. Press the Enter key at the end of each line.

5. **Click the New Document button.**

   Ha! I bet you thought you'd click the Print button. No way! The labels are typically more ugly than you think and you may want the chance to spiff them up a bit before you print.

   The labels appear as a document in Word (see Figure 9-6). Each label is surrounded by a little box, and the label text appears in the box. Now here's some things you can do:

   You can now format the labels, if you like. Press Ctrl+A to select the entire document (it's only a page long) and then change the font to something more pleasing. Refer to Chapter 10 for more information.

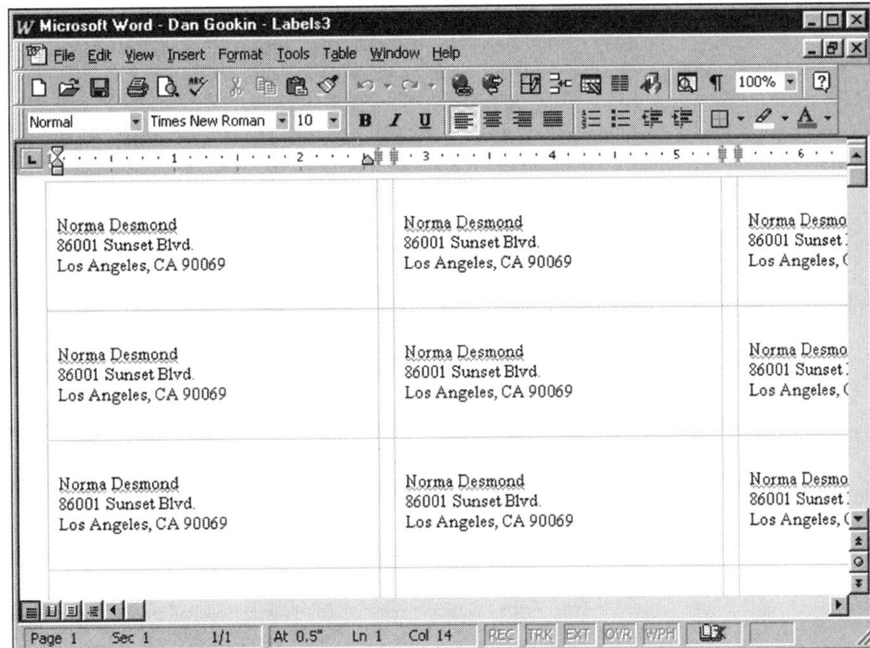

Figure 9-6: Labels await inspection in Word.

Don't mess with the margins or paragraph formatting. This is all carefully tuned to print on the labels you specified.

You can edit the labels. Sure, they all look the same, but if you like you can type in a few new names or other information in several of the little boxes.

You may want to review Chapter 14 on tables before you do any extensive editing. (Essentially the labels are all stored in a huge table in Word.)

6. **Print the document.**

Make sure that your printer is on and ready to print, and that you have the proper type of label-printing material in the printer, right-side up and all that. Then print your document as you normally would. Click the li'l Print button and the labels soon unfurl from your printer ready for lickin' and stickin'.

- You do not have to save this document to disk, unless you just like the labels and want to keep them around. Just press Ctrl+W to close the document and type N, no save.
- If you're serious about printing lots of labels, consider getting the label-printing program Avery distributes. I think it's called Avery Label Pro. Like any specific piece of software, this program does its job much better than Word's jack-of-all-trades approach.
- When you get into labels, you typically get into databases. If you need to print lots of differing labels and store and sort the names you print, what you really need is a database program. Many of these programs are on the market, from those that do just about everything for you, to specific mailing list programs, to complex databases and programming languages — something for everyone on the nerd spectrum.

Part II

Formatting (Or Making Your Prose Look Less Ugly)

In this part . . .

Formatting is the art of making your document look less ugly. It's the second part of word processing, coming right after the writing part, yet often consuming far more time. After all, text is text. Your word processor is capable of taking plain, boring text and making it look pretty. You can change the text style, size, and emphasis. You can adjust the margins, make tables, add pictures, and create all that excess that impresses people, especially those who don't care about content (which probably includes most of your superiors). Ah, let me tell you, nothing makes you swell with pride like a well-formatted document.

This part of the book tells you how to format your document, making it look pretty. Unlike writing, which is a pretty straightforward, whack-the-keyboard kind of thing, there are many strange and ugly commands plus some ancient rituals you must go through to get your text looking "just so." This part of the book describes those techniques, setting everything out for you in as clear a manner as possible.

Chapter 10

Formatting Characters

In This Chapter

- Changing the font
- Formatting text bold, italics, and underline
- Using text attributes
- Changing text size
- Making superscript text
- Making subscript text
- Undoing text formatting
- Changing to upper- and lowercase
- Doing the Font dialog box

The most basic thing you can format in a document is a character. *Characters* include letters, words, text in paragraphs, and weird Uncle Lloyd, who trims the hair in his ears with a butane lighter. You can format characters to be bold, underlined, italicized, little, big, in different fonts, or in an Easter bunny suit at Thanksgiving dinner. Word gives you a magnificent amount of control over the appearance of your text and enables you to generate documents that are truly professional in quality — and fool everyone in the process.

Changing the Font

One of the fun things about Word is its capability to use lots of different fonts. Sure, text can be made bold, italic, underlined, big, little, and on and on, but adjusting the font to match your mood takes expression to an entirely new level.

To switch to a different font, follow these steps:

1. **Arouse the font box on the Formatting toolbar.**

   Click the down-arrow by the box with the mouse or press Ctrl+Shift+F and then Alt+↓. This step displays a little drop-down list of Windows fonts (see Figure 10-1).

Figure 10-1: Some fonts Word uses.

2. **Scroll down to the font you want.**

   They're listed by name in alphabetical order. Any fonts you've recently chosen appear at the top of the list, before the double bar (see Figure 10-1).

3. **Press Enter to choose a font.**

   Or click the font once with your mouse.

- Everything you type after choosing a new font appears on-screen in that font. It should print and look the same as well.
- You can change a font for text already in your document by first marking the text as a block (refer to Chapter 6) and then choosing the font you want from the font box.
- Want to see what the font looks like *before* you switch? Then you need to use the Font dialog box. See the last section in this chapter, "Doing the Font Dialog Box."
- If you know the name of the font you want, you can save time by typing the font name into the box on the toolbar. **But beware:** Word is not lenient on font name spelling mistakes.
- For text, Word assumes you want to use the Times New Roman font, which is okay — especially if you're a New Roman reading *The New York Times.* For headings, Word insists that you use Arial, which is a blockier font. The Courier font (also known as Courier New) looks like typewriter output.
- In Word, fonts are the responsibility of Windows alone. New fonts are installed with Windows Control Panel (though the procedure is really no big deal). Thousands of fonts are available for Windows, and they work in all Windows applications. (Windows users trade fonts like characters in cheesy sitcoms trade insults; contact a local computer club or scour the back of a computer magazine to look for some weird or interesting Windows fonts.)

Basic Formatting (Bold, Italics, Underline, and Stuff)

After picking out a font, the most basic way to format your text is to make it **bold**, *italic,* or underlined. Bold and underline could be done on a typewriter: bold by backing up and re-typing and underline by backing up and whacking the underline key. Italic was next-to-impossible, which is probably why it's the preferred way to emphasize your text when you're word processing. Underlining? Well, maybe when you're bored.

Boldly making bold text

To emphasize a word, you make it bold. Bold text is, well, bold. It's heavy. It carries a great deal of weight, stands out on the page, speaks its mind at public meetings, wears a cowboy hat; you know the type.

To make new text stand out, follow these steps:

1. **Press the Ctrl+B key combination.**

   This step activates bold mode, in which everything you type is bold. (You can also click the Bold tool in the Formatting toolbar to turn it on.)

2. **Type your bold text.**

   Go ahead; type away. La-la-la.

3. **Press Ctrl+B again.**

   This step turns off the bold character format; you can also click off the Bold tool. Now all the text you type will be normal.

- Everything you type after pressing Ctrl+B appears in boldface on-screen and in your printed document. However, if you wander with the toothpick cursor, you may turn off the Bold command. My advice is to do this: Press Ctrl+B, type bold stuff, press Ctrl+B, and type normal stuff.
- If you already have text on-screen and you want to make it bold, you have to mark it as a block and then make it bold. Mark the block of text, and then press Ctrl+B or click the Bold tool. See Chapter 6 for more information on marking blocks of text.

- When the Bold tool is depressed (it's crying or bemoaning something trivial), the text the toothpick cursor is nestled in has the bold attribute. (This feature helps when you can't tell by looking at the screen whether text is already bold.)

The boring difference between a bold font and bold text

In Windows, you can have bold fonts, such as Arial Rounded MT Bold, as well as the Bold text command. This concept sounds weird, but keep in mind that you're using a *computer,* and it's not supposed to be logical.

The difference between a bold font and the Bold command is that a bold font is designed to be bold. It looks better on the screen and when printed. Making text bold with the Bold command merely tells Windows to re-draw the current font, making it look fatter or darker. Although this approach works, the Bold command doesn't display or print the font as nicely as a font that was originally bold.

Obviously, using the Bold command is easier than switching to a bold font in the middle of a paragraph. But if you can, consider using a bold font for long expanses of text, titles, headings, or captions wherever possible. The Bold command is okay for making text bold in the middle of a sentence. But bold fonts always look better.

- Isn't "boldly" a weird-looking word?
- You can mix and match character formats; text can be bold and underlined or bold and italicized. To mix character formats, you have to press the proper keys to turn on those formats before typing the text. Yes, you may have to type several Word character-formatting commands before typing your text: Ctrl+B, Ctrl+I, and Ctrl+U for bold, italicized, and underlined text all at once, for example. The typing is a hassle, but everyone has to do it that way.

Making italicized text

Italics are replacing underlining as the preferred text-emphasis format. I'm not embarrassed to use italics to emphasize or highlight a title just because it looks so much better than shabby underlined text. It's light and wispy, poetic, and free. Underlining is what the DMV does when it feels creative.

To italicize your text, follow these steps:

1. **Press the Ctrl+I key combination.**

   Italics mode is on! (You can also click the Italic tool.)

2. **Type away to your heart's content!**

   Watch your delightfully right-leaning text march across the screen. Pat Buchanan, eat your heart out!

3. **Press Ctrl+I after you're done.**

   Italic formatting is turned off. (Or you can click the Italic tool again.)

- If the text you want to italicize is already on-screen, you must mark it as a block and then change the character format to italics. Mark the text as a block, following the instructions detailed in Chapter 6, and then press the Ctrl+I key combination or use the leaning *I* Italic tool.

- If you want to double up on a character font — make something italic and bold, for example — you can press both character-formatting keys while you hold down the Ctrl key. Holding down the Ctrl key and pressing I and then B seems easier than doing the Ctrl+I and Ctrl+B dance.

Underhandedly underlining text

Underlined text just isn't as popular as it used to be. Instead, people now use *italicized* text for subtle emphasis — unless you are writing a paper on War and Peace for that stodgy professor who thinks that all modern influence is of the devil. In that case, underline the title of major literary texts (or at least those by Tolstoy). And always, *always,* italicize titles by Danielle Steele. Everything in between is pretty much a judgment call.

To underline your text, follow these steps:

1. **Press the Ctrl+U key combination.**

   This step turns on the underline character format. (You can also use the Underline tool-button thing on the Formatting toolbar.)

2. **Type!**

   You're now free to type the text you want underlined.

3. **Press the Ctrl+U key combination again.**

   This step returns you to typing normal text. (Or click off the Underline tool button.)

If you already have text on-screen that you want to underline, you have to mark the text as a block and then press the Ctrl+U key combination to underline it. Refer to Chapter 6 for more information on marking text as a block (should you need it).

Text-attribute effects round-up

Bold, italics, and underlining are the most common ways to dress up a character. There are other ways, which are covered in this section, but bold, italics, and underline each have their own tool on the Formatting toolbar so they deserve special attention. Table 10-1 shows other, more esoteric ways of formatting characters along with their key combinations. I'm using a table here instead of witty paragraphs, because I'm trying to cut a few pages from this chapter.

Table 10-1 Text-Format Samples and Commands

Key Combination	*Applies This Format*
Ctrl+Shift+A	ALL CAPS
Ctrl+B	**Bold**
Ctrl+Shift+D	Double underline
Ctrl+Shift+H	Hidden text (it doesn't print — shhh!)
Ctrl+I	*Italics*
Ctrl+Shift+K	SMALL CAPS
Ctrl+U	Continuous underline
Ctrl+Shift+W	Word underline
Ctrl+=	Subscript
Ctrl+Shift + =	Superscript

- Applying one of the weird text formats shown in Table 10-1 is cinchy. Just follow the instructions from the preceding section, "Underhandedly underlining text," and substitute the proper shortcut from Table 10-1.
- Any of these neat-o formatting tricks can also be achieved by opening a dialog box. If you are feeling reckless, powerful, able to leap tall terminals in a single bound, skip ahead to the section "Doing the Font Dialog Box." Fair warning: Tying your fingers in knots with key combinations is much safer.
- Pay special attention to word underline and continuous underline. Some people like one and despise the other. If you prefer to underline only words, remember to use Ctrl+Shift+W and not Ctrl+U .

- Hidden text — what good is that? It's good for you, the writer, to put down some thoughts and then hide them when the document prints. Of course, you don't see the text on-screen either. To find hidden text, you must use the Find command (covered in Chapter 5) to locate the special hidden-text attribute. This information is in the section "Finding secret codes." You have to click the Format button, choose Font, and then click the Hidden box. (This information really should have been hidden to begin with.)

Big Text, Little Text, Text Size Effects

Attributes — bold, italics, underline, and so on — are only half the available character formats. The other half deal with the text size. By using these commands, you can make your text teensy or humongous.

- Before getting into this subject, you must become one with the official typesetting term for text size. It's *point.* That's what Word uses: point instead of text size. It's not point, as in "point your finger" or the "point on top of your head." It's point, which is a measurement of size. One point is equal to 1/72 inch. Typesetters . . .
- The bigger the point size, the larger the text.
- Most text is either 10 or 12 points in size.
- Headings are typically 14 to 24 points in size.
- Seventy-two points is equal to one inch-high letters. Golly!

Making text bigger or smaller

To change text size, follow these steps:

1. **Get at the point size box on the Formatting toolbar.**

   Two ways to do this: Click the mouse in the point size box or press Ctrl+Shift+P.

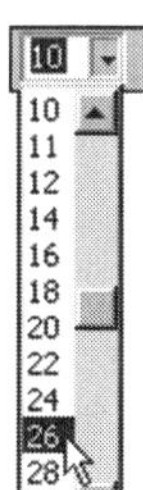

2. **Choose a new type size.**

   You can either type in the new point size and press Enter, or use your mouse and click the down-arrow by the side of the box and pluck out a new size from the list.

   The text you type from that moment on is in the new size.

Here are some things to remember about setting the point size:

- You can also use the drop-down button next to the point window to display the entire gamut of point options for your current font.
- Bigger numbers mean bigger text; smaller numbers mean smaller text.
- The average point size is 12 or sometimes 10.
- Most fonts can be sized from 1 point to 1,638 points.
- The author is 5,112 points tall.

If you want to apply a size format to text that is already on-screen, you have to mark those characters as a block before modifying the size.

To quickly change the size of a marked block, you can use the following shortcut keys:

Ctrl+]	Makes text one point size larger
Ctrl+[	Makes text one point size smaller

There really is no good mnemonic for this feature; you just have to commit it to memory.

Some fonts look ugly in certain point sizes. To ensure that the font looks good, you can use the following shortcut keys:

Ctrl+Shift+>	Makes the font larger in the next "look good" size
Ctrl+Shift+<	Makes the font smaller in the next "look good" size

Making superscript text

Superscript text is above the line (for example, the 10 in 2^{10}). To produce this effect, press Ctrl+Shift+= (the equal key) and then the text you want to superscript. Or mark a block of text and then press Ctrl+Shift+= to superscript the text in the block.

To return your text to normal, press Ctrl+spacebar.

Some people prefer superscript text that's a tad bit smaller than what Word gives you. Refer to the preceding section for information on changing the size of the text.

Here's a reason to be glad for Pepto-Bismol: Ctrl+Shift+= is the art of pressing the Ctrl and Shift keys at the same time — which anyone can do after a light lunch — and then pressing the equal key. Actually, Shift+= is the plus key. So this key combination is really Ctrl++ (or Control+plus sign). Ugh. I bet if they made a bigger keyboard, Microsoft would find things to do with all the keys, no sweat.

Making subscript text

Subscript text is below the line (for example, the 2 in $H_{2}0$). To subscript your text, press Ctrl+= (the equal key) and then type away. If you mark a block of text and then press Ctrl+=, all the text in the block is subscript. To return your text to normal, press Ctrl+spacebar (the long, boney key under your thumb).

Undoing All This Text-Formatting Nonsense

Sometimes, you have so many character attributes going that you don't know what to press to get back to normal text. This situation can be very frustrating. Fortunately, Word has lent a tiny ear to your cries for help. You can use the Reset Character text-formatting command to shut off everything — size and attribute formats — and return the text to normal. Here's how:

Press Ctrl+spacebar, the Reset Character shortcut.

Everything you type from that point on is normal (or at least has the normal attributes).

- You can press Ctrl+spacebar anywhere in your document to start typing in plain, boring text.
- You can also select a block and then press Ctrl+spacebar to remove all text formatting from that block.
- Another key combination for Ctrl+ spacebar is Ctrl+Shift+Z. That's actually easy to remember because Ctrl+Z is the Undo command; all you're doing is adding the Shift key, which may make sense — well, heck, if *any* of this makes sense.
- The only problem you may encounter with using Ctrl+spacebar is that it also restores the font. Well, that's good and bad news. It's good because you can also use Ctrl+spacebar to get rid of weird fonts. But it's bad because it changes the font back even when you don't want to.

- If you want to keep your fonts straight — and, indeed, all this formatting stuff — you should really look into creating a *style sheet* for your document. Refer to Chapter 15, "Formatting with Style."
- Pressing Ctrl+spacebar does not work on Cousin Melvin.

Changing the CASE of Your Text

Upper- and lowercase effects aren't considered part of a font, character attribute, or format. But still, the Word geniuses at Microsoft found room in their bustling bag o' tricks for a two-fingered command that lets you mix around in the case conversion of your text. And it doesn't even sound like procrastination, what-what?

To play with, er, I mean convert the case makeup of a block of text:

1. **Mark the text to convert as a block.**

   Refer to Chapter 6 for the best block-marking advice since the ancient Babylonians.

2. **Press Shift+F3.**

   This step capitalizes the first letter of a block or capitalizes every character in the block, or returns them all to their humble, lowercase origins.

3. **Continue pressing Shift+F3 until you have settled on the case you like most.**

   Yes, a veritable cornucopia of case conversion lies at your fingertips — Genie-in-a-Key-combo, I like to call it.

You don't have to mark a single word as a block of text for this trick: Just put the toothpick cursor somewhere in the middle of a word and press Shift+F3 to change that word's case.

Doing the Font Dialog Box

Too many choices can overwhelm you. Most people prefer simple, straightforward information — all the options explained right there on the menu, with pictures of what they look like. Or a smell may waft from two tables over and you point and say, "I want what the nun is having."

Then again, there are times when — if you know what you're doing — you want all the options right there at once. You know which levers you want pulled — the salad dressing and potato fixings and how burnt the meat should be — all at once. For those times, Word offers the Font dialog box (Figure 10-2), a place where almost all your character formatting can take place simultaneously. This dialog box is definitely not for the timid. But exciting and exotic things await you.

When you choose Format⇨Font, you open up the rather imposing Font dialog box. All sorts of interesting things happen here, most of which this chapter shows you how to do in other ways. But when you want it all done at once, this is the spot.

And the only true benefit to the Font dialog box is the Preview window at the bottom. That window shows you exactly how your choices affect text in your document — nifty, but probably not worth all the trouble.

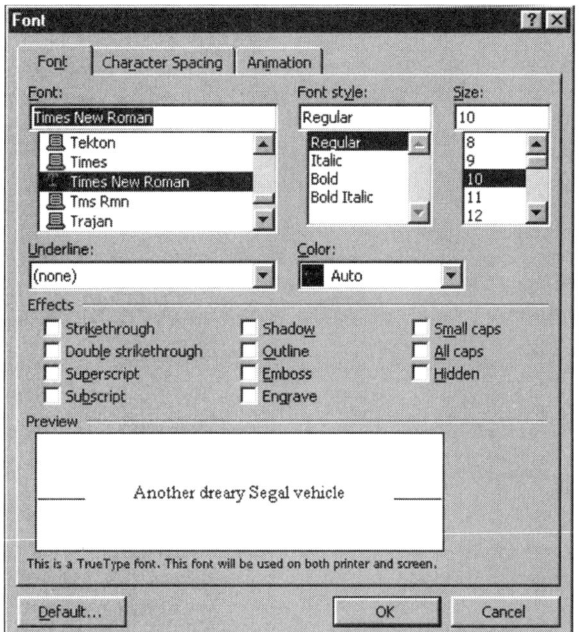

Figure 10-2: The Font dialog box.

Chapter 11

Formatting Sentences and Paragraphs

In This Chapter

- Justifying paragraphs (centering, justifying, and flushing)
- Changing line spacing
- Adding room between paragraphs
- Indenting a paragraph
- Making a hanging indent
- Double-indenting a paragraph
- A paragraph-formatting survival guide

Paragraph formatting is the second formatting step, after formatting your words. It's really easy because you can do only so much with a paragraph of text. As usual, Word takes care of all the details, centering things for you, aligning tab stops, even adding an extra puff of air between your paragraphs. And, as usual, Word does things in some of the strangest manners possible. This chapter does its best to cushion the blow.

Justifying Paragraphs

No, this section isn't an exercise from philosophy class. In typesetter lingo, justification refers to the way the text on either side of a paragraph lines up, or not. The following sections show you just how strangely Word can do things.

Centering a paragraph

I'm sure the artsy poet types will like centering all their text. It's just so symmetrical. For everyone else, centering a single line or block of text is usually done for document titles and headings. So if you feel the urge to center something, such as your soul in the cosmic plane, follow these steps:

1. **Press the Enter key to start a new line of text, the line you want to be centered.**

   This trick only works for new lines of text. If the text you want to center is already on-screen, refer to the bulleted list that follows these steps.

2. **Use the Center command's keyboard shortcut, Ctrl+E.**

   I know that E doesn't mean *center* in your brain. But the word *center* does have two *E*s in it. How about E means *equator?* Nah, that goes side to side. I give up.

   You can also center text by clicking the Center tool on the ribbon. It looks like the thing you yell into when you order burgers at a drive-thru.

3. **The cursor zips over to the center of the screen (or thereabouts).**

4. **Type your title or heading.**

   Don't boggle yourself as the text you type moves from the center of the screen out, cascading left and right like the Red Sea did in front of Charlton Heston.

5. **Press Enter after you're done.**

   That line you typed is centered.

If you want to center more than a line (a paragraph or more, for example), keep typing away. When you tire of seeing your text centered, press Ctrl+L to return to left justification or click the Left Align tool. (Left justification is the way text normally appears in Word; everything is even on the left side of the page on the left margin.)

- If the text you want to center has already been typed, click the mouse somewhere in that paragraph, and then press the Ctrl+E keyboard shortcut. Word centers that paragraph for you.
- If you want to center an expanse of text larger than one paragraph, select the text as a block first; see Chapter 6. Then press Ctrl+E to center that block.

- The Center command's keyboard shortcut, Ctrl+E, centers only paragraphs. If you want to center just one line at a time, you must end each line by pressing the Enter key — which makes that single line a paragraph.

- You cannot center words or letters unless they are their own paragraph. However, you can center text in the middle of a line by using the center tab. See the sidebar "Meddlesome nonsense about tab types" in Chapter 12.
- If you do manage to center your soul on the cosmic plain, you'll probably receive lots of respect and fame. If so, remember never to let your acolytes see you eat at Sizzler.

Make your text flush right

Flush right describes the way text aligns on-screen. (You soon discover that a great deal of flushing occurs in paragraph formatting.) Text is usually *flush left*, with everything lining up at the left margin. *Flush-right* text aligns at the right margin. In other words, all the text is slammed against the right side of the page — like picking up the paper and jerking it wildly until the text slides over.

- The flush right command is Ctrl+R. You can also click the Flush Right tool on the Formatting toolbar.
- To create a paragraph that's flush right, follow the instructions in the previous section but use the Ctrl+R shortcut key instead of Ctrl+E.
- When you type a new flush-right paragraph, the characters push right, always staying flush with the right side of the document. It's like writing in Hebrew!

- When you're done typing a flush-right paragraph, press Ctrl+L to return to left-justified text (normal flushing).
- To flush-right a paragraph of text you've already written, click the mouse inside that paragraph and press Ctrl+R or use the Flush Right tool.
- For flushing right more than a single paragraph of text, mark all the text as a block first and then use the Ctrl+R shortcut key. Refer to Chapter 6 for more information on marking blocks of text.

- The flush right command works only with paragraphs. You cannot flush words or individual lines of text unless they're paragraphs. You can, however, flush parts of a line right by using a right tab stop. See the sidebar "Flushing your dates right."
- Be careful not to flush large objects, cardboard, or other foreign objects when you're adjusting your text. Do not flush while the train is parked at the station.

Flushing your dates right

A good thing to flush right at the top of the document is the date. Most people start their letters this way. To flush right the date at the top of a document, follow these handy steps:

1. **Move to the top of the document to the line where you want to put the date (by pressing Ctrl+Home).**

   The date must be put on a blank line, so press the Enter key if the first line in your document isn't blank, and then press the Ctrl+Home again to move back to that first, blank line.

2. **Press Ctrl+R, the Flush Right shortcut key. The toothpick cursor zooms over to the right side of the page.**

3. **Press Alt+Shift+D. This step inserts the current date into your document.**

   (No need to memorize this command; just flag this page.)

4. **Press Enter.**

5. **Press Ctrl+L to go back to left justification.**

You can continue editing with the current date proudly flushed right at the top of the page.

- *Flush right* is a design term that means the same thing as *right align* or *right justification*.
- Typographers use words other than *justification.* They occasionally use the word *ragged* to describe how the text fits. For example, left justification is *ragged right;* right justification is *ragged left.* A rag top is a convertible with a soft top, and a rag bottom is any child still in diapers.

Giving a paragraph full justification

Full justification gives your paragraphs even sides, both left and right. It's the way text is formatted in most newspapers and magazines. And if you want to play like the big boys, you only need to know the full justification formatting key combination, Ctrl+J.

- To fully justify a paragraph of text, use the Ctrl+J keyboard shortcut or click the Full Justify tool on the Formatting toolbar.
- Follow the steps outlined in the section "Centering a paragraph" earlier in this chapter to fully justify a new paragraph of text.
- To justify an existing paragraph, click the mouse in that paragraph and then press Ctrl+J or use the Full Justify tool button on the toolbar.
- You can also mark several paragraphs — or your whole document — as a block and then use the Fully Justify shortcut key, Ctrl+J. See Chapter 6 for detailed block marking instructions.

- Word achieves full justification by inserting extra spaces and small pieces of wood (shims) between the words in a line of text.

- To return to left justification, press Ctrl+L or use the Left Justify tool. See the next section for more information.

Returning justification to normal (left justification)

Normally your paragraphs are formatted with left justification. If you've whacked out any paragraph and want to return to left justification, press Ctrl+L or use the left justify button on the Formatting toolbar. You can left-justify any existing paragraph of text, a block or text, or new text you type. Refer to the section "Centering a paragraph"; all the information there applies to left-justifying paragraphs as well as centering. Just use the Ctrl+L shortcut key instead of Ctrl+E.

Adding Vertical Air to Your Paragraphs

You can space out your text in an up-and-down fashion in two ways. The first, traditional method is to change the line spacing. On a typewriter, folks did that with multiple whacks of the line feed bar between sentences. With a word processor, there's nothing to whack — though whacking the monitor twice or thrice makes you feel good.

The second method for adding more space is simply to widen the spaces between your paragraphs. In the olden days, this was done by whacking the Return key on your typewriter one, two, or three times at the end of a paragraph. You can tell Word, however, to widen the spaces automatically. Yes, Word does save you from a lot of unnecessary whacking.

Changing line spacing

To change the line spacing for new text, you have three options:

- Press Ctrl+1 for single-spaced lines.

  Hold down the Ctrl key and press 1. (That's Ctrl and the one key, not the L key.) Release both keys, and Word single-spaces your text. Any text you type or a highlighted block on-screen is affected after you press Ctrl+1.

Unnecessary, more specific spacing stuff

If you want line spacing other than single, double, or 1½, you can choose the Format⇨Paragraph command. The Paragraph dialog box opens (see Figure 11-1). Make sure that the Indents and Spacing panel is in front (press Alt+I if it's not). Select Multiple in the Line Spacing box and the measurement you want in the At box. To triple space lines, for example, you select Multiple under Line Spacing and type **3** in the At box. This step sets the spacing to 3 lines.

- Press Ctrl+5 for 1½-spaced lines.

  The 1½ spacing means that your lines are between single and double spacing — which gives editors (and teachers) less room to mark up your stuff but still lets in all that air that makes the text readable. You press Ctrl+5 to get 1½ line spacing in your document or to change the spacing for a highlighted block.

- Press Ctrl+2 for double-spaced lines.

  Double spacing is often required by fussy editors who, without enough room in their precious 1-inch margins, want to write under, over, and between what you write. Press Ctrl+2 to make your text double spaced.

You can quickly change the spacing of a paragraph that is already in your text by placing the toothpick cursor anywhere in the paragraph and pressing the magical key commands!

- Only press the Enter key at the *end* of a paragraph. Word automatically adjusts the line spacing for you without you having to press Enter at the end of each line. Remember, this is *not* a typewriter.
- Ctrl+5 means 1½ line spacing, not 5 line spacing.
- Refer to Chapter 6 for information on marking a block. The Ctrl+1, Ctrl+2, and Ctrl+5 shortcuts affect any block marked on-screen.

- For your Ctrl+5 key press, don't use the 5 key on the numeric keypad; that's the command to select all the text in your document. Instead, use the 5 key hovering over the R and T keys on your keyboard.

Adding breathing room between paragraphs

Some people, myself included, are in the double-Enter habit. That is, you press Enter, Enter to end a paragraph, when all Word really needs is a single Enter. It's a similar disorder to pressing Space, Space after a period — an utterly useless affliction in the age of modern word processing, kind of like writing down your stutter.

If you want your paragraphs to automatically have some air around them — just like an insecure guy at the beach — you need only to tell Word to stick some padding down there. Here's how:

1. **Position the toothpick cursor in the paragraph you want more air around.**

   The air can be either above or below the paragraph. Oh, and you can select several paragraphs or your whole document if that's the way you want things. Refer to Chapter 6 for information on selecting stuff as a block.

2. **Choose Format➪Paragraph.**

   The Paragraph dialog box appears, as shown in Figure 11-1.

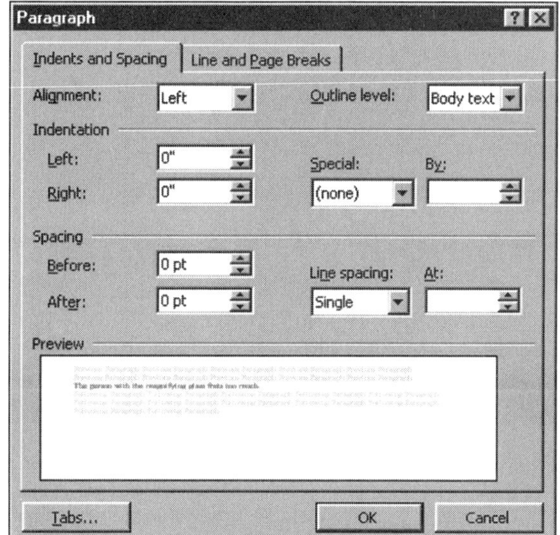

Figure 11-1: The Paragraph dialog box.

3. **Bring the Indents and Spacing panel forward.**

   Click that panel's tab or press Alt+I, if it isn't forward already. You'll want to concentrate on the area that says Spacing.

4. **Type in a value for spacing After.**

   Personally, I use the up- or down-arrows here. For example, to add space after every paragraph, I click twice on the down-arrow by that box. The value `12 pt` means that there will be just about one blank line after that paragraph.

A good way to remember the point nonsense is that Word adds one half line of blank space before or after a paragraph for each time you click one of the little arrows. (6 pt equals half a line of text.) You can also see how your text is modified by looking in the Preview box.

5. **Click OK.**

   Your paragraph has been modified. After you press the Enter key, you see the new air after your paragraph.

- You can also add space before a paragraph by adjusting the value in the Before box. (My advice is always to add the padding at the end of the paragraph, in the After box.)
- Changing a paragraph this way affects the current paragraph (the one the toothpick cursor is in), as well as any new paragraphs you type after that.
- To make a blank line between your paragraphs, follow the above steps and select 12 pt into the After box.
- Adding space before or after a paragraph isn't the same as double spacing the text inside the paragraph. In fact, adding space around a paragraph does not change the paragraph's line spacing one iota.

Changing a Paragraph's Indentation

Word can indent your paragraphs for you just as easily as a shopping cart can indent your car door. This is another one of those brain-lock issues many people suffer from. You probably indent each of your new paragraphs by pressing the Tab key. But Word ain't no typewriter; you don't need to whack the Tab key after you press Enter. Let Word do the indenting for you. And, as you might expect, there are several different ways to get this done, none of which is easy to remember.

Automatically indenting the first line

Word can automatically indent the first line of any paragraph you create. Here's how to set it up:

1. **Choose the Format⇨Paragraph command.**

   The Paragraph dialog box appears. Make sure that the Indents and Spacing panel is up front (like in Figure 11-1); press Alt+I if it's not.

2. **Locate the Special list box.**

   You find this in the Indentation area of the dialog box, off to the right.

3. **Select** `First line` **from the list.**
4. **In the By box type the length you want to indent the first line of every paragraph.**

   Unless you've messed with things, the box should automatically say `0.5"`, meaning Word automatically indents the first line of every paragraph a half inch. Type another value if you want your indents to be more or less outrageous.
5. **Click OK.**

   From that point on, all your paragraphs automatically have a first line indent as you've specified.

To remove the first line indent from a paragraph, repeat the steps, but select `(none)` from the drop-down list in Step 3. Then click the OK button.

Remember, when you've told Word to automatically indent your paragraphs you no longer need to start each one with the Tab key. See? Word is saving you valuable typing energy molecules.

Making a hanging indent

A hanging indent has committed no felonious crime. Instead, it's a paragraph in which the first line sticks out to the left and the rest of the paragraph is indented — like the paragraph has its tongue sticking out or it's a side view of a high diving board. To drive this point home, the following paragraph is shown in hanging indent style:

I'm sorry, Sheriff, but we just can't hang Big Vern. His darn neck's too big! We tried and tried, but every time he goes through the drop, the rope just slips on up 'round his head and he falls to the ground. Now Vern's legs are hurtin', and he's got a heck of a rope burn on his ears. Is that bad enough? Can't we just let him go?

To create such a beast for whatever frivolous reasons, follow these steps:

1. **Move the toothpick cursor into the paragraph you want to hang and indent.**

   Or you can position the cursor to where you want to type a new, hanging-indent paragraph. Or you can select a block, per the block-marking instructions in Chapter 6.
2. **Press Ctrl+T, the Hanging Indent shortcut.**

   Ta-da! You have a hanging indented paragraph.

   You can remember Ctrl+T because the English always hang felons just before Tea Time.

The Ctrl+T in Word moves the paragraph over to the first tab stop but keeps the first line in place.

- If you want to indent the paragraph even more, press the Ctrl+T key more than once.
- It's stupid that they have a shortcut key for a hanging indent but not for indenting the first line of a paragraph, which I feel that more people do more often than this hanging nonsense.

- To undo a hanging indent, press Ctrl+Shift+T. That's the unhang key combination, and your paragraph's neck will be put back in shape.

Indenting the whole paragraph

Indenting a paragraph means that you indent, or *nest,* the entire paragraph by aligning its left edge against a tab stop. Here's how you do it:

1. **Move the toothpick cursor anywhere in the paragraph.**

   The paragraph can already be on-screen, or you can be poised to type a new paragraph. Or you can try this command on a selected block of text (see Chapter 6).

2. **Press Ctrl+M, the Indent shortcut.**

   Ummm — indent! Ummm — indent! Say it over and over. It kinda works. (You can also click the Indent button on the Formatting toolbar.)

3. **Type your paragraph if you haven't already.**

   If the paragraph is blocked, it is indented to the next tab stop.

- To return the original margin, press Ctrl+Shift+M or, heck, Ctrl+Z, the Undo command (which is why it's there). You can also click the Unindent tool.
- To indent the paragraph to the next tab stop, press Ctrl+M again.
- Although the Ctrl+M and Ctrl+Shift+M shortcuts aren't mnemonic, their only difference is a Shift key. So when you get used to using them (hopefully before the afterlife), they're easy to remember.
- To indent both the right and left sides of a paragraph, see the following section, "Double indenting a paragraph."

Double indenting a paragraph

Sometimes an indent on the left just isn't enough. There are those days when you need to suck a paragraph in twice: once on the left and once on the right (for example, when you lift a quote from another paper but don't want to be accused of plagiarism). I do this to Abe Lincoln all the time. When I quote his stuff, I follow these steps:

1. **Move the toothpick cursor to the beginning of the paragraph.**

   If the paragraph hasn't been written yet, move the cursor to where you want to write the new text. Or just select a block of text you want to double-indent, following the block-marking rules so carefully laid out in Chapter 6.

2. **Choose the Format⇨Paragraph command.**

   The Paragraph dialog box appears. Make sure that the Indents and Spacing panel is in front. In the Indentation area, you see two items on the left side: Left and Right.

3. **Enter the amount of left and right indentation.**

   Click the Left box. Type a value, such as **.5** to indent the paragraph a half-inch. Then click the Right box (or press the Tab key once) and type **.5** again. This step indents your paragraph half an inch from the left and right.

   You can also press the up- and down-arrows that cling to the right side of the box to spin numbers up and down with the mouse. Whee!

4. **Click OK.**

5. **Type your paragraph if you haven't already.**

Obviously, a double-indented paragraph should be inhaled equally from the left and right sides of the page; the numbers in the Left and Right boxes should be the same.

When you modify a paragraph in the Paragraph dialog box, notice the Preview box at the bottom of the card. Your paragraph's format is shown in dark ink on the sample page.

Paragraph-formatting survival guide

This table contains all the paragraph-formatting commands you can summon by holding down the Ctrl key and pressing a letter or number. By no means should you memorize this list.

Key Combo	Does This
Ctrl+E	Centers paragraphs
Ctrl+J	Fully justifies paragraphs
Ctrl+L	Left aligns (flush left)
Ctrl+R	Right aligns (flush right)
Ctrl+M	Indents text
Ctrl+Shift+M	Unindents text
Ctrl+T	Makes a hanging indent
Ctrl+Shift+T	Unhangs the indent
Ctrl+1	Single spaces lines
Ctrl+2	Double spaces lines
Ctrl+5	Makes 1 ½-space lines

Chapter 12

Setting Tabs and Margins

In This Chapter

- Using the ruler
- Setting tab stops
- Using the Tabs dialog box
- Removing tab stops
- Setting a leader tab
- Adjusting a paragraph's margins
- Adjusting margins for a whole page

Two weird word-processing holdouts from the typewriter age are tabs and margins. They're like a bad '60s band that just won't go away. But unlike a '60s band, which can be loud and smell bad, tabs and margins serve useful functions in a document. They are the second part of formatting sentences and paragraphs. So put on your fringed vest, headband, and blue granny glasses — time for some flashbacks to the era of typewriters. Peace. Love. Fight the man. Set a tab stop.

Who Died and Made This Thing Ruler?

Word's main throwback to the typewriter era is the ruler, which is the final strip/bar information on Word's screen (refer to Figure 1-3). The ruler is used to help you set tab stops as well as adjust on-the-fly margin changes and indenting. All this is basic paragraph formatting stuff.

If you don't see the ruler on-screen, choose the View⇨Ruler command.

Figure 12-1 shows the typical Word ruler with a few things worth noting noted. You use these things in later sections in this chapter.

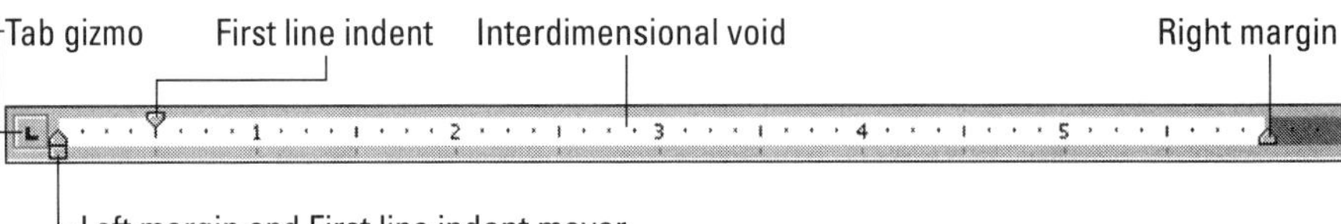

Figure 12-1: The typical Word ruler.

- The ruler is a mouse gizmo; you use the mouse to make changes on it. Even so, just about everything you can do to the ruler by using the mouse can also be done through various menu commands and whatnot. Still, the ruler makes a good visual aid.
- The Tab gizmo is used to select different types of tabs. You can then click the ruler to place a tab in a specific spot.
- You can drag the left, right, or first line markers to change a paragraph's indentation or margins.
- The changes you make on the ruler affect only the current paragraph in your document, the one the toothpick cursor is blinking in. To change more than one paragraph, you need to mark everything as a block. See Chapter 6.

The Tab Stops Here

Without otherwise consulting with you, Word presets tab stops in your document at half-inch intervals. Whenever you press the Tab key, the toothpick cursor hops over to the next half-inch *tab stop*. You can change this behavior, setting tab stops anywhere you like to allow your document to be formatted just the way you want. Like, hey man, it's do-your-own-thing time.

Adding new tab stops

To make a new tab stop for the current paragraph, follow these steps:

1. **Type the paragraph you want to stick the tabs into.**

   Big tip: When you begin to type the paragraph, first just press the Tab key and pretend (in your head) that the tab lined up just exactly where you wanted. Then continue typing the paragraph. If you do it this way, then setting your tabs and lining things up later will make a whole lotta sense.

2. **Make sure that the toothpick cursor is in the paragraph you want to change.**

Tabs are a paragraph-only thing. If you want to change the tab stops in more than one paragraph, mark the paragraphs you want to change. Refer to Chapter 6 for block-marking instructions.

3. **Click the mouse on the ruler where you want a new tab stop.**

   Figure 12-2 shows how a tab is being placed in a paragraph. See how the mouse pointer places the little plump L into the ruler? That's the tab being set. (Also notice how the text has already been typed with the Tab key separating the items. This approach makes it easier to set the tab.)

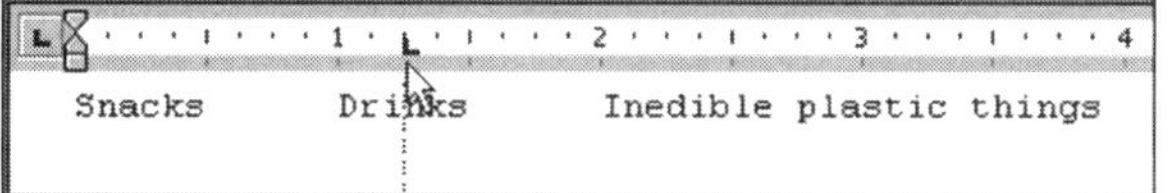

Figure 12-2: A tab is being set.

- After you set the tab, you can change its position by dragging the tab left or right on the ruler. When you do, a dotted line extends down into your text to help you line things up (see Figure 12-2).
- The fat L tab is a left tab, the most common tab you set in Word. See the sidebar "Meddlesome nonsense about tab types" for more information on the different types of tabs you can set.

- When I'm working with many tabs, I usually press the Tab key only once between each column of information. Then I select all the paragraphs and drag the tab indicators around so that each of my columns aligns. Using one tab instead of two or three is much easier to edit. And using one tab lets me do fancy stuff, like sorting and math.
- If you're typing anything with columns and rows of organized information, consider using Word's Table command instead of messing with tabs all over creation. See Chapter 14 for more information.

Setting a gang of tabs all at once

If you need to set a group of tabs, say six of them each 1½ inches apart, you're probably better off using the Tabs dialog box than messing with the ruler. Choose Format⇨Tabs and the Tabs dialog box appears in all its glory (see Figure 12-3).

The Tabs dialog box is a beast, but this box can be handy when you need to be precise. The following list tells you a few things you can do here. After you're done, click the OK button to set your tabs. And remember that the tabs you set affect only the current paragraph or any paragraphs you have marked as a block.

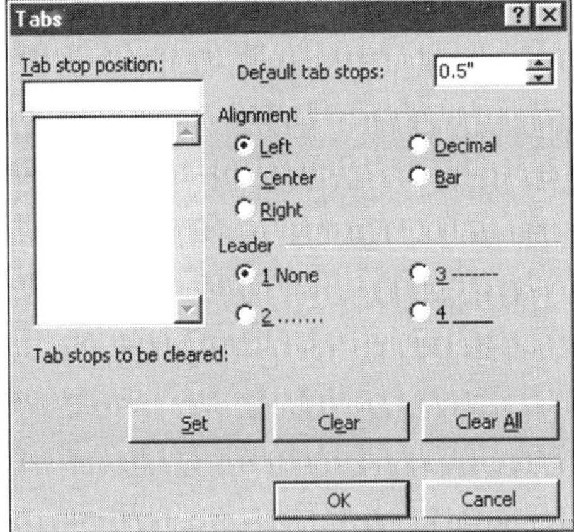

Figure 12-3: The Tabs dialog box.

- If you need to set a row of tabs, say, each 3/4 of an inch apart, type **0.75"** into the Default tab stops box, and then click the OK button. Word automatically figures the tab stops and sets them for you.
- For setting precise tab stops, type measurements for each tab stop into the Tab stop position box. For example, type **1**, click the Set button; type **1.67**, click Set; type **2.25**, click Set, and so on. Each tab stop is added to the list of tab stops in the Tabs dialog box. Click OK to set them for your paragraph.
- If you make a mistake, click the tab stop you want to remove and then the Clear button.
- To get rid of all your tab stops, click the Clear All button.

- You can still set tabs by using the ruler, which is better when you're just futzing around. The Tabs dialog box is best for setting precise tabs.

Killing off a tab stop

If you decide that you don't want the tab after all, you can drag it off the ruler altogether; grab it with the mouse and drag it up or down. Thwoop! It's gone.

You can also zap all your tab stops at once by summoning the Tabs dialog box (Format⇨Tabs) and clicking the Clear All button; then click OK.

Setting fearless leader tabs

The leader tab is interesting but not required for most writing. This tab produces a row of dots when you press Tab. You see this all the time in indexes or tables of contents. Word gives you the choice of three different leaders:

Meddlesome nonsense about tab types

Word uses four different types of tabs, as depicted by four different icons that can appear on the far-left side of the ruler. Whichever one you see determines which types of tabs are set. And to see a different tab, click the tab gizmo with your mouse. This list shows what each type does:

- The most common tab is the left tab, the plump L. This tab works like the Tab key on a typewriter: Press the Tab key and the new text appears at the next tab stop. No mental hang-ups here.
- The right tab causes text to line up right justified at that tab stop. This tab gives you leeway to do some fancy paragraph justification on a single line, which you can read about in Chapter 24, "Your Basic Desktop Publishing Stuff."
- The center tab stop centers text on the tab stop — good for one-word columns or titles. Again, see Chapter 24.
- The decimal tab aligns numbers by their decimals. The number is right justified before you press the period key and then left justified on the decimal. So say, for example, that you set one of these jobbies on a line. You press the Tab key and the toothpick cursor hops over to the right spot. Type **$123** and the text is right justified (pushed out to the left). Then type a period, which lines up at the tab stop, and the rest of the number (say, **45**), which moves out to the right like normal. That way, you can line up a column of numbers when each of them is of a different size.

Fearless dot leader tabs 147

Zipper line leader tabs - - - - - - - - - - - - - - 147

U-boat underline leader tabs __________ 147

To set up a fearless leader tab, follow these steps:

1. **Position the toothpick cursor on the line where you want to have your leader tabs.**

   For example, you've been asked by a local rest home to index the dictionary. You're starting the index in a new document in Word.

2. **Set a tab stop on the ruler.**

   Click the mouse at the number 3 on the ruler, which sets a stop at 3 inches in from the page's left margin. A plump L appears on the ruler.

3. **Choose the Format⇨Tabs command.**

   You see the Tabs dialog box, as shown in Figure 12-3. Focus in on the Leader area.

4. **Choose the style of fearless leader tab you want.**

   Click the appropriate style, as presented at the beginning of this section. My personal favorite is the dotted underline, which you can select by pressing the Alt+2 key combination.

5. **Click OK.**

6. **Type the text to appear before the tab stop:**

   ```
   Words beginning with the letter A
   ```

7. **Press the Tab key.**

   Zwoop! The toothpick cursor jumps to your tab stop and leaves a trail of, well, "stuff" in its wake, as shown in Figure 12-4. That's your dot leader (or dash leader or underline leader).

Words beginning with the letter A.................................

Figure 12-4: Dot leader tabs.

8. **Type the reference, page number, or whatever.**

   ```
   Page one
   ```

9. **Press Enter to end that line.**

Setting the dot leader tabs doesn't work unless you manually stick in your own tab stops, as discussed in "The Tab Stops Here," earlier in this chapter.

You can adjust the tab stops after setting them if some of the text doesn't line up. Remember, to adjust the tab stops for more than one paragraph at a time, you need to select everything as a block. See Chapter 6.

Marginal Information

Actually, Word offers two different sets of margins. The first ones are found to the left and right of each paragraph. These are the paragraph margins. Page margins also exist, which tell Word where to set the text on each page you print.

Now this duplicate margin information sure sounds dumb. However, you really do need two sets of margins. The page margins are for your whole document, top to bottom. You probably don't want to change those; just set them once and forget about them. But paragraph margins may change as you compose your document. You may want wide margins at one spot and narrow margins at another.

Adjusting a paragraph's margins

You can adjust the margins for any ding-dong paragraph in your document, or for a group of paragraphs should you select them all as a block. To do this, move the left and right margin doojobbies on the ruler; point your mouse at either one of them and drag them left or right to make your paragraph appear just so.

- Figure 12-1 shows you where the margin doojobbies are on the ruler.
- The left and right margin doojobbies are on the bottom of the ruler.
- The one doojobbie on the top of the ruler (to the left) sets the indentation of the first line in your paragraph.
- The little rectangular doojobbie below the left margin doojobbie allows you to move both the left margin and first line indent at the same time.

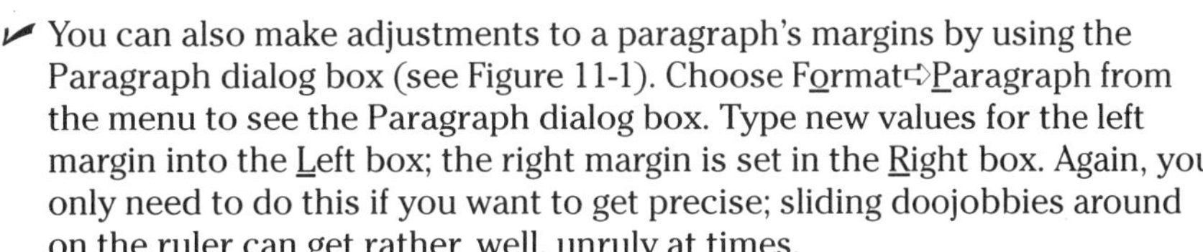

- You can also make adjustments to a paragraph's margins by using the Paragraph dialog box (see Figure 11-1). Choose Format➪Paragraph from the menu to see the Paragraph dialog box. Type new values for the left margin into the Left box; the right margin is set in the Right box. Again, you only need to do this if you want to get precise; sliding doojobbies around on the ruler can get rather, well, unruly at times.

Adjusting margins for a page

Every page has margins. This is the air around your document — that inch of breathing space that sets off the text from the rest of the page. Word automatically sets your margins at 1 inch from the right, left, top, and bottom of the page. Most English teachers and book editors want things like this because they love to scribble in margins (they even write that way on blank sheets of paper). In Word, you can adjust the margins to suit any fussy professional.

To change the margins, follow these steps:

1. **If you want to change "from here on," move the toothpick cursor to the place in your text where you want the new page margins to start.**

   It's best to set the new margins at the top of the document, top of a page, or beginning of a paragraph (or the beginning of a new formatting section). If, on the other hand, you want to change all of the document, where you place the cursor doesn't matter.

2. **Choose the File➪Page Setup command.**

   The Page Setup dialog box appears, as shown in Figure 12-5. Click the Margins tab if it's not up front.

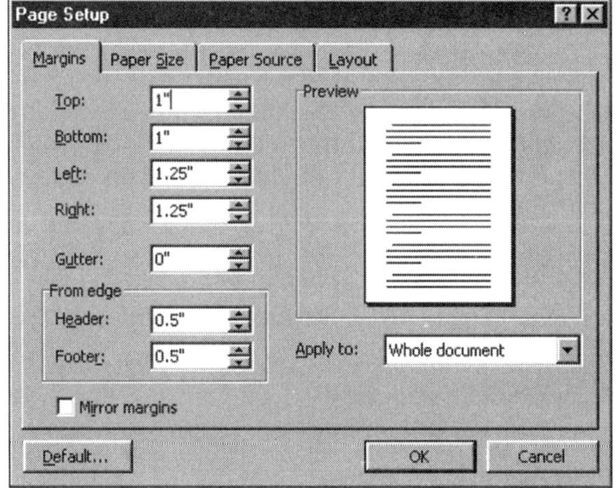

Figure 12-5: The Page Setup dialog box.

3. **Enter the new measurements for the Top, Bottom, Left, and Right page margins.**

   Type the new values in the appropriate boxes. For example, a value of `1"` in all the boxes sets all margins to 1 inch. A value of `2.5"` sets a $2^1/_2$-inch margin. You don't need to type the inch symbol (").

   The Preview window shows you how your margins affect the page.

4. **Choose Whole document or This point forward from the Apply to drop-down list.**

   You have two basic choices when setting a page's margins. You can change your whole document, from beginning to end, top to bottom, bow to stern. Or you can change the margins from the toothpick cursor's position onward (This point forward).

   If your document is split into formatting sections, you can also choose to apply the margin to change to the current section (This section); see Chapter 13 for more information on sections.

5. **Click OK.**

   Your new margins appear.

- If you want to print on three-hole paper, set the left margin to 2 or 2.5 inches. This setting allows enough room for the little holes, and it offsets the text nicely when you open up something in a three-ring notebook or binder.
- Keep in mind that most laser printers cannot print on the outside half-inch of a piece of paper — top, bottom, left, and right. This space is an absolute margin; although you can tell Word to set a margin of 0 inches right and 0 inches left, text still does not print there. Instead, choose .5 inches minimum for the left and right margins.

- The Gutter box inside the Page Setup dialog box applies more to documents printed on two pages and intended to be bound in a booklike format. The Gutter box is a *bonus margin* that appears on the left side of right-facing pages and vice versa. No need to put your mind in the gutter.
- If your homework comes out to three pages and the teacher wants four, bring in the margins. Set the left and right margins to 1.5 inches each. Then change the line spacing to 1.5. Refer to the section "Changing line spacing" in Chapter 11. (You can also choose a larger font; check out the section on text size effects in Chapter 10.)
- You can have several page margins set for different parts of your document. To do this, you must split your document up into formatting sections, and then assign a different page margin to each section. Chapter 13 covers splitting up a document into formatting sections — which is a rather advanced concept.

Chapter 13

Formatting Pages and Documents

In This Chapter

- Starting a new page with a hard page break
- Creating a section break
- Setting the page size
- Choosing Landscape or Portrait layout
- Centering a page, top to bottom
- Automatically numbering your pages
- Changing page numbers
- Adding a header or footer
- Editing a header or footer
- Using footnotes

At last, the formatting circus has come to this. Formatting pages and documents isn't as common as formatting characters or paragraphs. This major-league stuff affects your entire document, and it can be really handy: headers and footers, page numbers — even footnotes. This is the stuff of which professional-looking documents are made. This chapter explains it all so carefully that even we amateurs fool them.

Breaking Up Your Document

Formatting your document is not usually a top-down thing. After all, most documents are not one long Great Wall of Text. There are little breaks, puffs of air between paragraphs, and different sections in each document typically have their own look and feel. To accomplish these tricks, knowing how Word lets you break up a document into smaller, formattable pieces helps. The following sections outline how that task can be done without cutting yourself on anything sharp.

Starting a new page (a "hard page" break)

You can choose two ways to start a new page in Word:

- Keep pressing the Enter key until you see the row o' dots that denotes the start of a new page. Needless to say, this method is tacky and wrong.
- Press Ctrl+Enter, the hard page break key combination. Ctrl+Enter inserts a tighter row of dots than you normally see between two pages. Also, the tight row of dots actually says `Page Break` right in the middle to remind you that it's artificial. This method is the preferred way to start a new page.

  This line shows a Word hard page break (in Normal view):

..........................Page Break..........................

Keep these things in mind when you're dealing with hard page breaks:

- The hard page break works just like a regular page break does, although you control where it lives in your document: Move the toothpick cursor to where you want the hard page break and press Ctrl+Enter.
- Pressing Ctrl+Enter inserts a hard page-break *character* in your document. That character stays there, always creating a hard page break no matter how much you edit the text on previous pages.
- You can delete a hard page break by pressing the Backspace or Delete keys. If you do this accidentally, just press Ctrl+Enter again, or you can press Ctrl+Z keys to undelete.
- Don't fall into the trap of using hard page breaks to adjust your page numbering. You can use *the power of the computer* to alter your page numbers without having to mess with page formatting. See "Where to stick the page number?" later in this chapter.

Taking a section break

Books have chapters and parts to break up major plot lines. Formatting has something called a *section break* that serves the same function. Word uses all kinds of different breaks: page breaks, column breaks, and section breaks, but not lunch breaks.

You can use a section break when you want to apply different types of formatting to several different parts of a document. You may want different margins to appear in different places, a banner headline, different numbers of columns, or whatever. You can accomplish these tasks by inserting a section break. It's kinda like building an island: All types of weird formatting can live on it, isolated from the rest of the document.

No, a section break isn't a common, everyday thing, but if you get heavily into formatting, you'll be thankful for it.

To insert a section break, do this:

1. **Position the toothpick cursor where you want the break to occur.**
2. **Choose the Insert⇨Break command.**

   The Break dialog box opens, as shown in Figure 13-1.

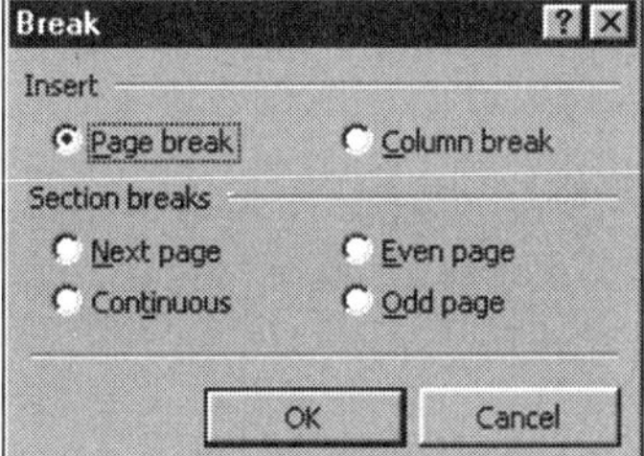

Figure 13-1: The Break dialog box.

3. **Choose your break from the Section breaks area.**

   Click Next page if you want the new section to start on a fresh page. This step has the dual effect of inserting a hard page break and starting a new formatting section. You would use this option, for example, to center text on a title page (see the section "Centering a page, top to bottom" later in this chapter).

   Choose Continuous if you want to insert the break wherever you happen to be. Generally, you select this option when Next page isn't what you want.

   The Even page and Odd page options are rarely used.

4. **Click OK.**

   A double line of dots appears on-screen with the notation `End of Section` in the middle. Lo, you have your section break. Let the new formatting commence!

This is a what a Next Page section break looks like:

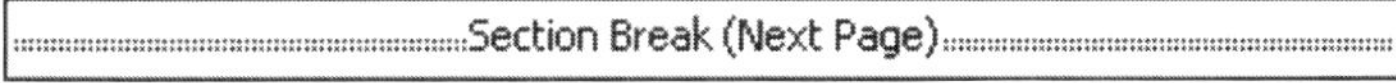

- Section breaks also provide a great way to divide a multipart document. For example, the title page can be a section; the introduction, Chapter 1, and Appendix A all can be made into sections. You can then use Word's Go To command to zoom to each section. Refer to Chapter 3 for more information on the Go To command.
- You can delete a section break with the Backspace or Delete keys. If you do this accidentally, you lose any special formatting that you applied to the section. Press the Undo command, Ctrl+Z, before you do anything else.
- You can also use the Break dialog box to insert a Page Break, but Ctrl+Enter is much quicker; refer to the preceding section.

Messing with the Whole Page and Nothing but the Page

Finally, it comes to this: The following sections tell you how to format a page. Not what's on the page, the page itself. You can choose only three things: the size of the paper you're printing on, whether you're printing normal or sideways, and whether or not you want to center text on the page from top to bottom. Word has a cryptic command for each of these tasks.

Setting the page size

Most printing takes place on a standard, 8½-x-11-inch sheet of paper. But Word lets you change the paper size to anything you want — from an envelope to some weird-size sheet of paper. The following steps describe how you change the paper size to the legal 8½-x-14-inch sheet of paper:

1. **Position the toothpick cursor at the top of your document or at the top of a page on which you want to start using the new paper size.**
2. **Choose the File⇨Page Setup command.**

   The Page Setup dialog box appears. Make sure that the Paper Size panel is in front, as shown in Figure 13-2. If not, click that tab or press the Alt+S key combination.
3. **Click the Paper size drop-down list.**

   The list drops down.
4. **Select a new paper size from the list.**

   For example, `Legal 8½ x 14` in for legal-sized paper. Other standard sizes are listed there as well.

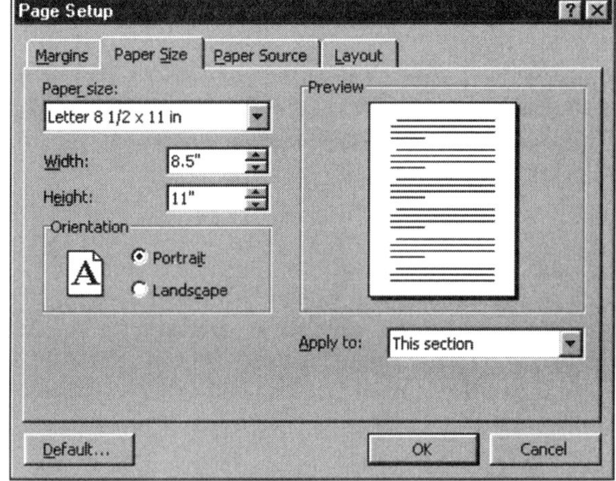

Figure 13-2: The Page Setup dialog box, Paper Size panel.

Select this new paper size by clicking it with your mouse.

5. **Select what part of your document you want the new page size to apply to from the Apply to drop-down list.**

   Select Whole document or This point forward. Of if you're using document sections, select This section.

6. **Click OK.**

   Okay. Type away on the new size of paper.

- If you're printing an odd-sized piece of paper, remember to load it into your printer before you start printing. Some of the smarter printers even tell you which size of paper they want to print on. Mine does. It can be annoying at times.
- If the paper you're printing on isn't shown in the drop-down list, you can enter the measurements yourself. First select Custom size from the Paper size drop-down list. Then type the paper's width into the Width box and the height into the Height box.
- Keep an eye on the Preview window in the Page Setup dialog box. It changes to reflect the new paper size.
- The following section tells you how to print sideways on a sheet of paper. This technique really fools the relatives into thinking that you're a word-processing genius.
- Refer to Chapter 9 for information on printing envelopes. (There's a special command for doing that; no sense in finagling a new paper size here.)

Landscape and Portrait

Word usually prints up and down on a piece of paper — which is how everyone is used to reading a page. However, Word can print sideways or long-ways on a page as well. In this case, the page's *orientation* is changed; rather than up-down, the paper is printed sideways.

The technical "I'm an important word-processing expert" terms for the two paper orientations are *Portrait mode* for the up-down paper and *Landscape mode* for sideways. A portrait picture is usually taller than it is long to accommodate our faces — unless someone has large ears on a jug-like head. Landscape is for those lovely oil paintings of seascapes or lakes and trees that are wider than they are tall — the kind Bob Ross used to paint (may he rest in peace — sniff, sniff).

To make Word print the long way on a sheet of paper — the Landscape mode — do the following:

1. **Choose File⇨Page Setup.**

   The Page Setup dialog box appears. Make sure that the Paper Size panel is forward if it's not already (press Alt+S to summon it). Refer to Figure 13-2.

2. **Choose Portrait or Landscape from the Orientation area.**

   The Sample document and the tiny icon change to reflect your perspective.

3. **Click OK.**

Avoid printing standard documents in Landscape mode. Scientists and other people in white lab coats who study such things have determined that human reading speed slows drastically when people must scan a long line of text. Reserve Landscape mode for printing lists, tables, and items for which normal paper is too narrow.

Centering a page, top to bottom

Nothing makes a document title nice and crisp like having it sit squat in the middle of a page. That's top-to-bottom middle as opposed to left-right middle. To achieve this feat, follow these steps:

1. **Move the toothpick cursor to the top of the page that contains the text that you want centered between the bottom and the top of the page.**

   The text should be on a page by itself — actually a section by itself. If the page that you want centered isn't the first page of the document, press Alt,I,B,N,Enter. This keystroke combination inserts the section and page break, and you see a double line on-screen (the section separator). That line marks a new page, the page that you want to center.

2. **Type the text that you want centered from top to bottom.**

   Refer to Chapter 10 for more information on formatting characters, making text big and fancy, or whatnot for your title or whatever text you want centered. If you also want the lines centered from left to right, refer to Chapter 11 for information on centering a line.

3. **Create a new section break.**

   You have to mark the end of the page you want centered with a section break. Press Alt,I,B,N,Enter. This step inserts a *next page* section break: a double line of dots that marks a new page and a new section.

   Press the ↑ arrow key to move the toothpick cursor back up into the section you just created.

4. **Choose the File➪Page Setup command.**

   The Page Setup dialog box appears. Make sure that the Layout panel is in front, as shown in Figure 13-3. If not, press Alt+L.

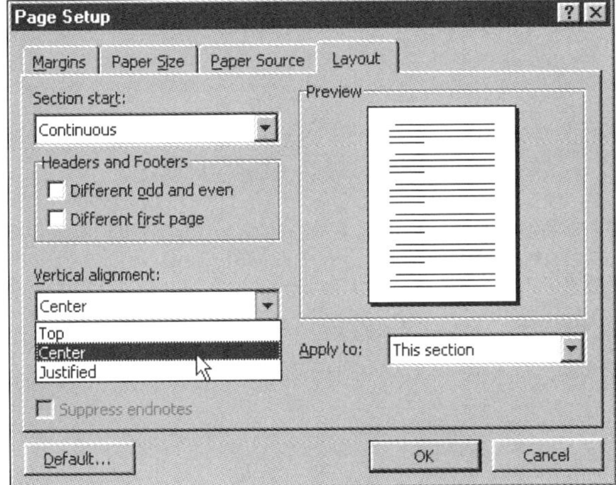

Figure 13-3: The Layout panel in the Page Setup dialog box.

   You should focus your laser beams on the lower-left corner, in the area roped in and named Vertical alignment.

5. **Click the Vertical alignment drop-down list.**

6. **Select** Center.

7. **Click OK.**

Normally, you get no visual feedback that you've centered a page on-screen. Choose the View➪Page Layout command to get a sneak peak at the centered page. (You may have to Zoom out to the *whole page* to see the title centered; see Chapter 30, "Face to Face with the Interface," to find out about the Zoom command.) Choose View➪Normal to return to Normal view.

All text on the page is centered from top to bottom with the Center page command. Keeping as little text on the page as possible — a title, description, and so forth — is a good idea.

Refer to "Taking a section break," earlier in this chapter, for more information on section breaks.

Page Numbering

Time to repeat the word-processing mantra:

Your word processor will number your pages for you.
Your word processor will number your pages for you.
Your word processor will number your pages for you.

Honest. Word does it all. It sticks the page number on the page and keeps the number there no matter how many pages you add or delete. There's *nothing* for you to do, other than tell Word where to stick the page number. Please, oh please, don't manually number anything in a word processor!

Where to stick the page number?

If your document is more than a page long, you should put page numbers on it. Word can do this for you automatically, providing you follow these steps:

1. **Choose the Insert⇨Page Numbers command.**

   The Page Numbers dialog box, shown in Figure 13-4, appears.

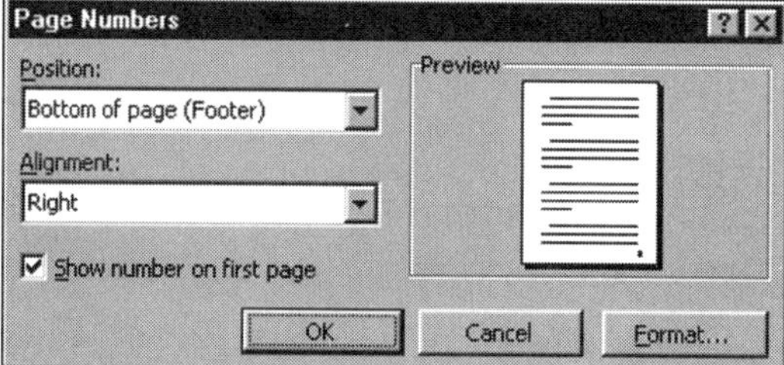

Figure 13-4: The Page Numbers dialog box.

2. **Where dost thou wantest thine page numbers?**

   Word can stick a page number in six possible places: either at the top or bottom of the page, on the left, on the right, or in the middle.

From the Position drop-down list, select Top of page (Header) or Bottom of page (Footer).

From the Alignment drop-down list, select Left, Center, or Right. (The Inside and Outside options are for different odd-even pages.)

Ponder this situation carefully and keep an eye on the Preview box — a slight change can drastically alter the power of your document.

3. **Choose OK.**

   The page numbers are inserted.

You can also create page numbering by sticking the page number command in a header or footer. See "Adding a header or footer," coming up soon in this chapter. If you do end up putting the page number in a header or footer, you don't have to use the Page Numbers command.

If you want to get fancier page numbers, click the Format button in the Page Numbers dialog box. This step opens the Page Number Format dialog box. From there, you can select various ways to display the page numbers from the Number Format drop-down list — even those cute little *ii*s and *xx*s.

'Nother tip: If you don't want a page number on your first page (say, the title page), click in the box by Show number on first page, located in the Page Numbers dialog box (see Figure 13-4). That tells Word *not* to stick an ugly "1" on the bottom of your pristine title page.

Starting off with a different page number

To start numbering your pages with a new page number, heed the instructions in the previous section to conjure up the Page Numbers dialog box. That must be done first since, obviously, there's no need to change page numbers when your document doesn't have them in the first place. Like, *duh.*

Follow these steps:

1. **Click the Format button in the Page Numbers dialog box.**

   Clicking this button opens the Page Number Format dialog box, shown in Figure 13-5. (Refer to the preceding section for the commands to summon the Page Number dialog box.)

2. **Click the Start at radio button.**

   Type the page number you want to begin with into the box. You can also press the arrows to wheel up and down. Whee!

3. **Click OK to close the Page Number Format dialog box.**

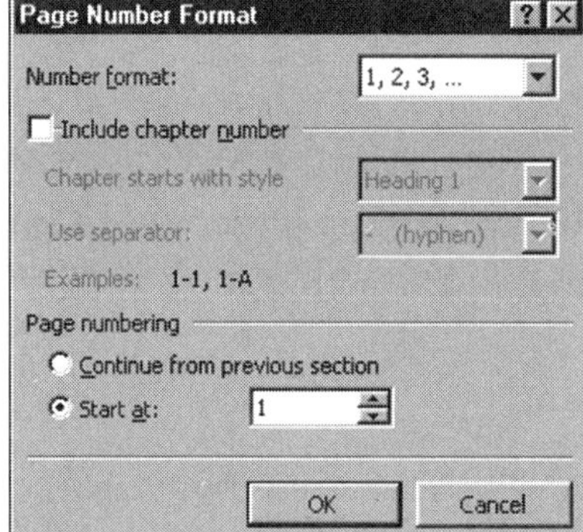

Figure 13-5: The Page Number Format dialog box.

4. **Click OK to close the Page Numbers dialog box.**

You see the new page numbers reflected on the status bar's little nonsense line. Time to fool everyone!

This procedure is something that you may want to do for the second, third, or later chapters in a book. By setting a new page number, the page numbers in all chapters are continuous.

The Joys of Headers and Footers

A header is not a quickly poured beer. Instead, it's text that runs along the top of every page in your document. For example, the top of each page in this book has the section name or chapter name. Those are *headers.* You can stick headers on your work, complete with a title, your name, date, page number, dirty limericks — you name it.

The *footer* is text that appears on the bottom of every page. Good footers include page numbers, a chapter or document title, and odor-eaters. The footer is created by using exactly the same steps used to create a header.

Adding a header or footer

Headers and footers can make any document shine. You don't need to use them both; you can use just one or the other. Either way, the same command is used to add or play with them.

To add a header or footer, follow these steps:

1. **Choose the View⇨Header and Footer command.**

   The document window changes, and you're given a sneak peek at your document's header (or footer), roped off with the title Header or Footer up there in the left corner. Also visible is the floating Header and Footer toolbar. Witness Figure 13-6 for an example.

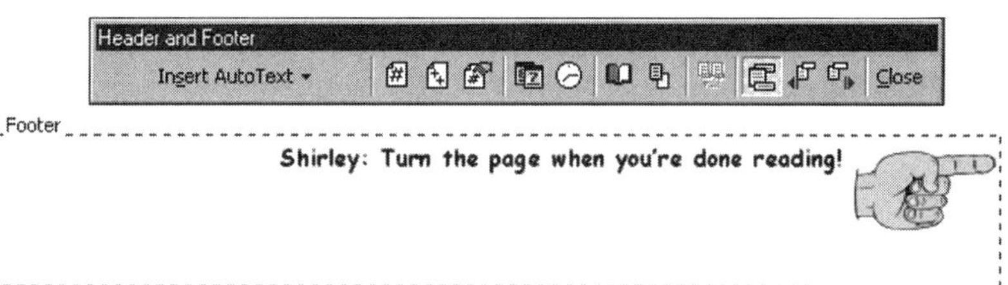

Figure 13-6: A sample footer with the Header and Footer toolbar.

2. **Click the Switch Between Header/Footer icon to choose either the Header or Footer for editing.**

   Click the button once to switch back and forth.

3. **Enter your header or footer text.**

   The text can also be formatted just as though it were a separate document by using most of the tools in the Standard and Formatting toolbars as well as instructions lovingly described in Chapters 10 and 11.

   The footer is already formatted with a center tab stop (see Chapter 12), which enables you to press the Tab key, type some text, and have the text automatically centered at the bottom of each page. This tab stop isn't required, but it's thoughtful of Microsoft to set it up that way.

4. **Use the buttons in the Header and Footer toolbar for special items.**

   Hover the mouse pointer over each button to see a brief explanation of its function (just like on the big toolbars!). These buttons are described in detail in the sidebar "The Header and Footer toolbar unbuttoned."

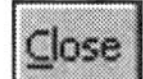

5. **Click the Close button after you are done.**

   You're back in your document. The header and/or footer is/are there, but you can't see it/them until you print or choose the File⇨Print Preview command (or use the Preview button on the Standard toolbar) or if you view your document in Page Layout mode.

You can put anything in a header or footer that you can put in a document, including graphics (see Figure 13-6). This capability is especially useful if you want a logo to appear on each page. See Part IV of this book for information on Word and graphics.

Here are some tips for adding headers or footers:

- If you want to insert the page number in the header or footer, put the toothpick cursor where you want it to appear and press the Page Numbers button on the Header and Footer toolbar. The number 1 appears in the header text, but it is replaced by the current page number when the document is printed.
- You probably will want to put some text in front of the page number because a number sitting all by itself tends to get lonely. You can get real creative and type the word **Page** and a space before you click the # button, or you can come up with some interesting text on your own.

- To insert the current date or time into the header or footer, click the Date or Time buttons on the Header and Footer toolbar.
- To see your header or footer displayed on-screen, choose View⇨Page Layout. In Page Layout mode, you can see your header or footer, but they appear washed out — in gray text and not very appealing. Choose View⇨Normal to return to the normal way you look at Word.

You can have two headers, odd and even, running on different pages — and the same with footers. From the Header and Footer toolbar, click the Page Setup button. The Page Setup dialog box opens. On the Layout panel, look in the Headers and Footers area and check Different odd and even. Click OK. Create an odd and an even header (or footer) in turn, according to the preceding steps, and they print differently on odd and even pages.

This odd-even stuff has nothing to do with the last number in your car's license plate or the last number in your address.

To prevent the header or footer from appearing on the first page of text, which usually is the title page, click the Page Setup button on the Header and Footer toolbar. Then check Different first page and click OK. In your document, move to the first page header (First Page Header) and leave it blank. This procedure places an empty header on the first page; the header appears on all the other pages as ordered. You can also use this option to place a different header on the first page — a graphic, for example. See Part IV of this book to find out about placing graphics in a document.

A header is a section-long thing. You can change parts of a header, such as a chapter name or number, from section to section, without changing other parts of the header, like the page number. Refer to the section "Taking a section break," earlier in this chapter, for more information on sections.

I've always hated all that fuzz on top of a stein of beer. But recently, I was in Germany and had a beer connoisseur tell me that it is an imperative part of a good beer. Hmm. Of course, this from a nation where they drink their beer *warm*. Yech.

Editing a header or footer

To edit a header or footer you have already created, follow these steps:

1. **Go to the page that has the header or footer you want to edit.**

   If you want to change the odd-page header, go to an odd page; if you want to edit the first-page footer, go to the first page.

2. **Choose View⇨Header and Footer.**

   Or press the Alt,V,H key combination. The Header and Footer screen appears.

3. **If necessary, click the Switch Between Header/Footer button to move to the header or footer you want to edit.**

4. **Make any changes or corrections.**

   Make these changes as you would edit any text on-screen.

5. **Click Close after you're done.**

Editing a header or footer changes how it looks for your entire document; not just for the current page. And you don't have to move the cursor to the tippy-top of your document before editing a header or footer.

You can also edit a header or footer from Page Layout view: Choose View⇨Page Layout or click the Page Layout button. This command adjusts the way Word displays your document and exposes the thinly veiled text sequestered in your headers or footers. If you double-click the mouse pointer on the grayed header or footer text, the magical window of header and footer editing opportunity reopens.

Using Footnotes

Some folks seem to think that footnotes are pretty advanced stuff. Pooh! Many people need them in their documents. I mean, academics use them all the time and look how many people consider them "experts."

The Header and Footer toolbar unbuttoned

One little, two little, twelve little buttons on the Header and Footer floating palette of button joy. This table shows the official picture, title, and function for each of them:

Button	*Official Name*	*Purpose in Life*
	Switch Between Header/Footer	Like the name says
	Show Previous	Views previous header or footer
	Show Next	Views next header or footer
	Same as Previous	Copies previous header or footer to this header or footer
	Page Number	Inserts page number into the header or footer
	Insert Number of	Inserts the length of your document in pages (use with the page number to make a 1/3 type of footer).
	Page Number Format	See "Where to stick the page number?" earlier in this chapter.
	Date	Inserts current date into header or footer
	Time	Inserts current time into header or footer
	Page Setup	Grants you access to Word's Page Layout dialog box
	Show/Hide Document Text	Allows you to view the main document's text along with the header or footer
Close	Close	Returns you to your document and closes the Header and Footer screen

The Show Next, Show Previous, and Same as Previous buttons are necessary because Word allows you to have several different headers and footers in the same document. Want a new header on page 17? Create it. Actually, you can have dozens of different headers and footers (though that's kind of impractical). The Show Next, Show Previous, and Same as Previous buttons let you switch between the different headers and footers.

Rather than create footnotes obtusely, follow these handy steps:

1. **Position the toothpick cursor in your document where you want the footnote to be referenced.**

   The tiny number that refers to the footnote goes here. For example[1].

2. **Choose the Insert⇨Footnote command.**

   You see the Footnote and Endnote dialog box. It's kind of boring, so I'm not putting a figure of it in this book.

   There is a lot of other stuff to do here. But since most of the time you'll want a footnote to appear on the bottom of the page that references it, you don't need to do anything else in the Footnote and Endnote dialog box. (See the list at the end of this section for more information, like if you want an endnote instead of a footnote.)

3. **Click OK.**

   A new area magically appears at the bottom of your page. The toothpick cursor sits there, ready for you to . . .

4. **Type your footnote.**

   You can place in a footnote anything you can place in a document — charts, graphs, pictures, and even text.

5. **Click the Close button.**

Figure 13-7 shows what a footnote might look like. Keep in mind that no one reads footnotes, so you can usually stick anything you want down there.

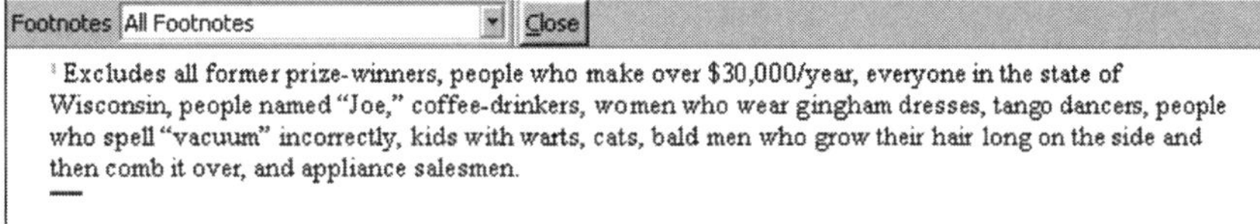

Figure 13-7: A sample footnote.

Here are some non-footnote footnote notes:

- To view or edit footnotes, choose View⇨Footnotes.
- To quick-edit a footnote, double-click the footnote number on the page. The footnote text edit area opens.

[1]Distracting, isn't it?

- To delete a footnote, highlight the footnote's number in your document and press the Delete key. Word magically renumbers any remaining footnotes for you.
- An endnote is like a footnote, but they all appear at the end of your document. To create an endnote, select Endnote in the Footnote and Endnote dialog box before Step 3 in the preceding list.

- You can change the location of footnotes in your document by clicking the Options button in the Footnote dialog box. In the Footnote Options dialog box you can choose where you want the footnotes to appear: on the bottom of the page where the footnote is referenced or beneath the text that contains the reference. Endnotes — the other panel — can be placed at the end of the current section or at the end of the document.
- You can actually insert graphics into a footnote, just as you can a header or footer. Think how embarrassed those academics will be, seething with jealousy at your wondrously creative, graphical footnotes! Part IV of this book contains such information on inserting graphics into your document.

If you decide that some little fact would be better footnoted from another place in the text, you can cut (Ctrl+X), copy (Ctrl+C), and paste (Ctrl+V) footnotes easier even than normal text! Just block the number that denotes the footnote, move it to its new home, and — voilà — Word moves the rest. Better than U-Haul!

Chapter 14
Tables and Columns

In This Chapter

- Creating a table
- Changing the table
- Adjusting a table's column width
- Automatically formatting a table
- Arranging your text into columns

Remember those old TV commercials where they told you over and over again what kind of a *deal* you were getting?

But wait! There's more!

In Word, you can format everything you could possibly dream of formatting in your document: fonts, sentences, paragraphs, pages, margins, tabs, headers, footers, footnotes. . . .

But wait! There's more!

Tired of fussing with tab stops and text awkwardly stuffed into uneven rows and columns? Egads! That's not the way to present organized information! Instead, you need Word's handy Table command. You can line up that text into neat rows and columns quicker than a Ginsu knife slices through a lead pipe. Now how much would you pay for that? Don't answer!

But wait! There's more!

Columns can come marching your way in Word, giving your documents the look of professionally desktop-published stuff. It's easy, say, to turn a document on its side (Landscape mode), tell Word to do the three column march and, lo, you have a brochure.

Now how much would you pay for all this?

Don't answer that! You've already paid for it. Time to figure out how it all works.

Cobbling Tables Together

A table is this thing with four legs on which you set things — but not your elbows when Grandma is watching. In Word, a *table* is a list of items with several rows all lined up in neat little columns. In the primitive days, you made tables happen by using the Tab key and your handy frustration tool. Face it: Making things align can be maddening — even in a word processor and even if you think that you know what you're doing.

Coming to your rescue, of course, is Word. "It's Table Man, Ma, and he's here to rescue us!" Word has an able Table command. This command lets you create this prison-like grid of rows and columns. Into each cubbyhole, or *cell,* you can type information or store society's miscreants, and everything is aligned nice and neat and suitable for framing. The printed result looks very impressive, and if you do things right, your table is even sturdy enough to eat off of.

Creating a table (the traditional, boring way)

To create a table in your document, follow these steps:

1. **Place the toothpick cursor on the spot in the text where you want the table.**

   The table is created and inserted into your text (like pasting in a block — a *cell block*). You fill in the table *after* you create it.

2. **Choose the Table⇨Insert Table command.**

   Yes, Word has its own Table menu. How handy. Choosing the Insert Table command from that menu opens the Insert Table dialog box, as shown in Figure 14-1.

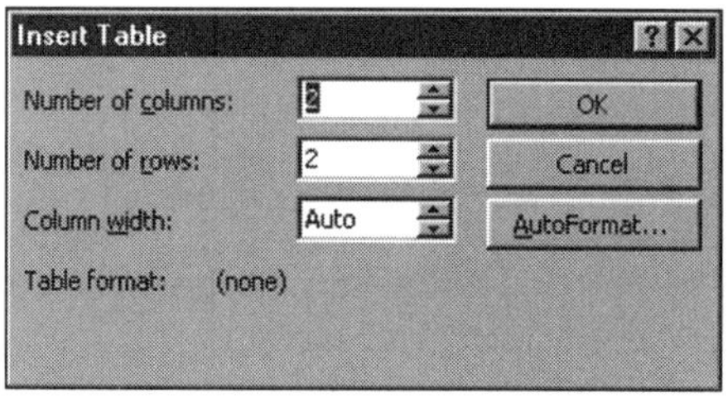

Figure 14-1: The Insert Table dialog box.

3. **Enter the number of columns into the first box.**

   For example, type **3**. You have three columns going across.

4. **Prcss the Tab key.**

   The cursor moves to the next box.

5. **Enter the number of rows into the second box.**

   For example, type **5**. You have five rows, marching down.

   Three columns? Five rows? Who knows? Accuracy isn't a big issue at this stage; you can change your table after it's created if you goof up. (I do this all the time.)

6. **Click OK to leave the Insert Table mini-dialog boxlet.**

   Welcome to prison! After you tell Word how many rows and columns to make, the program builds a table and shows it to you on-screen (something like Figure 14-2, but not filled in).

   Tables look like spreadsheets and smell like spreadsheets, and if I weren't afraid of electrocuting myself, I'd tell you whether they taste like spreadsheets. You're still in Word, however.

7. **Fill in the table.**

   Use crayons on your screen or, better still, see the next section for table-filling-in instructions.

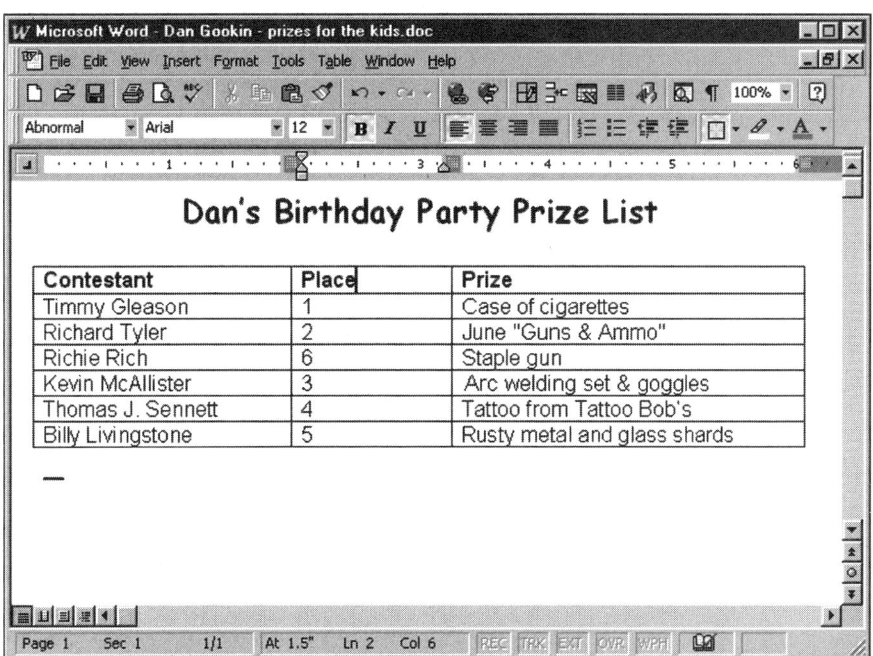

Contestant	Place	Prize
Timmy Gleason	1	Case of cigarettes
Richard Tyler	2	June "Guns & Ammo"
Richie Rich	6	Staple gun
Kevin McAllister	3	Arc welding set & goggles
Thomas J. Sennett	4	Tattoo from Tattoo Bob's
Billy Livingstone	5	Rusty metal and glass shards

Figure 14-2: A table is born.

If you can't see your table, choose Table➪Gridlines to display the cell borders.

If the grid you see around your table doesn't print, you need to add a table border. Likewise, you can remove the border around your text if you don't want it there. See Chapter 24, "Your Basic Desktop Publishing Stuff" for more information on borders in Word.

Use a table in your document whenever you have information that must be organized in rows and columns. This feature works much better than using the Tab key on several lines because adjusting the table's rows and columns is easier than fussing with tab stops.

You can always add or delete columns and rows to your table after you create it. See "Changing a Table," later in this chapter.

Alas, Word does not have a handy Chair command. (Although rumor has it that Microsoft is working on barstools.)

Creating a table (the unconventional way)

Why do you need two ways to create the same table? Because there must be an easy way and a hard way. So here's another way to create a table in your document. This method could be easier than the steps listed in the preceding section, and it could be harder. Anyway, it's a more mousy alternative:

1. **Place the toothpick cursor on the spot in the text where you want your table.**

   This step marks the spot where the table's prison-like skeleton appears.

2. **Click the Table button on the Standard toolbar.**

   A grid drops down, looking similar to the maze of questions that daunts *Jeopardy* players but looking much more like Figure 14-3. Using this grid is how you can graphically set your table's dimensions with the mouse.

3. **Use the mouse to set the table's size.**

   Drag down and to the right to create a table with a given number of rows and columns. The precise values appear at the bottom of the grid.

4. **Release the mouse.**

   Your table is inserted into the document, at the perfect size.

Refer to the previous sections for any tips worth noting.

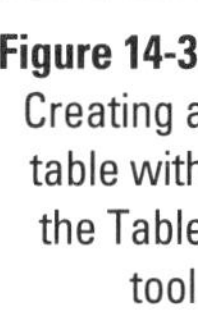
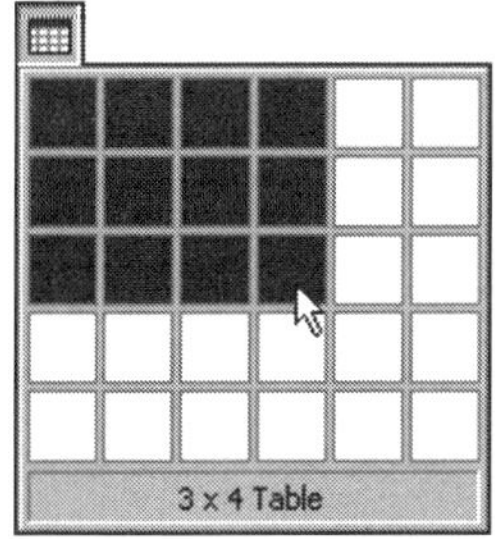

Figure 14-3: Creating a table with the Table tool.

Putting stuff in a table

An empty table sits in your document. But before you break out the MinWax and clean it up, why not set the table?

The table is divided into rows and columns. Where they meet is called a *cell* — just like they have in prison but without the TV and metal toilet. Your job is to fill in the various cells with text, graphics, or whatever. Here are some pointers:

- Press the Tab key to move from cell to cell. Pressing the Enter key just puts a new paragraph of text in the same cell. (Each cell is like its own little document.)
- The Shift+Tab combination moves you backward between the cells.
- If you press the Tab key in the last bottom-right cell, a new row of cells is added.
- If you press Shift+Enter, you can start writing text on a new line without starting a new paragraph. (Shift+Enter is the new line keyboard shortcut which, unlike the Enter key alone, doesn't really start a new paragraph. Weird, huh?)
- You can press the cursor keys to move from cell to cell as well (how swell). But if the cell contains text, pressing the cursor keys makes the toothpick cursor dawdle through the words. After all, you can still use the cursor keys to edit text in the cells. (Using the Tab key to move from cell to cell is best.)
- Text-formatting commands also work in the cells. You can boldface, underline, italicize, center, flush left, and so on. Refer to Chapters 10 and 11 for the details. The formatting affects the text in only one cell at a time — or in the cells that you collectively mark as a block.
- You can apply styles to text in a table. See Chapter 15 for the details.
- To format a row or column all at once, you have to select it first. Just click the mouse in that row or column and choose either Table⇨Select Row or Table⇨Select Column.

- To utterly remove the table from your document, highlight the whole darn thing as a block and then choose Table⇨Delete columns. The table is blown to smithereens.
- To erase a cell's contents in a table, mark it as a block and press the Delete key.

Changing a Table

Suppose that you create a card table but really need a dining room table — or one of those long dual-time-zone tables rich people eat at — or, because you are participating in a back-to-nature movement, no table at all. You have decided to squat down on your haunches around the fire when you eat. (A granola friend once told me that this method was really great for your lower back, but after about five minutes, I lost all feeling in my legs.) Anyway, whatever you decide, any table can be changed and adjusted after it has been created.

Adding and deleting rows and columns

To add rows to your table, follow these steps:

1. **Stick the toothpick cursor in the row above the spot where you want your new row.**
2. **Click the Insert Rows tool.**

   This tool appears on the toolbar, replacing the Insert Table tool whenever the toothpick cursor lurks in a table.

   Thud! The government of the People's Democratic Republic of Word is proud to be adding brand-new story to existing workers' apartment complex.
3. **Repeat Steps 1 and 2 to add as many rows as you want.**

   You can also use the Table⇨Insert Rows command, which does the same thing. But, eh, why bother?

To delete rows from your table, follow these steps:

1. **Highlight the row that you want to delete.**

   Move the cursor into the row and choose Table⇨Select Row.
2. **Choose the Table⇨Delete Rows command.**
3. **Repeat Steps 1 and 2 to blast away as many rows as you want.**

To add columns to your table, follow these steps:

1. **Move the toothpick cursor into the column to the left of the spot where you want the new column to be added.**
2. **Choose Table⇨Select Column.**
3. **Choose the Table⇨Insert Columns command.**
4. **Repeat Step 3 to add as many columns as you want.**

Doubtless you need to adjust the width of the table's columns after adding new columns. See the following section, "Adjusting the column width," for the details.

To delete columns from your table, follow these steps:

1. **Highlight the column that you want to delete.**

   Move the toothpick cursor to that column.
2. **Pluck out Table⇨Select Column from the menu.**
3. **Choose the Table⇨Delete Columns command.**
4. **Repeat Step 3 to blast away as many columns as you want.**

Here are some things to keep in mind about rows and columns:

- You can also select columns by moving the mouse cursor above the column until it changes shape, to a down-pointing arrow. Point the arrow at the row and click the left mouse button. You can select multiple columns by dragging the mouse across them.
- New rows are inserted *below* the current row in a table, which is the highlighted row or the one that the toothpick cursor is in.
- New columns are inserted *to the right* of the current column in a table.

Adjusting the column width

Columns, like my waistline, tend to get fatter and, unlike my waistline, thinner too. Fortunately, changing the width of a column in Word is a heck of a lot easier than going on a diet.

To adjust the width of a column, follow these steps:

1. **Put the toothpick cursor anywhere in the table, in the column that you want to change.**
2. **Choose the Table⇨Cell Height and Width command.**

This step opens the cute little Cell Height and Width dialog box. Click the tab for Column, or press Alt+C, so that your dialog box looks like the one shown in Figure 14-4.

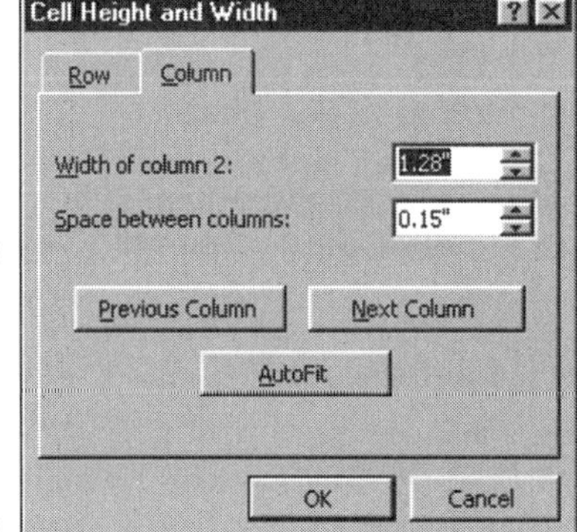

Figure 14-4: The Cell Height and Width dialog box.

3. **Click the AutoFit button.**

   This step lines up all the columns according to the width of the widest text item in that column — ideal for wide columns with skinny text.

   The dialog box vanishes, and your column is perfectly adjusted.

If you want to make several, or all, of the columns the same width, select them before you open the Column Width dialog box. Any changes you make apply to all the selected columns.

You can also change the column width by using the mouse. Place the mouse cursor on the border between columns, and the cursor changes its shape into something that looks like a railroad track with arrows pointing east and west. Hold down the left mouse button and drag the column border to a new size.

If you look up at the ruler when the toothpick cursor is in the table, you see that each column is given its own miniruler. You can adjust the column width by using the mouse and the tiny washboard doojobbie. When you hover the mouse over the washboard, the cursor changes to a left-right pointing arrow. Drag the washboard left or right to change the size of a column.

Automatically spiffing-out your table

Word contains a deep well of formatting tricks, some of which you can use on any old table you create to make it look really, really nice — like someone who actually cared created the thing. To make this happen you need to use the Table AutoFormat command. It's cinchy.

Stick the toothpick cursor in any table, preferably one you've already filled in. Then choose Table➪Table AutoFormat from the menu. The Table AutoFormat dialog box appears, as shown in Figure 14-5.

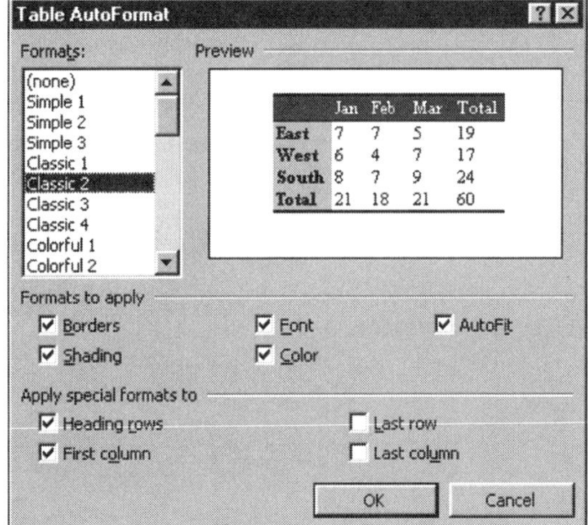

Figure 14-5: The Table AutoFormat dialog box.

Just keep your eyeballs focused on the sample table shown in the Preview. Then click your mouse on each consecutive item in the Formats scrolling list. Each one of those items automatically spiffs up your table to look like the sample shown in the Preview window.

After you find a table format you like, click the OK button.

You can goof around with other options in this dialog box on your own spare time.

Mustering Text into Columns

Columns — especially those you can see right on your screen — are one of those features all the magazines, gurus, and other pseudopundits demanded for their word processors. Do we need them? No. Can Word do them? Yes. Do you want to mess with this? Sure, why not? It will give you something to do while the electric chair recharges.

Before I divulge my Word column secrets, here's a healthy bit of advice: The best way to make columns is in a desktop publishing package, such as PageMaker, QuarkXPress, or any of the other fine products geared to such tasks. Those programs are designed for playing with text and making columns much easier to use than Word does (although figuring out the instructions is like playing an eternal chess match with a guy who wears a size 12 hat). In Word, columns remain more of a curiosity than anything you or I want to spend more than 15 minutes of our time on.

To start columns in your document, follow these next steps. If your text has already been written, Word puts it all in column format. Otherwise, any new text you create is placed in columns automagically.

1. **Move the toothpick cursor to where you want the columns to start.**
2. **Choose the Format⇨Columns command.**

   The Columns dialog box opens, as shown in Figure 14-6.

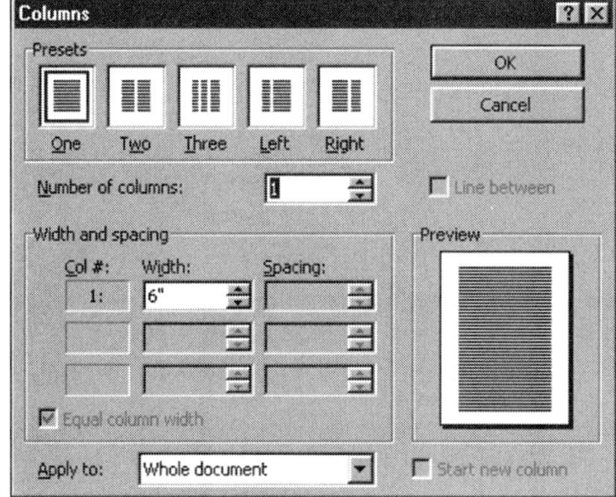

Figure 14-6: The Columns dialog box.

3. **Enter the number of columns that you want.**

   Or click one of the illustrated, ready-to-wear buttons. (Two columns is sufficient enough to impress anyone. More columns make your text skinnier and may be harder to read.)
4. **If you want a pretty line between the columns of text, check the Line between box.**

   The display says Line between, not Pretty Line between (though it should).
5. **Open the Apply To drop-down list and choose to apply the columns to the whole document or just from now on (this point forward).**
6. **If you want to start a new column right from where you are, check the Start new column box.**

   This step tells Word to put a column break in the document.

7. **Click the OK button.**

   Okay!

Word shows you your columns right there on-screen. That feat is at least $15 of the purchase price right there!

In a hurry? You can use the Columns tool. Click the tool, and a baby box of columns appears. Click and drag the mouse to indicate how many text columns you want. When you release the mouse button, the columns appear.

The space between columns is called the *gutter.* Unless you have a bunch of columns or a great deal of space to fill, leave this setting at .5" — half an inch. This amount of white space is pleasing to the eye without being too much of a good thing.

Editing text in columns is a pain. The cursor seems to hop all over the place and takes an eternity to move from one column to another. I'm just complaining here because I'm bored and fresh out of rainy-day, popsicle-stick projects.

Using the mouse to poke the cursor to a new spot on a column seems to work nicely.

To get rid of columns, go back and change the number of columns to one. Neat, huh? (Or click the Undo tool or press the Undo shortcut, Ctrl+Z.)

The three-column text format works nicely on Landscape paper. This method is how most brochures are created. Refer to Chapter 13 for information on selecting Landscape paper.

All the text and paragraph formatting mentioned in this part of the book also applies to text and paragraphs in columns. The difference is that your column margins — not the page margins — now mark the left and right sides of your text for paragraph formatting.

Chapter 15
Formatting with Style

In This Chapter

- Using the Style command
- Creating a style
- Using a style
- Using the Heading styles
- Changing a style
- Copying character formatting

Want to stand out from the crowd? Then do what I do: Eat massive quantities of garlic. Nothing else makes you stand alone like that. When you're word processing, however, garlic won't help much (unless you buy garlic paper — refer to a funky former-hippie neighborhood in your town for a shop that carries the stuff). Instead, you can stand out by using Word's Style command.

No matter how pretty your undies are, style — in Word anyway — is not what you wear or even how you wear it. A style is a series of formatting instructions — bold, centered, sideways — that are named and stored for future use. Suppose that you have a series of paragraphs that you want indented in bold, tiny type with a box drawn around each paragraph — oh, and an extra line placed at the end of each paragraph. You can create a style that slaps on all these formats with a single keystroke. Styles may be advanced stuff, but they certainly can save time.

Using the Style Command

Styles bring all your formatting (character, paragraph, tabs, and so on) together under one roof — or in one dialog box, which is the case with Word. That one roof is found in the Format menu: the Style command. When you choose Format⇨Style, you see the Style dialog box, shown in Figure 15-1.

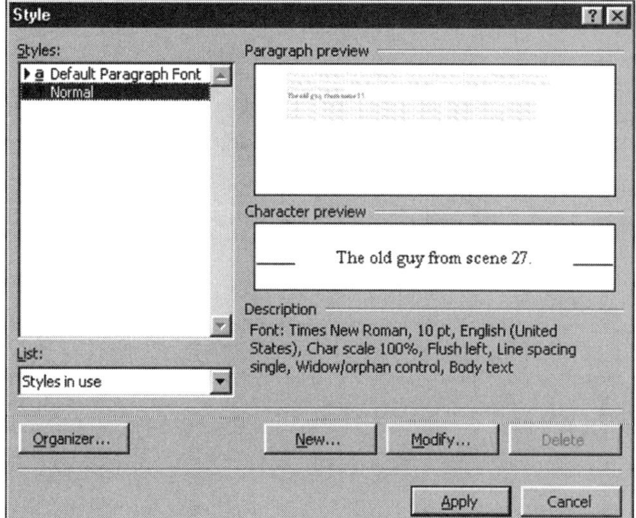

Figure 15-1: The Style dialog box.

Four items are worth noting in the Style dialog box: Styles, Description, and the Paragraph preview and Character preview windows.

The Styles scrolling list displays easy-to-remember names assigned to each style. Word always starts with the Default Paragraph Font and Normal styles, which are plain, boring text on-screen styles. You can use the Styles list to select a new style for your document or just to see what's available.

The Description area (below the Character preview) is the technical mumbo jumbo description of the style. For example, the description area may specify bold, list tab stops, or mention fonts and such. No need to rest your weary eyes there for long.

Two preview windows show style effects on both paragraph and character formatting.

- You can use Word without ever messing with styles. Only if you want to get truly fancy should you ever bother with this stuff. (Refer to Chapter 17 on automatic formatting if you're truly lazy and really don't care.)
- Styles are combinations of character, paragraph, and other formatting, all saved under an easy-to-remember name.
- The idea behind a style is that you don't have to keep selecting font (character) and paragraph formatting while you're working on your document.

For example, the style for this bulleted list is saved under the name Indent. I formatted the main text preceding this list under the style named Body. That way I can write this text without having to constantly mess with the font and character dialog boxes. I just say "Gimme the Body style" and Word dutifully obeys.

- The Normal style is Word's standard style, the one that always appears when you open a new document. Yeah, the Normal style is pretty plain and ugly, but you can add your own styles to make your text fairly fancy if you like.
- The Styles list actually shows two types of styles. Styles with a paragraph marker (¶) by them control both font and paragraph formatting. Styles with an underlined A (a) affect only font (character) formatting. Refer to "Creating a character-only style" later in this chapter for the details.
- Use the List drop-down box to see some or all of the styles you have available. When Styles in use is displayed, you only see those styles that belong to your current document (as in Figure 15-1). If you select All styles from the list, you see tons and tons of styles, almost to the point of driving you mad.

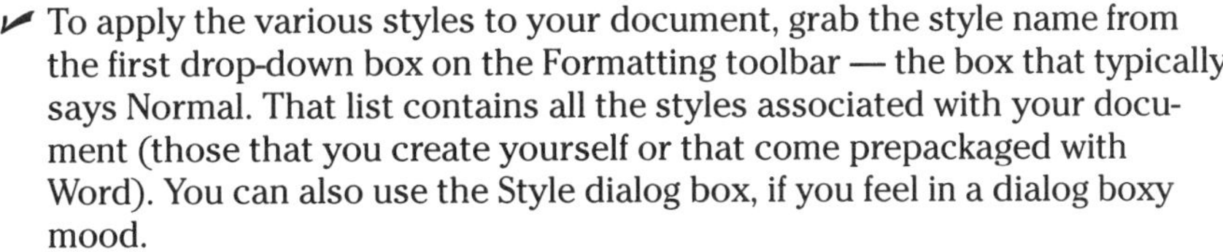

- To apply the various styles to your document, grab the style name from the first drop-down box on the Formatting toolbar — the box that typically says Normal. That list contains all the styles associated with your document (those that you create yourself or that come prepackaged with Word). You can also use the Style dialog box, if you feel in a dialog boxy mood.
- When you choose a new style, it applies to the paragraph that the toothpick cursor is in or any block you select on-screen.
- For more information on font or character formatting, refer to Chapter 10.
- Refer to Chapter 11 for the details on paragraph formatting.
- If you mess with outlines, Word also tosses in the Heading 1, Heading 2, and Heading 3 styles. See the section "Using the built-in Heading styles" later in this chapter for more information on those styles.

Creating a new style

New styles are easy to create. Just follow these loosely outlined steps:

1. **Type a paragraph of text.**

   You don't need a whole paragraph; a single line will do. Just remember to press Enter at the end of the line, which makes Word believe you typed an entire paragraph.

2. **Mark your paragraph as a block.**

   See Chapter 6 to find out how to mark a block of text.

3. **Format the block.**

   Select your character formatting. Select a font and select a point size to make the text big or little. See Chapter 10 for more information on character formatting.

   Stick to fonts and sizes for your character formatting; avoid bold, italics, or underline unless you want them applied to all of your text. (Only select bold, underline, and similar character formats if you want them applied to the *entire* paragraph; typically those formats are word-only things.)

   Select the paragraph formatting for your style. See Chapter 11 for the details. Indent, center, or apply whatever formatting you want to apply to your style.

4. **Press Ctrl+Shift+S.**

   This key combination activates the Style command. Actually, it highlights the Style drop-down box on the Formatting toolbar — the one that usually says Normal.

5. **Type a name for your style.**

   A brief, descriptive, one-word title does nicely. For example, if you create an indented paragraph that you want to use to list things, name the style **List.** Or if you create a special musical style, name it **Liszt.**

6. **Press Enter.**

   The style is added to Word's repertoire of styles for your document.

- To use the style — to *apply* it to other paragraphs in your document — refer to "Using a style," later in this chapter.

- Give your style a name that is descriptive of the style's function. Names like Indented List or Table Body Text are great because it's easy to remember what they do. Names like Ira or Gopple-bop are somewhat less desirable.
- The styles that you create are only available to the document in which they're created.
- If you create scads of styles you love and want to use them for several documents, you need to create what's called a *template*. Chapter 16 covers this procedure in "Creating a Document Template to Store Your Styles."

- You can also create a style by using the Style dialog box, though this method requires more mental work than following the preceding steps. Choose Format⇨Style. Click the New button. The New Style dialog box opens. Click the Format button to see a menu that allows you to play with the Font, Paragraph, Tabs, and much more. Click OK after setting the Font, Paragraph, or whatever, and then click the Name box in the New Style dialog box to give your style a name. Click OK and then the Close button to return to your document.

Creating a character-only style

You'll notice that some styles listed in the Styles list are marked with an underlined A, like this: a. That moniker flags character-only styles. What these styles do is affect only the font and not the paragraph formatting. So if you have a centered block of text and only want to change the font to big, ugly text, you can do so by selecting the Big Ugly character-only style, which leaves the paragraph formatting alone.

To create a character-only style, follow these steps:

1. **Choose Format⇨Style.**

   The Style dialog box appears (refer to Figure 15-1).

2. **Click the New... button.**

   The New Style dialog box appears (see Figure 15-2). This dialog box allows you to create a new style — familiar turf if you've already done this procedure.

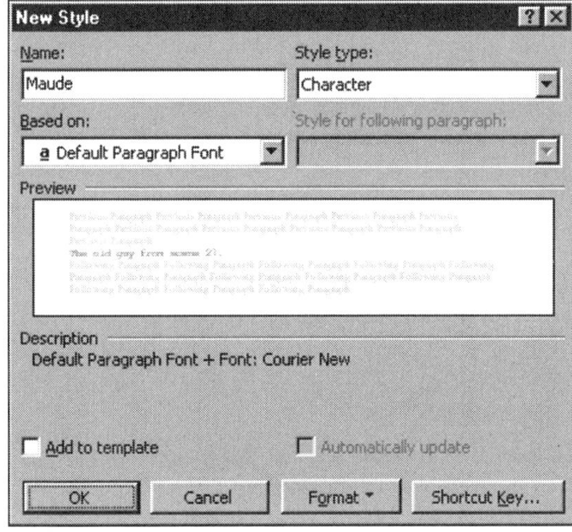

Figure 15-2: The New Style dialog box.

3. **In the Name box, type a name for the style.**

   Be clever. If, for example, the character style applies small caps in a stocky font, name it **Stubby**.

4. **In the Style type drop-down list, select Character.**

   This selection gears everything in the New Style dialog box to accept only character and font-related formatting stuff.

5. **Use the Format button to select the font formats that you want.**

   Only three options are available: Font, Border, and Language.

   Forget Border. Forget Language.

   Font brings up the Font dialog box, where you can set the various character attributes — similar to what I cover in Chapter 10 of this book.

6. **Click OK after you're done defining the character style.**
7. **Click the Close button in the Style dialog box.**

   And you're done.

- Character style names appear with an underlined A (a) by them in the Style list.
- The special character styles don't affect any paragraph formatting. Selecting a character style only changes the font, style, size, underlining, bold, and so on.
- Also refer to "Stealing Character Formatting," later in this chapter, for a shortcut method of applying font formats.

Giving your style a shortcut key

Styles allow you the advantage of quickly formatting a paragraph of text. Style shortcut keys make formatting even better because pressing Alt+Shift+B to get at the Body style is often faster than messing with the Style drop-down list or dialog box — especially when you have a gob of styles you're messing with.

To give your style a name, follow these steps:

1. **Choose Format⇨Style.**

   Style dialog box, come on down!

2. **Select a style for which you want a shortcut key.**

   Highlight that style in the list by clicking it once with the mouse.

3. **Click the Modify button.**

   The Modify Style dialog box appears.

4. **Click the Shortcut Key button.**

   A cryptic Customize Keyboard dialog box appears. Don't waste any time trying to explore here. Just move on to Step 5.

5. **Press your Shortcut key combination.**

   Using Ctrl+Shift+letter or Alt+Shift+letter or Ctrl+Alt+letter key combinations is best, where "letter" is a letter key on the keyboard. For example, press Ctrl+Alt+B for your Body style shortcut key.

You'll notice that the key combination you press appears in the Press New Shortcut Key box (see the middle left side of the dialog box). If you make a mistake, press the Backspace key to erase.

6. **Check to see that the combination isn't already in use.**

   For example, Word uses Ctrl+B as the Bold character formatting shortcut key. This key combination appears under the heading `Currently Assigned To`, which shows up under the Press New Shortcut Key box. Keep an eye on that box! If something else uses the shortcut key, press the Backspace key and go back to Step 5.

   If the key isn't used by anything, you see `[unassigned]` displayed under the `Currently Assigned To` heading.

7. **Click the Assign button.**

8. **Click the Close button.**

   The Customize dialog box sulks away (but remember that there are no losers on *The Price is Right!*).

9. **Click the OK button.**

   The Modify Style dialog box huffs off.

10. **Click the Close button in the Style dialog box.**

    Congratulations; you now have a usable shortcut key for your style.

I use the Ctrl+Alt key combinations along with a letter key for my style shortcuts. When I write a magazine article, Ctrl+Alt+B is the Body style; I use Ctrl+Alt+T for "type this in stuff" style and Ctrl+Alt+C for my Caption style. The notion here is to make the shortcut keys kinda match the style name.

Information on using a style — *applying the style,* if you work for Microsoft tech support — is covered in the next section.

Using a style

You don't *use* a style as much as you *apply* it. The character and paragraph formatting carefully stored inside the style is applied to text on-screen, text in a block, or text that you're about to write. Using a style is easy:

1. **Know what you're applying the style to.**

   If it's a paragraph already on-screen, just stick the toothpick cursor somewhere in that paragraph. Otherwise, the style is applied to any new text you type.

2. Select a style from the Formatting toolbar.

Click the down-arrow button beside the first drop-down list — the "Normal" list. Select your style from that list. From the keyboard, press Ctrl+Shift+S and then the down-arrow key to see the styles. You see a gaggle of styles displayed, some in the styles they apply themselves! (See Figure 15-3.)

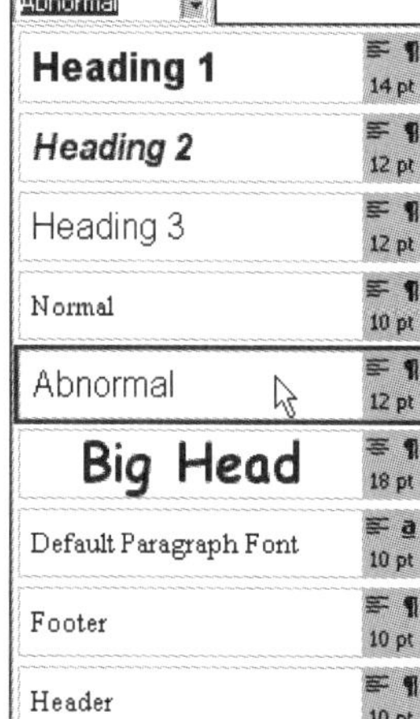

Figure 15-3: The Style drop-down list in action.

- Highlight a style name and click it with the mouse or press the Enter key. You can also type the style name directly into the box if you can spell.
- Applying a style is a paragraph-level thing. You can't put a style in just a single word in a paragraph; the style takes over the whole paragraph instead.
- You can also apply a style by using a shortcut key, provided you've created one for that style. Refer to the long, boring instructions in the preceding section for the details.
- To apply a style to your entire document, choose Edit⇨Select All. Then select the style you want for *everything.*
- Herds of styles can be collected in things called *Style Galleries.*
- Refer to "Creating a new style," earlier in this chapter, for information on creating your own special styles for a document.
- Sometimes you can develop a style so sophisticated that it won't show on your monitor. If you exceed the capabilities of your printer or graphics card, you may see some strange stuff. Don't get excited, it's not the '60s all over again.

"Uh, what does the Modify Style dialog box mean?"

As you're goofing with styles, you may stumble upon the Modify Style dialog box, which tries in its own awkward way to explain the following: "Excuse me, but you selected some text and a style, but they don't match. Should I pretend that the style should match the text from here on, or should I reformat the text to match the style?" An interesting question.

The way Word puts it is `Update the style to reflect recent changes?` You probably don't want to select this option. Highlighting this option and clicking OK means that the style you already created will match the selected text. (Of course, if that's what you want, click OK.)

The other option is `Reapply the formatting of the style to the selection.` Equally confusing, this option means that Word formats your highlighted text to match the style you selected. You probably want to choose this option; it keeps your style intact.

As a final word, be thankful for Word's Undo command. No matter what you select in the Modify Style dialog box, the Undo command can return your text to normal (or the way it was before).

Using the built-in Heading styles

Word comes with three built-in Heading styles. You can, and should, use these styles if you plan on breaking up your text with different headings. For example, this chapter has main headings, such as "Using the Style Command" and then subheadings, like "Using the built-in Heading styles." In Word, the main headings would be formatted using the built-in Heading 1 style; the subheads by using the built-in Heading 2 styles.

Granted, the Heading styles are boring as they come out of the box. But you can change them to suit your document's needs. Refer to the very next section for information on changing a style's look and smell.

There are a few advantages to using the Heading styles. The first is that you will see the headings listed when you drag the elevator button in the scroll bar. Also, you can use the browsing buttons (below the vertical scroll bar) to hop through your document, stopping at various Heading styles. All this is covered in Chapter 3, if you're interested.

Honestly, though, you don't *really* have to use the Heading styles. There are those advantages mentioned above. But if you really want to create your own, fun styles, don't let the Heading styles get in your way.

- Heading styles, like the Normal and Default Paragraph Font styles, cannot be deleted from your document.
- There are actually many Heading styles Word can use, from Heading 1 on down through Heading 9. These mostly come into play when you use Word's outlining feature. See Chapter 28, "Organizing Your Thots."

Changing the style

Styles change. Bell bottoms were once the rage, but now, well now they mostly define West Greenwich Village from the East. (Or is it the other way around?)

Times New Roman — the bane of the Normal style — is a wonderful font . . . if you're into bow ties and think that Merengue is a salted tequila drink or an ex-Nazi who lived in Brazil. Still, Times New Roman is a workhorse that is used by everyone for almost everything. Maybe you want to put this font out to pasture and use a different font in your Normal style. If so, you can change it.

Here are the instructions for changing a style — any style, not just the Normal style.

1. **Choose the Format⇨Style command.**

   Well, Howdy Mr. Style dialog box, how are the wife and kids?

2. **Select a style to change from the Styles list.**

   Click that style once with your mouse.

3. **Click the Modify button.**

   The Modify Style box erupts on the screen.

4. **Click the Format button.**

   A list of formatting options drops down. Font, Paragraph, Tabs, Border, Physique, Rx. It's all there. Figure 15-4 shows what it looks like.

5. **Choose the part of the style that you want to change.**

   For example, choose Font from the drop-down menu to open the Font formatting dialog box. There you can change the font, size, or any of the other things controlled in the font box (see Chapter 10). Other menu items lurking on the Format button menu allow you to change other formatting aspects.

6. **Click OK.**

   Clicking OK closes whichever dialog box you opened to modify some aspect of a style. If, for example, you opened the Font dialog box, clicking its OK button closes that box and returns you to the Style dialog box.

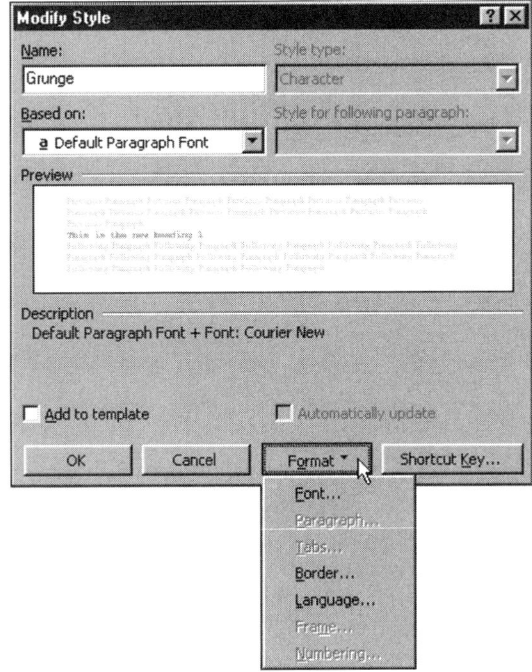

Figure 15-4: The Modify Style dialog box with its Format button hanging open.

7. **Repeat Steps 4, 5, and 6 as necessary to change the style.**
8. **Click OK in the Modify Style box after you're done.**
9. **Oh, and click Close in the Style dialog box to get back at your document.**

- Changing styles is advanced stuff — not recommended for the timid. It's entirely possible to use Word without bothering with styles at all, which is the way most people use the program.
- Changing a style means that all paragraphs in your document that have that style change, which is a great way to change a font throughout a document without having to select everything and manually pick out a new font.
- You don't like the result? Click the Undo button (or press Ctrl+Z) to make it all go away and return to your original headache.

Stealing Character Formatting

To heck with styles! Suppose that you created a neat character format and want to copy it to other text in your document. For example

Outrageous text!

The format appeals to you, and you imagine that it would be effective elsewhere. To copy the character's format only — which sorta fits in with all this style nonsense — heed the following:

1. **Jab the toothpick cursor in the middle of the text that has the character (font) formatting that you want to copy.**

   No need to select anything as a block here.

2. **Click the Format Painter button on the Standard toolbar.**

   The cursor changes to a paintbrush–I-beam pointer, depicted at left. This special cursor is used to highlight text in your document. That text then takes on new character attributes.

3. **Hunt for the text that you want to change.**

   Refer to Chapter 2 for information on Word's navigation keys.

4. **Highlight the text.**

   Drag the mouse over the text that you want to change. You must use the mouse here.

5. **Release the mouse button.**

   Voilà! The text is changed.

- Painting the character format in this manner only works once. To repaint with the same format, repeat the preceding steps or refer to the next section. Or . . .
- Double-click the Format Painter button in Step 2. That way, the format painter cursor stays active, ready to paint lots of text. So after Step 5, you can continue changing text (repeat Steps 3, 4, and 5 as often as you like). Press the Esc key to cancel your Dutch Boy frenzy.
- If you tire of the mouse, you can use the Ctrl+Shift+C key command to copy the character format from a highlighted block to another location in your document. Use the Ctrl+Shift+V key combination to paste the character format elsewhere. Just highlight the text in your document and press Ctrl+Shift+V to paste in the font formatting.
- You can sorta kinda remember Ctrl+Shift+C to copy character formatting and Ctrl+Shift+V to paste because Ctrl+C and Ctrl+V are the copy and paste shortcut keys. Sorta kinda.
- Don't confuse the format painter with the highlighting tool, which is described in Chapter 27.

Chapter 16

Templates and Wizards

In This Chapter

- Creating a document template
- Using a template
- Changing a template
- Using Wizards to create o' so lovely documents

Templates and Wizards both deal with the same thing: creating pretty-looking documents without requiring a third-degree black belt in typesetting. Templates are more of the old-fashioned way of doing things. A template is a collection of styles and other items that make writing certain types of documents easier. For example, the Department of Transportation uses these huge STOP templates that they lay down at intersections. The workers just spray paint over the template and a huge STOP appears on the roadway. Word's templates work sorta like that.

Wizards are more magical — more along the lines of what used to be called *artificial intelligence* in computing circles. Well, it turns out that artificial intelligence is nothing more than the computer doing its job by helping you do your job. In the case of Word, Wizards help you set up and write sample documents, sometimes even filling in the words for you. Wizards are like magic, and they're ideal for us lazy-minded typists who really want to dazzle with a minimum of effort.

Creating a Document Template to Store Your Styles

Styles are a collection of paragraph and font attributes that you store under one convenient name. Chapter 15 has all the details on how they're created and used.

Often times, you want to store a bunch of your styles so that you can use them over and over. For example, you may want to keep all the styles you used in the *American Gun Nut Newsletter*. To do this task, you create a *document template,* actually a special type of document. In the template, you can store all your styles, which allows you to use them again and again without the bother of recreating them each time.

You create a document template like you do any new document. Start by creating a new document in Word:

1. **Choose the File⇨New command.**

   You must choose the New command from the File menu; clicking the New button on the Standard toolbar doesn't do the job.

   The New dialog box opens, numbing your brain because it's just way too complex (see Figure 16-1).

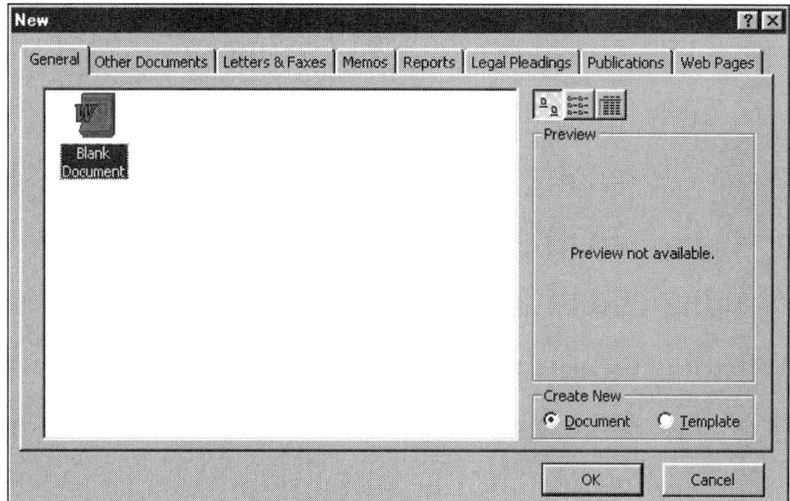

Figure 16-1: The New dialog box stuns you.

2. **Scan for the Create New area in the New dialog box.**

   You have two radio buttons: Document and Template.

   I would also refer you to the sidebar "Sticking your template into the proper panel," but you don't have to go there at this very moment.

3. **Click the Template button.**

   Clicking the mouse on the Template button puts a little dot there.

4. **Click OK.**

   You see what looks like a new document on-screen. Don't be fooled. It's really a document template thing. (The title bar of the new document indicates that you are working on a template.)

5. **Create the styles for your new document template.**

   Follow the instructions for creating styles in Chapter 15, but create a number of styles that you want to save or use for particular documents. For example, this book has a document template that includes styles for the main text, numbered lists, figure captions, section headings, and a bunch of other stuff I routinely ignore.

6. **Save the document template to disk.**

   Choose File➪Save As. The Save As dialog box appears. Type a name for your template, keeping in mind that you should be descriptive here but that you don't need to use the word "template" because Word keeps track of that for you, and click OK. Then you can close the template document, and you're done.

- Word's document templates are saved in a special template folder on your hard drive. Don't try to save them any place else.
- To use a document template when you create a new document, refer to "Using a document template," later in this chapter.
- After creating a new template, you see its name appear in the New dialog box's General panel (joining the Blank Document shown in Figure 16-1). Choosing that template for a new document is a cinch, but I leave the details up to "Using a document template," just a few pages from here.
- You can find more information on saving stuff to disk, including all-important filename info in Chapter 8.

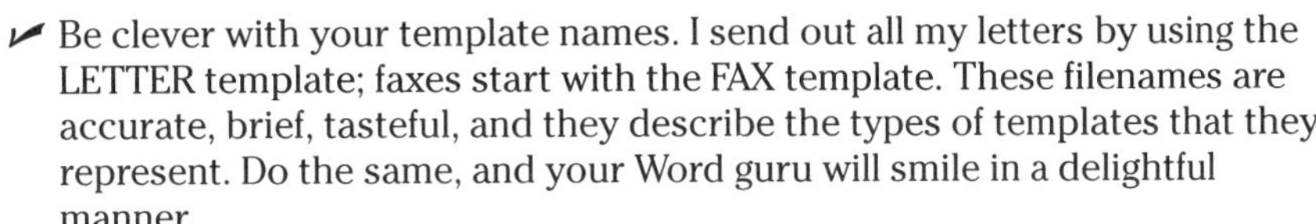

- Be clever with your template names. I send out all my letters by using the LETTER template; faxes start with the FAX template. These filenames are accurate, brief, tasteful, and they describe the types of templates that they represent. Do the same, and your Word guru will smile in a delightful manner.
- Word actually comes with a slew of templates ready for the taking. Refer to "Using a document template," later in this chapter.

Creating a template complete with text

There's no rule that says your document templates must contain only styles. They can also store text, especially text you may use over and over again in certain types of documents. For example, a common type of Word template may contain letterhead, which allows you to use that template for your correspondence.

Sticking your template into the proper panel

The New dialog box contains several panels, each of which has its own panel along the top; you know, typical Windows 95 "let's see how much crapola we can stuff into a single dialog box" kind of stuff. Review Figure 16-1 to see what I'm talking about.

Each of those panels, General, Letters & Faxes, Memos, and so on, contains a different type of document template, a different way to start out something new in Word. For example, the Letters & Faxes panel contains templates the boys and girls at Microsoft have already created for you — templates designed to start off your letters and faxes with the utmost of ease. (You can even find Wizards in there. See the section "Chickening Out and Using a Wizard," later in this chapter.)

After you create a new template, you can try to put it where it belongs by choosing the appropriate folder when you save the template to disk. Of course, you don't really have to; feel free to stick all your templates into the General panel, which is what I do (and I'm not that bad of a person).

I have a FAX template that I use to send out faxes; the first part of this template (the To, From, and Re lines) is already typed, which saves me valuable typing energy molecules that I can otherwise use to get down to business.

To create a template complete with text, follow these steps:

1. **Do everything outlined in the preceding section, steps 1 through 5.**

   Gee, a direction like that saves the author a lot of typing energy molecules.

2. **Before saving your document template to disk, type some text that you want to be part of the template.**

   Anything you type will be saved to disk along with the template's styles. You can, for example, create your own letterhead, provided you read various other chapters in this book. Or if you're doing a li'l newsletter, you can create the parts of it that don't change from issue to issue, such as the sample shown in Figure 16-2.

3. **Save the template to disk, as outlined in the preceding section.**

   Give it a clever name, something like LETTER or LETTERHEAD or even NEWSLETTER.

   You don't have to use the word "template" in the name, because Word keeps document templates separate from normal documents.

- You can store lots of text in a document template if you like — anything you normally type into a Word document. However, the idea here is to be brief. A specific template isn't as useful as a general one.

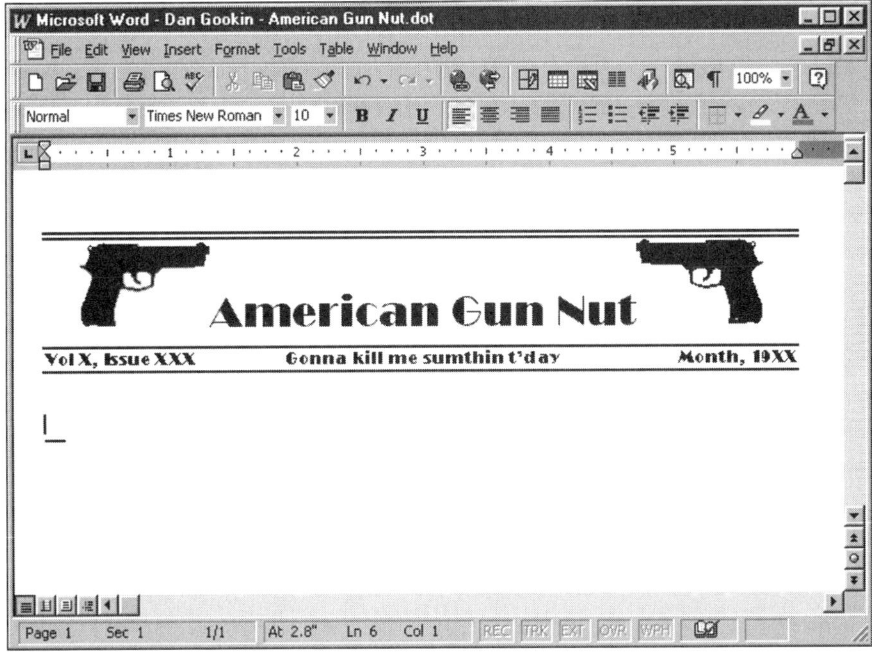

Figure 16-2: A sample template containing text and graphics.

- You can also stuff graphics into a document template. Refer to Part IV of this book for information on using graphics in your documents.
- Please refer to Chapter 21 for information on Mail Merge — a distant concept from document templates, although the two can be easily confused.

Using a document template

Oh, this is really dumb. To use a document template, follow these steps:

1. **Choose File⇨New.**

   The New dialog box opens. You must use the File⇨New command to see the New dialog box; pressing Ctrl+N or clicking the New button on the toolbar just doesn't do the trick.

2. **Select the template that you want from the assortment presented.**

   First look for the panel that describes the kind of document you want to create. If you're creating your own templates, however, they should all live in the General panel. Pluck out the proper template for whatever job you're trying to do.

   The Normal template is Word's own boring normal template (which should be renamed *Yawn*).

Sticking the current date into a template

Any text that you type into a template becomes a permanent part of that template. This situation isn't good news when you want to add the date to a template, as today's date may differ from the date you actually use the template. Fortunately, there is a solution. Though the procedure is a bit cumbersome, the following steps enable you to set an updating date *field* into your template:

1. **Position the toothpick cursor where you want the date.**
2. **Choose InsertÍField. The Field dialog box appears.**
3. **From the Categories area, select Date and Time.**
4. **From the Field Names area, select Date.**
5. **Click the Options button.**

   The Field Options dialog box appears. (Make sure that the General Switches panel is forward; click that panel if it's not.)

6. **Select a date format from the Date-Time list.**

   The letters d, M, and y stand for the day, month, and year. The format MMMM d, yyyy prints the month, day, and year in the full (unabbreviated) format.

7. **Click the Add to Field button.**
8. **Click the OK button.**

   The Field Options dialog box zooms outta sight.

9. **Click the OK button in the Field dialog box to make that box go away.**

Your template now has a date field in it, which looks like the current date, but this field is not the same thing as normal text. Instead, a field is like a mini-block of text that always displays the current date. (You must highlight the block — select it — to delete it; you cannot edit the date field like normal text.)

3. **Click OK.**

   Word starts up a document, complete with that template's information, fonts, styles, and whatnot, all ready for use. You can take advantage of any styles stuffed into the template and view, use, or edit any text saved in the template.

- Special templates are given the surname wizard. Refer to "Chickening Out and Using a Wizard," later in this chapter, for more information on them.
- Opening a document with a template does not change the template; your new document is merely using the template's styles and any text it already has. To change a template, refer to the next section.
- Golly, don't templates make Word kind of easy? Only, of course, if the entire document template and style fiasco hasn't already induced brainlock.

Changing a document template

Changing or editing a document template is identical to changing or editing a normal document. The difference is that a template is opened instead of the document. Yes, Word can deal with this task quite easily. Problem: You need to negotiate various folders on your hard drive, which is an E-ticket ride in Windows.

1. **Open the template by choosing File⇨Open.**

   The Open dialog box appears.

2. **In the Open dialog box, select Document Templates from the Files of type drop-down box.**

   You can find the Files of type drop-down box in the lower-left corner of the Open dialog box.

   This option directs Word to list only document templates in the Open dialog box file window.

3. **Find your template folder.**

   Word ensconces all its templates in a special folder. You need to use the Look in drop-down box to help you find this folder. (See Chapter 20, "Managing Files," for more information on using this device if you need to, though it's a standard Windows doohickey.)

   Here is the path you need to take to find your templates folder:

   Look in drive C. Use the Look in list to pluck out your `(C:)` hard drive.

   Look in the Program Files folder; double-click that folder to open it.

   Look in the Microsoft Office folder.

   Look in the Templates folder.

   Look in any folder you may have your template stored in, such as Letters & Faxes or Other Documents. You can see templates saved in the General panel without having to open any more folders.

4. **Open the template that you want to edit.**

   Double-click its filename.

   When you open the template, it appears in Word just like any other document — though it's really a template. (Sneaky.)

5. **Make your changes.**

   You edit the template just as you would any other document. Bear in mind that it is a template that you're editing and not a real document. Any style changes or text editing affect the template and are saved to disk as a template again.

6. **Save the modified template by choosing File➪Save.**

   Or choose File➪Save As to assign the modified template a new name and maintain the original template.

7. **Close the template document by choosing File➪Close.**

- Any changes that you make to a document template do not affect any documents already created with that template. The changes do, however, affect any new documents that you create.
- The Normal template is a special beast. Any change that you make to the Normal template affects all other templates that you use. The moral of this story is not to mess with the Normal template.

Chickening Out and Using a Wizard

If all this template-style-formatting nonsense has you in a tizzy, sit down and have a cup of tea. And while you're at it, prepare to let Word do all the formatting work. This is possible, with desirable results, thanks to the wonderful Wizards of Word.

A wizard enables you to create a near-perfect document automatically. All you need to do is select various options and make adjustments from a handy and informative dialog box. Word does the rest of the work.

To use a Word wizard, follow these steps:

1. **Choose File➪New.**

   This command opens the New dialog box (refer back to Figure 16-1).

2. **Hunt down a wizard.**

   A number of wizards come prepackaged with Word. Of course, none of them hides in the General panel. To find a wizard, click another panel in the New dialog box, for example, the Letters & Faxes panel.

   Wizards live along with templates, though the wizards have the word "wizard" in their name. You can find the Fax wizard, Letter wizard, Memo wizard, Lizard wizard, and maybe the Wizard of Oz if you look hard enough.

   Whatever wizard you select, highlight it in the template list; click the wizard's icon once with your mouse.

3. **Click OK.**

   Word hums and churns for a few minutes. It's thinking — no doubt a painful process. Give it time.

4. **Be enlightened by the Wizard dialog box.**

   A sample of one of the Wizard dialog boxes appears in Figure 16-3. Most of them look the same. Wizard dialog boxes offer questions to answer, maybe a preview window to peruse (which gives you an idea of what the finished document will look like), plus four helpful buttons: Cancel, <Back, Next> and Finish.

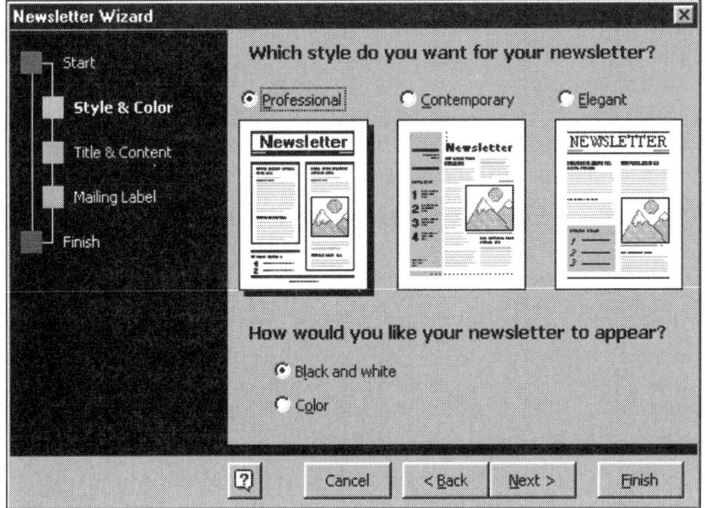

Figure 16-3: The wizard helps you create a something or other.

   Generally speaking, repeat the following two steps as often as required to create your document:

5. **Select one of the options to help the Wizard create your document.**

   The wizard helps you, but only if you first help the wizard. Answer any questions it poses you. For example, in Figure 16-3, you get to select the format for a newsletter.

   Feel free to play with the options and make different choices to see how it affects your document.

   Some options may require you to do a bit of typing, such as entering your name, return address, hat size, and so on.

   Some of the options may have you enter measurements. Don't fuss over this part of the process; just guess! A preview window helps with your guesses. And you can always use this book to help you reformat things later.

   If you're dissatisfied with the choice you're given, click the <Back button and start again with a new option.

6. **Click the Next> button.**

   This button moves you along to the next stage of creating your document, giving you more options from which to select. At this point, continue with Step 5 and select more options.

   Eventually, you see a `Those are all the answers the wizard needs to create your whatever` message. You'll also notice that the Next> button is dimmed. Word is ready to slap together your document.

7. **Click the Finish button.**

   The wizard prepares your document and presents it to you for editing and further primping.

- Wizard. Wizard. Wizard. It's one of those words that gets weirder and weirder the more you say it.

- Even though a wizard created your document, you still must save it to disk after you're done. In fact, most wizards may just start you on your way. After that point, you work with the document just like any other in Word. Don't forget to save!
- Some wizards may not ask you questions at all. Instead, a new document appears with lots of text that reads `Click here and type whatever.` Do it: Click the text and enter the appropriate information (which replaces the `Click here` text).
- The Tools menu offers a Letter Wizard item. This command is merely a shortcut for the Letter Wizard you can also summon through the New dialog box. I don't know why they added it as a menu item. If you choose the Letter Wizard command, just follow your annoying little Assistant's advice and answer the various questions in the dialog box.
- Some wizards even fill in text for you. These are super-cheating wizards. The Stephen King wizard, for example, writes his books for him in under a day.
- There. I managed to finish this entire section with only one silly reference to the *Wizard of Oz*.

Chapter 17

Some Automatic Formatting Tricks

In This Chapter

- Using AutoFormat
- Creating automatically formatted lists
- Creating automatically formatted headings
- Creating automatically formatted borders

Now that you have a computer, you really need to buy another to help keep you and the first computer organized. It seems that way sometimes. Actually, my biggest beef with computers is that they're just so darn stupid. For example, some things should be obvious to a computer: The first word of a sentence is capitalized; if you type `1.` to start a list, the computer should automatically type `2.` for you on the next line; and computers should recognize that the alluring smell of a kraut dog doesn't portend well for the digestive system.

This chapter is about automatic formatting jazz. There's actually an AutoFormat command in Word. Not only that, sometimes Word actually grows brains beneath its bone-laden skull, figures out what you're doing, and helps you finish the job. That's so amazing; it's almost enough to make you forget that you're using a computer.

Word capitalizes the first letter of a sentence for you automagically. See Chapter 7 for information on the AutoCorrect command.

Using AutoFormat

Word's AutoFormat command has absolutely nothing to do with formatting in the sense of font or paragraph formatting. No, what AutoFormat really does is clean up your document, remove excess spaces, add spaces where needed, and other minor housekeeping chores. Yes, it removes the slop most of us add to our documents without thinking about it.

Before AutoFormat can do its job, you need to create the document's text. Write! Write! Write! Write your letter, memo, chapter, poem, whatever. Then follow these steps:

1. **Save your document to disk.**

   This step is most important, and it's something you should be doing all the time. Save your document before you AutoFormat it. Refer to Chapter 1 for the details on saving.

2. **Choose Format⇨AutoFormat.**

   The AutoFormat dialog box appears, as shown in Figure 17-1.

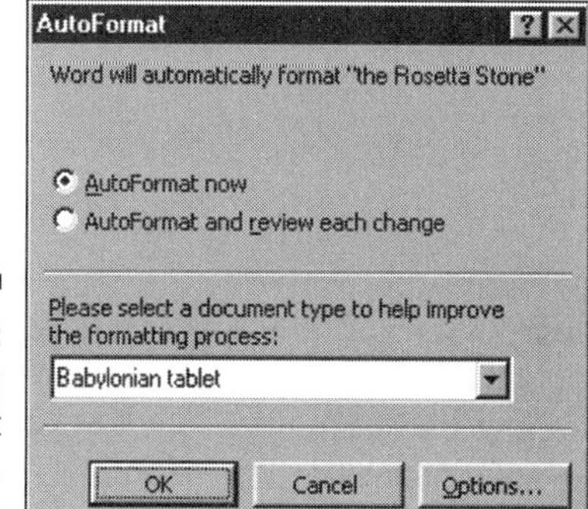

Figure 17-1: The AutoFormat dialog box.

3. **Click OK.**

   Ook! Eep! Ack!

4. **Formatting completed.**

   Word has carefully massaged and adjusted your document. You may find new headings, bulleted lists, and other amazing, whiz-bang things automatically done to your text.

- If you like, you can click AutoFormat and review each change button in the AutoFormat dialog box to see exactly what needs to be done before AutoFormat does its job.
- If your text is kinda boring, it won't appear as though AutoFormat did anything. Don't despair. AutoFormat is good at creating headings and bulleted lists, but it can't read your mind.
- You can always use the Undo command if you detest what AutoFormat did to your document. (Alas, there is no Detest command.)
- The AutoFormat tool has nothing to do with formatting your document, as in character or paragraph formatting.
- If you're interested in formatting your document automatically, refer to the section on wizards in Chapter 16.

Automatic Formatting as It Happens

Sometimes Word can be so smart it's scary. A long time ago, just having a program remind you to save before you quit was thought to be miraculous. But now . . . why just the other day Word reminded me that I forgot to floss the night before and, boy, though that blackberry cobbler looked tempting, I am several stones over my ideal weight. Scary stuff.

Making the automatic formatting thing happen as you work

You must direct Word to be smart. The program cannot do it on its own. To take advantage of the many automagical things Word can do, follow these steps:

1. **Choose Format⇨AutoFormat.**

   The AutoFormat dialog box exposes itself on the screen.

2. **Click the Options button lurking in the bottom-right corner.**

   The AutoCorrect dialog box appears. (Microsoft had to stick the AutoFormat stuff somewhere. They both start with Auto. And they both have a capital letter in the middle.)

3. **Click the AutoFormat As You Type tab.**

   What you see looks something like Figure 17-2.

4. **Because you don't know what the options do, check them all on.**

   Click the box by each option to put a check mark in it. This activates all the features, some of which are highlighted in the following sections.

5. **Click OK and then click OK again.**

   Close both the dialog boxes you left hanging open. Now you're ready to start playing, beginning in the next section.

- Make sure that you switch on the Headings, Borders, Tables, Automatic bulleted lists, and Automatic numbered lists items before you work through the remaining sections in this chapter.
- The "Straight quotes" with “smart quotes” option tells Word to change the boring straight quote marks into the more stylish “double” and ‘single’ style quote marks. Face it: The " and ' smell of Smith Corona.
- The Ordinals (1st) with superscript option tells Word to change your text so that when you type **2nd**, the program immediately formats it as 2nd. No pencil could ever be that smart.

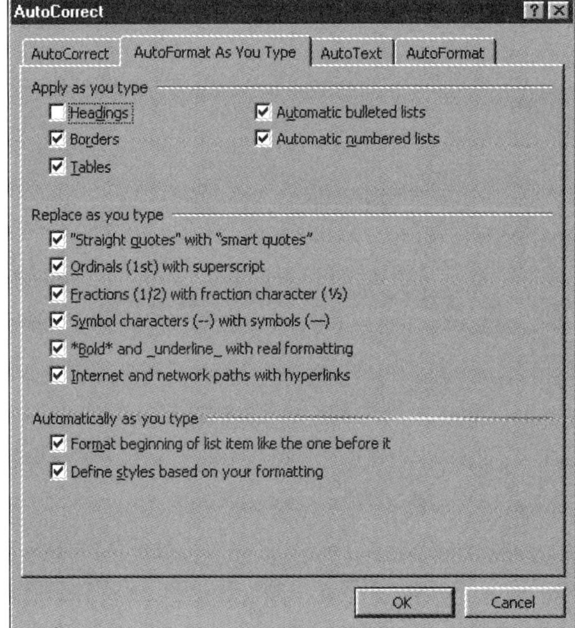

Figure 17-2: The AutoCorrect dialog box, AutoFormat thing front and present.

- The Fractions (1/2) with fraction character (½) directs Word to change what you would type as 1/2 with the nifty ½ symbol. Again, you lose a degree of dorkiness in your text.
- The Symbol characters (--) with symbols (—) option is a little less obvious to figure out. Such a symbol would be ™ (TM), for example. There must be a list of them somewhere, but I've yet to find it.
- *Bold* and _underline_ come in handier when you use Word to compose e-mail messages (though I've yet to figure this one out fully).
- Internet and network paths with hyperlinks and everything after it: Don't bother. Check it on. Maybe someday it will help.

Automatic numbered lists

The best way to understand this adventure is to *live* it. Heed the following steps:

1. **Start a new document in Word.**

   The simplest way to do that is to press the Ctrl+N key combination. No messing around here.

2. **Type the following:**

```
Things to do today:
```

Press the Enter key to start a new line. Then type:

```
1. Bury the body in the cellar.
```

Now — prepare yourself — press the Enter key to end that line. You see the following:

```
2.
```

Not only does Word automatically give you a 2, but it reformats the previous line as indented text. Amazing. Stupendous. Definitely worth $25 of the purchase price.

3. **Deal with your annoying Assistant.**

   Because this may or may not be what you want to do, your annoying Assistant appears to ask a question of you (see Figure 17-3). Click OK if you want to keep numbering your list or choose `No, change it back to how it was` if you don't want a numbered list. (For more information on the annoying Assistant, see Chapter 25.)

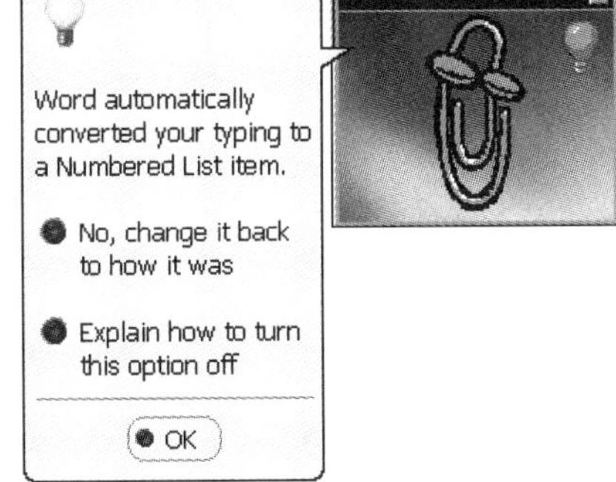

Figure 17-3: Your annoying Assistant asks what's next.

4. **Keep typing your list.**

   If you elected to continue typing your list, type away! Word adds a new number every time you press the Enter key to start a new paragraph.

5. **Press Enter and then Backspace after you're done.**

   When you're done, press the Backspace key after you press Enter the last time. Word instantly forgets that it was helping you out and returns to its original, rude mode.

This trick also works for letters (and Roman numerals, too). Just start something with a letter and a period and Word picks up at the next line with the next letter in the alphabet and another period.

Automatic headings

This is simple. To stick an automatic heading into your document, type the heading and then press the Enter key twice. No need to apply any formatting; Word instantly converts the line you typed into the Heading 1 format.

- See Chapter 15 for more information on the Heading 1 style. You can change this style to be more suitable to your document if you like.
- Personally, I think this is a silly option. For me, it's easier to format my own headings, primarily because I use A, B, and C level headings, and this trick doesn't apply to those lesser headings.

Automatic borders

In the old Smith Corona days of yore, we would fancy up our documents by woodpeckering a line of hyphens, underlines, or equal signs. It brings back kind of a sentimental tear to the eye, especially for me, because I pressed the keys so hard that ripping the paper out of the typewriter often ripped the paper in two. Not with a word processor, though.

If you want a single-line border, right margin to left across your page, type three hyphens and press the Enter key:

```
---
```

Then press the Enter key. Word instantly transmutes the three little hyphens into a solid line.

Want a double line? Then use three equal signs:

```
===
```

Press the Enter key and Word draws a double line from one edge of the screen to the next.

Again, this is really a cheap and dirty trick. If you really want to get fancy with borders, check out Chapter 24.

Part III

Working with Documents

"HOW'S THAT FOR FAST SCROLLING?"

In this part . . .

Document — it sounds too important to be something you create in a word processor. What I write is *stuff.* Documents are reserved for formal occasions, official purposes, for important people to shred in times of urgency. Yet they had to call the stuff you create in a word processor something. Using the term *document* just makes you feel better. And it may also justify all the contortions you must go through to get the stupid thing to look just so. After all, you don't toil with a penciled grocery list. But a well-formatted shopping agenda with fancy fonts and all — why that's a document!

This part of the book concentrates on document-level things, including viewing your documents in Word as well as organizing how they're stored on disk. As a bonus, I also tossed in a chapter on the sordid story of Mail Merge, which is definitely a document-thing, yet right up there next to paying taxes in mental agony and grief.

Chapter 18

More Than a File — a Document

In This Chapter

- Working on several documents simultaneously
- Seeing more than one document
- Working on two or more parts of the same document
- Using the old split-screen trick

Word lives to serve the document, kind of the way parents (unbeknownst to them) live to serve their children. When a document is up all night, you're there. When a document develops aches and pains, you're there. When your document throws up all over the printer, you're there. But documents aren't there to torture us. They're there for us to love. Oh, I'm getting carried away. . . .

Truly, a *document* is what you see on-screen in Word. It's the text you create and edit, the formatting you apply, and the end result that's printed. But a document is also a file you store on-disk for later retrieval, editing, or printing.

"Just how big can my document be?"

Word can handle any size document you want to dream up, from the 23rd Psalm on a postage stamp to a document thousands of pages long. Granted, both of those examples are rather extreme, but in practice you never really have to worry about Word coming up and telling you: "This is your last page, better tell Sally Jane whether or not she inherits the ranch and marries Sheriff Randy or just stick in a cliff-hanger and start over with a new document."

Most documents are usually 2 to 6 pages long, which you can see by looking at Word's status bar (the fraction part, the number on the left is how long your document is). Refer to Figure 1-3 for where to look. I've used Word to edit documents several hundred pages in length, but at that size Windows tends to get sluggish and moody. Smaller-sized documents are better in that respect.

If you're writing a book, try to split up the chapters into separate Word documents. For example, this chapter is its own Word document on my computer; the entire book is actually several dozen documents on disk, one document per chapter.

Working on Several Documents Simultaneously

This is handy: Word lets you work on up to a zillion documents at once. Well, actually, you can work on several documents at once, though only nine of them show up in the Window menu. Still nine is a bunch — a whole Brady Bunch, if you count Alice the indentured servant.

In Word, each document is stored in its own window on-screen. Normally that "window" uses the whole screen, so that document is all you see in Word. To see other documents, you access the Window menu (Alt, W). From there, select a number, 1 through 9, corresponding to the document you want to see.

Word politely shows you the document name, right after its number in the menu. Figure 18-1 shows what the Window menu looks like with a bunch of documents open. If more than nine documents are open, an extra menu item, More Windows, appears. Choose it to see a dialog box from which you can select your documents from a scrolling list.

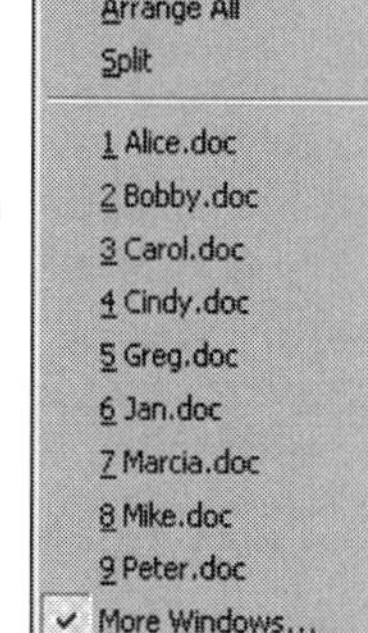

Figure 18-1: Use the Window menu to track open documents.

- To switch from one document to another, select its name from the Window menu by using the mouse or the keyboard. The names are alphabetized for your convenience.
- If you press Ctrl+Shift+F6, you are taken to the next window; Ctrl+F6 takes you to the previous window. If you only have two windows open at a time, Ctrl+F6 makes for a keen shortcut to skip-to-my-lou between them.
- The goings on in one document are independent of any other: Printing, spell checking, and formatting affect only the document you can see on-screen.

- You can copy a block from one document to the other. Just mark the block in the first document, copy it (Ctrl+C), open the second document, and paste it in (Ctrl+V). (Don't forget that you can use the Copy and Paste buttons.) Refer to Chapter 6 for detailed block action.

Seeing more than one document

You can arrange all your documents on-screen by choosing Window⇨Arrange All. This command puts each document into its own mini-window — officially known as the Multi-Document Interface by Windows Well-Wishers.

- Although you can see more than one document at a time, you can work on only one at a time: the document with the highlighted title bar. You can work on other documents by clicking them with the mouse or by pressing Ctrl+F6.
- After the windows have been arranged, you can manipulate their size with the mouse and change their position.
-  Clicking a mini-window's Maximize button restores Word to its normal, full-screen view.
- The Window⇨Arrange All command works great for two or three documents — when you're comparing text, for example. Arranging more documents than three makes the viewing area so small that it's of little use.

Working on two, or more, parts of the same document

You can look at two or more different parts of the same document — yes, the *same* document — by choosing the Window⇨New Window command. This creates another window on-screen in which you find another copy of your document. Unlike having different documents open in separate windows, each copy of this document is connected to the other; changes that you make in one of the copies are immediately included in the other.

- This feature is useful for cutting and pasting text or graphics between sections of the same document, especially when you have a very long document.
- The title bar tells you which copy of your document you're looking at by displaying a colon and a number after the filename. For example, this document is `CHAPTER 18:1` in one window and `CHAPTER 18:2` in the second window.
- You can move back and forth between these windows by using Ctrl+F6.

- You cannot use the File➪Close command to close one window. Instead, click the window's Close button (the Microsoft Word icon in the upper-right corner) or press the Ctrl+W key combination. (The File➪Close command closes the document and, therefore, *both* windows.)
- Another way to view two parts of the same document is by using the old split-screen trick. This feature is discussed . . . why, it's right here.

Using the old split-screen trick

Splitting the screen allows you to view two parts of your document in one window. No need to bother with extra windows here. In fact, I prefer to use Word with as little junk on-screen as possible. So when I need to view two parts of the same document, I just split the screen — Moses-like — and then undo the rift when I'm done. You can accomplish the same splitting-screen feat by following these steps:

1. **Place the mouse cursor on the little gray thing located just above the up-arrow button on the vertical scroll bar (on the upper-right side of your document).**

   Oh, brother. Just refer to Figure 18-2 to see what I'm talking about.

Figure 18-2: The little gray thing you use to split a window.

   When you find the sweet spot, the mouse pointer changes shape and looks like a pair of horizontal lines with arrows pointing down and up.

2. **Hold down the left mouse button and drag the pointer down.**

   As you drag, a line drags with you and slices the document window in half. That marks the spot where the screen splits.

3. **Release the mouse button.**

   Your screen looks something like Figure 18-3.

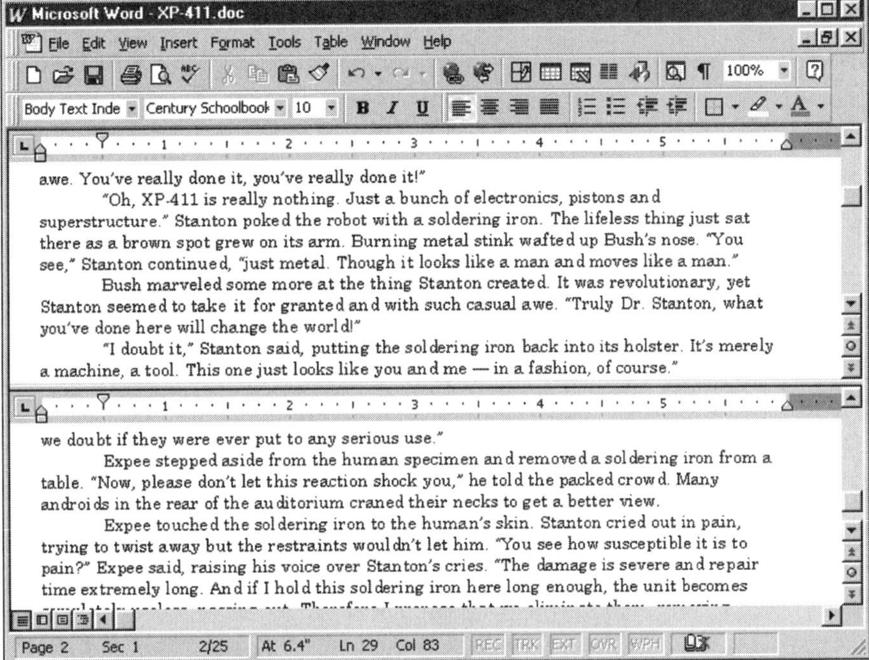

Figure 18-3: Splitting the screen.

- Each section of the screen can be manipulated separately and scrolled up or down. But the windows still represent the same document; changes that you make in one of the copies are immediately included in the others.
- This feature is useful for cutting and pasting text or graphics between parts of the same document.
- To undo a split screen, put the cursor on the little gray area and drag it back up to the ruler.
- You can also choose Window➪Split to split your screen and Window➪Remove Split to undo it.

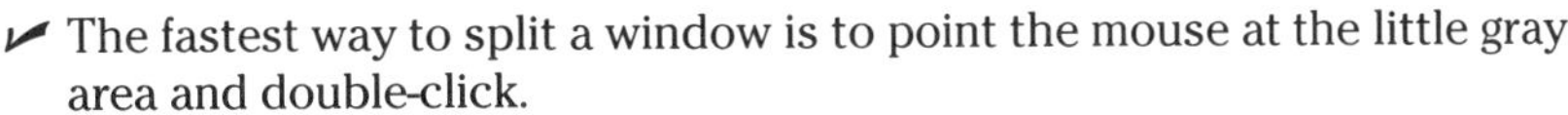

- The fastest way to split a window is to point the mouse at the little gray area and double-click.

Chapter 19

Importing and Exporting Documents

In This Chapter

- Loading a text file
- Saving a text file
- Loading documents created by alien word processors
- Saving documents in alien formats
- Saving documents in older Word formats

Word isn't the only word processor in the world (though Microsoft is trying *very* hard . . .). Other folks use other word processors, and occasionally you may tangle with the files that they create. When you do, you need to *import* their weird word-processing files into Word so that you can do something with them. Likewise, you can *export* your Word documents into weird word-processing formats. And you don't need those big dinosaur cranes to do it.

Another thing worthy of import or export to or from Word are ASCII files. These are boring, plain text format files. Because they lack formatting, they come in handy for exchanging files between programs and different computers. Oh, and Windows itself requires plain text files when it's feeling discrete. Droll stuff, but required reading.

Loading a Text File

A text file is a special, non-document file that lacks any formatting or anything creative, like an old Eastern Bloc housing project. You can load this type of document into Word for editing if you like. Follow these steps:

1. **Do the Open command.**

   Choose File⇨Open or press Ctrl+O, the Open shortcut. The Open Document dialog box appears.

2. **In the Files of type drop-box, select Text Files.**

   Click the mouse on the down-arrow by the Files of type drop-down box. From the list that drops down, click the mouse once on the Text Files item. This step tells Word to display only text files in the Open dialog box.

3. **Hunt down the text file you want to load.**

   Use the controls in the dialog box to hunt down the file that you want on your hard drive. Chapter 20 contains more information on how you can use the Open dialog box to see files in another folder or on another hard drive.

4. **Click the text file's icon once with the mouse.**

5. **Click Open.**

   The text file appears on-screen, ready for editing just like any Word document — although the formatting is really cruddy because the file was boring, plain text to begin with.

- Additional information on opening Word document files lurks in Chapter 8.
- Text files are also called *ASCII* files. ASCII is a technospeak acronym that loosely translates to English as "a text file." You pronounce it *ask-EE*.
- Other terms for text files include DOS text file, plain text file, and unformatted file.

- Not every text file is a "TXT" file as Word insists. Some have specific names. Generally speaking, when you're told to open such a file, you are given the file's full name, something like `CONFIG.INI` or something. In those cases, just type the file's name into the Open dialog box's File name text box. Or just find your computer guru and tell them to edit the file for you. Use a can of Jolt Cola as a bribe.

Saving a Text File

Because some applications need to have files in a text format, you need to train Word in how to save them that way. Otherwise, Word assumes that you're saving a Word document to disk and junks up the text file with lots of curious Word stuff. Because this procedure is about saving a text file, also known as saving a file in ASCII format, you've got to be more careful.

To save a text file to disk, follow the same instructions as for saving any document to disk, as outlined in Chapter 8. However, in the Save as type box, you should choose the Text Only format. Other than that, everything pretty much works the same.

But aha! You might be told that it is merely a plain text file and that none of the formatting you applied will be saved to disk. (Remember, plain text files do not contain formatting, so it was probably silly of you to add it in the first place.) When this happens, you most likely see a dialog box displayed, such as the one shown in Figure 19-1. Click Yes to save the file as a text file.

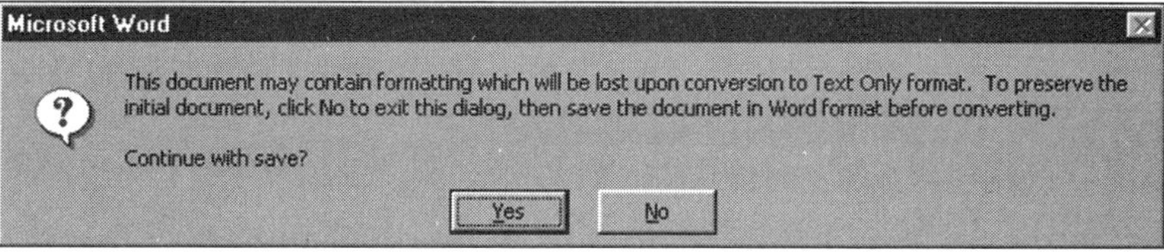

Figure 19-1: Uh-oh! Do you really want to save a text file?

- Word really doesn't want you to save documents as text files. It assumes that's not what you want to do, because text files are unformatted and ugly and, honestly, Word is just plain bossy.
- If your annoying little Assistant is visible, it displays the warning message shown in Figure 19-1. See Chapter 25 for more information on the annoying Assistant.

- Click Yes to save the file as a text file.
- If you click No, Word allows you to save the file as a Word document, which might not be what you really want.

- If the file must be saved with a name that doesn't end in TXT, remember to re-type the name into the File name box inside the Save As dialog box. Just click the mouse in that box and retype the name as the file should be saved. Be very careful with this step, because programs that insist on specific filenames are usually very important and fussy at the same time.
- Text Only and MS-DOS Text are the same format, mostly likely what you need. The "with line breaks" formats are only needed if you're told to save something to disk in a plain text format with "line breaks."
- You can save a document as a text file *and* a Word document file. First, save the file to disk as a Word document by selecting Word Document from the Save as type box. Then save the file to disk as a text file by selecting Text Only from that list. You'll have a text file, which is what you want, and a Word file, which contains secret codes and prints out really purty.
- Fortunately, the days of having to save things in a text-only format are waning fast.

Understanding the ASCII thing

Word saves documents to disk in its own special file format. That format includes your text — the basic characters that you type — plus information about formatting, bold, underline, graphics, and anything else you toss into the document. These elements are all saved to disk so that the next time you use Word, you get back your formatting for editing, printing, or whatever.

Every word processor has its own different document file format. So your Word documents are considered *alien* to other word processors, which use their own non-Word format. It's been this way since the dawn of the PC, so to keep the confusion low, a common text format was developed. It's called the *plain text* or *ASCII* format.

ASCII is an acronym for something I need not mention because there will be no test on this material, and you'd probably forget what the acronym stands for two minutes from now. What's more important than knowing what it represents is knowing how to pronounce it: *ASK-EE.* It's not *ask-two.* It's *ASK-EE.*

An ASCII file contains only text — no formatting codes, no bold, underline, graphics, or anything. Just text. It's also called the *plain text* format or sometimes the *MS-DOS* or *DOS text* format. Whatever you call it, an ASCII file contains only text.

Because ASCII files aren't littered with word processing codes, any word processor can read the text. In a way, ASCII files are the Esperanto of document files. Any word processor can read an ASCII file and display its contents. The text looks ugly, but it's better than nothing.

Loading Documents Created by Alien Word Processors

Suppose that crazy Earl gives you a disk full of his favorite limericks. Of course, Earl is crazy, so crazy that he actually uses WordPerfect. Without thinking about it, Earl has handed you a disk full of WordPerfect documents, and it's making you silly.

Don't panic; Word can safely read Earl's limerick files, although he saved them in that wacko WordPerfect file format. To retrieve the files, just follow the steps outlined in "Loading a Text File," earlier in this chapter. However, in Step 2 select WordPerfect 5.x (or 6.x) from the Files of type drop-down box. That tells Word to only display those types of files in the Open dialog box, which makes it easier for you to pluck out Earl's wacky limericks.

When they're opened, Word recognizes the WordPerfect documents and automatically converts them into Word format. The same holds true for any other word processing document; just select its type from the list, and you'll be fine.

- Not only can Word read WordPerfect documents, it also recognizes several other popular document formats instantly.
- If you're unsure as to what format a document is in, choose All Files from the Files of type drop-down box. That displays every file on disk. Word lets you know whether or not it can be opened after you click the Open button. (No damage can be done.)
- Nothing's perfect. The alien document you open in Word may require some fixing up, adjusting fonts, and whatnot. This kind of task is at most a minor bother; at least you don't have to retype anything.
- Occasionally, Word finds something so utterly bizarre that the program won't recognize it. When this situation occurs, you can try to open the document, but it's probably better to ask the person who created the document to save it in ASCII format.

- Another common document format is the *Rich Text Format (RTF)*. This format is better than ASCII because it keeps track of underline, bold, and other formatting. If you'll be sharing files often with other weirdo word processors, try to get everyone to settle on a common format, like Rich Text Format. Better still, get everyone to settle on Word.
- Word won't recognize anything written in a newer version than itself. Sorta like how professors don't like to call on that smarty-pants who always thinks that he has all the answers.

Saving Documents in Alien Formats

Now comes the time for you to give Earl your collection of leper jokes. Alas, those are all saved to disk in Word format. You could be lax like Earl and just hand him a diskette full of Word documents. But then he'd call you up and complain or ramble on and on about some new word-processor conversion program he found. Because you don't have the time for that, just do him a favor and save the file in his own word processor's format.

To save any document in an alien word processor format, use the File⇨Save As command and select that format from the Save as type drop-down list at the bottom of the Save As dialog box. If the alien word processor format isn't listed, select Text Only or Rich Text Format, or see the sidebar "But I don't have any alien formats!" for more information.

If you've opened an alien word-processing file to disk, Word saves it back to disk in that alien format. If you want to save the document as a Word document, you must choose the File⇨Save As command and, at the bottom of the Save As dialog box, select Word Document from the Save as type drop-down list. Otherwise Word just saves the document to disk in its original, alien format.

But I don't have any alien formats!

Rather than wait in the Nevada desert for the aliens to arrive, you can add more alien word processor formats into Word's repertoire at any time. All you need is the original CD or stack-o-diskettes that came with Word or Microsoft Office. Contained therein you can find a whole gaggle of conversion formats, but you need to install them which, of course, requires some time and lots of agony.

Best advice: Have the same person who installed Word on your PC install the new formats.

Second best advice: If you installed Word, you can do it yourself. Recognizing that I'm going to be brief (because this is, after all, a "Technical Stuff" sidebar): Quit Word if you're using it right now. Open Windows Control Panel and then click the Add/Remove Programs icon. Select Word or Microsoft Office from the scrolling list in the Install/Uninstall panel, and then click the Add/Remove button. Insert your CD or disks when prompted.

The Setup program eventually displays a dialog box with an Add/Remove button. Click it. Click the item that reads Converters and Filters, and then click the Change Option button. Click Text Converters, and then click the Change Option button in the next dialog box. Finally, you see a scrolling list of Word processor types. Click the word processor type you want to convert from, putting a check mark in its box. After you're done, keep clicking the OK button to close various dialog boxes until the Setup program installs your converters. After you're all the way done, Windows may ask to reset your computer. Do so.

You'll notice that the selection of word processing formats is rather limited. If the type you need isn't there, use the Rich Text Format option for exchanging files with alien word processors. If the other person's word processor doesn't accept the Rich Text Format, you have to settle for Text Only. Ugh.

Saving Documents for Older Versions of Word

If you're working with someone who uses an older version of Word, such as Word 95 or Microsoft Word 6.0 or earlier, you need to save your documents in a special format to exchange them. Just select the proper Word format from the Save as type list at the bottom of the Save As dialog box. This rule does not apply for opening the files, but if you want some poor loser who is still using Word 6.0 to read your stuff, you have to be nice and save in that particular format.

Chapter 20

Managing Files

In This Chapter

- Naming files
- Finding a place for your work
- Creating a new folder
- Using another folder
- Working with favorite folders and files
- Finding files in Word
- Finding text in files
- Looking at documents on-disk
- Working with groups of files
- Opening files
- Printing files
- Saving or closing several documents simultaneously

The more you work in Word, the more documents you create. And because you always save those documents to disk, the more files you make, which is how a hard drive gets full of stuff: You create it. In a way, your hard drive is like your closet; it's full of stuff. Unless you have a handy closet organizer — like the one I bought on TV for three low, low payments of $29.95 — things are going to get messy. This chapter tackles the subject of files — using and organizing them.

Naming Your Documents

When you save your precious work to disk, which is always a good idea, you need to give your document a specific type of filename. This requirement has nothing to do with Word; point your fingers of blame at Windows.

- A filename can be any length, from one single character to up to 255 characters long. Of course, it would be ridiculous to name a document with that many characters.
- Shorter, more descriptive filenames are always best.
- You can use any combination of letters or numbers to name your file. Extra points are awarded for being clever. Upper- and lowercase letters look different on the screen but are the same according to Windows.
- A filename can start with a number. In fact, the name of this file, the document that contains this chapter, is 20 (two zero). This name is a perfectly legit filename — and descriptive because it tells me what this file contains. (A better name would be CHAPTER 20, but I personally find the CHAPTER part redundant.)
- Filenames can contain spaces, periods, and all manner of punctuation and symbols, save for the following assortment:

```
\ : * ? " < > | /
```

- If you're from the old school, forget everything you ever knew about filename extensions. That's all handled internally by Windows now. Ignore extensions. Don't put .DOC at the end of your files! Just, no, never mind.
- Examples of good and bad filenames are provided in Chapter 1, in the section "Save Your Stuff!"

Optional other ways you can mess with files

Windows, being so bold and mighty, offers you several chances to mess with the files you create. I won't bother to list them all here, but two popular activities — renaming and deleting files — can be done through the convenience of an Open or Save As dialog box Word tosses up on the screen.

To rename a file or document you see lurking in any Open or Save As dialog box, click the file's name once with your mouse. Press the F2 key. Windows selects the filename for editing or changing to suit your whim.

One word of warning: If the file you see ends with a dot and a three-letter filename extension, do not change it. That part of the filename is important to Windows, and it will even warn you if you try to change it. If you don't see the dot and three-letter extension, you can rename any file fearlessly.

And if you want to delete any file, blowing it to smithereens, just click it once in any Open or Save As dialog box and press your keyboard's Delete key. Windows may ask if you really, *really* want to delete the file. Click Yes, and it's gone. (Need I mention that you should be careful when deleting any file?)

Making a Place for Your Work

A hard drive can be a rugged and unforgiving place — like the parking lot at Nordstroms during a shoe sale. Trouble looms like the last pair of off-white pumps at under $10. Unless there is some semblance of organization, chaos rules.

To work your hard drive effectively, you need organization; organization's a big deal. There are special places on your hard drive called *folders*. These things are like holding bins for files. All files of a certain type can be stored in — and retrieved from — their own folder.

Normally, Word saves all your documents in a folder called (shockingly) My Documents. Everything you save goes there; Word looks there when you use the Open command.

You can create other folders as necessary. For example, if you want to write a book, you can create a folder for all the chapters and other documents related to that book. That's part of Hard Disk Organization, which is an optional thing but it helps keep your hard drive orderly.

If you don't create extra folders, eventually the My Documents folder will be burdened with thousands of documents. It will take you hours to find things. Some folks look for missing documents for days. It just makes sense to create new folders for your stuff; the next section covers the procedure.

In prehistoric times, *folders* were known as *directories,* or sometimes the nautical *subdirectory* term was used. There is no difference, other than the fact that the guy saying *directory* is a DOS geek.

Creating a New Folder

To keep organized, you may need to create new folders for your new projects. For example, suppose that you just started your plan to take over the entertainment industry. Heck, you're going to need a new folder to put in all those memos and extortion letters. Here's how you'd do that:

1. **Summon the Save As dialog box.**

   Obviously, having something to save first helps, such as that first letter to Steven Spielberg. The Save As dialog box is where you get to create a new folder. Choose File⇨Save As; the normal Save command just doesn't cut it here.

2. **Click the Create New Folder button.**

This happy guy lives in the top row of the Save As dialog box. Click him once to see the New Folder dialog box. (The New Folder dialog box is horrifically boring so I won't show it here.)

3. **Type a name for your new folder.**

Be descriptive. Be creative. Short and sweet. To the point. (Try real hard to achieve this goal if you're a lawyer.)

Word automatically suggests the name New Folder for your new folder. What a joke! Anyone who has a folder named New Folder on their hard drive should be taken out and forced to use DOS on an 8088 for the rest of their corporeal existence.

Have the folder name reflect its contents.

4. **Click OK.**

Through the magic of the computer, your new folder is created, sitting right there on the screen for you to marvel at.

5. **Marvel at it.**

6. **Double-click the folder to open it.**

After all, this is a file-saving exercise here. You open your folder by double-clicking it. The Save As dialog box then displays the contents (nothing).

7. **Continue saving your document.**

You don't really have to save a document every time you create a folder. You can click the Cancel button in the Save As dialog box to return to your work. The next time you do go to save (or open for that matter), you will be using the new folder you just created.

- New folders can only be created in the Save As dialog box. I mean, like *duh*. If you created a new folder in the Open dialog box, there wouldn't be anything in the folder for you to open. Some people . . . .
- You can also create new folders using Windows Explorer or the My Computer thing. Refer to your favorite book on Windows for more information on that process.
- Folders are named just like files. Same rules. See the first section of this chapter for the nitty-gritties.
- You'll get a lot of mileage out of naming a folder Junk or Misc.

Using Another Folder

If you're going to go mad with various folders on your hard drive, you'll need to access them whenever you want to see the documents they hold. For example, all those files stacking up in your Extortion folder will seem lost — unless you can somehow tell Word to look in there for those files when you use the Open command. Here's how:

1. **Summon the Open command.**

   Choose File⇨Open, press Ctrl+O, or tickle the Open button on the toolbar. However you manage it, you soon see the Open dialog box swing into full view, as shown in Figure 20-1.

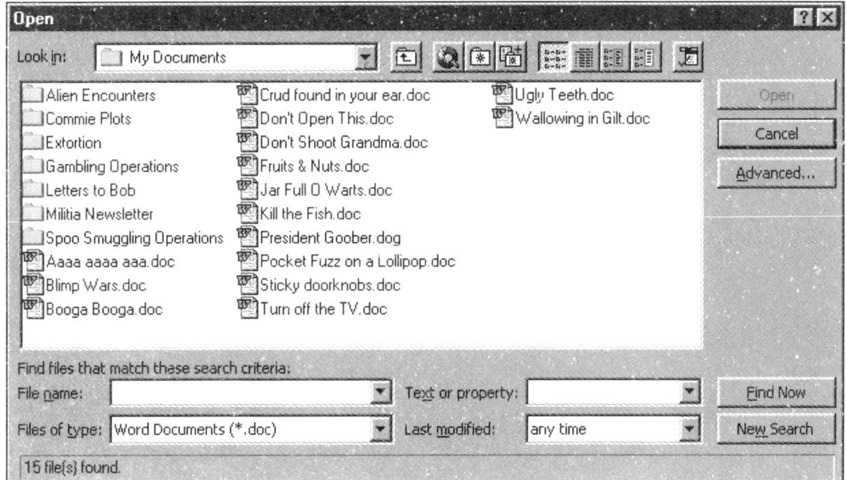

Figure 20-1: The Open dialog box.

2. **First, see which folder you're using.**

   The folder's name appears in the Look in drop-down box at the top of the dialog box. In Figure 20-1, the My Documents folder appears in the box, which is where Word normally wants to save stuff.

   If you're already in the folder that you want to be in, skip to Step 6 (which means that you're more-or-less done).

3. **Select the disk drive that you want from the Look in drop-down list.**

   Click the down-arrow button or press Alt+I. Select a drive from the list. If you select a floppy drive, ensure that you have a disk in the drive *before* you select it.

   If you only have one hard drive, C, select it as well. Looking for your folder from the top down is best.

4. **Select your folder from those listed in the dialog box.**

   You may have to scroll through the list to find the folder that you want. When you find the folder you want, such as the My Document folder (which should be on drive C), double-click it with the mouse to open it.

5. **Keep repeating Step 4 until you find the folder you're looking for.**

   For example, you may have to open My Documents, then Projects, then Memos to finally see the documents stored in the Memos folder.

6. **Open your document.**

   Refer to Chapter 8 for more information on opening a document.

- You can follow these same steps if you want to save a file in a specific folder on a specific hard drive. The only difference is that you'd be using the Save As dialog box instead of the Open dialog box. Otherwise, it all works the same.
- Some folders contain other folders. To see their contents, double-click the folder's name in the Open dialog box.
- The files in each folder appear in the big window in the middle of both the Open dialog box and the Save As dialog box.
- Each disk in your system has its own set of folders. If you can't find the folder that you want on one disk, try another. For example, scope out drive D if drive C turns out to be a dud.

- If you want more detailed information about working with folders and the Save As or Open dialog boxes, refer to *PCs For Dummies,* 4th Edition, Chapter 8.

Making a folder one of your favorites

This folder nonsense is useful but bothersome. Personally, I hate trudging around my hard drive looking for stuff in distant folders. Sure, I'm organized. But I hate messing with the darn Open dialog box, wading through folders. Mr. PC Guru, can you help me?

Why, yes, gentle reader. If you have one or more folders that are dear to your heart, you can add them to a List-O-Favorites for quick and easy access. First, find the folder as you normally would (see the preceding section) and then click the Add to Favorites button in the Open dialog box. You see a menu, such as the one shown in Figure 20-2.

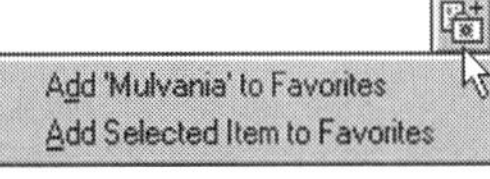

Figure 20-2: Adding a folder to your List-O-Favorites.

If you want to add the current folder to the list, choose the first menu item. If you want to add a file, select it first and then choose the second menu item. The next section tells you how you can easily access those folders (or files).

Using a favorite folder

After collecting a few favorite folders or files (see the preceding section), you can access them quicker than a sleeping cat jumping off a ringing phone. In either the Save As or Open dialog boxes, click the Look in Favorites button. Word then displays a list of the folders and files you placed in your favorites stockpile, from which you can easily pluck what you want.

Finding Files in Word

It's really hard to lose a file so thoroughly that Word can't find it, even if you have an absolutely horrid memory. I often find it difficult to remember which documents contain the information that I want and also where the heck I put that file anyway. Of course, I often find all sorts of things next to the milk in the refrigerator. Cereal fairies is what I think. In any case, it's possible to tweak the Open dialog box so that you can easily find any old file, no matter where you stuffed it. To do so, follow these steps:

1. **Summon the Open dialog box.**

   Press Ctrl+O.

2. **Select a disk drive from the Look in drop-down list.**

   Pluck out any old drive. For most of us, that's just drive C. However, on an older computer I was fond of putting all my word-processing stuff on drive D.

3. **Make sure that you have selected Word Documents (*.doc) from the Files of type drop-down list.**

   If you don't double-check this, Word may find *every* file on your hard drive (which is dumb) or no files at all (which is sad).

4. **Click the Commands and Settings button.**

   This little guy is located at the top of the Open dialog box. Clicking him once with the mouse displays a heretofore hidden menu (not that the icon on the button offered any hints or anything).

5. **Choose Search Subfolders.**

   Click that menu item once with the mouse.

   Word churns and hums.

Eventually, you see a cascading list of folders and Word documents — every document that lives on your disk drive. Figure 20-3 shows what the list may look like.

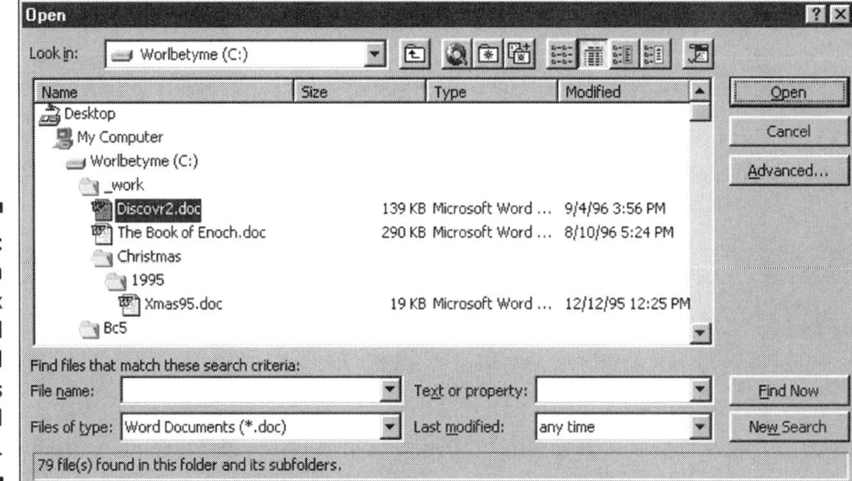

Figure 20-3: The Open dialog box displays all the Word documents on your hard drive.

6. Find your document.

Use the scroll bar to scan through the list or obey some of the hints offered in the following bullets:

- Displaying files this way makes the Open dialog box work a bit like Windows Explorer. You can even open and close folders and disk drives by double-clicking them. This capability makes the list a bit more manageable.

- To look for a file when you know it contains some specific bit of text, type that text into the Text or property box and then click the Find Now button. Word takes a while to locate the specific document(s), but this delay can be a godsend if you forget what a document is called but remember some bit of text inside.
- If Word finds no matching files, the list will be empty. The dreadful text `0 file(s) found in this folder and subfolders` appears. Weep bitterly and curse the computer. Or maybe try again with another word that you're *certain* is in your file.
- After you find the file that you want, highlight it and click the Open button to open it into Word.
- Don't forget that you can search other drives for your files as well. Just select another disk drive in Step 2.

- The Open dialog box stays in the find all files mode until you turn it off. Click the Commands and Settings button again and choose Search Subfolders. This returns the Open dialog box's operation back to normal (more-or-less).
- Likewise, the Open dialog box continues to show files that contain only text listed in the Text or property box. Click once in that box and press the Delete key, and then click the Find Now button to return the Open dialog box to normal operation.

Looking at Documents on Disk

Wouldn't it be nice if you could look into a document before you loaded it, like getting a sneak preview? This task is entirely possible using the Preview button in the Open dialog box.

Follow the steps for peering into a file's contents before opening it:

1. **Choose File⇨Open.**

   Or use your favorite alternative to get at the Open dialog box.

2. **Click the Preview button.**

   Pictured at left, click once with your mouse.

3. **A special preview window opens in the Open dialog box.**

   Figure 20-4 shows you what it sort of looks like. Now you can see the contents of any file you click in the left side of the dialog box. Use the scroll bar to peruse before you open.

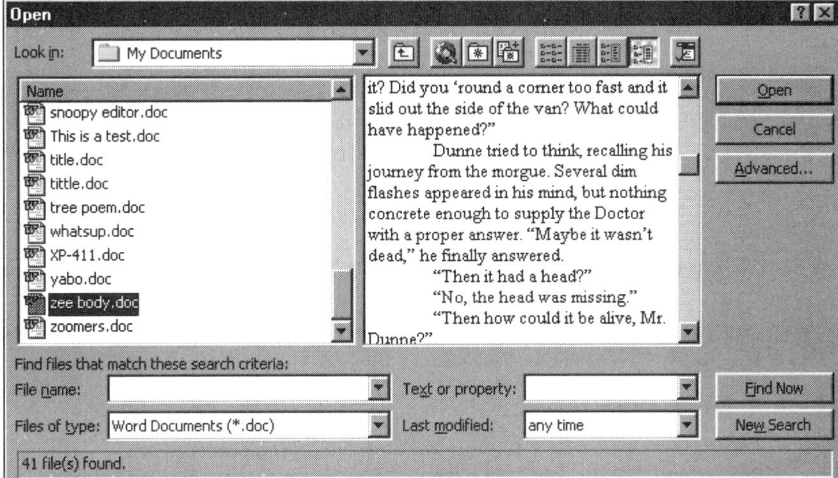

Figure 20-4: The Open dialog box with its preview window hanging out.

4. **Open the file.**

   Click the Open button when you like what you see.

The Open dialog box stays in preview mode until you switch it back to regular mode. Click the mouse on the List button to return to the way things were before.

Working with Groups of Files

The Open dialog box enables you to work with files individually or in groups. To work with a group of files, you must select them with the mouse, which follows the typical Windows metaphor for selecting several items in a group:

1. **Press the Ctrl key and click each document that you want.**

   The item becomes highlighted and selected.

2. **Repeat Step 1 for each additional item that you want in your group.**

   Et cetera and so on.

- When you have the preview window active, it displays only the contents of the last file in the group. See the previous section, "Looking at Documents on Disk," for information on the preview mode.
- You can only select a group of files in one folder. However, if you follow the instructions in "Finding Files in Word," earlier in this chapter, you can select files from all over your hard drive.

Opening files

Here's how you would open more than one file at a time using the Open dialog box:

1. **Select the file or group of files that you want to open from those shown in the Open dialog box's window.**

   Refer to "Finding Files in Word" and "Working with Groups of Files" for the details.

2. **Click the Open button.**

   The files open, and Word places each into its own document window.

3. **Work away!**

- There is a limit on the number of files Word can work with at once. No, I don't know what the maximum number is — but you will! You'll see some odd error message about not enough memory or "heap" space or something bizarre. Don't panic. Close a few windows — maybe even quit Word — and start over.
- Refer to the section "Saving a gang of documents simultaneously" later in this chapter for information on saving all your files at once.
- Wow — doing it all at once. I'm sure that such a concept was promised in a computer brochure somewhere.

Printing files

You can print one or several documents without opening them in the Open dialog box. To do so, obey the following steps:

1. **Select the file or group of files that you want to print from the Open dialog box.**

   Instructions in "Finding Files in Word" and "Working with Groups of Files" tell you how to locate the files and highlight them.

2. **Click the Commands and Settings button.**

   A drop-down menu appears.

3. **Choose the Print command.**

   The Print dialog box appears.

4. **Click OK to print your document(s).**

- Make sure that your printer is on and ready to print before you click the OK button in the Print dialog box.
- Chapter 9 offers more information on printing. Chapter 9's information on the Print dialog box applies here as well.

Saving a gang of documents simultaneously

To save a multitude of documents all at once, you could switch to each window and incant the File⇨Save command. Or you could be sneaky and do the following:

1. **Press and hold the Shift key — either one.**
2. **Choose the File menu.**
3. **Choose the Save All item.**

Normally, you would choose the Save item. But because you pressed the Shift key before choosing the File menu, it magically became the Save All menu item.

There is no prompting, and no wait and see. Everything is just saved to disk as fast as your PC can handle it.

- If a file has not yet been saved, you are prompted to give it a name. Refer to "Saving a Document to Disk (the First Time)," in Chapter 8 for more information.
- There is no keyboard shortcut for the Save All command.

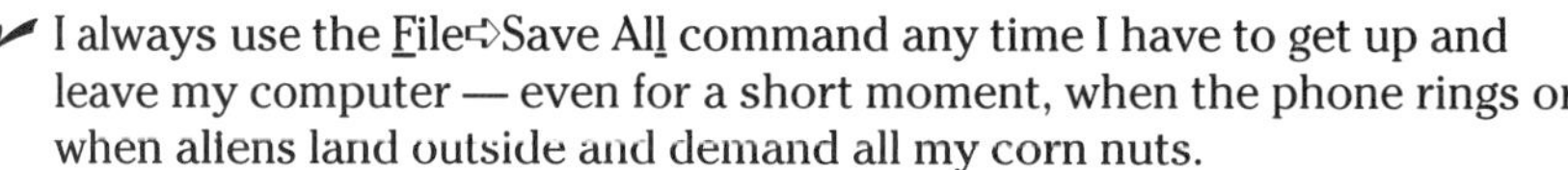

- I always use the File⇨Save All command any time I have to get up and leave my computer — even for a short moment, when the phone rings or when aliens land outside and demand all my corn nuts.

Closing a gang of documents simultaneously

You can conjure up a Close All command just like the Save All command. The difference is that you choose the Close All item from the menu; just press the Shift key (either one) before you click the File menu with your mouse. Then choose the Close All item and — Thwoop! — all your open documents are closed.

- Refer to the previous section for more information (if you need it) on how to use the Shift key before choosing the File menu.
- Word still asks whether you want to save any unsaved documents before it closes them. See Chapter 8, "Saving a Document to Disk (The First Time)."

Chapter 21

Mail Merge (Or Form Letters to Fool Everyone)

In This Chapter

- Understanding mail merge
- Using the Mail Merge command
- Preparing the main document
- Preparing the data file
- Adding data to the data file
- Inserting the fields
- Merge mania!

Mail merge is an old word-processing concept, supposedly developed by Mel Murch, an early PC telemarketer. Mel had to send out dozens of letters every day to potential customers. But no one read the letters because Mel's stilted writing style combined with his ugly printer output gave everything away. Mel knew that if he could only customize each letter, making it look like he took pains to type everything personally, he'd get a few replies — maybe even a sympathetic English teacher would show him the difference between it's and its.

Mail merge hasn't changed much since the early days of the PC; it's just as ugly and painful to do as it was back in Mel's day. In fact, even though the author of this book considers himself a Word expert, he constantly refers to this chapter whenever he needs to do a mail merge. Yes, it's that obscure. But mail merge is incredibly handy and not that painful providing you follow the helpful hints outlined in this chapter.

Understanding Mail Merge

There are three ways to handle Word's (or anybody's) mail merge:

- Read this chapter and then go out and have a drink.
- Skip this chapter and go straight to the booze.
- Hire a professional to do mail merge for you while you're drying out at the Betty Ford Center.

I'll outline the first part of the first approach here. The second approach you can attempt on your own. The third approach shouldn't be necessary since most high-powered people usually hire people to write for them, as well as people to go to detox for them.

Mail merge is the process of taking a single form letter, stirring in a list of names and other information, and combining (merging) everything into a final set of documents, each of which is customized and almost personal.

The file that contains the names and other information should be called the list file. Alas, Microsoft has called it the *data source,* which is what every good boy and girl should call it from now on. Say, "data source."

The file that contains the form letter should be called the form letter. Microsoft refers to it as the *main document.* No, I didn't make this up. Get used to it. Say, "main document."

You start by typing the main document, creating it as you would any other document, complete with formatting and other mumbo-jumbo. But leave blank those spots where you would put the address, "Dear Mr. Zipplebip," or anything else that changes from letter to letter. Eventually, you can stick some special fill-in-the-blanks codes into the main document.

Oh, and the fill-in-the-blank codes should be called fill-in-the-blank codes, but Microsoft wants you to know them as *fields* (another term that I didn't make up). Everyone say, "fields." Kind of like "Mrs. Fields' Cookies." Everyone say, "cookies."

The data source is a file (kind of) that contains the names, addresses, and other information to fill in the blanks in the main document. Unlike the main document, however, the data source document is created by using a special format. It's almost like filling in names in a database program. (In fact, that's exactly what it is.)

The names, addresses, and other information in the data file composes what's called a *record.* Everyone say, "record."

Word creates a custom letter by using each of the fields in a record to fill in the blanks in a main document and create a unique document. Everyone say, "Golly, that's awfully complex and pointless for me to memorize. Why don't I just go ahead and work through the remaining sections of this chapter until I get everything right. Then I can forget all this until next time."

Please don't feel that my emphasis on intoxication in this section's first three steps is to be taken lightly. In fact, I take all my drinking seriously.

Using the Mail Merge Command

Start your mail merging mania by choosing Tools⇨Mail Merge. This command opens the Mail Merge Helper dialog box, depicted in Figure 21-1. Don't let the title fool you.

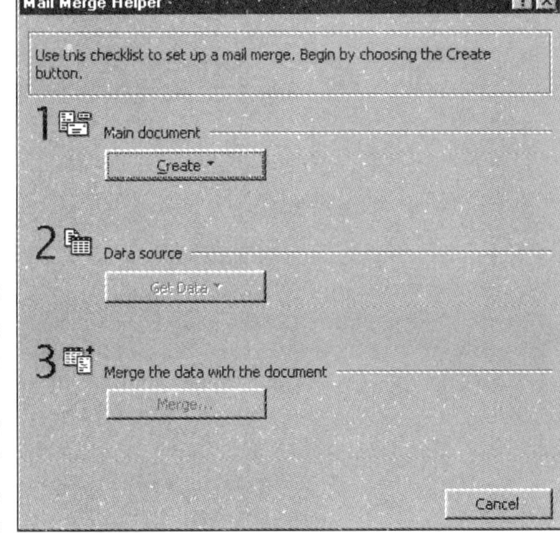

Figure 21-1: The misnamed Mail Merge Helper dialog box.

You mail merge in three steps, as shown in the Mail Merge Helper dialog box. First comes the Main document, and then the Data source, and finally the actual merging.

- Don't let the Spartan nature of the Mail Merge Helper dialog box mislead you. Other buttons and gadgets appear as you get into it. I mean, the dialog box may look like Jeff Goldblum now, but in a few minutes, you'll have the horrid Brundlefly to deal with. Truly, it's frightening.
- Yeah, there are really more than three steps to this whole operation — lots more.
- Please continue reading with the next section.

Preparing the main document (the fill-in-the-blanks part)

The main document is the fill-in-the-blanks document. Don't freak out if you've already created that document (self-starter, eh?). Just follow along, and I'll show you when to do what:

1. **Click the Create button in the Mail Merge Helper dialog box.**

   A drop-down list drops down.

2. **Select Form Letters from the list.**

   Another, annoying dialog box appears. Ignore it and . . .

3. **Choose how to create your main document.**

   If your main document is all ready to go in Word (right up there on the screen), click the Active Window button.

   If you need to create a new fill-in-the-blanks document, click the New Main Document button.

4. **Click the new Edit button, which just appeared out of thin air next to the Create button.**

   See? I told you the dialog box gets crowded. It gets worse.

5. **Choose the only item in the new Edit button's menu.**

   The item is `Form Letter`, followed by `Document# item` or the name of the document you're already working on in Word.

6. **Edit your document.**

   You're now allowed to edit your form letter document. The Mail Merge Help dialog box disappears, and the Mail Merge toolbar shows its ugly face, as shown in Figure 21-2.

- The main document contains all the fill-in-the-blanks stuff. Don't bother putting them in just now; you do this task in a later step. However, keep in mind what you want to go where.
- In my main documents, I usually stick the replaceable, fill-in-the-blanks stuff with ALL CAPS so that I can find the items more easily later (see Figure 21-2).
- The new toolbar you see on your screen (see Figure 21-2) is the Mail Merge toolbar. Don't bother messing with it; none of its buttons work at this point. (The attempt is an exercise in frustration, which makes you wonder why the toolbar is there in the first place.)

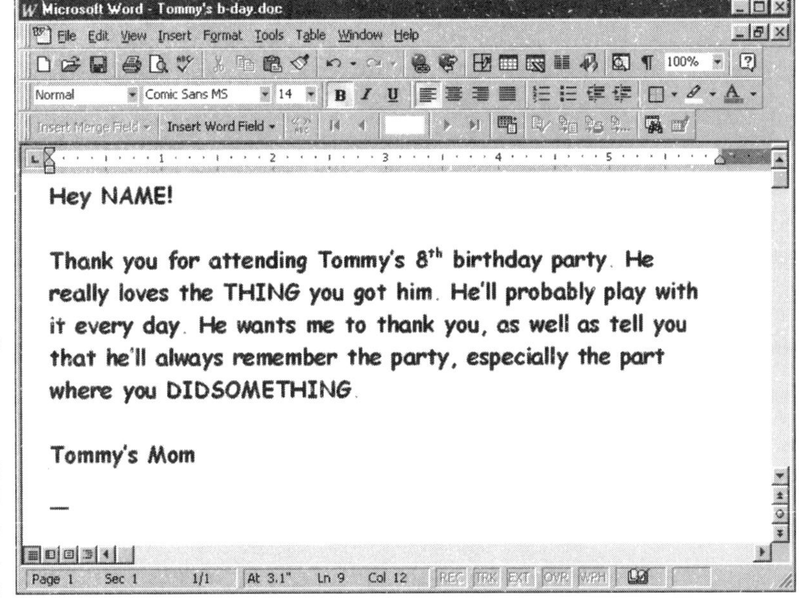

Figure 21-2: A sample main document and the Mail Merge toolbar.

Preparing the data source (the list of names and such part)

A data source is not a traditional Word document. It is a database table of sorts, which includes information stored in *fields* and *records*. Each field contains a tidbit of text that fills in a blank in the main document. A collection of fields — one form letter — is what makes up a record. Don't sweat the details or the jargon. Word handles the details. I'll ease you through the jargon.

To start a data source, follow these steps:

1. **Choose Tools⇨Mail Merge.**

   The Mail Merge Help dialog box appears again. Don't bother checking with Figure 21-1; the thing has transformed again. Mostly in Step 1, you see a new button plus some new information. As usual, ignore the details and keep reading with the next step.

2. **Click the Get Data button.**

   A drop-down list appears.

3. **Select Create Data Source from the list.**

   The Create Data Source dialog box appears, full of mirth and merriment (see Figure 21-3). This place is where you create the fields — the fill-in-the-blank items.

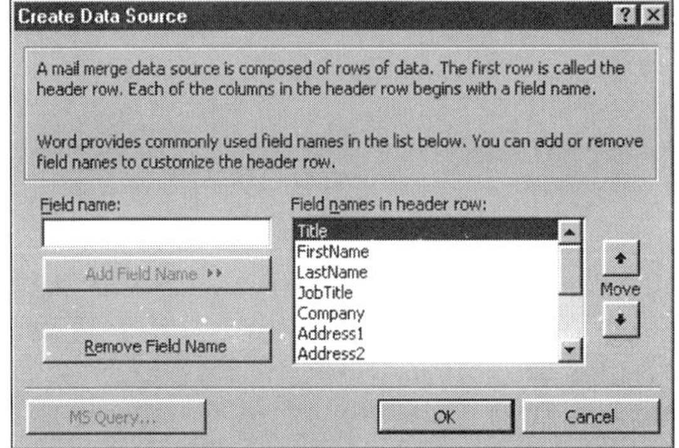

Figure 21-3: The Create Data Source dialog box.

To be helpful, Word has already dreamt up a whole parade of field names. Your first duty is to erase them all.

4. **Keep clicking the Remove Field Name button until all the names Word concocted in the Field names in header row list are gone, gone, gone.**

   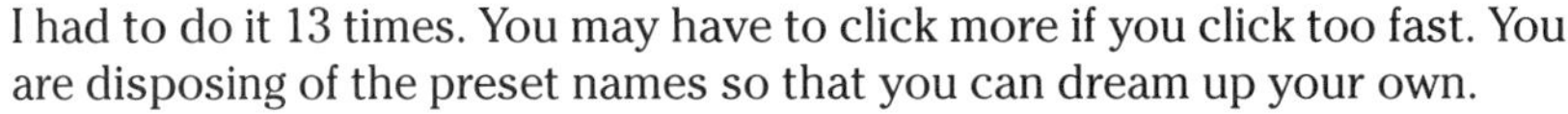

   I had to do it 13 times. You may have to click more if you click too fast. You are disposing of the preset names so that you can dream up your own.

5. **Type a field name into the Field name box.**

   Here are some suggestions for making this step make sense:

   - The field should be named to reflect the kind of information that it will contain. For example, a field named firstname would contain first names.
   - No two fields can have the same name.
   - A field name must begin with a letter.
   - A field name can contain up to 20 letters, numbers, and underscored characters.
   - You cannot use spaces or punctuation marks in field names.
   - When entering addresses, always make separate fields for the city, state, and zip codes.

6. **Click the Add Field Name button after typing your field name.**

   For example, type **name** into the Field name box and then click the Add Field Name button. This command inserts the field that you created into the list shown in the Field names in header row box.

7. **Repeat Steps 5 and 6 for each field that you want to include in your data file.**

   In my example (see Figure 21-2), I have NAME, THING, and DIDSOMETHING. I had to go through Steps 5 and 6 three times. For more-detailed form letters, you may be stuck here for an eternity.

8. **Click the OK button when you're done creating field names.**

   The Save As Data Source dialog box appears. This dialog box works just like the Save As dialog box to save a document. In fact, that's what you're doing: saving your data source document to disk.

9. **Give your data source document a name.**

   Be clever. I called my thank-you note document TOMMY'S B-DAY. I call the data source document, which contains names, gifts, and stuff, GIFT LIST.

10. **Click the Save button.**

    Another annoying dialog box appears after your data source has been saved to disk. Don't read it! Just . . .

11. **Click the Edit Data Source button.**

    The Data Form dialog box appears and . . . you're ready to continue reading with the next section.

Adding data to the data source

Because you're obeying step-by-step instructions here, editing the fill-in-the-blanks information — which is technically called "adding data to the data source" — is done via the handy Data Form dialog box, shown in Figure 21-4. The following steps tell you how to fill in the blanks.

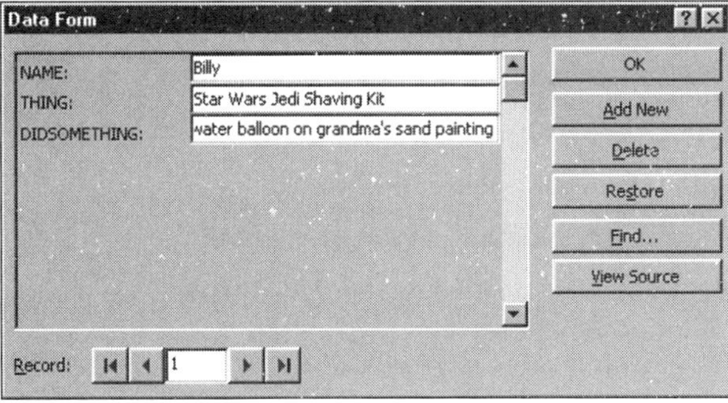

Figure 21-4: The Data Form dialog box.

1. **Fill in the blanks.**

   Each field in your document needs information. For a NAME field, type a name. Then type other necessary information as displayed in the Data Form dialog box: street, zip code, phone number, hat size, and so on. Use the Tab key to move from box to box.

2. **When you've filled in all the blanks, click the Add New button.**

   You don't have to click the Add New button after typing the last record. Instead, go right on to Step 4.

3. **Repeat Steps 1 and 2 for every person to whom you want to mail your form letter.**
4. **After you're done, click the OK button.**

   Clicking OK sends the Data Form dialog box away, saving all the information to disk.

- Remember to click the Add New button after entering a record; the OK button is only clicked when you're done typing all the records.
- Data is pronounced *DAY-ta*.
- The names for the boxes in the Data Form dialog box are the field names that you created in the preceding section.
- Move from box to box by pressing the Tab key.
- You can use the Record buttons to scan and modify information that you've already entered.
- If you need to reexamine or edit the data source file, refer to the very next section.

Editing the data source file

If you need to look at your data source information, for recreational examination or editing, you can follow these steps:

1. **Choose Tools⇨Mail Merge.**

   The Mail Merge dialog box from Hell appears (refer to Figure 21-1).

2. **Under Step 2, Data source, in the dialog box, click the Edit button.**

   A menu with one item should drop down.

3. **Click the highlighted Data item or press Enter.**

   You see the Data Form dialog box displayed. There you can peruse or edit your information as you see fit.

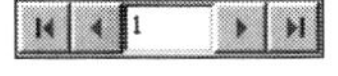

Use the Record buttons to scan the various records. You can use the Delete button to remove a record. Edit the text in the fields and click the OK button after you're done.

- From the Mail Merge toolbar, you can click the View Data Source button to see the Data Source dialog box.

- The data source file is secretly attached to your main document. After you go to save your main document, Word will ask if you also want to save the data source. Always do so. That way you can re-use the form letter and edit the data source file at any time in the future.

Inserting fields into the main document

You need to place the fields — the blanks — into your main document. That's done after you fill in your data source file (see the previous sections) and is accomplished by following these steps:

1. **Position the toothpick cursor where you want the field to be placed.**

   For example, you want a name field after the *Dear* in your letter's greeting, so position the cursor between the *Dear* and the colon.

   If you used ALL CAPS words to mark your fill-in-the-blanks stuff (as I did in Figure 21-2), select those place holders with your mouse; drag the mouse over the ALL CAPS text to highlight it.

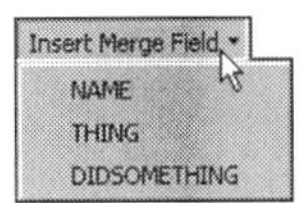

2. **Click the huge Insert Merge Field button in the Mail Merge toolbar.**

   A list of your fields drops down.

3. **Select the field that you want to place in the document.**

   A special cryptic code is inserted into your document, representing that field. For example, the FIRSTNAME field may look like `<<firstname>>` in the main document, which is what Word thinks of as a "blank" for fill-in-the-blanks stuff.

4. **Continue adding fields until the document is complete.**

   Repeat Steps 1, 2, and 3 as necessary to create all the blank spots in your document.

- You can have more than one field on a line.
- A tad bit of editing may be required after the field. I typically have to add a space, comma, colon, or whatever after fields as Word inserts them.
- Don't worry if the formatting looks too funny with the `<<Fields>>` in your document. Things get formatted nicely when Word fills in the blanks — *after* merging.
- To delete an unwanted field, select it with the mouse and press the Delete key. You can't use the Delete or Backspace keys by themselves! You must highlight a field and then delete it.

Merge mania!

After creating the main and data files, you're ready to merge away! Ensure that the main document whatever has been saved to disk: Save! Now you're ready to merge, which is actually the simplest part of all this mail merging nonsense. Follow these steps:

1. **Choose Tools⇨Mail Merge.**

   Golly, that dialog box has gotten busy. Fortunately, this is the last time it will offend you.

2. **Click the Merge button, near the bottom of the dialog box by the third step.**

   The Merge dialog box appears. Dally here later after you have the whole process down pat.

3. **Click the Merge button in the Merge dialog box.**

   As if by magic, Word creates several documents merging your main document with the information that you put into your data source. All the new documents appear, one after the other, on the screen in front of you in Word. Congratulations; you've just merged.

- Word merges the names and other information from the data file into the main document and creates lots of little, customized documents in one great big document file. That's what you see on-screen right now. Your options at this point are to review all the documents, save them, or print them. You made it!

- The merged documents are tossed into a new file; one that hasn't yet been saved. Save that file now!
- Viewing several merges before printing is a good idea. Check for punctuation and spacing.
- The main file appears several times on-screen, with information from the data file plugged into each copy. All files are separated by section breaks or hard page breaks.
- If your merge isn't humongous, you should save your mail merge in this on-screen format.
- You can print right from the screen view of the merged files by selecting File⇨Print.
- Now you know how to get those custom, uniquely crafted documents out to the foolhardy who actually think that you took the time to compose a personal letter. Ha! Isn't mail merge great?

- Always examine the results of the merge. Some things may not fit properly, and some editing will no doubt be required.

Part IV
Working with Graphics

In this part . . .

Word processing is words, text, written expression. So why should anyone give a hoot about graphics? After all, you struggle to write; now do they want you to struggle to draw? Will a stick man holding a balloon enhance your quarterly report that much?

Welcome to the '90s, where a word processor must also be a graphics processor in order to meet the stuffy demands of the computer software industry. Fortunately, this task isn't as rough as it could be. Windows lives and breathes graphics, so sprucing up your document with a few pictures (most of which come premade as clip art), graphs, or complex formatting along the lines of desktop publishing isn't painful torture. It's all covered in this part of the book in a typically cheery manner. Be prepared to make your writing not only literary, but flowery as well.

Chapter 22

Putting Purty Pictures into Your Documents

In This Chapter

- Using the Insert Picture command
- Inserting the image into a table
- Moving an image in your document
- Changing an image's size
- Cropping an image
- Wrapping text around an image
- Putting a border around an image

If a picture were really worth a thousand words, we'd never get some artist types to shut up. And you know how much they love to talk. Go visit a coffee bistro sometime to find out. Make sure that you're not carrying any weapons with you.

Blissfully, you don't have to become an artist to tastefully accent your Word documents with graphics. Heck, you don't even have to be tasteful about it. All you need to do is choose the proper image (or create your own, if you're reading this in a coffee house) and then slap it down in Word just like cut and paste in kindergarten. Word lets you do it with a minimum of effort, as this chapter shows.

Spruce Up Your Dull Text with Graphics

You can add a graphic to any Word document in three ways:

- Just paste it in wherever the toothpick cursor happens to be.
- Put it in a table.
- Tape it to your monitor.

The first method is the most popular, and I'll bet you never thought of the second method (though it's really handy). The third method works just fine, as long as you never scroll your screen and your printer has ESP.

- Pasting is the latter half of copy-and-paste. You start by finding or creating an image in another program, one suited to graphics. Then you *copy* the image. Windows remembers it. Then you *paste* it into Word. This procedure works like copying and pasting text, and the same Ctrl+C (Copy) and Ctrl+V (Paste) keys are used in all Windows programs for this purpose.
- In addition to copy and paste, you can also use the Insert⇨Picture command to slap down a number of interesting graphical things into a document. This is probably the most common way you'll stick graphics into your documents, because the Insert⇨Picture command is linked to a collection of pre-made graphics that come with Word.
- Windows comes with a simple painting program called MS Paint. You can use MS Paint to create interesting, albeit primitive, images for use in Word.
- Graphics come from several places. You can create the image in a graphics program, buy a disk full of images or *clip art,* or use a device called a *scanner* to electronically convert pictures and other printed images into graphics files you can store in the computer.
- Inserting an image into a table works just like pasting text at the toothpick cursor's position. The difference is that the image fits snugly into a cell in a table. Refer to Chapter 12 for more information on tables; your local hardware store has lots of books on making chairs and lawn furniture.
- Putting an image into a frame is nice because you can write text *around* the image. Otherwise, the image kinda sits by itself, all lonely without text to insulate it.

Inserting an image into a document

To stick a graphic already created — which is called "clip art" because "graphic already created" is too awkward to say every time — on disk into your text, follow these whimsical steps:

1. **Position the toothpick cursor in the spot where you want your picture.**

   If any text is already there, it is shoved aside to make room for the graphic.

2. **Choose the Insert⇨Picture⇨From File command.**

   You see the Insert Picture dialog box, as shown in Figure 22-1.

3. **Make sure that the Preview Picture box is visible.**

   Click the Preview button if you don't see the preview window displayed. And while you're at it, make sure that All Pictures is selected from the Files of type list box.

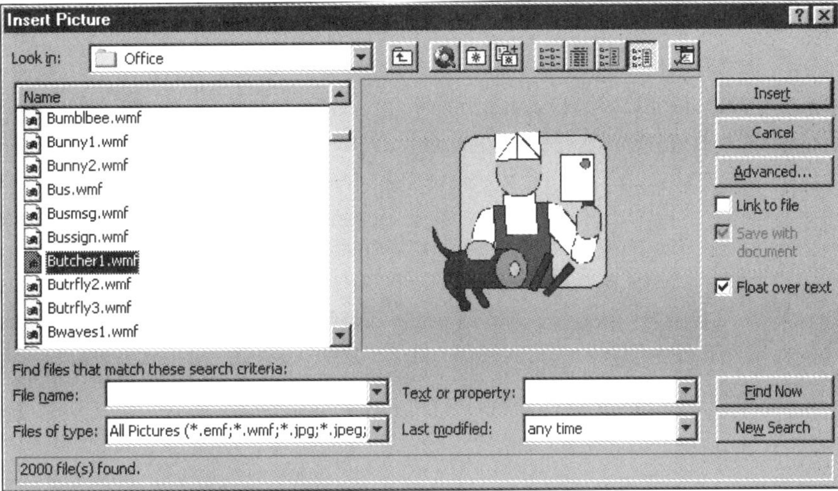

Figure 22-1: The Insert Picture dialog box.

4. **Navigate through the drives and folders until you find the image that you want.**

   This step is optional. Word automatically shows you a slew of its own clip-art images right away. Only if you want to find an image saved elsewhere do you need to scour.

5. **Select the image.**

   Click the image with your mouse. Just click once. A preview of the graphic appears on the right side of the dialog box (see Figure 22-1).

6. **Click the Insert button.**

   Splat! The image is pasted into your document, wherever your cursor happened to be. Now you may want to adjust the picture, which is covered in the section "Tweaking the Image," later in this chapter.

- I know, the Insert⇨Picture⇨Clip Art command seems more logical. But that one only works if you install clip art with Word. Otherwise, you get a nasty error message. The Insert⇨Pictures⇨From File command always works.
- If you don't see any images on your hard drive, see the sidebar, "Waaa! I don't have any Word clip art."
- "Ugh! That wasn't the image I wanted." Hurry and choose the Edit⇨Undo command or press Ctrl+Z, and try again.

- You don't have to use the Insert⇨Picture command if you copy and paste an image. To do that, create the image in another Windows application, select it for copying, and then return to Word and paste.

- Some images are colorful on-screen. Unless you have a color printer, they only print in black, white, and — with a laser printer — shades of gray.
- A cool thing to stick at the end of a letter is your signature. Use a desktop scanner to create your John Hancock. Save it as a file on disk and then follow the previous steps to insert it at the proper place in your document.
- Word automatically shifts into Page view whenever you mess with graphics. That's why you see an extra ruler on the side of your document. Choose View⇨Normal to return to Normal view, though you may not see your graphical image in Normal view. You just can't win.
- This method of inserting a graphic may frustrate you because the graphic and the text may not behave well together. Don't worry; Word has not left you high and dry. See "Tweaking the Image" later in this chapter, but also look into the sections "Slapping it in a table" for other ways to stick an image into your document.
- Although they're not really "graphics," Word has an assortment of oddball characters that you can insert into your text, right along with the normal human characters. For example, the ☺ or the ♥ symbol are ever popular with hippie-wanna-bes. Refer to Chapter 26 for more information on Word's oddball characters.

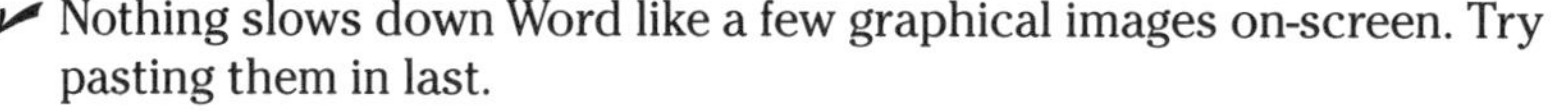

- Nothing slows down Word like a few graphical images on-screen. Try pasting them in last.

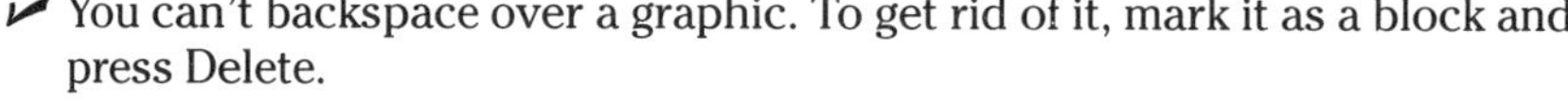

- You can't backspace over a graphic. To get rid of it, mark it as a block and press Delete.

Slapping it in a table

Tables are wonderful places for a graphic. You can put your image of, say, your favorite politician in a cell and place text in any cell before or after the graphic. This keeps everything neat without interfering much with the text before or after the table. Figure 22-2 shows what I mean.

To insert a graphic in a table, follow these steps:

1. **Make the table.**

   Refer to Chapter 14 to find out about tables. Keep in mind that it's okay to make a table with only one row and two columns (as shown in Figure 22-2). You can put the image in one column and text in the other.

2. **Follow the instructions in the preceding section for inserting a picture into your document.**

   The main difference here is that you position the toothpick cursor in the cell where you want your picture. Otherwise, it all works the same.

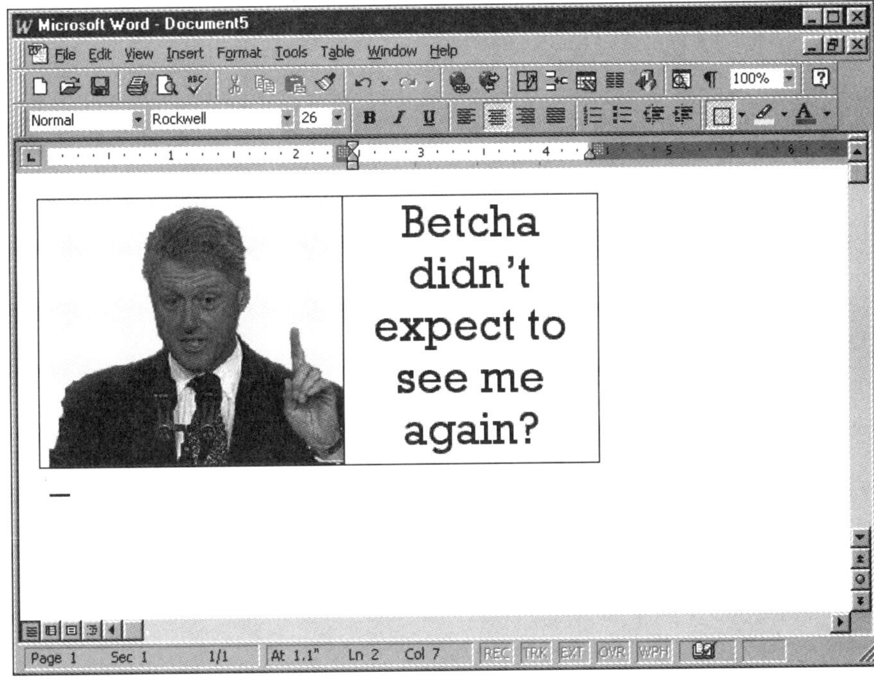

Figure 22-2: Text and graphics mix nicely in a sneaky table.

- If the image has already been saved in the Windows Clipboard (you copied it from another program), you just need to press Ctrl+V, the Paste command, in step 2, and you're done.
- You can grab the edges of a cell in a table to change the cell's size or position.
- To change the size of your image, see "Tweaking the Image," later in this chapter.

"Waaa! I don't have any Word clip art"

Installing the clip-art images is optional and may not have been done if your PC doesn't have enough disk space. But you can make amends. If you want to add the images, you just need to rerun the Word (or Microsoft Office) setup program and then choose to install the images. This sort of works like installing a new text converter, which is covered in Chapter 19, only you're installing clip-art images.

You can also buy a diskette or (preferably) a CD-ROM chock full o'clip-art images. My in-laws bought me the Corel Gallery 2 CD-ROM clip-art disk for Christmas last year, and it works just fine with Word. (Drop several notes around your house so that some of your noncomputer relatives will get the hint.)

Tweaking the Image

Unless you're a graphical pro (in which case you probably bought the wrong book), you need to tweak just about every image you slap into your document. And, ho boy, Word does some frustrating things with images. Fortunately, there's always some hidden way to fix things.

- The following sections are listed more-or-less in the order you'll probably need them to adjust any image in your document. If you haven't already, choose View⇨Page Layout from the menu. This places your document in Page Layout view (duh), which is best for tweaking graphics.
- You tweak a graphical image by using your mouse. Whenever you click a graphic in your document, the Picture toolbar appears. If anything on that toolbar is important, it is discussed in the following sections.
- After you're done tweaking your graphic, just click the mouse on some text. That throws you back into text editing mode. You can also choose View⇨Normal to switch back to the Normal view, where most graphics don't show up.
- Graphics in a table are always visible. Yet another graphics-in-a-table tip for you.

Moving an image hither and thither

To move an image around on the page, drag it by using your mouse. Just point the mouse at the graphic and press and hold the left button. The mouse pointer changes to an arrow with a compass thing on it. Drag the image around in your text and then release the mouse button to plop the image in a new location.

If you plan on doing any major dragging around a page, choose View⇨Zoom and then double-click the Whole page item in the Zoom dialog box. This displays the entire page in Word's window, which makes it less of a drag to drag graphics around.

If you need to move an image from one page to another, I recommend cutting and then pasting the image: Click the image once to select it and then press Ctrl+X to cut. Scroll to the page you want the image on, poke the toothpick cursor in the right spot, and press Ctrl+V to paste.

Changing an image's size

I don't know about you, but all my graphics are way too big when I insert them. Changing their size is a cinch: Just click the image with the mouse cursor. The graphic is enveloped in a box with eight tiny *handles* on it. You use your mouse to drag the handles and adjust the image's size. In Figure 22-3, the eight handles are around the middle image, Cup o' Joe.

Figure 22-3: Grab one of the eight handles to change an image's size.

Generally speaking, grab one of the handles with the mouse and drag toward or away from the image. So, grab the top handle to make the image taller or shorter. Grab the side handle to make the image narrower or fatter. The corner handles move in two directions (diagonally) simultaneously.

- The graphic can be *scaled* (made larger or smaller without distortion) by dragging one of the corner handles.
- To change the size of a graphic in a uniform direction (from the center out), press the Ctrl key before dragging one of the handles. (Play with this for a while to see what I'm talking about.)
- You can make a graphic fatter and taller or shorter and thinner by dragging the left, right, top or bottom sides. This is how one graphic of a coffee cup was changed three different ways in Figure 22-3.
- If adjusting the image's size just isn't enough, you can do some pretty fancy editing of the image by double-clicking it with the mouse. This opens a link between the image and the program that made it — or a program that can work with the image. Usually, Microsoft Draw opens, although MS Paint sometimes does instead. Chapter 23 offers some basic information on using Microsoft Draw.

Cropping an image

To grow corn on your image, do the following:

No. Wait. That's the wrong type of crop. When you work with graphics, cropping an image means changing its size without making the image smaller or larger. Grandma does this all the time when she takes pictures of the family; she crops off everyone's head. It's like using a pair of scissors to cut a chunk from a picture. Figure 22-4 shows a before-and-after-crop job.

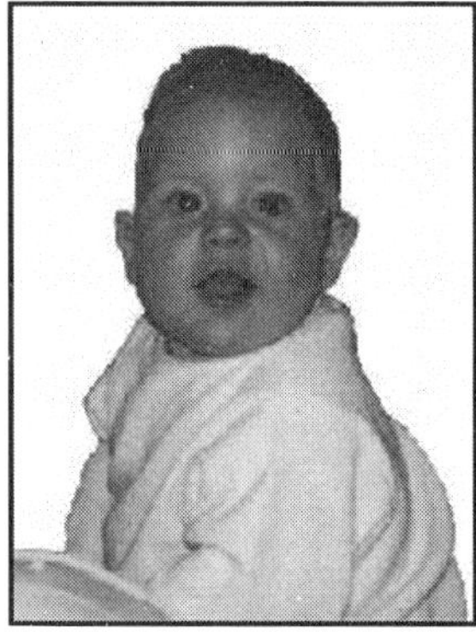
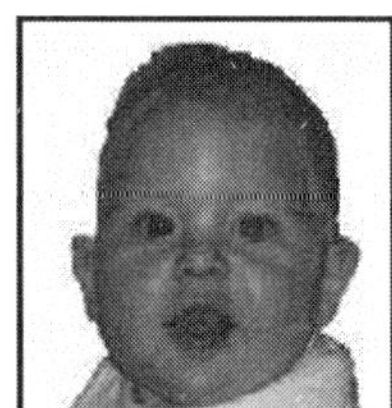

Figure 22-4: Jeremiah before and after cropping.

You crop an image just like you re-size one (see the preceding section). The difference is that you must switch the mouse pointer into crop mode. Follow these steps:

1. **Click the image once to select it.**

   This has the dual benefits of putting eight little handles on the image as well as displaying the Picture toolbar.

2. **Click the Crop tool on the Picture toolbar.**

   Click it once. You're now in cropping mode, which works a lot like re-sizing an image.

3. **Drag one of the image's handles to crop.**

   Point the mouse at one of the handles. The mouse pointer changes to a weird crop-like thing that must register only in the minds of graphic artists. Anyway, you move the mouse inward to crop.

   I usually use the outside (left, right, top, bottom) handles to crop. The corner handles never quite crop the way I want them to.

4. **After you're done cropping, click the Crop tool again to turn that mode off.**

   Again, the weird mouse pointer should remind you that you're in cropping mode. If not, you can always un-crop by dragging one of the handles back out to where you want it.

Text wrapping (or avoiding the "image floating over my text" syndrome)

It may frustrate you to no end to see your graphics "floating" over your text. This is because Word treats graphics like separate objects in a document, like different pieces of clear plastic laying one atop the other. However, you can lock your graphic into the text layer if you want, even make the text flow around the graphic like cars avoiding a ladder on the freeway. Here's how:

1. **Choose View➪Page Layout from the menu.**

   This step switches you into Page Layout view, where you can see your graphic and any text at the same time.

   You may also want to zoom out to see more of your document at once. Choose View➪Zoom and then double-click Whole Page in the Zoom dialog box. This action displays the whole page in Word's window, with text very teensy tiny and your graphics all there for the world to see.

2. **Click once on the image you want to change.**

   This step selects the image, putting the eight little handles 'round it, and shows you the Picture toolbar.

3. **Click the Text Wrapping tool.**

   A drop-down menu is displayed, shown in Figure 22-5.

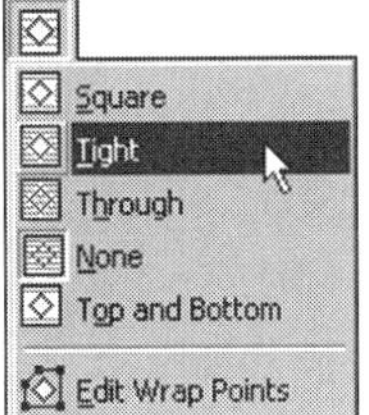

Figure 22-5: Options for wrapping text around an image.

4. **Select the type of text wrapping you want.**

   For example, choose Tight to have the text hug your image on all sides; choose Square to have your image appear in a box-like thing. Floating an image over your text is done by selecting the Through or None options.

The Edit Wrap Points item works just like the Tight item. However, the image appears in the document with dozens of tiny handles on it. In a dramatic effort to waste serious time, you can drag each handle to adjust how the text wraps around your image. Me? I just select the Tight option and let Word do the work.

5. **You're done.**

   Unless you choose the Edit Wrap Points item, you're done with text wrapping. If you did choose Edit Wrap Points, press the Esc key on your keyboard to exit that mode. (You need to click your graphic again to re-edit things.)

You'll notice that you can move a graphic after selecting a wrapping option and the text in your document jiggles to accommodate it. That's because wrapping options are attached to each graphic in your document like lint to an all-day sucker stuck in a kid's pocket. The only way to change the way the graphics and text interact is to repeat the preceding steps and select a new type of text wrapping.

Because graphics live on various "layers" in Word you may notice that sometimes your graphics overlap. To move one image in front of or behind another image, right-click that image by using your mouse. From the shortcut menu that appears, choose the Order submenu and then Bring to Front or Send to Back or any of the other fine options to change the way your images overlap.

Putting a pretty border around your graphic

Some graphics are just too naked to sit on a page by themselves. Take Figure 22-4, for example. Jeremiah is sitting before a white background. To prevent each image from looking muddled, a black border was applied. You can do the same to any image you have in your document. Heed:

1. **Click once on the graphic to select it.**

   The image grows its eight handles, and the Picture toolbar lurks into view.

2. **Click the Line Style tool.**

   A drop-down menu of lines and styles is displayed.

3. **Pluck out the line style you want to border your graphic.**

   Click it with your mouse. The picture grows a border.

If you select the More Lines option from the bottom of the Line Style tool's menu you see the Colors and Lines panel in the Format Picture dialog box. From there, you can select even more line styles and whatnot to format your picture. Click the OK button when you're happy with your selections in the Format Picture dialog box.

Chapter 23

Cute Li'l Programs for Doing Cute Li'l Things

In This Chapter

- Activating AutoShapes
- Working with WordArt
- Faking fun facts with Microsoft Chart
- Drawing Pictures in Word

As if word processing wasn't enough by itself, Word is also capable of stupendous graphical feats. These are accomplished by a host of little programs that attach themselves to Word like sucker fishes on a shark waiting for a free meal. Most of these programs are graphical in nature, which is why they're in this part of the book. Each one allows you to insert a special graphical whatnot into your document, enhancing its appeal and earning you praise beyond the document's mere textual content. And being praised for how things look is *really* what life is all about, huh?

Activating AutoShapes

AutoShapes are basically graphics, simple images that may come in handy in your document. They're a part of the Microsoft Draw program included with Word, which is covered later in this chapter. But Draw is a pain to use. So rather than make your stick figures and arrows yourself, you can use AutoShape images that are already created. See? It's all about saving time *and* looking good.

No document *needs* AutoShapes. But if you feel like spicing something up with some simple graphics and you don't have an M.F.A. in Italian Post Renaissance Art History, you can do the following:

1. **Choose Insert⇨Picture⇨AutoShapes.**

   Word switches into Draw mode, growing an extra Draw toolbar you can employ to make Word behave like an honest-to-goodness drawing program. But because you choose the AutoShapes command, you also see the AutoShapes toolbar.

2. **Pick a style of shape from the toolbar.**

   Click your mouse on any button in the AutoShapes toolbar. Each button represents a whole slew of shapes. When you click one of the buttons, you see a drop-down menu showing each of the shapes, which is shown in Figure 23-1.

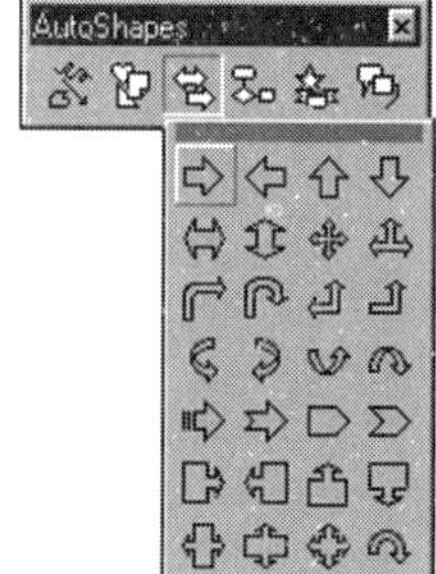

Figure 23-1: The AutoShapes toolbar with its arrow shapes hanging down.

3. **Choose the shape you want from the drop-down menu.**

   I'm kinda fond of arrows in my text, so I chose a nice fat arrow from the third button, Block Arrows.

   The mouse pointer changes to a crosshair (a thin plus-thing if you've never looked through a periscope on a submarine).

4. **Drag the mouse to draw the AutoShape in your document.**

   Start in the upper-left corner and drag down to the right, creating a huge (or not-so-huge) rectangle. The shape you selected appears as you drag down and to the right, becoming larger, longer, or squatter depending on how you drag the mouse.

   Release the mouse button, and Word draws the shape to fill that rectangle. The shape is selected with eight *handles* on it for re-sizing or cropping.

You can move, re-size, wrap text around, or otherwise fiddle with the graphic image after it's been created. First, select the image by clicking on it with your mouse. Then choose View⇨Toolbars⇨Picture from the menu. Refer to "Tweaking the Image" in Chapter 22 for more information on what you can do with the graphic image. (AutoShape images work just like any other graphics in your document.)

You can also use the Draw toolbar to further manipulate the AutoShape image. Refer to the last section in this chapter.

If you want to dispense with drawing and return to editing your document's text, choose View⇨Toolbars⇨Drawing from the menu and then View⇨Toolbars⇨AutoShapes. You may also want to switch back to Normal view: Choose View⇨Normal.

Working with WordArt

WordArt is sadly neglected by most Word users. This is too bad, because WordArt can quickly add a lot of dazzle to your documents. And it's a fun place to waste time.

WordArt produces a graphical object in your text. It's not text, it's a graphic! For formatting text in strange manners, you really need to use the character formatting rules and regulations outlined in Chapter 9. WordArt is art. No, better: WordArt is *arte*.

To put WordArt into your document, follow these steps:

1. **Position the toothpick cursor in the spot in your document where you want the WordArt to appear.**

   It can really be anywhere: at the start of a line, in the middle of a paragraph, or on a line by itself. Whatever the case, move the toothpick cursor to that location first.

2. **Choose the Insert⇨Picture⇨WordArt command.**

   The WordArt Gallery dialog box appears, showing you the colors and variety of WordArt you can create like a lipstick display at a cosmetics counter (see Figure 23-2).

   What you're looking for in the WordArt Gallery dialog box is a *style,* the way the words bend and flare and the way the letters are formatted and colored.

3. **Click the style you like and then click OK.**

   Select a style from the assortment in the WordArt Gallery dialog box and then click the OK button. The Edit WordArt Text dialog box appears, which is too boring to show in this book.

4. **Type the text you want "artified" into the box.**

   What you type replaces the `Your Text Here` in the box. You can also select a different font from the Font list, a text size from the Size list, or bold and italic formatting, all found in the Edit WordArt Text dialog box.

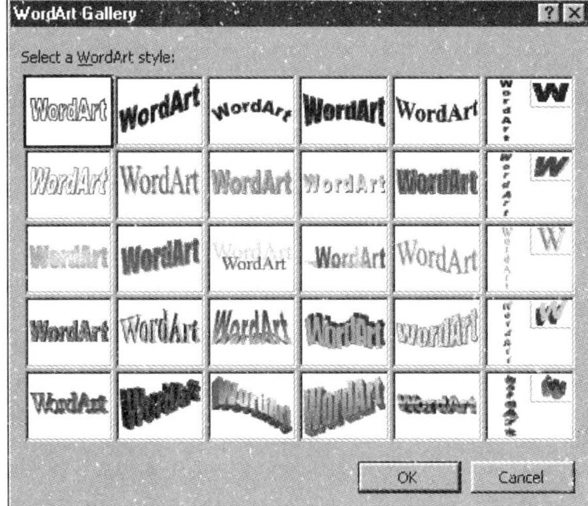

Figure 23-2: The WordArt Gallery lipstick case dialog box.

5. **Click OK.**

   The Edit WordArt Text dialog box goes away, and your WordArt appears in your document (see Figure 23-3). Also appearing for a limited time only: The WordArt toolbar, which allows you to further modify the WordArt image in your document.

Figure 23-3: WordArt in a document.

6. **Tweak your WordArt (if necessary).**

   The bulleted list at the end of these steps has more information.

7. **Click the mouse back in your document to return to text editing mode.**

   After you're done fussing with your WordArt, just point the mouse at some text in your document and click. This step makes the WordArt toolbar go away and returns you to text-editing mode. You may also wish to switch back to Normal view; choose View⇨Normal from the menu.

- WordArt works like other graphics in your document. You can move it around, wrap text around it, and so on. Refer to "Tweaking the Image" in Chapter 22 for more information. Mostly, though, you'll probably use the WordArt toolbar to change the image.

- You can use the WordArt toolbar to do the following. Just click the WordArt graphic in your document and then choose one of the following buttons from the WordArt toolbar.

- Click the Edit Text button to return to the Edit WordArt Text dialog box to change the WordArt text, font, size, and so on. Click OK after you're done.

- The WordArt Shape button displays a drop-down list of different layouts for your WordArt text — a more detailed version than you can find in the WordArt Gallery. Just select a shape, and your WordArt text is reformatted to fit into that shape.
- Click the Format WordArt button to display the Format WordArt dialog box, very similar to the Format Graphics toolbox (briefly covered in the last chapter). Each panel of the toolbox controls a different aspect of the WordArt you create: Color, Size, Position, (Text) Wrapping, and so on. Use this toolbox to make fine adjustments to your WordArt.
- If you want to wrap text around your WordArt, click the Format WordArt button and, in the Format WordArt dialog box, choose the way you want text to wrap around your WordArt from the Wrapping panel. These are the same options presented for wrapping text around a graphic, as covered in Chapter 22, the section "Text wrapping (or avoiding the "image floating over my text" syndrome)."

- Refer to Chapter 24 for information on creating a drop cap in your document. You might assume that WordArt could handle this task, but the Drop Cap command does the job much better.

Faking Fun Facts with Microsoft Chart

Nothing can spin the dust off numbers better than a real cool graph. You don't even need to mess with a spreadsheet or futz with a chart program. Everything can be done neatly from within Word, thanks to Microsoft Chart — yet another li'l program they tossed into Word "just because."

To insert a chart into your document, follow these steps:

1. **Move the toothpick cursor to the place you want to insert the chart.**

   Charts are big square things. Word inserts the big square thing into your document, so move your cursor where you want the graph *before* you start.

   Of course, you can always move the chart later, wrap text around it and so forth, just like any other graphic. But do that later. For now:

2. **Choose the Insert⇨Picture⇨Chart command.**

   A chart is slapped into your document (complete with bogus data), and a new Datasheet window appears (complete with bogus data).

3. **Replace the sample data with the information that you want displayed.**

   To delete a column or row of the bogus data, click the column or row letter or number. This step selects the whole column or row. Then press the Delete key.

   Type new information, row and column. If you're used to working with a spreadsheet, it works the same here (except for the math part, only text is displayed).

   Don't worry about making it perfect; you can always come back to edit the datasheet at any time.

   Right now, Word has the chart set up as a two-dimensional bar graph. You can change the chart later, if you like. First you have to enter the information for the graph. In Figure 23-4, I've created a pie chart. You'll note that pie charts require only one row of information. The columns represent each slice of the pie.

4. **Close the Datasheet window.**

   Click the mouse on its X close button. This returns you to your document where you can tweak with the chart you just created.

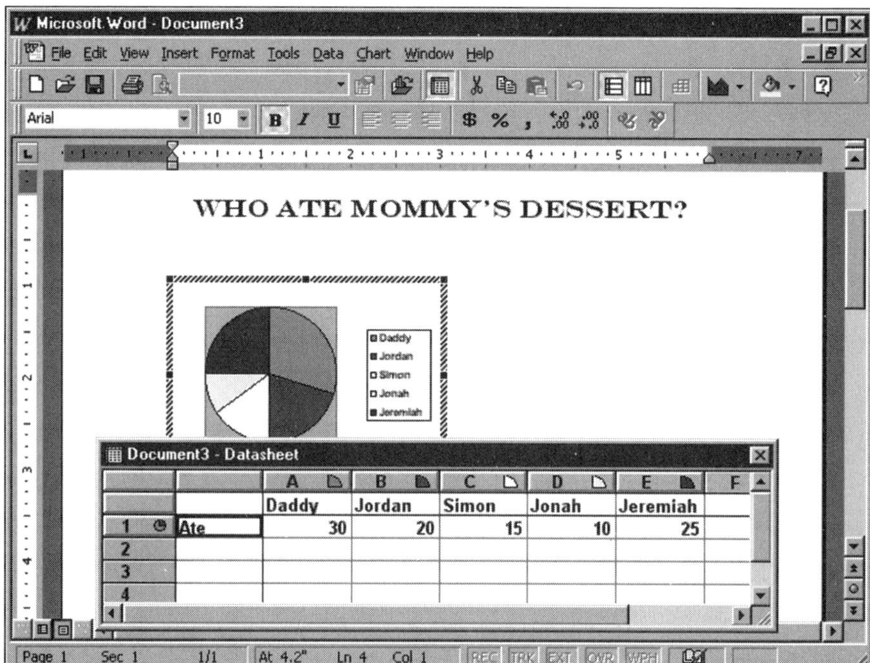

Figure 23-4: A sample chart in a document.

5. **Select the chart for changing, if you like.**

   To change the chart, make sure it's selected. The chart should have a thick hatched border and black "handles" on it, as shown in Figure 23-4. If not, double-click the chart with your mouse to select it.

6. **Right-click the chart to display its shortcut menu.**

   Point the mouse at a blank area of the chart; not on the chart itself or the legend, but still within the hatched boarder. Here's a hint: Hold the mouse still and it should say `Chart Area` below the mouse pointer. After you're there, right-click the mouse to display the Chart's shortcut menu, as shown in Figure 23-5.

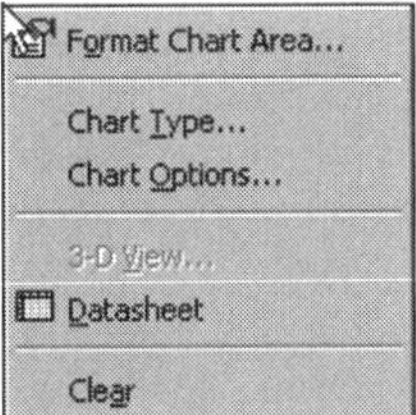

Figure 23-5: The Chart shortcut menu.

7. **Click Chart Type to choose a new type of graph.**

   This displays the Chart Type dialog box, where you can pluck out a new type of graph, either a bar chart, pie graph, doughnut — all sorts of interesting options. Click the OK button after you're done.

8. **You're done!**

   Click the mouse outside the graph's area (click your document). Your document now has a beautiful graph, suitable for framing.

- To re-edit your chart's data, summon the Chart shortcut menu (Step 6 above) and choose Datasheet.
- After the chart appears in your document, it can be treated like a graphic. If you click the graphic-object, it will be outlined like a graphic window frame. You can use standard graphic tweaking methods on the chart; refer to Chapter 22 for more information.

- You can make a graphical chart from data already in your document. Suppose that you have numbers sitting in a table. To make it into a Microsoft Chart thing, mark the entire table as a block and choose Insert⇨Picture⇨Chart. Continue with step 4 in the preceding list, because Word uses the information from your table instead of bogus data to help create your chart.

✓ Whenever you double-click a chart for editing, Word's Standard toolbar changes to a special Chart toolbar. You can use some of the buttons on that toolbar to handle your basic chart functions, such as the View Datasheet button and Chart Type drop-down menu button. Clicking outside the chart (to un-select it) restores the Standard toolbar back to normal.

Drawing Pictures in Word (The Ultimate Word Processing Sacrilege)

If you feel the need to break out and draw something in your word processor, you can. Word sports a special Drawing mode that allows you to insert circles, lines, arrows, and other blocky artwork at your whim. Inserting artwork could really be the subject of an entire book, so bear with me if the following run-through is overly brief.

Before diving into this, be aware that a drawing program is different from a paint program, such as MS Paint. Painting programs splash pixels on the screen — small dots of color, just like electronic crayons. Drawing programs work with *objects,* or collections of points and lines that can easily be resized, moved, and grouped to form interesting things and so on. Blah, blah, blah.

To activate Word's drawing mode, click the mouse on the Drawing button on the Standard toolbar. You can also choose View⇨Toolbars⇨Drawing from the menu. That's because the drawing mode is really nothing more than an extra toolbar that contains various drawing things, as shown in Figure 23-6.

The Drawing toolbar is divided into several areas. The middle area contains tools you can use to draw various lines, arrows, squares, and circles. The right area contains controls for colors, line width, and three-dimensional effects.

Click the arrow tool to manipulate any images you create, changing their location and stuff like that. Also, you cannot change an object's color or line thickness unless it's selected.

If you don't like something you created, select it with the arrow tool and press the Delete key. Poof! It's gone.

You can put text into your drawing by using the Text Box button. Unlike a paint program, the text you create appears in its own box. The text can be edited later just like you were editing text in Word. Use the Format⇨Font command to change the text style.

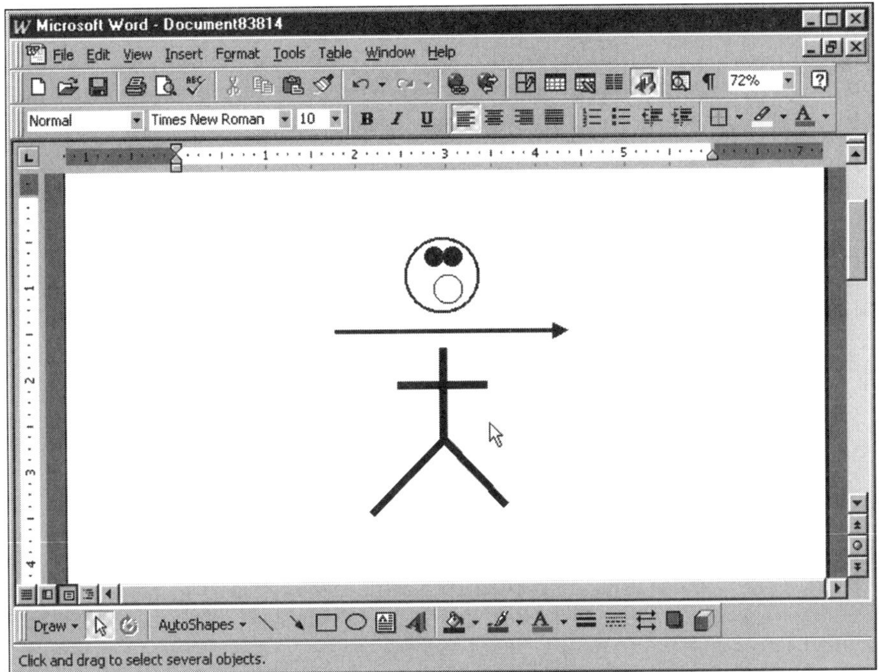

Figure 23-6: Word in its Drawing mode.

You can also create WordArt or insert an AutoShape by clicking the appropriate button on the toolbar. See previous sections in this chapter for more information.

After you're done, click the Drawing button again to rid yourself of the Drawing toolbar and return to document editing mode. You see whatever graphic you created right there in your document.

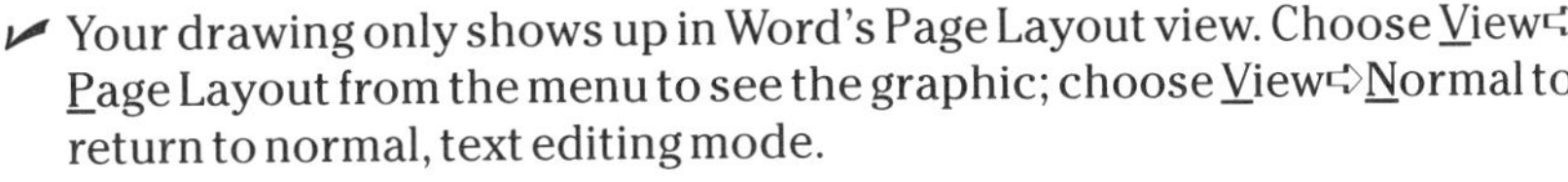

- Your drawing only shows up in Word's Page Layout view. Choose View⇨Page Layout from the menu to see the graphic; choose View⇨Normal to return to normal, text editing mode.

- Because the Drawing tools only create simple shapes, you may want to group some of them together for easy manipulation. To do this, select a bunch of objects and click the Draw button to display a pop-up menu. Choose Group from that menu to group together your objects. I did this in Figure 23-6 to create the stick-man image (well, his head and body separately).
- The Drawing tools are good but best used for simple illustrations. If you need complex or detailed drawing, my advice is to pick up a nice illustration package for your computer, such as Adobe Illustrator.

- When your drawing is in your document, it behaves like any other graphic. Refer to Chapter 22 for some general graphic-tweaking information.

- To edit the graphic in Picture again, click the Drawing button. Then you can use the tools to manipulate or edit your drawing objects.

Chapter 24

Your Basic Desktop Publishing Stuff

In This Chapter

- Dropping the cap
- Creating cool document titles
- Formatting text just so
- Centering your title perfectly
- Using the Borders and Shading command
- Drawing a box around your text
- Putting less than a box around your text
- Shading your text
- Printing white on black

Some graphical things you can do with your document don't involve graphics at all. Instead, these items approach that fuzzy border between word processing and desktop publishing. Indeed, this part of the book would have been considered desktop publishing just a few years ago. So what else is there besides fancy graphics and text? There are boxes — and interesting ways to slap fancy titles and other things into your document. It's not really graphics; it's more along the lines of your basic DTP (desktop publishing) stuff.

Making a Drop Cap

A drop cap is where the first letter of a report, article, chapter, or story appears in a larger and more interesting font than the other characters. Figure 24-1 shows an example. This trick, which requires hours of painstaking work and adjustments in other word processors, is a snap in Word. Just use the handy Drop Cap command, nestled in the Format menu.

Figure 24-1: A cap is dropped at the start of a novel.

> It was a dark and stormy night. Suddenly, a champagne cork shot out! It was the group of programmers sitting in the next booth, celebrating the release of Microsoft Word '97, the 8th version of Word (which is really only the 4th version of Word because they skipped versions 3 through 5). "Ha, ha," they said, "Ha, ha."

Here are some steps you can follow to start your stuff off with a drop cap:

1. **Position the toothpick cursor at the start of your text.**

   Not the title. Not just anywhere. Put the toothpick cursor on the first paragraph of text. It also helps if this paragraph is left justified and not indented with a tab or any of the tricky formatting discussed in Chapter 11.

   By the way, you *do* have to write something here; the Drop Cap command isn't available until you have some text down on paper. (This is to thwart the efforts of writer's block-plagued authors who'd rather diddle with the Drop Cap feature than start writing anything.)

2. **Select the first character of the first word.**

   For example, the *O* in "Once upon a time."

3. **Choose Format⇨Drop Cap.**

   The Drop Cap dialog box appears, as depicted in Figure 24-2.

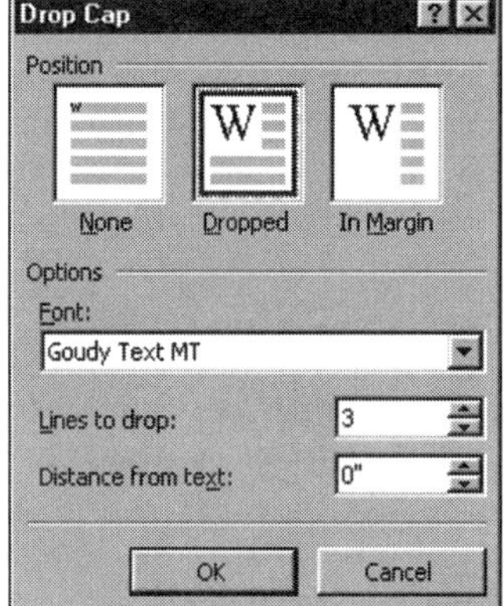

Figure 24-2: The Drop Cap dialog box.

4. **Select a drop cap style.**

   The first one, None, isn't a drop cap at all. The second style is Dropped and the third is In Margin. I prefer the Dropped style myself. Click the box you prefer.

5. **Select a Font if you wish.**

   Oh, and you can mess around with the other options if you like. Writer's block is a terrible thing . . . .

6. **Click OK.**

   Word switches your document to Page Layout view to see the drop cap in action (that is, if you're not already in Page Layout view).

   The drop cap is selected and shown inside a hatched box with eight black handles. Don't mess with it!

7. **Click the mouse in your text (not on the drop cap) and continue editing.**

   You're free to go on with your work.

- The drop cap looks best in Page Layout view, where it appears with a little chain link fence around it. Choose View⇨Page Layout.

- If you switch back to Normal view (View⇨Normal), the drop capped letter appears on the line above your text. Funky, but that's the way Word does it. Don't try to fix it; instead, return to Page Layout view to see the drop cap more properly.
- By the way, Chapter 29 talks about the Page Layout and Normal commands.
- A drop cap is not a graphic or graphical object (see Chapter 22). To fix it, you must follow the above steps again and make adjustments in the Drop Cap dialog box.
- Flourishy drop caps seem to work best for pretentious stuff. Otherwise, choose a big, blocky font for your drop caps.
- You can undo a drop cap by clicking on its box and then choosing Format⇨Drop Cap. In the Drop Cap dialog box, double-click the None position, and the drop cap vanishes.

Using the Borders and Shading Command

You can make document titles more interesting by putting a box around them — or maybe just some lines along the top and bottom or some fancy shading, as seen in Figure 24-3. You can do this to any text in Word. If you want to set aside a paragraph of text from the rest of the page, for example, you can box it or shade it. Just choose the Format⇨Borders and Shading command.

Figure 24-3: A fancy border around a document title.

Putting a box around your text

If you're creating a title, you can draw a nice square box around it. Or you can draw a box around any paragraph or group of paragraphs in any document or even a graphic. To do so, follow these steps:

1. **Mark the paragraph you want to box as a block.**

   Use the handy block-marking instructions in Chapter 6 to carry out this deed. You can mark any text, such as a title you want to snazz up. If you need to mark more than one paragraph, select them all as a block.

2. **Choose the Format⇨Borders and Shading command.**

   The Borders and Shading dialog box opens, as shown in Figure 24-4.

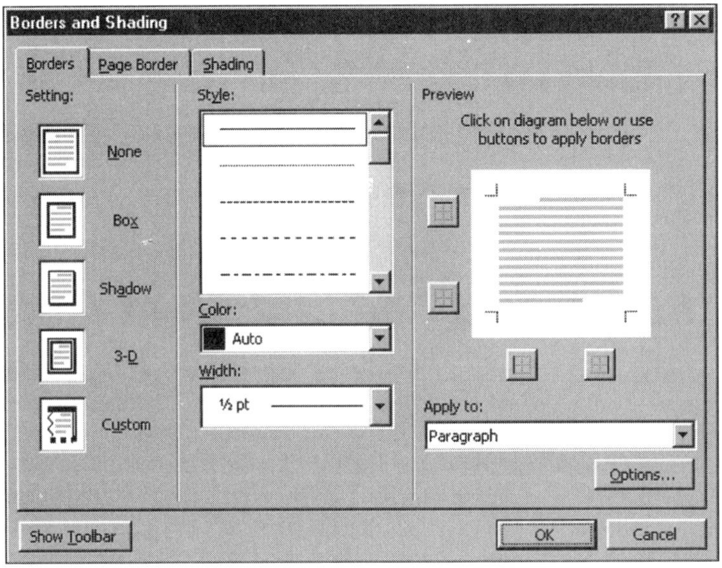

Figure 24-4: The Borders and Shading dialog box.

3. **Make sure that the Borders tab is up front.**

   Click the Borders tab if it's not.

4. **Select the type of border you want from the Setting column.**

   Four preset, easy-to-use, pop-n-fresh border styles are available; don't bother with the Custom style until you fully figure this out. Just click the style of paragraph border you want. My favorite is Shadow.

   Observe the Preview window to see how the border affects your text.

5. **Click OK.**

   Your title now has a box around it.

- Word draws lines around only full paragraphs of text — not bits and pieces.
- The left and right lines of the border are set equal to the left and right margins. So if you want a tighter border around your title, move in your margins.
- You can also use these techniques to spruce up any table you may create in your text. See Chapter 14.

- To change the line style, such as the style shown in Figure 24-3, select a different line type from the Style scrolling list. You can also set a color for the border from the Color drop-down menu, as well as set the line width from the Width drop-down thingamabob.
- To remove any border from your highlighted text, select the None item from the Setting column and then click OK.

Putting less than a box around your text

In Figure 24-5, the boxed title has lines only on the top and bottom. To make that happen with your title or any other text, follow Steps 1, 2, and 3 as outlined in the preceding section. And then do the following:

1. **Click the Box icon to put a box around your text.**

   Yeah, this isn't how you want to end up, but it's how you must start. (Just click once — don't double-click here.)

2. **Select a line style from the Style area in the Paragraph Borders and Shading dialog box.**

   You can choose from several thicknesses and double or single line patterns. Click the line style you want. Notice that the text in the preview box changes to match the line style you select.

   You can also mess with the Color and Width doohickeys if you feel like it. Oh, play, play, play. What's the point in doing any work?

Figure 24-5: A document title with borders at the top and bottom.

PANICKY FINANCIAL NEWSLETTER

THINGS ARE GOING DOWN, DOWN, DOWN.

VOL. 13. FRIDAY, JUNE 13, 1998.

3. **Now focus on the preview box.**

   The box tells Word where to put lines around your text — top, bottom, left, right, middle, and so on.

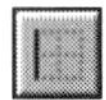

4. **Click the mouse on the left and right sides of the border in the Border preview box.**

   Or you can click the left and right border buttons. Either way it eliminates the lines on the outside of your text.

5. **Click OK after you finish making your box.**

   The box is now missing two sides, so it's really not much of a box at all and will probably spill all of its contents if you tip it the wrong way, so be careful.

Putting a border around the entire page

Not only can you rope titles and paragraphs, but you can put a border around each page in your document. Now that may sound hokey, but if you're making a newsletter or award or something cheesy like that, the border can come in handy.

To stick a border around your document, choose Format⇨Borders and Shading and then click the Page Border tab to view that panel. I'm not including a figure here because this panel looks and operates just like the Borders panel; see the previous two sections for more information.

The only difference you find in the Page Border panel is the Apply to drop-down list in the lower-right corner. Before you click OK, you need to tell Word which parts of your document need a page border. Then click OK.

- Select Whole document from the Apply to list to have a border on every page.
- Other options in the Apply to list deal with sections in your document. For example, if you want to border only one page out of many, you need to make that page its own section. Refer to Chapter 13 for more information on creating a section break in your document.

Using the Border button on the toolbar

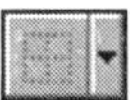

If you ever need to slap down a quickie border on your paragraph (or in a table), you can take advantage of the Border button on the toolbar and it's handy quick-o palette of line options. Just click the down-arrow by the button, and you see a selection of line types, top, bottom, outside (see Figure 24-6). Pick one from the list and whichever paragraph the toothpick cursor is on, or whichever paragraphs are selected, will grow that line.

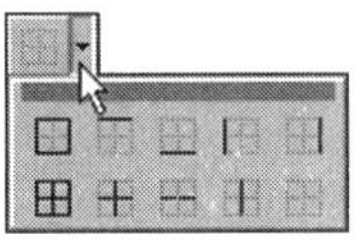

Figure 24-6: Your paragraph border selection, courtesy of the toolbar's Border button.

- The line style, selected in the Borders and Shading dialog box, is what's applied when you choose the shortcut buttons from the Border button on the toolbar.
- So, if you don't like the line style, choose Format⇨Borders and Shading from the menu to change it.

- To remove all borders from a paragraph, click the Border button on the toolbar and click the No Border button.
- The Border button on the toolbar only affects paragraphs, not the entire page.

Shading your text

The neatest Border dialog box effect of them all is shading your text — or a title, such as the sample shown in Figure 24-7. You can shade a title with or without a border around it. Use these steps:

1. **Mark your text or entire title as a block.**

   Refer to Chapter 6 for efficient block-marking instructions. If you want the shaded area to cover more than the title line, highlight the lines before and after the title.

Figure 24-7: A sample document title with a border and shading.

2. **Choose Format⇨Borders and Shading.**

   The Paragraph Borders and Shading dialog box appears, but . . .

3. **Make sure that the Shading panel is up front.**

   Click the Shading tab with your mouse if it's not. The Shading panel jumps to the front, as shown in Figure 24-8.

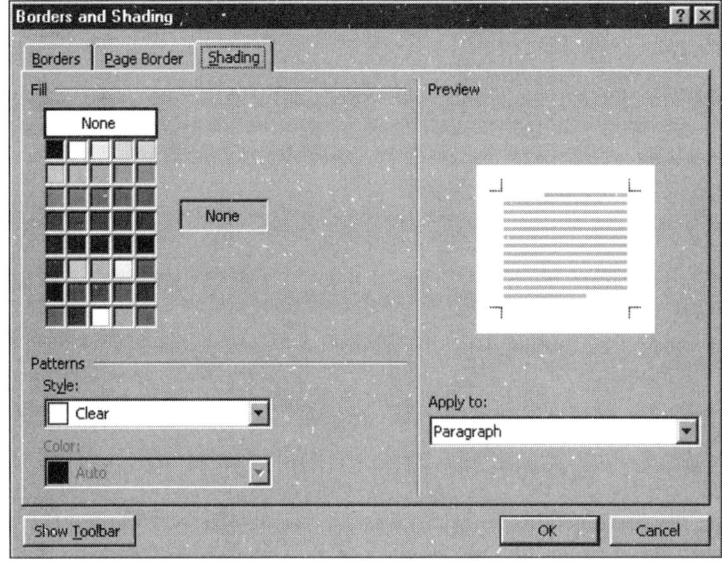

Figure 24-8: The Shading panel in the Borders and Shading dialog box.

4. **Select a shading from the Style drop-down list.**

   Shading patterns (in percentages of black) vary from 5 percent to 95 percent (including clear and solid). A value of 50 percent is equal parts black and white — solid gray. The 95 percent value is almost solid black. Other patterns appear at the end of the list, but you don't care about them.

The best values to select for shading your text are 10 percent, 20 percent, or 30 percent. I prefer 20 percent because it prints on my laser printer — not too dark to overpower the title text but still dark enough to see that it's the all-important shading that's so hard to do in other word processors.

6. **Click OK.**

   Your text appears shaded on-screen. Everyone will wonder how you did it.

- Nope, just because you visited the Border dialog box doesn't mean that you have to put a border around your text.
- If the shading stinks (and we're all allowed a little latitude for screwing up here), you can remove it. Just follow the steps outlined previously, but select None in the Shading panel in Step 5.
- At the bottom of the list of styles, you can find some shading patterns as well. Choose something to match the drapes.
- Shaded titles look best when they're at the top of your first page — not on a page by themselves.

Printing white on black

After shading, the next most fun thing to do is print white text on a black background. This is a very bold move and stands out prominently in your text — like being hit in the face with a cinder block. So don't use this technique casually.

This section for telepath seating only.

To produce white-on-black text, you must do two things. First, you must create a black background; and second, you must create white-colored text. Here is how you create a black background:

1. **Mark your text as a block.**

   It's best to start with text you've already written. At some point here, you will have black text on a black background, which you cannot see. If you already have the text written, it is easier to see after you're done. (See Chapter 6 for block-marking instructions.)

2. **Choose Format⇨Borders and Shading.**

   The Paragraph Borders and Shading dialog box appears.

3. **Making sure that the Shading panel is forward.**

   Click the Shading tab if it's not. The Shading dialog card reshuffles itself to the top of the pile.

4. **Click the black square in the upper-left part of the Fill area.**

   That's the first square in the first column; you can see the word Black appear in the box to the right of the color grid.

5. **Click OK to exit the Borders and Shading dialog box.**

Now you don't see anything on-screen because you have black text on a black background. (Actually, with the block highlighted, you see what looks like a large white block floating over a black block. Don't freak!)

With the block of text still highlighted, you need to change the text color to white. This step is done by using the Text color tool on the formatting toolbar.

1. **Click the Font Color tool on the toolbar.**

   A drop-down menu appears.

2. **Make sure that the Font panel is up front.**

   Click the Font tab if it's not.

3. **Look for the Color drop-down list in the dialog box, just above dead-center.**

4. **Click the down-arrow by the Color drop-down list.**

   You see a bunch of colors displayed.

5. **Select White from the list.**

   This is the color you want; white text over the black background you already created.

6. **Click OK.**

   You can now unhighlight your block. The text appears on-screen and printed in *inverse* white letters on a black background.

- Yes, although I said you can't print in color in Chapter 9, you can print with white text on a black background.
- I don't recommend reversing vast stretches of text. White text on a black background prints poorly on most computer printers. This stuff is best used for titles or to highlight smaller blocks of text.
- You cannot highlight a word or part of a paragraph with white text on a black background. The black background can be applied only to an entire paragraph.
- When you highlight a block of white text on a black background, it appears on-screen normally. That is, the reversed text appears inverted — or black on white — when you mark it as a block. This can really goof you up, so just try not to go mental when you highlight reversed text.

- You can use the white-on-black text sample you created to make a white-on-black *style* in Word. Highlight that text; then press Ctrl+Shift+S. In the Style box, type **Inverse** or some other appropriate name for the style. Press Enter, and you've added that style to your document. Refer to Chapter 15 for more information on styles.

Part V
Strange Things Living Under the Hood

"GENTLEMEN, I SAY RATHER THAN FIX THE 'BUGS', WE CHANGE THE DOCUMENTATION AND CALL THEM 'FEATURES'."

In this part . . .

There is no such thing as "just a word processor" any more. Word processing involves more than just words. It's graphics. It's formatting. It's columns and tables. It's a whole lotta weird and strange stuff that you may not ever use but they toss in there anyway. And with every new version of Word, they toss more and more weird stuff into the pot. You would think a good chef would limit his ingredients. But no. In the kitchen of Word, there are huge pots, and loads of new stuff regularly gets dumped into them every day. *M'on back!*

I'm not condemning everything. Obviously, the stuff covered in this part of the book has its own charm or virtue. Your Office Assistant and Help system are useful. And I use the outlining function all the time. The truly bad and ugly stuff you can read about in Chapter 35, "Ten Features You Don't Use but Paid for Anyway." The stuff here may be strange and obtuse, but you may wind up using it, or at least wanting to know about it, at some point in time.

Chapter 25

Your Annoying Little Assistant

In This Chapter

- Activating your little helper dude
- Asking your Assistant for help
- Changing your Assistant
- Animating your Assistant
- Using Word's Help system
- Using context-sensitive help

Everyone needs a little help now and then. With computer programs, the emphasis is on "a little" because what help they do offer isn't much and is often only helpful to the people who wrote the program and not the people who use it. Still, software developers feel compelled to add "help" features to their programs. In fact, the recent trend is to move all the stuff that used to be in the manual into a help feature. Not that doing so makes the information more lucid; it's just more accessible.

Word has lots of help available for you. Nothing you find in Word will help you as much as this book does, though. Although this book concentrates on the things you do, Word's Help is more of a list or documentation of what the program does. And then there's the Office Assistant, the latest trend in computers trying to be helpful. Honestly, until the thing grows arms and reaches around to scratch your back, I'll take a good book on the subject any day.

Little Helper Dude

When you first start Word, a little window appears containing the Microsoft Office Assistant (see Figure 25-1). Don't get excited. It's not a robot. It's not like having a real expert. Instead, the little helper dude is there as a way to get help in Word. Oh, and the Assistant can be amusing or annoying depending on how much of a deadline you're on.

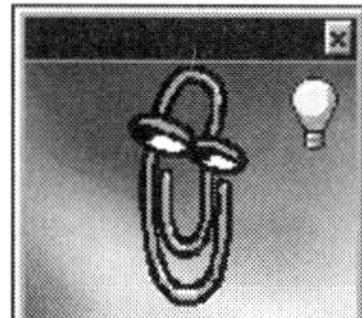

Figure 25-1: The paper clip helper dude.

Optional history of your annoying Assistant

Microsoft strives to make its programs lucid and useful. At least, they say they do. To help them out, they occasionally bring in real people to test-drive software and offer suggestions. In one such situation, the real human test-driving the program saw a little animated dog appear and tell him what to do next. The human was impressed and wanted the dog around all the time to tell him what to do. And thus begat Bob.

Bob was a Microsoft program designed to make using Windows easier. (And Windows was designed to make using DOS easier.) Bob was a basic set of computer programs with an animated character who sat in the lower part of your screen and told you how to do things. The idea sounds great, but it had two important flaws that led to its failure (besides the fact that it was overpriced and required too much computing horsepower to run).

The first flaw with Bob was that the program assumed that you are stupid. You're not. Computers may intimidate you, and they definitely frustrate you. But you know what it is you want to do, you just don't know how to tell the computer to do the job. Having a program that treats you like a kindergartner doesn't help any.

The second flaw with Bob was the little animated dog — which could also be any of a number of animated characters, including Bob himself. While it's nice to get advice about using a computer, it's downright rude to have the computer itself giving you the advice. What you need is a *human* voice, either right next to you or in a book like this, but not the computer itself. Having the computer itself help you out is like playing poker against someone who's beating you and also offering suggestions on how you can play better. (Why Microsoft never picked up on that I'll never know.)

Now even though Bob was a failure, Microsoft wasn't going to let all that Bob technology go to waste. Digging through the messy leftover Bob pulp, they rescued the little Assistants and tossed them into Microsoft Office 97, of which Word is a part. So there you have the reasons behind the annoying little Assistant. Whether you want to use him or not is still up to you.

If you don't see your annoying little Assistant, click the Office Assistant button on the toolbar. The Assistant appears and asks a question, something like Figure 25-2. You can type a question if you want or press the Esc key to get back to your writing.

Figure 25-2: The Assistant asks what you would like to do.

To make your Assistant go away, click the X button in his window's upper-right corner. Mr. Paper Clip dances a jig and then vanishes back into the toolbar. Good-bye and good riddance.

- After you turn the Assistant off, he'll stay off until you turn him on again.
- Turning the Assistant off in Word also turns him off in all your other Microsoft Office applications. Likewise, turning him on in another Office program turns him on again in Word.
- The Assistant may do strange and different things while you're working. He usually does something unique when you print, save, or other standard Wordy things.
- The dog Assistant (Power Pup) has the cutest animation while he's printing. See "Changing your Assistant" below for more information on choosing another Assistant, like the dog.

- When the Assistant is visible, it asks you most of the questions that would otherwise appear in a dialog box. For example, if you try to close a document without saving, it's the Assistant who asks if you want to save the document. (When the Assistant has been banished, you see a similar warning but in a dialog box.)
- After a period of non-use, the Assistant withers into a smaller box. This response is normal. Don't think he's dying on you or anything.
- You can change the Assistant's window size, from smaller to larger. Just point the mouse at one of the window's corners and drag it in or out. Unfortunately, the window only comes in two sizes. You can't make it really huge in an attempt to scare your cat.
- I refer to all the Assistants as "him," which doesn't accurately reflect the Assistant's true sex, but it's the proper pronoun for English.

- Normally, the Assistant gets out of the way if his window covers the part of your document you're working on. If not, click once on the Assistant and click the Options button. In the Office Assistant dialog box, click the Move when in the way check box (to put a check there) and then click OK.

Asking your Assistant for help

There are two ways to squeeze information from the Assistant, neither of which involves a rubber hose or magnets. The first way is to click him once. This method displays a cartoon bubble full of suggestions plus a box for you to type a question (refer to Figure 25-2). For example, you could type **How do I adjust my margins?**, press the Enter key, and the Assistant displays a list of options.

The second way to get help from the Assistant, especially in a dialog box, is to press the F1 key. This key displays the Assistant along with a cartoon bubble full of items relating to the dialog box or whatever area of Word you're working in.

- The F1 key is Word's Help key.
- Peruse the list of options displayed in the cartoon bubble. When you find one you like, click its little blue button. That action displays more information, tips, or general help. Refer to later sections in this chapter about Word's Help system for additional information.

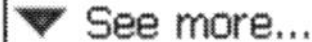

- If you see the `See more` item, click it to see more options.
- If you don't find what you're looking for, or you're suddenly hit by lightning and know the answer through divine intervention, click the Close button. That closes the cartoon bubble, but does not (as logic would imply) close your Assistant's window.

How about a tip?

To see if your Assistant is truly bursting with information, ask him for a handy tip. Okay, so the tip may not be so handy. Anyway, just click your Assistant's window and click the Tips button from the cartoon bubble. A useful, sometimes relevant, tip appears on the screen, similar to what you see in Figure 25-3.

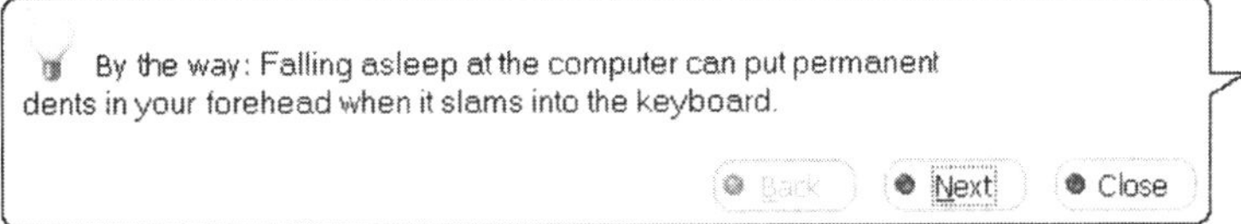

Figure 25-3: Word imparts some of its wisdom.

You can click the Next or Back buttons to get more tips. Click the Close button when you tire of the knowledge nugget and get back to work.

Changing your Assistant

Welcome to the Bob leftovers (refer to the sidebar "Optional history of your annoying Assistant"). Microsoft Office comes with a tiny army of Assistants for you to choose from. Each one looks different, sings a different tune, and does a different dance. Other than that, they all perform the same job. When the paper clip doesn't thrill, you can activate one of his siblings by taking the following steps.

1. **Right-click your mouse on the Assistant.**

   A shortcut menu appears, as shown in Figure 25-4.

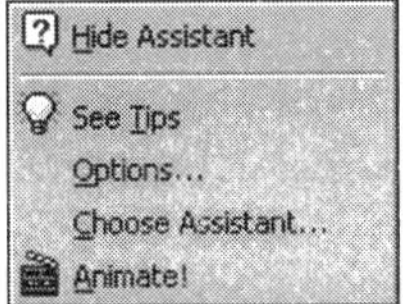

Figure 25-4: Your Assistant's shortcut menu.

   Refer to the section "Little Helper Dude" earlier in this chapter if you don't see your Assistant.

   A right-click is when you click the mouse's right button, the one you don't normally click. This is a common Windows 95 thing, so get used to it.

2. **Click the Choose Assistant item.**

   The Clippit Office Assistant dialog box appears with the Gallery panel up front. Here is where you find out that the paper clip Assistant's real name is "Clippit" — like a combination of "clap it shut" and "stop it."

3. **Click the Next> button to tour the rogues gallery of office Assistants.**

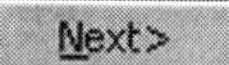

   Keep clicking the Next> button, or press Alt+N, until you find an Assistant that pleases you. I won't draw any connections here between choosing an Assistant and mail-order brides.

4. **After you find the Assistant you want, click the OK button.**

   That Assistant becomes your new leach — I mean, uh, personal helper — from then on.

- Some Assistants are more animated and colorful than others.
- Whenever you change your Assistant in Word, you change him for all your Microsoft Office programs. Likewise, changing the Assistant in Excel also changes him in Word. It's a group-happy thing.
- My favorite Assistant is the Genius, a.k.a. Einstein. Nice animation, but he makes very annoying sounds, so I had to turn him off.
- The dog is pretty funny.
- The stupidest Assistant has to be Office Logo. I also hate the Mother Nature one.
- It wouldn't surprise me if Microsoft adds or removes Assistants in the future, so you may find some new ones, favorites and stupids, in later releases of Word.

- By the way, if you detest your Assistant's noise-making, click him once and click the Options button. In the Options panel of the Office Assistant dialog box, click the Make sounds check box to remove the check mark, and then click OK.

Wasting time with your Assistant

In the several months I've been using this latest version of Word, I have put my Assistant through a lot of torture. There is really little you can do to make him suffer, though. On the other hand, he is capable of some tricks. No, I'm not talking about the random things the Assistant may do while you're working (which is annoying enough). I'm talking about *ordering* him to be goofy. Here's how:

1. **Right-click your mouse on the Assistant.**

   This step summons his shortcut menu, as shown in Figure 25-4.

2. **Choose Animate.**

   Your annoying little Assistant does something. It may be something big (such as Einstein warping into the next dimension), or it may be something brief and silly (such as Einstein ordering the perfect glass of wine to go with his veal medallions, shown in Figure 25-5).

Figure 25-5: The Office Assistant doing something goofy.

3. **Keep repeating Steps 1 and 2 until you're no longer bored.**

   Each Assistant has a wealth of animated goodies. Keep selecting the Animate option from his shortcut menu until you've seen them all.

4. **Get back to work.**

Getting Help in Word

After your annoying Assistant, your next line of defense in Word's help battle is the Help system itself. This feature is actually a part of Windows more than a part of Word; like Windows itself and all Windows programs, Word sports a "Help system," which is a little program designed to toss methods and documentation at you as if you're a monkey in a psychology experiment yearning for another M&M.

Seriously, help is available in Word. In the old days, help was the stuff they used to print in a manual. Today, helpful information is in the computer and comes out in text of various colors and sizes with weird doodads that the following sections all carefully try to explain.

The Help menu (won't really help you)

If you click Help on the menu bar, you open the Word Help menu. Alas, if you're looking for real help, you're not going to find it here.

The first item in the Help menu, Microsoft Word Help, merely activates your annoying little Assistant (see the first half of this chapter).

The second item in the Help menu, Contents and Index, is what actually starts the Help system, which is covered in the next section.

If you're a former WordPerfect user, you can try to take a stab at the WordPerfect Help item. Of course, I have no idea what it's doing here; if you were once a WordPerfect user you probably need more help with Word than you do with WordPerfect. I mean, some people . . . .

The Word Help system

If you want to use the Word Help system itself, as opposed to typing angrily at your annoying little Assistant, you need to choose Help⇨Contents and Index from the menu. This displays the Help Topics: Microsoft Word dialog box, as shown in Figure 25-6.

Figure 25-6: The Word Help Topics dialog box.

The Help Contents panel basically shows you what would have (should have) been the Word manual. Topics are displayed like chapters in a book; double-click one of the li'l book icons to open that chapter and see the document — or even more chapters — nestled inside. Some of the information actually borders on being useful.

The index panel contains an alphabetical list of topics related to Word. To see this panel, click the Index tab. You can search through the list of topics alphabetically, or type whatever you're interested in to move through the list a tad bit more swiftly. Personally, I prefer this method because it gets me right to where I want to go.

- After selecting a topic from the index panel, you'll probably see another dialog box with even more choices; select the one that best applies to whatever it is you need help with.
- Ignore the Find panel. It's not worth the trouble.

- After you're done with Help, you must close its window. Click the Close button in the Help window's upper-right corner.

Help system tips

The Help system is really a collection of different methods for showing you how to do things. Most good books on Windows can tell you how it works. Here are some highlights:

- Click the mouse on text with a green, dotted underline to see a pop-up help bubble explaining the term or offering more information. The mouse pointer changes to a pointy-hand whenever you hover it over this type of text.
- Occasionally, Word may show you a large image, such as the one in Figure 25-7. The image shows you a bunch of stuff you can do in Word. Just click part of the image or one of the captions for more information.

- Some items in the Help system may have a little How button by them (see the margin). Click this button to have Word show you additional information or steps required to accomplish some task or ritual.
- Another type of button you may find is the Show Me button. Clicking this little goober actually carries out the task being described (choosing a menu item, picking an option in a dialog box, or whatever).
- To review the various places you've been in the Help system, click the Back button on the Help system's window.

- If you want a printed copy of the Help system's instructions, click the Options button in the Help system window and choose the Print Topic item. Click OK in the Print dialog box to print your help topic.

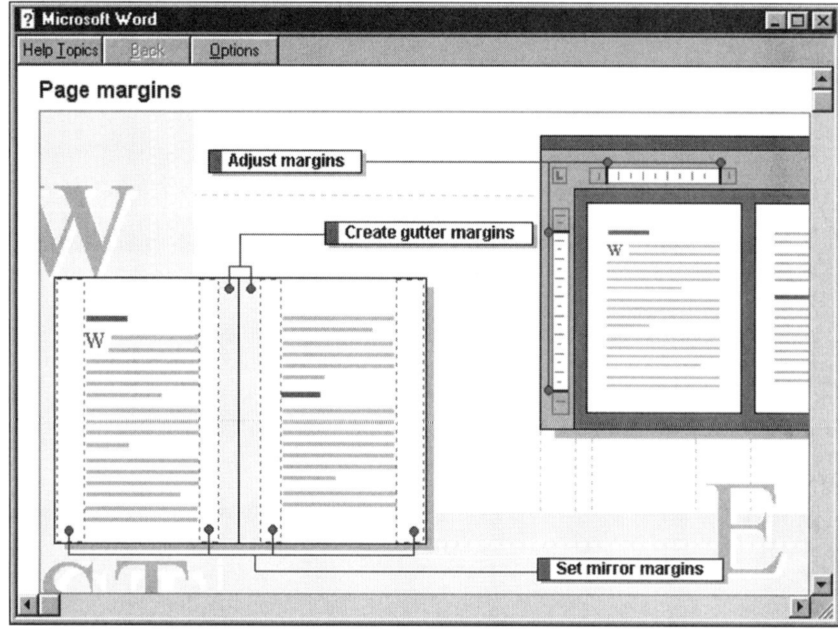

Figure 25-7: Word showing you what's what for page margins.

The joys of context-sensitive help

Word can give you help with what you're doing when you're doing it. So if you're mired deep in a nest of nasty dialog boxes, you can easily find out what's what by activating context-sensitive help. This step even works if you're not mired in a nest of nasty dialog boxes.

To get context-sensitive help in a dialog box, click the little question-mark button in the upper-right corner of the dialog box window. The mouse pointer changes into a question mark/arrow thing. Point and shoot for help.

Likewise, when you're not in a dialog box, you can use the Shift + F1 key combination. That, too, changes the mouse pointer into a question mark/arrow thing for context-sensitive help. Just point and shoot. For example, point the arrow at the scissors on the toolbar and click the mouse. You find out that the scissors are used to cut text, not to give you a haircut.

- For a briefer, more simplistic, and generally less helpful explanation of what some of the doodads on-screen do, hover the mouse pointer over the icon in question. In a moment, a cryptic couple of words appear, which unfortunately tell you only what the button or tool is and not what it does.

- If the computer rudely beeps at you when you click, assume that no help is available for that item.
- Yet another way to get help on something in a dialog box is to right-click the mouse on it. This typically displays a pop-up box telling you what it is you're pointing at and how it works.
- Press the Escape key to change the mouse pointer back to normal if you don't really need context-sensitive help.

Chapter 26

Extra Special Typing Tricks

In This Chapter

- Inserting oddball and, er, special characters
- Typing foreign characters
- Discovering AutoText
- Using AutoText
- Creating an AutoText entry
- Editing AutoText entries
- Deleting AutoText entries

Having a word processor makes writing — actually *composing* documents — easier. No argument. But one thing they haven't improved upon is the drudgery of typing. Even though you may have the fastest computer running the best word processing software in the history of the universe, you still type at your keyboard the same way they did in the 1920s.

Rather than wait for Oprah to do a special on Poor Slobs Who Own Pentium 5000s and Hate to Type, you can put Word to work making things easier for you. This can happen in one of two ways. First, you can use Word to easily type special and weird symbols — characters even Superman's X-ray vision doesn't see on the keyboard. Second, you can use the power of AutoText to have Word automatically type common phrases for you. Both of these quantum leaps in typing technology are thoroughly discussed in this handy chapter (which took me only three key presses on my keyboard to create).

Inserting Oddball and Special Characters

Look over your keyboard's keys. Yeah, it has the letters of the alphabet plus numbers and some weird symbols. Word can display all those characters just fine; you see them on your screen every day.

But there are several dozen to several hundred additional, interesting characters you can stick into your document as well. No, I'm not talking about creative writing and adding dotty Aunt Doris in the middle of Chapter 6. No, these oddball characters are things you can't type at the keyboard. Word lets you insert them into your document by using the Insert➪Symbol command. Here's how you work it:

1. **Position the toothpick cursor where you want the oddball character to appear.**
2. **Choose the Insert➪Symbol command.**

   Use the mouse or press Alt,I,S. You see the Symbol dialog box, as shown in Figure 26-1. (If the Special Characters panel appears, click the Symbols tab with the mouse.)

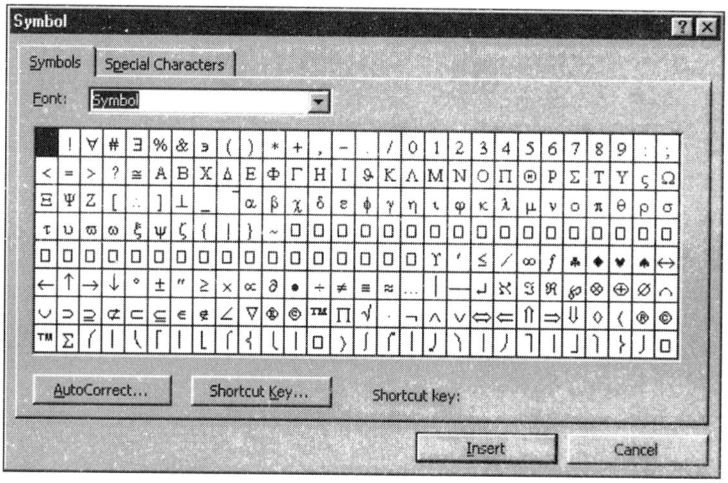

Figure 26-1: The Symbol dialog box.

3. **Choose the symbol you want.**

   Point the mouse at the symbol that interests you and then double-click that character. Or you can press the cursor keys to move a highlight box around and then press Enter.
4. **The oddball character is inserted into your text.**

   Well, I'll be @#$%&ed!

Here are some tips for inserting special characters:

- ✓ To get a good look at a particular symbol, point the mouse cursor at it and press and hold the mouse button. That one symbol is magnified.
- ✓ Just about any installed font containing symbols appears in the drop-down list at the top of the Symbol dialog box. To look at other symbols, click the down-arrow next to the Font box and select a different symbol set by clicking its name. The best symbols can be found in the various Wingdings fonts.

Assigning a shortcut key to the symbols you love most

If you see a symbol you like in the Symbol dialog box, you can assign a shortcut key to it. This step gives that weird symbol, which you would otherwise be unable to type at the keyboard, a special key combination you can, well, type at the keyboard.

For example, I assigned the shortcut key Ctrl+; (Ctrl and the semicolon key) to the check mark symbol because I use the ✓ a lot in my writing. Here's how you could do the same:

1. **Summon the Symbol dialog box.**

   Choose the Insert⇨Symbol command or press Alt, I, S. The Symbol dialog box appears (see Figure 26-1).

2. **Find the symbol you love best.**

   Refer to the preceding section.

   Remember that you can choose special symbols from other fonts as well. Click the down-arrow by the Font drop-down list to see the lot of 'em.

3. **Click the symbol once with your mouse.**

4. **Click the Shortcut Key button.**

   A Customize Keyboard dialog box appears. Don't mess with anything here, just . . .

5. **Press the key combination you want to assign to that key.**

   You need to be clever here. I can promise you that all the Ctrl and Alt key combinations are already used by Word. You need to use a Ctrl+Shift or Alt+Shift key in combination with some other key on the keyboard.

   After pressing your key combination, you see it displayed in the Press new shortcut key box. Immediately, look below that box to see if any other command is using that key combination.

For example, if I use Ctrl+` (the accent grave, above the Tab key) combination, the Press new shortcut key box displays `Ctrl+'`. But below that, Word tells me that the shortcut is already assigned to the `[prefix key]`. But if I press Alt+‘, Word tells me that the key combo is `[unassigned]` and okay to use.

6. **Click the Assign button after you find the right key combination.**

Now you can use that key combination as a shortcut for the special symbol in your document.

Be sure to read the next section before you go nuts with assigning shortcut keys to symbols when they may already have them.

Be careful when assigning new shortcut keys! Do not reassign a key combination that's already used in Word. If you do, you have to contact a Word expert to assign the key combination back. Keep in mind that nearly all the simple key combinations — anything with Ctrl or Alt plus a letter or number — is probably used by Word somehow.

Some special characters you may need from time to time

Peeking out from behind the Symbol dialog box is the Special Characters panel. This side of the Symbol dialog box contains some common symbols you may want to use in your Word documents, more of the kind of stuff an English teacher might use (as opposed to a cursing cartoon character).

The Special Characters panel is used the same way as the Symbol dialog box: Click the Special Characters tab and then find the symbol you want. Or, if you can remember such things and have long, spindly fingers, refer to each character's special key combination. Some of the more common ones are shown in Table 26-1.

Table 26-1 Special Symbols and Their Shortcut Keys

Key Combination	*Weird Thing That Appears*
Alt+Ctrl+- (minus key)	— (em dash)
Ctrl+_	Non-breaking hyphen
Ctrl+Shift+spacebar	Non-breaking space
Alt+Ctrl+C	©
Alt+Ctrl+R	®
Alt+Ctrl+T	™

- Use an em dash in place of a double hyphen. Press Alt+Ctrl and the minus key next to your keyboard's numeric keypad.
- The non-breaking hyphen (Ctrl+_, which is the underline character, not the hyphen) can be used when you don't want Word to wrap something like a phone number or a part number from a catalog.
- Use a non-breaking space (Ctrl+Shift+spacebar) when you don't want two words split between two lines.

- The Wordmeisters at Microsoft have also added some symbols to AutoCorrect's repertoire. For example, you can type **:-)** (a happy face) and Word magically transforms it into the little smiley symbol, ☺. Refer to Chapter 7 for more information on AutoCorrect.

Weirdo foreign characters you can type

In addition to the shortcut keys shown in Table 26-1, there are also special key combinations you can use to insert foreign characters into your document. No, I'm not talking about Andre the large Albanian who is probably a spy. I'm talking accented vowels and letters of the alphabet. For example, if you ever have to type the following:

```
En bök for oss vanliga användare!
```

you merely need to know how to use Word's special *prefix keys.*

A prefix key is a key combination you press *before* pressing a regular key on the keyboard. The end result is an accented character. For example, Ctrl+Shift+: (colon) is the prefix key used to get the ü character that appears in so many German films. Other prefix keys are listed in Table 26-2.

Table 26-2 Prefix Keys and Foreign Characters

Prefix Key	*Characters Affected*	*Results*
Ctrl+' (apostrophe)	a, e, i, o, u, d, A, E, I, O, U, D	á, é, í, ó, ú, ∂, Á, É, Í, Ó, Ú, Đ
Ctrl+` (accent grave)	a, e, i, o, u, A, E, I, O, U	à, è, ì, ò, ù, À, È, Ì, Ò, Ù
Ctrl+Shift+: (colon)	a, e, i, o, u, y, A, E, I, O, U, Y	ä, ë, ï, ö, ü, ÿ, Ä, Ë, Ï, Ö, Ü, Ÿ
Ctrl+Shift+^ (caret)	a, e, i, o, u, A, E, I, O, U	â, ê, î, ô, û, Â, Ê, Î, Ô, Û
Ctrl+Shift+~ (tilde)	a, n, o A, N, O	ã, ñ, õ, Ã, Ñ, Õ
Ctrl+Shift+&	a, o, s, A, O	æ, œ, ß, Æ, Œ
Ctrl+Shift+@	a, A	å, Å
Ctrl+, (comma)	c, C	ç, Ç
Ctrl+/	o, O	ø, Ø

To use a prefix key, follow these steps:

1. **Discover which character you yearn to insert into your document.**

   Say you wish to type the ever-popular French word voilà into your document. It's not voila, it's *voilà* with a left-slant over the A.

2. **Type the proper prefix key *before* typing the vowel.**

   For the A in voilà, it's the accent grave thing (in the upper-left part of your keyboard). Type Ctrl+\` .

3. **Type the vowel or character to be modified.**

   Type the A in voilà. The prefix character forces Word to insert the proper foreign dinglenob, and you're set.

4. **Continue typing and using the prefix keys as necessary.**

   Do this until you tire of typing foreign words, though they really do look impressive and could mean anything to anyone who doesn't speak that language.

- Don't confuse the Ctrl+\` and Ctrl+' prefix keys. The first one is the accent grave — the backwards apostrophe — found above the Tab key on your keyboard. The second one is the apostrophe key, which adds a right-leaning slant thing above the vowels.
- Ctrl+Shift+^ is the same as Ctrl+Shift+6 on your keyboard.
- The ~ (tilde) key is found above the Tab key on your keyboard, the same key as the accent grave.
- If you need wacky inverse punctuation on your foreign typing, try these combos:

  Alt+Ctrl+Shift+? is the upside-down question mark, ¿

  Alt+Ctrl+Shift+1 is the upside-down exclamation point, ¡

- You must type a little s to get the German ß symbol; it's Ctrl+Shift+&, s.

- If you plan on doing any extensive typing in a foreign language, look into switching Windows' keyboard layout. This switch gives you easier access to those foreign characters used most in a particular language, without having to remember these weirdo prefix keys. Consult your favorite book on Windows for the how-tos.

All about AutoText (Required Reading If You Haven't a Clue)

AutoText is a shortcut. Word can automatically type text for you when you give it only a teensy-tiny hint of what you want. It's like expanding a balloon but without the huffing and puffing. You type **balloon**, tap Word's AutoText magic wand, and the word *balloon* is expanded into something like "a bag of stretchy stuff filled with hot air. . . ."

The idea behind AutoText is this: To make the typing job easier, Word lets you type shortcuts that can be expanded into longer text. That's all it is. That, and being incredibly handy when you have the same thing — or something complex — to type again and again.

This list shows you some tips for using AutoText:

- You must create an AutoText *entry* before you can use the AutoText command. Word has created a bunch of these for you, but you can also create new ones on your own.
- The AutoText entry is nothing more than a bunch of text, a *boilerplate* if you know what I mean. That text is assigned a special shortcut word by using the Insert⇨AutoText command. The details are outlined in the following sections.
- AutoText entries become a part of the document template. See Chapter 16 for more information on document templates.
- Word has already created some AutoText entries for you. You may see these cartoon bubbles appear as you type short words. The entries are annoying at first, but easily ignored.
- AutoText is not AutoCorrect. The latter swallows whole words and replaces them with correctly spelled alternatives. AutoText takes word fragments and expands them into longer phrases and paragraphs — all with a flick of your wrist.

AutoText in action

To put an AutoText entry in a document, follow these steps:

1. **Put the toothpick cursor where you want the AutoText entry to be placed.**
2. **Type the shortcut word.**

   You assign a shortcut word when you create an AutoText entry. If you haven't done so yet, type the following to see what I mean.

   ```
   To wh
   ```

After typing **To wh**, an AutoText bubble appears over your text, as shown in Figure 26-2. That's the *To Whom It May Concern* entry, which comes already created with Word. If you were using your own AutoText entry here, you would type in your own shortcut word.

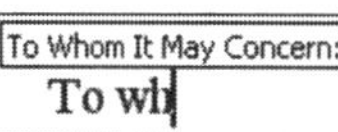

Figure 26-2: AutoText comes to the rescue (or annoys you).

3. **Press the Enter key.**

   The AutoText entry is slapped into the document and replaces the shortcut word. So *wh* is magically transformed into his full obnoxious name.

- If you don't want the AutoText entry inserted, just keep typing. Pressing any key except for Enter (or F3), tells AutoText to "go take a hike."
- Not all AutoText entries display a preview bubble. For some you must type the shortcut word and then press the F3 key to activate AutoText.
- If you press the F3 key and Word beeps at you, the toothpick cursor is not on an AutoText entry. Try moving the cursor back onto the word, or checking to make sure that you really typed an AutoText shortcut.

- F3 is the AutoText key — not that it makes any sense. That was just the next function key on the list when the Word programming staff showed up that morning.
- If you do continue with To Whom It May Concern, Word asks you if you need help creating a letter. Your annoying Assistant appears and asks you a few questions. See Chapter 25 for more information on your annoying little Assistant.

Creating an AutoText entry

To create an AutoText entry, follow these steps:

1. **Type some text you want to use as an AutoText entry.**

   For example, type your company name. I'll use the names Meshach, Shadrach, and Abednego, a famous law firm in early Babylon.

   Type the full text in its expanded glory, the exact way you want Word to automatically type it for you later.

2. **Mark the text as a block.**

   Refer to Chapter 6 for the full details on marking a block of text. Keep in mind that all the text you mark is included in the AutoText entry. This means don't include any extra spaces or periods unless you want them, really want them.

3. **Press the Alt+F3 key combination.**

   The Create AutoText dialog box opens, as shown in Figure 26-3.

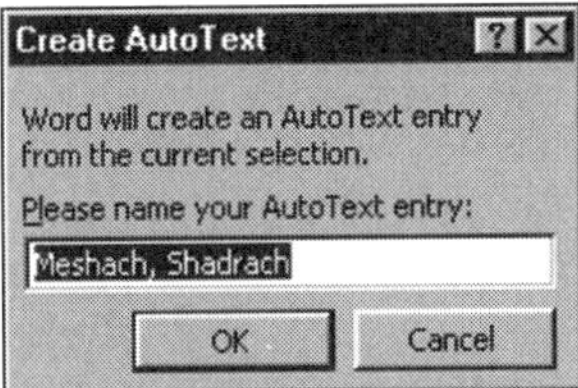

Figure 26-3: The Create AutoText dialog box.

4. **Give the AutoText entry a name.**

   Type the shortcut name, which can be very short. For example, for Meshach, Shadrach, and Abednego, you can type **mesh** in the dialog box.

   It's best if your shortcut is the first few letters of the longer phrase. If you type in some other shortcut name, the little AutoText cartoon bubble may not appear when you type the shortcut name in your document.

5. **Click OK.**

   You're done. The AutoText entry is now ready to be used, which is covered in the preceding section.

The shortcut word you type can be in upper- or lowercase. I usually keep everything in lowercase.

After you're done working on your document, Word asks whether you want to save the document and template changes; answer Yes to keep this AutoText entry you just created.

Changing AutoText text

Suppose that you create an AutoText entry (*me*) that has your name and address, just as you always type at the end of a letter. And though you hate messing with Word, one day you succumb to the idea of moving. You must update your *me* entry to reflect your new location. Here's how it's done:

1. **Put the toothpick cursor where you want the glossary entry to be placed.**

   You need to "go through the motions" here to make the operation run a bit smoother. Yes, this shortcut is not sanctioned in the manual. (But then again, that's why you're reading this book.)

2. **Type the shortcut word.**

   Do this just as though you were inserting the entry.

3. **Press the F3 key.**

   The AutoText entry is inserted into the document, at the place where the toothpick cursor is, to replace the shortcut word.

4. **Edit.**

   Make any changes you want to the AutoText entry just pasted into your document (type your new address, for example). After you're done, you re-save it by using the same name. The net effect here is that the original entry is changed, but the name is kept the same (to protect the guilty).

5. **Mark as a block on-screen the text you want included as the AutoText entry.**

6. **Press Alt+F3.**

   This is the AutoText shortcut, which is a lot easier than wasting mouse energy molecules getting back into the dialog box.

7. **Type the *same name* for the entry.**

   Such as *me*.

8. **Click OK.**

   You are asked whether you want to redefine the AutoText entry.

9. **Click Yes.**

   You're done. The entry has been edited in an underhanded but perfectly legal manner.

Deleting AutoText entries

Due to a nuclear accident, you suddenly grow eight more fingers on each hand. Suddenly, typing becomes a breeze (though you really do miss your hair). In that case, you may never have to use AutoText again, so you decide to remove a few entries. Here's how:

1. **Choose Insert⇨AutoText⇨AutoText.**

Your bony hands easily enable you to use the keyboard shortcut Alt, I, A, X. The AutoCorrect dialog box opens, AutoText panel forward, which lists all glossary entries (see Figure 26-4).

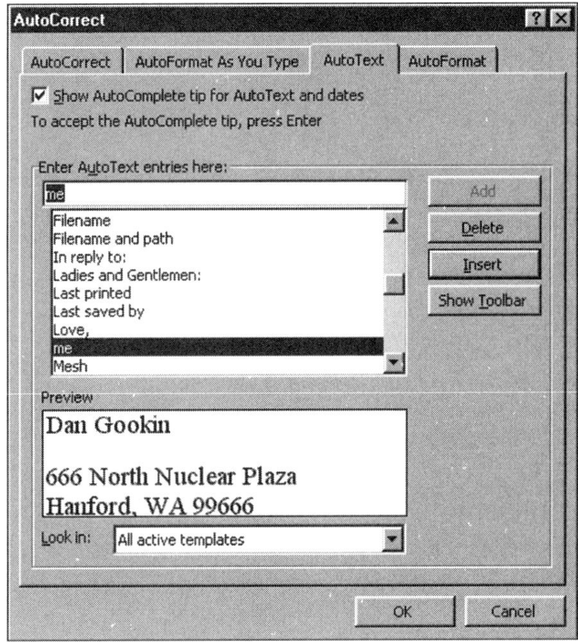

Figure 26-4: The AutoText panel lurks in the AutoCorrect dialog box.

2. **Click the name of the entry you want to delete.**

   Bye old me!

3. **Click the Delete button.**

   The AutoText entry's name is *removed* from the list.

4. **Click Close.**

   You continue typing away using only one hand, and, with the other hand, you merrily play the Hungarian Rhapsody on a nearby clavichord. That pain in your forehead is probably a third eye trying to poke through. Ah, the joys of nuclear contamination . . . .

Chapter 27

Let's Work This Out Together

In This Chapter

- Tracking changes as a document is edited
- Comparing two documents for changes
- Reviewing changes
- Sticking stick-on notes in a document
- Highlighting your text
- Un-highlighting your text

For me, writing is a solitary art. Sure, I've collaborated with others over the years, but it wasn't like both of us were sitting at the same computer, fighting over whose thumb got to whack the spacebar. In those instances, my fellow authors and I usually rely upon some of Word's cooperative tools to help us communicate. These are sneaky things authors can do to the text that the reader never sees. Without them, you'd often find things like the following in your reading materials:

```
Michael: Will Dr. Malcom ever finish his thoughts or shall
he always be interrupted?
```

But — aha! — with Word's Let's-work-this-out-together commands, you and all of China could write something, and no reader would be the wiser.

Sharing Work with Revision Marks

Every writer jealously guards his text. It's enough that someone must edit, some lowly editor who seethes with jealously over the fact that the noble writer is the one who gets all the fame and glory even though it's the editor who deserves the credit. Oh, editors can be nasty. [Hey! — Ed.] But other writers can be worse.

To help protect yourself against evil intrusion of your work by others, or just to see who's responsible for adding something stupid to a document, you can use one of Word's many revision tracking tools. The following sections outline two ways you can put them to use.

- You can either view the changes as you make them or compare an older version of a saved document with a newer version.
- Word shows what text has been changed right on the screen, usually in a different text color.
- Deleted text is shown crossed-out, ~~like this~~.
- New text appears underlined, <u>like this</u>.
- Figure 27-1 shows changed text on the screen if you need to see an example. To help you better find the changes, a line appears in the left margin next to the changed text.

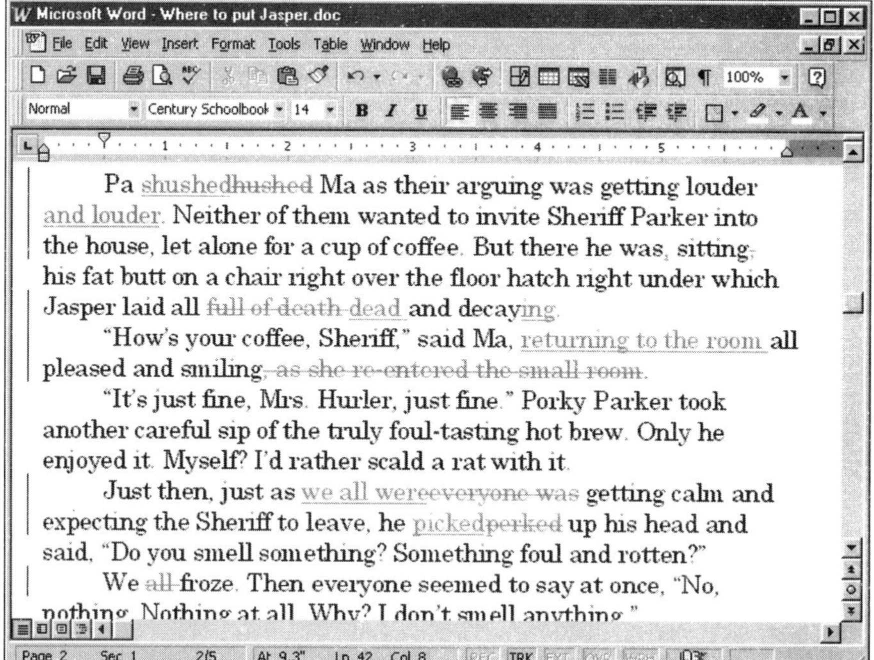

Figure 27-1: A document with changes-as-you-go.

Tracking changes as you make them

To visually keep track of any modifications you make to a document, follow these steps:

1. **Open the document you want to edit.**

   Refer to Chapter 8 for more information on opening documents. Opening the document as your first step is the best way to ensure that you track all the changes.

2. **Choose Tools⇨Track Changes⇨Highlight Changes from the menu.**

   The Highlight Changes dialog box appears (see Figure 27-2).

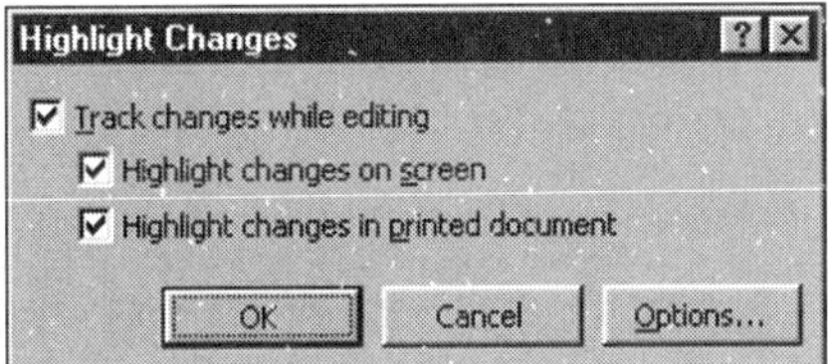

Figure 27-2: The Highlight Changes dialog box.

3. **Put a check mark in the Track changes while editing box.**

   Click the mouse in the box by Track changes while editing or press Alt+T. (You should also make sure that a check mark is in the box by Highlight changes on screen.)

4. **Click OK.**

   Word is now in change tracking mode.

- Different people reviewing your document leave different color revision marks. For example, if you send your document to Bill and then Diane, Bill's marks may show up in raging red and Diane's in logical lime.
- To see who made what corrections, just point the mouse over a bit of colored revision text. A cartoon bubble pops up explaining who made what change and when (as shown in Figure 27-3).
- After you're done editing or reviewing the changes, you can turn off the revision marks. To do this, choose Tools⇨Track Changes⇨Highlight Changes from the menu and click to remove the check mark by the Highlight changes on screen. Click OK to view your document in Normal mode.

Figure 27-3: Point the mouse at a revision to see who's responsible for it.

Dan Gookin, 10/7/96 11:34 AM:
Inserted
~~barfed~~ vomited

- After you're done marking up what was originally pretty good stuff, follow the preceding steps but remove the check mark by the Track changes while editing box.
- A quick shortcut for the preceding steps is to double-click the TRK thing on the status bar. When the TRK is bold, revision mark tracking is activated. If you double-click it again, you turn off the revision tracking.

Tracking changes between two versions of the same document

After the damage has already been done, you can review the cruel editing changes, deletions and general mayhem by comparing an edited document with the original. Unlike the on-the-fly revision marks made in the preceding section, this time you're comparing your original document with a fully edited copy. Here's how:

1. **Make sure that you have the edited document loaded and on the screen.**

   The original document should have been saved to disk. That's okay for now; you don't need to open it. Just open the edited document and have it on the screen in front of you. See Chapter 8 for more information on opening documents.

2. **Choose Tools⇨Track Changes⇨Compare Documents.**

   An Open dialog box appears, though it's named Select File to Compare With Current Document and not Open. Use your finely honed Open dialog box skills to locate the original document on disk.

3. **Click the Open button.**

   This step opens the modified version of your edited file.

   Word thinks long and hard.

4. **Peruse the changes.**

Eventually, you see the revision-marked-up result; the edited document on your screen is littered with revision marks, showing exactly what changes were made from the original. New text is underlined. Deleted text is crossed out (the strikethrough-text effect). Unchanged text remains the same. The edited result looks exactly like a document edited on-the-fly (see Figure 27-1), but here everything was done at once.

- You can continue to edit the document if you like. After all, it's your document.
- If you want to thumbs-up-or-down each revision, refer to the next section "Reviewing the changes."
- Revision marks can get in the way. To remove them, choose Tools⇨Track Changes⇨Highlight Changes and remove the check mark by the Highlight changes on screen option. Click OK.

Reviewing the changes

Don't plow on through a revised document, manually adding and subtracting things. Why not let Word do the work for you? This job is done by the Accept or Reject Changes dialog box, which lets you quickly browse through a document with revision marks to yeah-or-nay each little correction. Here's how:

1. **Move the toothpick cursor to the tippy top of your document. (Press Ctrl+Home.)**

   I'm assuming this is a document that has revision marks, otherwise this operation just won't work. Refer to the two previous sections for more information.

2. **Choose Tools⇨Track Changes⇨Accept or Reject Changes.**

   The Accept or Reject Change dialog box appears (Figure 27-4).

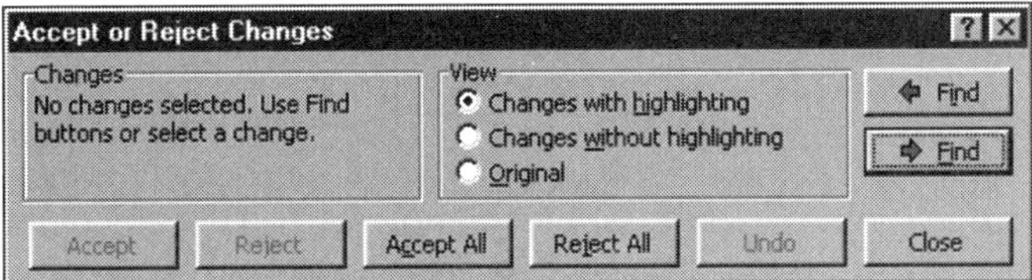

Figure 27-4: The Accept or Reject Change dialog box.

3. **Click the Find button.**

   Word ventures out into your document to find the next revision mark, which notes something that has been changed or added to your original document. Word stops at each deletion or addition, highlighting it for you on the screen.

4. **Click the Accept or Reject buttons.**

   Now pay attention:

   If you click Accept on a ~~strikethrough~~ word or phrase, you're telling Word to remove that phrase, to accept the edit or change from your original document.

   If you click Reject on a ~~strikethrough~~ word or phrase, you're telling Word to keep that phrase in your document.

   If you click Accept on an underlined word or phrase, you're telling Word to keep that addition to your original document.

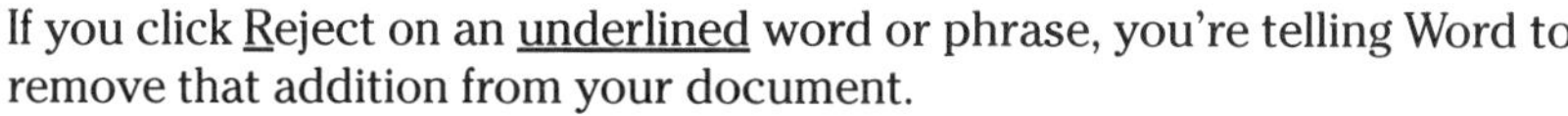

   If you click Reject on an underlined word or phrase, you're telling Word to remove that addition from your document.

   It works if you don't think of strikethrough and underline text together. Just look at each change and think Accept or Reject for each of them.

5. **Repeat Step 4 as necessary.**

   Or you can ignore the change and click the Find button to find the next instance.

   Click the Close button to make the Revisions dialog box revise itself outta here.

- If you goof, you can click the Undo button in the Accept or Reject Changes dialog box.
- You can click the Reject All button to do away with the all the revisions or corrections. I mean, *to hell with 'em!*
- Click the Accept All to keep all the changes at once. I mean, your editor *is* smarter than you are, and you should just blindly succumb to his superior knowledge.
- Going through this process removes all the revision marks from your document. If you want to re-review the revisions, you have to repeat the steps in the previous section for comparing two documents.

- Don't forget to save your revised text back to disk.

Stick-on Notes for Your Text

Revision marks are more of a way to track changes made to your document by evil people. Okay, maybe not evil, but people who change things without first making suggestions. If you're in a much more collaborative mood, or if you're reading someone else's work and you want to make a comment about it but don't want to make any changes, you can use a stick-on note.

Word's stick-on notes — or "comments" — are not the same as those stick-on notes you have stuck to your monitor like petals on a flower. Instead, they're pop-up notes you can stealthily insert into a document to tell someone else what you think, in a nice way of course. You can even make stick-on notes to yourself, because the notes don't print and sometimes you don't want "Pick up the kids at 3:30" to appear in the middle of a prospectus.

To stick a stick-on note into your document, follow these steps:

1. **Position the toothpick cursor where you want to annotate the text.**

   You can also select a block of text if your comment concerns some specific sentence or phrase.

2. **Choose Insert⇨Comment.**

   The screen instantly splits, just like you were writing a footnote (see Chapter 13). Your initials are inserted into the document, identifying you as the writer of the stick-on note.

3. **Type your comment.**

   Enter your comment in the lower portion of the screen, in the comments area. Type away!

4. **Click the Close button after you're done.**

   The annotation area disappears. The word the toothpick cursor was near in your document (or the selected block of text) becomes highlighted in yellow. That's your clue that a comment is there.

Repeat these steps to add more annotations to the text.

The beauty of all this is that the annotations remain mute until you want to see them. They don't print, and they show up on the screen as yellow text, which doesn't get in the way (much).

To read a stick-on note, just point (don't click) the mouse at it. The mouse cursor changes to the insertion pointer plus a little sort-of stick-on note thing (see the margin). Just hold the mouse still and the stick-on note pops up on the screen, similar to what you see in Figure 27-5. The name of the person who wrote the note appears above it, and then comes the note's contents.

Move the mouse away from the yellow text to make the stick-on note disappear.

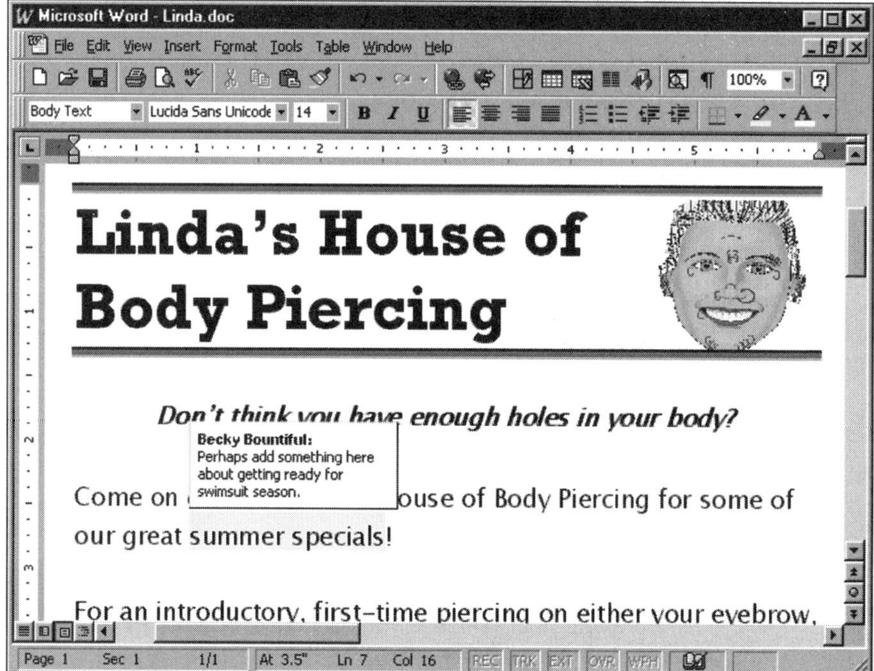

Figure 27-5: A pop-up note on the screen.

- If you want to see all the comments in a document at once, choose View⇨Comments from the menu. This action splits the screen (just like when you created the comments), but shows you every one of them. Jump around through your document by clicking the mouse on the initials that start each annotation. For example, click `[DG4]` to see which part of your text the fourth comment DG made pertains to.
- Obviously, if the Comments command in the View menu is dimmed, your document contains no comments. Whoopee!
- To edit a comment, right-click the mouse on the yellow text. From the shortcut menu that pops-up, choose Edit Comment. The screen splits, and the toothpick cursor hops on down to the comment area where you can edit the comment.
- To delete a comment, right-click the mouse on the yellow comment text and choose Delete Comment from the shortcut menu.
- Yes, the comments don't print — no way to get them to print, either. Unless, of course, you select Comments from the Print what part of the Print dialog box. But don't let me ever catch you doing that in real life.
- In older versions of Word, comments were called *annotations* — same thing, more expensive word.

- The little Tape Cassette button on the annotation area's split bar allows you to actually record comments in your text. Too many things can go wrong if you try, so I won't elaborate on it here.
- If you want to change your initials used in Word (and who doesn't), choose Tools⇨Options. The Options dialog box appears. Click the User Information tab to bring its panel forward. Type your new initials into the Initials box. Click OK.

Whipping Out the Yellow Highlighter

There's an old joke about computers that you can always tell when a so-and-so uses a word processor because there is White Out on the screen. Har, har.

There's no need to worry about smearing your monitor with White Out because Word erases text automatically. But one thing you are likely to goop the screen with is a yellow marking pen. I've been tempted to do this ever since I used to watch Hobo Kelly on TV and actually drew an umbrella for Mr. Wuzzle so he wouldn't get wet in the rain. With Word, however, you don't need to fear your father whomping you because you used an indelible pen on the new color TV.

Using the highlighter

To highlight your text (on-screen, electronically, of course), click the Highlight button on the formatting toolbar. Click!

Now you've entered Highlighting mode. The mouse pointer changes to something I can't describe verbally but can picture in the left margin. When you drag the mouse over your text, that text becomes highlighted — just like you can do with a highlighter on regular paper — amazing what those whiz kids at Microsoft can come up with. . . .

- To stop highlighting text, click the Highlight button again or press the Esc key.
- You can also highlight a block of text by first marking the block and then clicking the Highlight button. See Chapter 6 for all the proper block-marking instructions.
- The highlighted text prints, so be careful with it. If you don't have a color printer, highlighted text prints black on gray on your hard copy.
- See the next section for information on removing the highlight from your text.

- As with other tools described in this chapter, highlighting is great for sharing your work with others. Personally, I use it to mark text that needs fixing or something that may need my attention later on. Hopefully, the bright yellow text will catch my eye on the screen.
- The yellow highlighter color is almost the same as the yellow used to identify a stick-on note. For that reason, if you're using both stick-on notes and highlighter, try using a different highlighter color.

- If you click the down arrow by the Highlight button, you can choose other colors for your highlighted text. And to think that an office supply store would charge you an extra $1.20 for each color. . . .

Removing highlighter

You tried rubbing, you tried buffing, and still that darn highlighter doesn't come out of your text.

Relax. To un-highlight your text, you have two options:

First, select the None color from the Highlight drop-down list. Click the down-arrow by the Highlight button and then click the top color, None. Then go around to all your highlighted text and paint over it again with the None color.

Second, mark the highlighted text as a block and then click the Highlight button and select the "None" color. To remove all the highlighting from your document, follow these steps:

1. **Mark your entire document as a block.**

   Press the Ctrl+A key combination.

2. **Select "None" as the highlight color.**

   Click the down-arrow by the Highlight button on the toolbar and select None from the menu.

Your text transforms from an ugly, used college text book with marking all over the place, into a nice, clean, fresh-as-a-daisy document.

Chapter 28

Organizing Your Thots

In This Chapter

- Starting a new outline
- Adding topics
- Making subtopics
- Creating a text topic
- Looking at all or some of your outline
- Reorganizing your outline
- Printing the outline

All my high school teachers used to urge me to create outlines for my papers. I thought this was silly, and I was correct. If you're writing a three-page paper on why Winnie the Pooh loves honey, you don't really need an outline. But if you're working on something long and involved, you probably need an outline to help you organize your thoughts. In fact, I don't write anything any more without some form of outline.

Outlines in a computer are wonderful. They help by allowing you to view your work from far away or close up. For example, you can view only the major topics in your outline and hide all the details, or you can choose to see everything all at once. Either way, starting off something big with an outline helps you keep your thoughts organized and create a more cohesive document. And who doesn't love the word cohesive?

Making Up a New Outline

I was recently hired by the Disney Corporation to write a script for the musical cartoon version of *Ivan the Terrible* (starring Howard Stern in the title role). Tim Rice and Elton John are doing the music, so I have to weave the tragic, yet humorous story of Ivan through seven musical numbers — including the big dance number in the dungeon. I definitely need to shuffle my ideas into an outline to help me understand it.

You start a new outline like any other document in Word. In fact, an outline *is* just another document. The only difference is in how Word displays the outline on the screen. Follow these steps:

1. **Start a new document.**

Press Ctrl+N or click the New button on the toolbar. (Don't bother with File➪New because that command adds another, annoying step you don't really need here.)

The new document stares at you like the blinding white headlights of an oncoming truck with a dozing driver.

2. **Switch to the Outline view.**

Ah. The secret. Choose View➪Outline or click the Outline View button crowded into the lower-left corner of the window. See Figure 28-1 (though this figure has a lot of text in it that you won't see on your screen right now).

Two amazing things happen: First, you get to see the Outlining toolbar, which helps you work your outline. Second, a hollow minus sign appears before the toothpick cursor. This minus sign means that you're typing a *topic* in the outline and the topic has no *subtopics* (which has nothing to do with naval vessels, by the way).

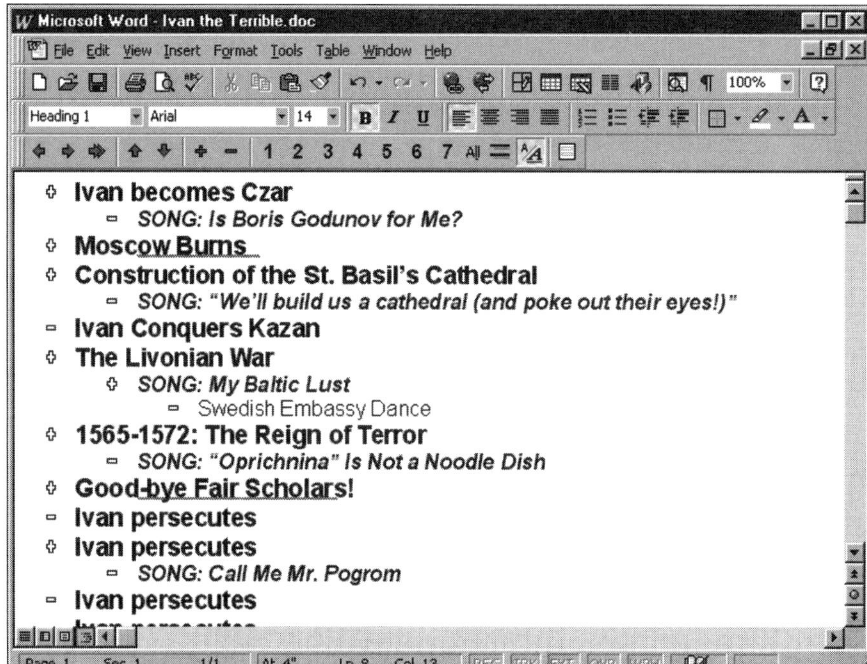

Figure 28-1: A typical outline.

3. **You're ready to start your outline, the details of which are covered in the next few sections.**

- Word's outlining function is merely a different way to look at a document. It's possible to shift back into Normal view or Page Layout view, but not really necessary when you're working on an outline.

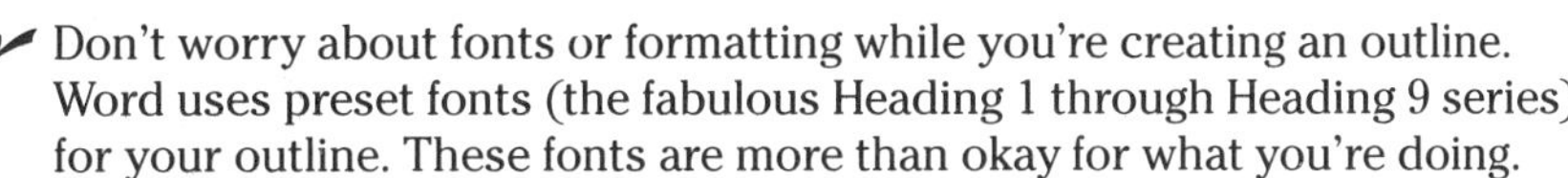

- Don't worry about fonts or formatting while you're creating an outline. Word uses preset fonts (the fabulous Heading 1 through Heading 9 series) for your outline. These fonts are more than okay for what you're doing.
- All Word's normal commands work in the outline mode. You can use the cursor keys, delete text, spell check, save, insert oddball characters, print, and so on.
- The only commands that don't work normally are the block-marking commands. In Outline mode, Word lets you mark only a paragraph (which is a topic) as a block. You can't mark words or parts of paragraphs. This limitation is only a minor inconvenience and is actually a blessing when you get to shuffling around your topics in the outline.

Adding topics to your outline

An outline is composed of topics and subtopics. The main topics are your main ideas, with the subtopics describing the details. You should start your outline by adding the main topics. To do so, just type them out.

In Figure 28-2, you see several topics typed out, each on a line by itself. Pressing Enter after typing a topic produces a new hollow hyphen at which you can type your next topic.

- **Pick up Jordan from football**
- **Get dry cleaning**
- **Stop by ATM machine**
- **Get pizza**
- **Dump toxic waste barrels into river**
- **Get video**
- **Get gas**

Figure 28-2: Level one topics.

- Press Enter at the end of each topic. This tells Word that you're done typing information for that topic and want to move on to the next topic.
- Pressing Enter creates another topic at the same *level* as the first topic. To create a subtopic, refer to the next section.

- A topic can be a single word, a few words, a complete sentence, or a big paragraph. However, your main topics should be short and descriptive, like in a book's table of contents.
- You can split a topic by putting the toothpick cursor somewhere in its middle and pressing the Enter key.
- To join two topics, put the toothpick cursor at the end of the first topic and press the Delete key. (This method works just like joining two paragraphs a regular document.)

- It doesn't matter if you get the order right at first or not. The beauty of creating your outline with a word processor is that you can rearrange your topics as your ideas solidify. My advice is just to start writing things down now and concentrate on organization later.
- An outline can be the plot to a novel, a speech you're giving, a recipe, an itinerary, a product development cycle — just about anything that requires more than one thought.

Working with subtopics

The purpose of an outline is to have more than one level of topic. For example, your main topic may be "Things wrapped in aluminum foil in the refrigerator," and the subtopics would be what those things actually are.

To create a subtopic, follow these steps:

1. **Position the cursor at the end of the main topic.**

   For example, if your main topic is "Things wrapped in aluminum foil in the refrigerator," click the mouse on that line to put the toothpick cursor there and then press the End key to move the cursor to the end of the line.

2. **Press the Enter key.**

   This step creates another topic, but at the same level! You need to move the topic over to the right one notch for it to become a subtopic.

3. **Move the subtopic over to the right one notch.**

   Click the Demote button or press Alt+Shift+→ to move the topic over.

   Instantly, the line of text moves over a tab stop, and the text style changes. Both of these visually indicate that you're working on a new topic level.

4. **Type your subtopic.**

   For example, type **moldy meatloaf** to continue with the fridge outline.

   Unlike creating main topics, you can get a little wordy with your subtopics. After all, the idea here is to expand upon the main topic. For example, if you're writing a speech, a subtopic would contain a more detailed sketch of your talk. Maybe not the talk itself, just more details.

5. **To create another subtopic, press the Enter key.**

   You're presented with another blank, subtopic line on which to jot down your brilliance.

Remember that each topic line should be an individual thought or idea. If your subtopic is:

```
old bologna sandwich and some corn bread
```

you should split it in two:

```
old bologna sandwich
corn bread
```

Each item is a different subtopic in the "Things wrapped in aluminum foil in the refrigerator" main topic.

- To make a topic into a subtopic, you *demote* it. Put the toothpick cursor in the topic and press Alt+Shift+→.

- To make a subtopic back into a topic, you *promote* it. Put the toothpick cursor in the topic and press Alt+Shift+← or click the Promote button.
- To create additional subtopics, just keep pressing the Enter key. This action continues to create topics at the same level. Only by demoting or promoting topics do they shift to another level.
- You'll notice that a main topic with a subtopic has a hollow+by it instead of a hollow minus.
- See "Viewing the Outline" for information on looking at different parts of your outline while hiding other parts.
- You can create a sub-subtopic simply by repeating the preceding steps for a subtopic. In fact, Word lets you organize on a number of levels. Most outlines, however, typically have maybe 4 or 5 levels max.

Adding a text topic

If you feel the need to break out and actually write a paragraph in your outline, you can do so. Although it's perfectly legit to write the paragraph on the topic level, what you should really do is stick in a text topic using the Demote to Body Text button. Here's how:

1. **Press the Enter key to start a new topic.**

   Do this just as you would create any new topic on a line by itself.

2. Click the Demote to Body Text button.

Or you can press Ctrl+Shift+N. What this step does is change the style to Normal (which is what the keyboard shortcut key does). In your outline, however, that style allows you to write a paragraph of text that isn't a heading. So you can write an actual bit of text for your speech, instructions in a list, or dialog from your novel.

- The Body Text style appears with a tiny hollow square by it, unlike topics that have hollow plus or minus signs by them.
- If you change you mind, you can promote or demote your Body Text to a topic or subtopic. Refer to the preceding section for which keys to press.
- Refer to Chapter 15 for more information on the Normal style.

Viewing the Outline

Unless you tell Word otherwise, it displays all the topics in your outline, top to bottom, everything. But this display really isn't part of the glory of outlining. What makes outlining on a computer special is that if you want to step back and see the Big Picture, you can do so.

For example, to see all the first-level topics in your outline, click the Show Heading 1 button. All the subtopics and text topics disappear, and you're left with only the main topics — the overview of your outline, which may sorta look like Figure 28-3.

- Ivan becomes Czar
- Moscow Burns
- Construction of the St. Basil's Cathedral
- Ivan Conquers Kazan
- The Livonian War
- 1565-1572: The Reign of Terror
- Good-bye Fair Scholars!
- Ivan persecutes
- Ivan persecutes
- Ivan persecutes
- Ivan persecutes
- Ivan meets his sorrowful death

Figure 28-3: Only top-level topics are shown here.

If a topic has subtopics, not only does it have a hollow plus sign by it, but you see a fuzzy line extending out over the last part of the topic name. I haven't met anyone yet who knows exactly what the fuzzy line is supposed to mean.

If you want to see your outline in more detail, click the Show Heading 2 or 3 button. Each button displays your outline at a different level.

The All button is used to expand your outline so that *everything* can be seen at once.

- Word automatically recognizes an outline document and immediately shifts into Outline view when it's loaded. Usually it displays *all* the topics, so if you're used to viewing only at level 1 or level 2, you have to click the appropriate button.
- You can view an Outline in normal view if you like, but it looks silly. (The outline looks silly, that is. It's not that you look silly looking at the outline in normal view.)

- You can open or close individual topics by double-clicking the hollow plus sign with the mouse. Using the keyboard, press Alt+Shift+Plus to open a topic; Alt+Shift+Minus to close it. (The Plus and Minus keys are the gray plus and minus keys on your keyboard's numeric keypad.)
- By the way, make sure that the Num Lock light is off (press the Num Lock key) before you use the keypad Plus and Minus keys.
- As your outline nears perfection, you can copy parts of it and paste them into other, new documents. This method is the way some writers create their books and novels; the document is merely a longer, more complete version of what starts as an outline.

Rearranging Topics

Just like shuffling the stack of 3 x 5 cards my high school teachers urged me to use when outlining, reorganizing your topics in a computer outline is a cinch. And it's more fun, too, because you're using a computer and not something that has your mother's recipes on the backside. (And, boy, was she mad!)

To move any topic in your outline, put the toothpick cursor in that topic and then click one of the following buttons:

- Click the Move Up button (or press Alt+Shift+↑) to move a topic up a line.

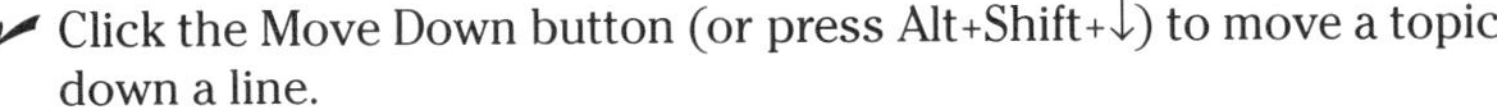

- Click the Move Down button (or press Alt+Shift+↓) to move a topic down a line.

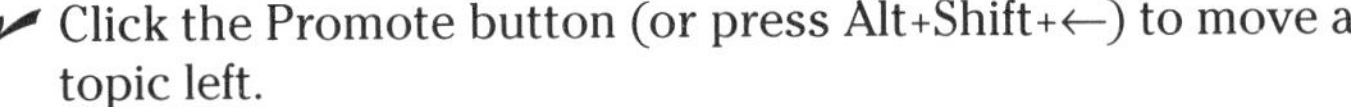

- Click the Promote button (or press Alt+Shift+←) to move a topic left.

- Click the Demote button (or press Alt+Shift+→) to move a topic right.

You can also use the mouse to move topics around: Drag the topic by its plus or minus sign and drop it off at the new location. Personally, I don't use this technique because my outlines are rather complex and moving topics in this manner becomes unwieldy.

If you select a group of topics as a block, you can move them around in your outline as a block. Only a topic and its subtopics can be selected in this manner, and keep in mind that you can only select topics in an outline, not individual bits of text.

It may be a good idea to switch to the All view in your outline before you start rearranging topics. That way you can see where things go and not miss any of the details.

Printing Your Outline

Printing your outline works just like printing any other document in Word. But because it's an outline, there is one difference: Only those visible topics in your outline print.

For example, if you only want to print the first two levels of your outline, click the Show Heading 2 button. This action hides all subtopics and when you print your outline, only the first and second topics are printed.

If you want your entire outline to print, click the All button before printing.

The outline shortcut key summary box

When I'm typing, I like my hands to remain on the keyboard. Because of this preference, I discovered the following key combinations that work when playing with an outline. Try them if you dare:

Key Combo	*Function*
Alt+Shift+→	Demote a topic
Alt+Shift+←	Promote a topic
Alt+Shift+↑	Shift a topic up one line
Alt+Shift+↓	Shift a topic down one line
Ctrl+Shift+N	Insert some body text
Alt+Shift+1	Display only top topics
Alt+Shift+2	Display first- and second-level topics
Alt+Shift+#	Display all topics up to number #
Alt+Shift+A	Display all topics
Alt+Shift+Plus (+)	Display all subtopics in the current topic
Alt+Shift+Minus (–)	Hide all subtopics in the current topic

Chapter 29

Word for the World Wide Web

In This Chapter

- Using Word as a Web browser
- Using Word to create HTML documents
- Inserting a hyperlink into a document
- Publishing a Web page
- Getting to know some Internet jargon

In Microsoft's ceaseless effort to turn every product they produce into some type of Internet-something-or-other, they've tossed a rambling collection of World Wide Web (WWW or "Web") features into Word.

For crying out loud, Word is a *word processor!* Microsoft should just give up on this Internet stuff and leave it to the professionals. But I digress.

Because the computer industry is all abuzz with everything Web and Internet, this chapter gives you the up-and-up on using Word to work the Web (keeping in mind, of course, that this is a book on *word processing* not Web publishing).

- If you don't care about the Web or don't even know what HTML is, then you can blithely skip this chapter.
- If you know what HTML editing is, then you're probably better off using a *real* HTML editor product — something like Microsoft FrontPage — instead of pretending that Word is an HTML editor.

Stumbling Into the Web with Word

Word has two utterly random things to do with the Internet and the Web: You can use Word to cruise the Web, viewing and editing various Web pages as you go, or you can use Word to create a Web page (HTML) document.

If you're careful, you'll never encounter any Web nonsense during your word-processing duties. In fact, you never really *need* to do any of this, which is why I stuck this chapter way, *way* in the back of this book.

Word as a feeble Web browser

To see Word in its Internet/Web cruising mode, click the Web button on the Standard toolbar. Or you can choose View⇨Toolbars⇨Web from the menu. The toolbar is shown (in floating palette mode) in Figure 29-1.

Figure 29-1: Word's wacky Web browsing toolbar.

Get rid of the Web toolbar by repeating either one of the actions mentioned above: Click on the toolbar button again or choose View⇨Toolbars⇨Web from the menu.

- You're seriously better off using a true Web browser, such as Netscape Navigator or Microsoft Internet Explorer instead of Word.
- Do you use Netscape to cruise the Web? If so, forget about using Word as a Web browser entirely. Trying to visit a Web page using Word only starts up Netscape. This is another example of Microsoft subtly twisting your arm to get you to switch over to their Internet Explorer.
- If you've ever browsed the Web before, you should recognize the Back, Forward, Stop, and Home buttons right away. If you've never browsed the Web before, then I hear the local Goodrich outlet is having a tire sale this weekend.

- You must configure Windows 95 to connect to the Internet before the Word Web-browsing feature really works. In fact, you should pretty much be an Internet maven before you even attempt to use the Word Web toolbar.
- What? You were expecting the computer to actually do something useful? They can't read minds, you know. In fact, they *refuse* to even try!

Word as an HTML editor

Whether or not you're connected to the Internet, you can use Word to create Web page documents. Of course, it helps if you are connected and, further, you know what an HTML document is and how to publish it on the Web. (Word can create nifty HTML documents, but it's up to you to publish them on the Web.)

To create an HTML document, either for the Web or just because you have only three days to live and you're too ethical to run up all your credit cards, follow these steps:

1. **Choose File⇨New.**

   The New dialog box appears.

2. **In the New dialog box, click on the Web Pages tab.**

   You'll see several options for creating a Web page, a few Web page templates, and the Web Page Wizard. Ah-ha!

3. **Open the Web Page Wizard icon.**

   Double-click on the Web Page Wizard icon to open it. A new document is created in Word, and you'll see the Web Page Wizard dialog box, as shown in Figure 29-2.

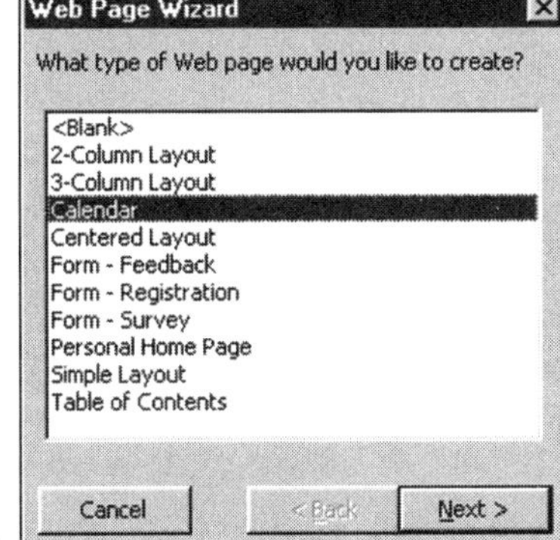

Figure 29-2: The Web Page Wizard dialog box.

4. **Choose a Web page style from the list.**

   For example, click on Personal Home Page. You'll notice the document in the background changes to reflect a preset Web page design — a starting point for you to fill in later.

5. **Click the Next button.**

6. Choose a visual style from the list.

Click on each of the various styles and observe the document behind the dialog box. See how it changes? Pick a style you think would just jazz the eyeballs off the people who come to visit the Web page.

7. Click the Finish button. You're done.

Your document is roughed-out on screen. You now need to customize it.

8. Edit the document.

First, find the present text, the `[Type Here]` stuff. Select that text by clicking on it once, then type in new text appropriate to your Web page.

- You can use all of the Word formatting commands to create your Web page. You can format fonts, paragraphs, insert graphics, tables, whatever.
- You can even use the Word character animation formatting options: Choose Format⇨Font from the menu and click on the Animation tab in the Font dialog box to see what's available.

- To create or change the background pattern, click on the Background button on the formatting toolbar. (It's a new button that appears when you're in HTML editing mode.) Choose a background fill color from the palette displayed, or click on the Fill Effects button to see a dialog box full of background textures you can choose from.

- Don't bother clicking on the Web Toolbar button. That activates the Word Web browsing mode, which won't help edit a Web page at all.
- See the next section for information on creating a hyperlink in your Web page. (You can only insert a hyperlink *after* you save the document to disk.)

9. Save the document to disk.

Because you used the Web Page Wizard to create your HTML document, Word automatically saves it in that format.

- You can also use Word to load an HTML document, such as some Web page you may have saved to disk. Just use the Open command and choose `HTML Document` from the Files of type drop-down list.
- If you want to save the document as a Word document, choose File⇨Save as Word Document from the menu.
- There is no reason under the sun to create an HTML document if you've never done it before or have no idea what's going on.

Inserting a hyperlink into your document

A Web page without hyperlinks would be, well, just information. And you can't have that, because raw information would spoil the *milieu* of the Web. So you should put a few hyperlinks into your HTML document. (Refer to the previous section for information on creating an HTML document in Word.)

After saving your HTML document, Word allows you to insert a hyperlink. Follow these steps:

1. **Select the text or graphic you want to use as a hyperlink.**

2. **Click the Hyperlink button on the standard toolbar.**

   The Insert Hyperlink dialog box appears (see Figure 29-3).

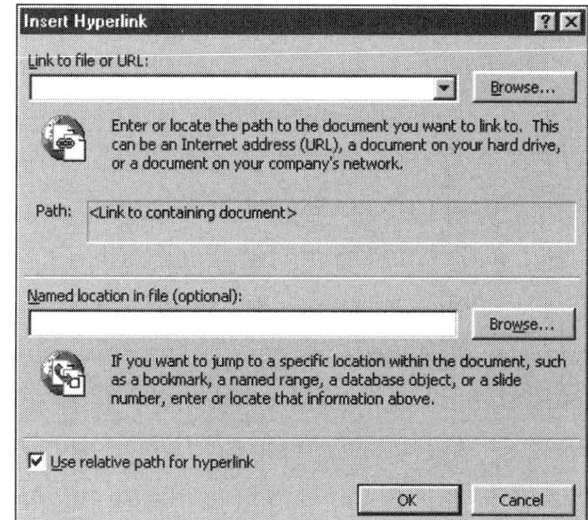

Figure 29-3: The Insert Hyperlink dialog box.

3. **Fill in the Insert Hyperlink dialog box.**

   To link to a Web page, type that Web page's address into the Link to file or URL input box.

4. **Click OK.**

   The link is created in your document. You'll notice that the text appears underlined and in another color (probably blue). That's a hyperlink.

- To edit a hyperlink you've already created, right-click on it. Then choose Hyperlink⇨Edit Hyperlink from the shortcut menu.
- You cannot access a hyperlink to the Internet unless you're connected to the Internet. Word may do this for you, and then again it may not.
- The Web page really doesn't work until it's published on the Internet. The next section has some choice words about that.

- You must select text or a graphic object before you click on the Hyperlink tool to create a hyperlink. Also, the HTML document must already be saved to disk before you can create a hyperlink to anything. Silly rule, but I didn't make it up.

Publishing Your Web Page

Publishing your Web page on the Internet should be as easy as saving a document to disk. Alas, it just ain't so.

To publish a Web page on the Internet, you need access to disk storage on an Internet computer, such as your Internet Service Provider's computer. Then you need a program to copy the HTML document from your computer to your disk storage on the ISP's computer. As you can probably guess, Word does *none* of this for you; you'll need other software to accomplish this task. I just can't help you here.

- Please don't accuse me of being feeble. This chapter is already four pages longer than I wanted it to be.
- As an HTML document editor, Word is okay. I've seen worse programs out there. But if you're truly serious about creating HTML documents and publishing them on the Web, then you should get software specifically designed to do so.

- Word is a *word processor*. You use it to create documents and such on your computer. It only does HTML like your doctor may dabble in stained glass work; it's an interesting hobby, but if you're serious you should consider using a professional.

Jargon Check

Here are some Web and Internet terms you would otherwise never find in a word-processing book.

HTML

Acronym for Hunting The Manic Lemur. Seriously, it's HyperText Markup Language and you pronounce it letters-only: Aytch-Tee-Em-El. Not a programming language, HTML is a *formatting* language. It's special codes and whatnots that live on a Web page that tell the Web browser how to display things.

Knowing HTML isn't necessary since you can use Word to create and format everything. You merely tell Word to save the thing as an HTML document and it inserts the proper HTML codes for you.

HTML is a very trendy acronym to use at an office cocktail party.

HTML document

Any document saved in HTML format. Word can both open and save files as HTML documents. If you're browsing the Web, you can save any Web page you visit to disk and then view or edit it with Word.

HTTP

A Web browser command that loads a Web page for scrutiny. HTTP stands for HyperText Transfer Protocol. It's simply a method for viewing documents on the Web. It's also the first part of a Web page address.

Hyperlink

A bit of text on a Web page that allows you to visit another Web page. Typically, you point the mouse at a hyperlink on a Web page and click to see more information or visit some other interesting spot on the Web.

Most hyperlinks appear as colored and underlined text on a Web page. However, graphic images can also be hyperlinks. Your best clue is that hovering the mouse over the text or image changes the mouse pointer to a little pointing hand instead of the normal arrow pointer.

Internet

A vast network of computers that exchange and store information. Lots of information. Tons of information. And all that information unorganized and not cataloged.

To use the Internet, you must have access to it. This requires a modem in your computer and a place for the modem to call. The best place to call is an Internet Service Provider (ISP), who connects you to the Internet and gives you access to all the information stored there. Yes, this costs money. (And it's not something Word can do for you; you need to sign up or subscribe to an ISP.)

You'll also need software to access the Internet. I recommend Netscape Navigator, though for some curious reason Word works best with Microsoft Internet Explorer.

Web

The World Wide Web, which is just a graphical, friendlier way to view the vast amount of information stored on the Internet. You typically need a program called a Web browser to view documents on the Web. Word supposedly can be used as a Web browser. Supposedly.

Web page

A document on the Web. Each document is called a *page*.

Web page address

The formal, long, complex identification for every Web page on the Internet. For example, Microsoft's Web page has the following address:

```
http://www.microsoft.com
```

Typing this address into a Web browser allows you to view that Web page.

Yaddi, yaddi

An Internet term for continuous nonsense. A high-tech relative to *blah-blah-blah*. Another term for sticking Internet software into a word processor, most probably as a random act of one-upmanship against the competition. A yaddi-yaddi typically holds no real benefit for the intended target audience of a product.

Part VI
Help Me, Mr. Wizard!

"OK, TECHNICALLY, THIS SHOULD WORK. JUDY, TYPE THE WORD 'GOODYEAR' IN ALL CAPS, BOLDFACE, AT 700-POINT TYPE SIZE."

In this part . . .

Word can feel your pain. After all, Word has to put up with the computer, printer, Windows, and all that other nonsense you must live with day to day. Who knows what causes things to go goofy all of the sudden? Phases of the moon? The evil eye? You suddenly become a character in a Fellini movie?

Fortunately, some people — yes, real people — actually enjoy using computers. Further, they enjoy helping you with your computer problems. Call them wizards or gurus, it helps to keep one handy when you need some extra assistance with your PC or Word. And when they're not available (why does the phone always ring and ring?), you can rely on the chapters in this part of the book to help you get through your troubles.

Chapter 30

Face to Face with the Interface

In This Chapter

- Looking at your document
- Adding toolbars
- Converting between toolbars and floating palettes
- Getting rid of the spots between words
- Muffling Word's obnoxious sounds
- There's a line down the left side of my screen!
- The ruler changed into a line of arrows, numbers, and whatnot!
- Zooming about

By now, you probably have noticed that approaching Word and the strange and unusual ways that it shows stuff on your screen is about as calming as having the waiter personally assure you that the food is supposed to taste that way, and nothing is wrong. Meanwhile, you hear a siren approaching, and the cook rushes to the bathroom holding his mouth with one hand and his stomach with the other. Don't you agree that there are too many buttons, icons, gizmos, and whatzits? Don't answer too quickly because there are even more than that — including some wild things that you've never seen and probably don't want to see. This chapter mulls over the lot, explains just what's what on-screen, and tells you whether it's important and why.

Looking at Your Document

The way you look at your document is controlled by Word's View menu, as shown in Figure 30-1. The View menu contains all sorts of options for controlling the display: the way your document appears, various optional goodies that you may see along with your document, and how big the document looks (set by the Zoom command). These and other items are discussed in the check mark list that follows, as well as in the rest of this chapter.

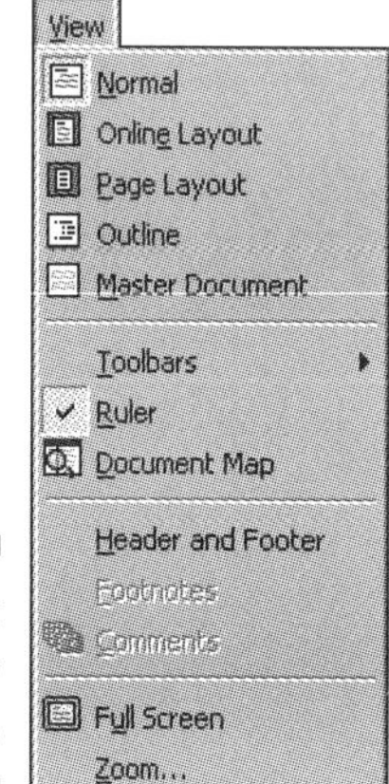

Figure 30-1: The View menu.

- The Normal command sets Word to look at your document in the Normal view — what you probably want most of the time while you work in Word. The Normal View icon, at the far-left end of the bottom horizontal scroll bar, also switches you to this view.

- Don't choose the View⇨Outline layout command or click its button on the bottom of Word's window. Using that view isn't covered in this book, and if you choose it, the view buttons on the bottom of the window vanish. Choose View⇨Normal to return to sanity.

- The Page Layout command directs Word to let you see your entire document, including the header and footer plus the graphics and other effects that may not look proper in the Normal view. Clicking the Page Layout icon on the horizontal scroll bar also activates this view.
- In Page Layout view, a second, vertical ruler appears along the left side of your document. You also see a misty gray region to the top and bottom of each "page" in your document. That void is made of the same stuff that they find in the Bermuda Triangle.
- Several Word commands automatically shift you into Page Layout view.
- The Outline command shifts Word into the Outline mode, which is covered in Chapter 28 (though it's really an advanced topic, many readers insisted). The last of the three view buttons on the horizontal scroll bar switches on Outline view.
- I touch on the Master Document view in Chapter 35.

- The interesting Full Screen command in the View menu lets you look at your document without being encumbered by menus, toolbars, or any other whatnot. This command is well suited for the white-page purists among us. Click the only remaining button on-screen to return yourself to the safety of the normal mode.

- Other commands in the View menu are discussed elsewhere in this chapter.
- Yet another check mark item.
- Chapter 18 offers information on working with document windows, splitting them, Windexing them, and so on.

Looking for Mr. Toolbar

Toolbars come and toolbars go. They appear when you use special Word commands or enter secret operating modes, and then they disappear. That's great, because Word has over a dozen toolbars and all of them on the screen at once would mean that you'd be using a toolbar program and not a word processor. That's not very productive.

The following sections tell you just about everything you need to know about toolbars in Word.

- Review Chapter 1 for information on the toolbars Word shows you most of the time: The Standard toolbar, Formatting toolbar, and the ruler (though the ruler isn't really a toolbar).
- Toolbars are controlled via the View⇨Toolbars submenu.

- Word lets you customize any toolbar, adding or removing buttons as you see fit. This is an advanced topic, not covered in this book. The following sections let you go wacky enough with toolbars.

Summoning toolbars

You control toolbars in Word — and there are many of them — with the View⇨Toolbars submenu. On that submenu, you find a list of all the toolbars Word has to offer, depicted in Figure 30-2.

To display a toolbar, choose its name from the submenu. A check mark appears by those toolbars already visible. Choosing a toolbar's name again removes the check mark from the box, making the toolbar go away. This is standard menu-check mark stuff.

- A quick way to get at the toolbars submenu is to right-click the mouse on any toolbar in Word. That action displays a pop-up toolbars submenu, from which you can switch various toolbars on or off.
- Toolbars can appear as a strip of buttons across the screen (like the Standard and Formatting toolbars), as *floating palettes,* or buttons in their own wee windows. See the section "It's a toolbar! It's a palette!" for more information.

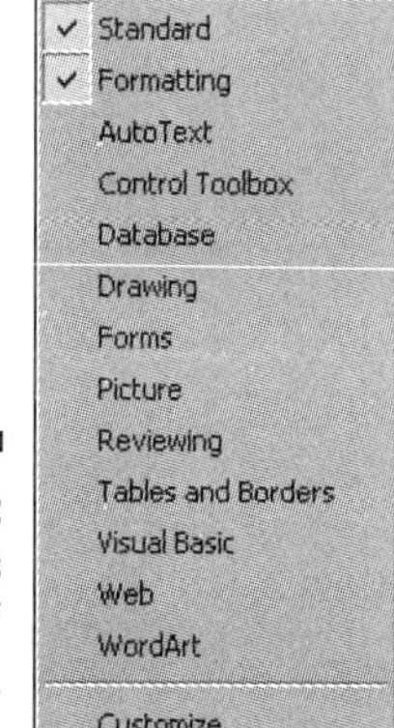

Figure 30-2: Word's submenu o' toolbars.

- The ruler is not a toolbar, yet it's controlled through the View menu. To see the ruler or to hide it, choose View➪Ruler. Like a toolbar, a check mark by the Ruler item means that the ruler is visible; no check mark means that it has abdicated.
- Some toolbars appear automatically when you're working on specific things in Word. For example, the Picture toolbar appears when you're working with Microsoft Picture (see Chapter 23).
- Word has some toolbars that don't appear in the View➪Toolbars submenu. For example, the Merge toolbar appears only when you're merging documents (see Chapter 21); you cannot choose it from the menu (see Figure 30-2).

- Having tons of toolbars sates the button gluttons, but too many toolbars leave little room on the screen for your all-important text. Typically, you only need the Standard and Formatting toolbars. Everything else is just for show.

It's a toolbar! It's a palette!

Every toolbar in Word can also serve as a floating palette, a little mini-window that always hovers over the top of all the other windows in Word. Figure 30-3 shows the AutoText toolbar as a toolbar and as a floating palette. On its own, Word determines whether or not the toolbar shows up one way or the other. But you can change that arrangement at any time.

To convert a toolbar into a floating palette, drag the toolbar by the two little bumps on its far left side (see the margin). Dragging the toolbar a little ways merely moves its location, but if you drag it far enough, it changes into a floating palette.

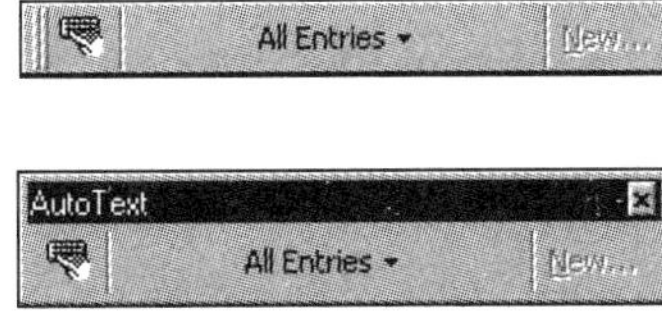

Figure 30-3: The AutoText toolbar and floating palette duet.

To convert a floating palette into a toolbar, drag the palette up to the top of Word's window, where the other palettes live. The floating palette automatically changes into a toolbar.

You can also drag toolbars/floating palettes to the bottom of Word's window, below the horizontal scroll bar.

Floating palettes are moved around like any window in Windows; just drag the palette by its title bar (on top).

To close a floating palette window, click its wee X close button.

Out, Damn Spots!

This•can•be•very•annoying.¶

What you see on your screen when your text looks like the preceding line are *non-printing characters*. These symbols represent spaces (produced by the space bar), end-of-paragraph marks (the Enter key), and tabs. The symbols show up on-screen but — fortunately — not when printed. You can feel two ways about these characters:

- The marks let you see things that would otherwise be invisible, such as rogue tabs and spaces and other stuff that may foul up your document if you don't see them.
- The marks look gross on-screen; who wants to edit a document that looks like it has the chicken pox?

¶ You turn off the specks from the Standard toolbar. Click the Show/Hide button, the *paragraph* symbol. Doing so shuts off the effect.

- The keyboard shortcut for the Show/Hide button is Ctrl+Shift+8 (that's the 8 key on the keyboard not on the numeric keypad).
- A good way to clean up rogue spaces in a document is to use the AutoFormat command. Refer to Chapter 17.

"I Can't Stand All the Silly Noises!"

The Macintosh was really the first PC to fully utilize its little speaker. I remember a program — and I'm not making up this name — called MacPuke. It did nothing, other than play the sound of someone retching every time someone ejected a floppy disk. Oh, I must have laughed and laughed. But after a while the sound got very annoying to me. I almost enjoyed removing MacPuke as much as I did installing it.

Windows makes noise if your PC has a sound card installed. That's okay. I can live with the occasional ding or cha-cha-cha. But then along comes Word, and the PC is singing like a monk who just broke a 20-year vow of silence. *Will you PLEASE shut up already!*

To stifle Word and its cacophony of noises, follow these steps:

1. **Choose Tools⇨Options.**

   The knotty-looking Options dialog box appears in all its Halloween frighteningness.

2. **Click the General tab.**

   This moves all the gizmos in that panel up to the front.

3. **Remove the check mark by the Provide feedback with sound item.**

   Click the mouse in the box by that item to remove the check mark.

4. **Click OK.**

   The Options dialog box is gone, and so is the noise.

You can always restore the sounds by repeating the preceding steps to put the check mark back.

- The number one sound culprit is your annoying Office Assistant. I hate The Genius's scribbling when I'm in the Options dialog box. Unfortunately, resetting the sound item in the Options dialog box does not mute your annoying Office Assistant. You have to get rid of him altogether, which is covered in Chapter 25.
- You can always make Windows mute as an ice cube by muting the speaker. Click the mouse on the little yellow speaker icon on the right side of Windows' taskbar. Click the mouse in the button by Mute to zero-out all your PC's sounds.
- Hey: You can always unplug your PC's speakers and throw them out a window.

- You can change the sounds associated with each event. This task is done in the Windows Control Panel by using the Sounds icon. Any good book on Windows tells you how it works. The sounds associated with Word are kept in the Microsoft Office area.
- Changing the sounds in Word also changes them for all of Microsoft Office. So if you like the noise Excel makes, you have to re-activate the sounds when you use Excel, and then turn them off again when you get back to Word.

"There's a Line down the Left Side of My Screen!"

Ah, that annoying line down the left side of the screen doesn't mean that your monitor is out of whack. Instead, you have discovered the *style area*. That thing shows you what style is applied to what paragraph, and there's really no reason to have it visible.

To turn off the style area, follow these steps:

1. **Choose Tools⇨Options.**

   The Options dialog box appears.

2. **Coax the View panel into coming forth.**

   Click the View tab with the mouse.

3. **Look for the Style Area Width item.**

   It's in the lower-left corner of the dialog box, hiding from you.

4. **Type the number** 0 **(zero) into the box.**

   Or use your mouse and the spinner buttons to reset the value to zero.

   You've just set the width of the style area thing to zero inches, which effectively makes it nonexistent. Yeah!

5. **Click OK.**

   The style area is forever gone.

Although the style area is annoying, having it visible can really help you edit strange documents. If you're having trouble applying styles to your document, you can switch the style area back on. Just follow the preceding steps again and enter a value of .5 or 1 for a half-inch or inch-wide style area.

"The Ruler Changed into a Line of Arrows, Numbers, and Whatnot!"

When the strange things mentioned in the title of this section happen, you've simply discovered Outline view. This feature is a really neat gizmo designed especially by Microsoft for people who really, really love to outline stuff.

Chapter 28 covers Word's outlining function. But if you accidentally stumble onto the Outline view and see those weird arrows instead of a ruler, you can choose View⇨Normal to return to Normal view.

Zooming About

The Zoom command at the bottom of the View menu controls how big your document's text looks. No, the command doesn't change the text size — that's done in the Font menu. Instead, the Zoom command controls how much of your text you see at once. Follow these steps for a quick demonstration:

1. **Choose View⇨Zoom.**

   The Zoom dialog box appears, looking much like the one depicted in Figure 30-4.

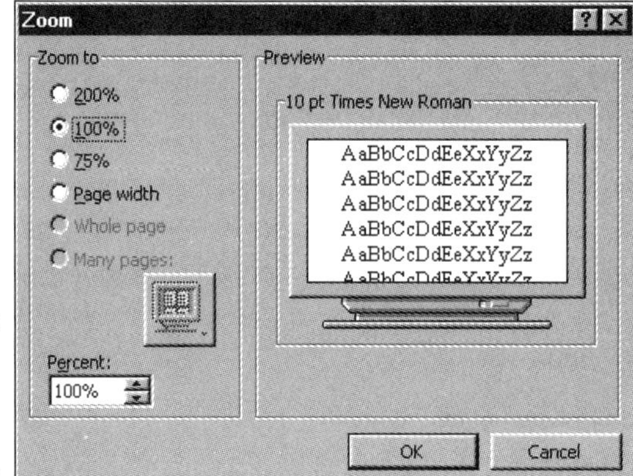

Figure 30-4: The Zoom dialog box.

2. **Select a Zoom size from the Zoom to area.**

   For example, 200% makes your text look real big — ideal for Grandpa. The Page width option sets the zoom so that you see your entire document from left to right margins.

You can set individual percent sizes using the Percent box.

3. **Click OK to view your document at a new size on-screen.**

- The Whole Page and Many Pages options in the Zoom dialog box are only available when you're in Page Layout view. Choose View⇨Page Layout and then select the Zoom command to play, er, experiment with those options.
- When zooming takes you too far out, your text changes to shaded blocks, called *greeking.* Although not keen for editing, zooming out that far gives you a good idea of how your document looks on the page before printing.
- A Zoom drop-down list appears on the Standard toolbar, way over to the right. Click it to quickly set a Zoom size for your document.
- The Zoom command does not make the *zoom* noise when selected.

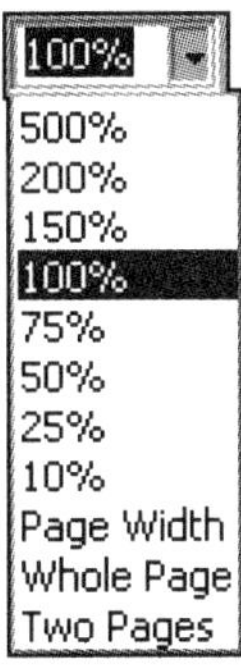

Chapter 31

Learning to Love Your Printer

In This Chapter

- Selecting a printer
- Canceling a print job
- Feeding the printer paper
- Unjamming the printer
- Stopping incessant double-spacing!
- Changing ribbons and toner
- "Where did the weird characters come from?"

Is the printer your friend? Perhaps. And if there can't be love between you, maybe you both could come to an understanding? Maybe try for Oprah's "Computer Peripherals and Their Owners, a Love-Hate Relationship?" show.

Unfortunately, friend or foe, the printer is just as stupid as the computer, which means that you must beat it with a stick a few times to get it to behave, or else you wind up hitting yourself in the head with the same stick. But give yourself a second of repose and consider leafing through this chapter before causing yourself or your printer any physical harm.

Choosing Another Printer (If You Have More Than One to Choose From)

Betcha didn't know that your computer can have more than one printer attached. Granted, you'd have to be rich, silly, or decapitated to *want* more than one printer, but the PC can handle two printers at once, three if you're resolute about it. And you need not be rich, either. Perhaps you have an older dot matrix you kept after buying a laser printer. And then there are those of us in an office on a network with dozens of printers to select from. *It's printer madness!*

After someone has properly set up your computer to recognize and work with multiple printers, you can direct Word to use one or more of them at any time. So you can zip out drafts on the dot matrix printer next to you and save the massive laser printer down the hall for pristine work, like your resume. To do so — and this only works if you have more than one printer installed in Windows — follow these steps:

1. **Choose the File⇨Print command.**

   Or, better yet, press Ctrl+P, the Print shortcut. Do not use the Print button on the toolbar for this because you need to see the Print dialog box.

   The top area of the dialog box describes your current printer, called the *default printer* by those who really don't know what the word *default* means.

2. **Click the down-arrow on the Name list box.**

   The Name list box is at the top of the Printer area. When you click the down-arrow, a list of the printers Windows knows about is displayed (Figure 31-1).

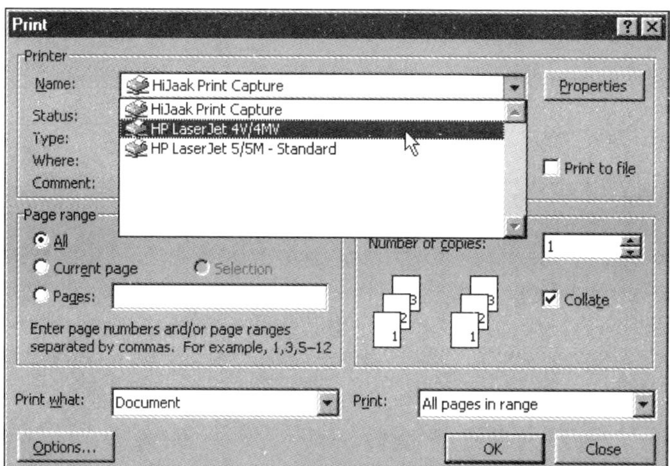

Figure 31-1: The Print dialog box.

3. **Select the printer that you want to use.**

   Click once on the printer's name.

4. **Click Close.**

   Clicking the Close button confirms that you've changed the printer, but does not tell Word to print. If you want to print as well as change the printer, click the OK button.

Instantly, Word is alerted to your new printer. You're done. That's it.

- Selecting a printer is necessary only if you have more than one printer connected to your PC.
- Word remembers which printer you last chose and continues to use that printer until you tell it to change again.
- To change the printer back, just pick another printer, following the same steps. Remember to click the Close button to verify your change; if you click OK, Word prints the current document.
- You can also select a Fax card from the Print Setup dialog box, which is one way you can send faxes with Word.
- Information on setting up multiple printers in Windows can be found in *PCs For Dummies,* 4th Edition, from IDG Books Worldwide, Inc.

Canceling a Print Job

Sometimes you print something and then change your mind. This happens all the time. (Rumor has it that Gutenberg originally wanted to print a cart parts wall calendar with an etching of a wood nymph.) Or maybe your printer is so slow that you repeatedly press Ctrl+P, Enter too many times. Then you find yourself accidentally printing several dozen copies of the same document. Ugh.

Because Word simply passes off its printing jobs to Windows, there is no obvious way to cancel printing. It can be done if you're crafty, however. Follow these steps:

1. **Locate the li'l printer dude by the current time on the taskbar.**

   This little cuss only appears when Windows is sending something to the printer. Depending on how much you're printing and how fast your printer is, you may not even see it at all. If you don't, you're out of luck and you may as well quit right now and eat some ice cream.

2. **Double-click the little printer guy.**

   This step opens up your printer's window (see Figure 31-2) and displays a list of documents waiting to be printed. The top document in the list is currently printing; other documents are waiting in the queue (which is the way the British say "line").

3. **Click the name of your Word document "job" in the Print Manager's list.**

   Documents in the list are called *print jobs.* Your task is to fire one of them.

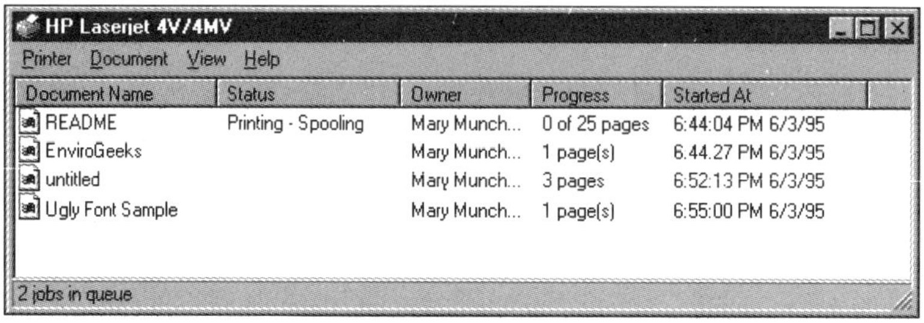

HP Laserjet 4V/4MV

Printer Document View Help

Document Name	Status	Owner	Progress	Started At
README	Printing - Spooling	Mary Munch...	0 of 25 pages	6:44:04 PM 6/3/95
EnviroGeeks		Mary Munch...	1 page(s)	6:44:27 PM 6/3/95
untitled		Mary Munch...	3 pages	6:52:13 PM 6/3/95
Ugly Font Sample		Mary Munch...	1 page(s)	6:55:00 PM 6/3/95

2 jobs in queue

Figure 31-2: Documents waiting in your printer's queue.

4. **Choose Document⇨Cancel Printing.**

   You may be asked whether you really want to terminate the employee, er, print job. Click the OK button.

   If you're using a network printer, you may not be able to cancel the document. Oh well.

5. **Cancel more print jobs if you are in an especially vicious mood.**

   Repeat Steps 3 and 4 for each job you want to fire.

6. **Close your printer's window after you're done.**

   Choose Printer⇨Close to remove that window from the desktop. You are zapped back to Word, ready for more editing action.

Obviously, canceling a print job is the act of a desperate person. In its efforts to make life easy for computer users, Windows tries hard to help us change our minds. Canceling something that's printing may or may not work as planned. My advice is just to be careful with the Print command in the first place.

Feeding It Paper

The way the paper feeds into your printer depends on which printer you have. Some printers eat paper one page at a time. Other printers may suck up continuous sheets of *fan-fold* paper directly from the box (the spaghetti approach). And laser printers delicately lift one sheet of paper at a time from their paper tray and then weld the image to the page by using dusty toner and inferno-like temperatures. Printing can be quite dramatic.

Whichever way your printer eats paper, make sure that you have a lot on hand. The end result of a word processor's labors is the printed document. So buy a box or two of paper at a time. I'm serious: You'll save money and trips to the store in the long run. And I suggest that you look for a huge paper store or supplier and buy your printer paper from them instead of an office supply or computer store. The prices are better.

- Try to get 20 lb. paper. The 18 lb. paper is too thin. I like 25 lb. paper, which is thicker and holds up very well, but it's more expensive. Paper that's too thick, such as card stock, may get stuck in your printer.
- Colored papers and fancy stuff are okay.
- Do not print on erasable bond paper! This paper is awful. After all, the point behind erasable bond is that you can erase it, which doesn't happen much with a computer printer.
- Avoid fancy, dusted paper in a laser printer. Some expensive papers are coated with a powder. This powder comes off in a laser printer and gums up the works.
- Special laser paper is designed for a laser printer. It's more expensive, but it looks *maaaarvelous*.
- Only buy the two-part or three-part fan-fold papers if you need them. These may contain carbon paper and are commonly used for printing invoices and orders. Also, the old green bar paper makes for lousy correspondence. It has nerd written all over it.
- If you need to print labels in your laser printer, get special laser printer labels. I recommend Avery labels.
- Laser printers can print on clear transparencies — but only those specially designed for use in a laser printer. Anything less than this kind will melt inside your printer, and you'll have to clean out the gunk. If you are going to print transparencies, it's cheaper to print on a piece of paper and then have the image photocopied onto transparency film, anyway.
- Always buy double-ply toilet tissue. It's comfier.

Unjamming the Printer

One brand of Jam you'll never find the Smuckers label on is Printer Jam. This is what happens at 5:00 when too many people are trying to get home, and they all print at once. Because printers don't have on-ramp stop lights, the paper gets all bunched up inside the printer, and the printer sits there looking dumb with the word "Jam" flashing on its panel. Something like that.

If you have a dot-matrix printer and the paper jams, turn the printer off. (You may also need to cancel the print job; refer to the proper section earlier in this chapter.) Rewind the knob to reverse-feed the paper back out of the printer. Don't pull on the paper, or it will tear, and you'll have to take the printer apart to get the paper out. (If dismantling the printer becomes necessary, call someone else for help.)

For laser printers, you need to pop open the lid, find the errant piece of paper, remove it, and then slam the lid down shut. Watch out for various hot things inside your printer; be careful about what you touch. You don't need to cancel printing here because laser printers have more brain cells than their dot-matrix cousins. However, you may need to reprint the page that got jammed in the printer. Refer to Chapter 9, the section "Printing a Specific Page."

If the jam was caused by using thick paper, retrying the operation probably won't work. Use thinner paper.

Don't put any Smuckers into a printer when it's panel is flashing "Jam" over and over.

Stopping Incessant Double-Spacing!

Nothing is quite as disenchanting as a printer that constantly produces double-spaced documents, whether you want them or not. This problem is terribly annoying, but it has a handy, one-time solution — if you kept your printer manual when you bought your printer.

Somewhere on your printer is a tiny switch. That switch controls whether your printer double-spaces all the time or only single-spaces. Right now, the switch is set to double-space no matter what. You need to find that switch and turn it off.

- Sometimes, the little switches are on the back or side of your printer; sometimes they're actually inside your printer.
- Turn your printer off and unplug it before you flip the switch. Cutting the power is especially important if the switch is inside the printer. It also prevents people from trying to print while your fingers are in the way of the printer's buzz saw-like gears.
- The switch may be referred to as "LF after CR" or "Line feed after carriage return" or "Add LF" or "Stop double-spacing!" or something along those lines.

Changing Ribbons and Toner

Always have a good ribbon or toner cartridge in your printer. Always! Many printers use ribbons; laser printers use toner cartridges. This aspect of printing is something that you should never skimp on, lest the Printer Pixies come to you in your dreams and smear ink on your fingers.

- Keep a supply of two or three extra ribbons or toner cartridges. The extra supplies will hold you in case you need a new one over a working weekend.
- When the ribbon gets old and faded, replace it. Some places may offer re-inking services for your ribbon. This service works if the ribbon fabric can hold the new ink. If your ribbon is threadbare, you need to buy a new one.

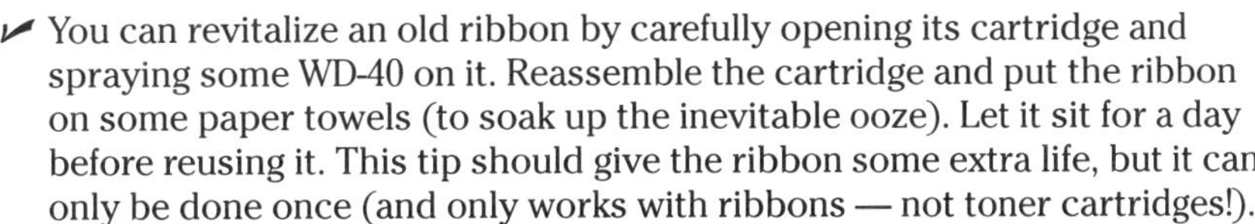

- You can revitalize an old ribbon by carefully opening its cartridge and spraying some WD-40 on it. Reassemble the cartridge and put the ribbon on some paper towels (to soak up the inevitable ooze). Let it sit for a day before reusing it. This tip should give the ribbon some extra life, but it can only be done once (and only works with ribbons — not toner cartridges!).

- Ink printers use ink cartridges. Replace the ink cartridges when they run low on ink, just as you should replace a ribbon or toner cartridge.

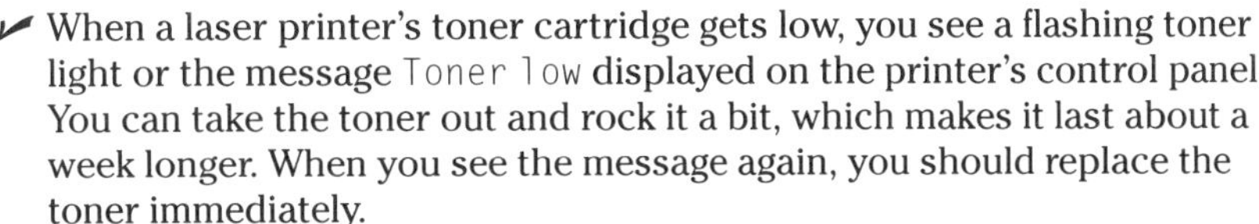

- When a laser printer's toner cartridge gets low, you see a flashing toner light or the message `Toner low` displayed on the printer's control panel. You can take the toner out and rock it a bit, which makes it last about a week longer. When you see the message again, you should replace the toner immediately.
- There are services that offer toner recharging. For a nominal fee, they take your old toner cartridges and refill them with new toner. You can then use the toner cartridge again and squeeze some more money out of it. Nothing is wrong with this service, and I recommend it as a good cost-saving measure. But never recharge a toner cartridge more than once, nor should you do business with anyone who says that it's okay.

"Where Did the Weird Characters Come From?"

If strange characters appear on your output — almost like the printer burped — it's a sign that Word may not be set up to use your printer properly. Those stray @ and # characters that appear on paper but not on-screen indicate that your printer may not be properly installed.

Installing your printer is a job best done by your computer guru. You need to know the manufacturer, make, and model number of your printer, and then run the special Printer Setup program that came with Windows. *PCs For Dummies,* 4th Edition, tells you how to do this, should you be so bold.

Chapter 32

Help Me! I'm Stuck!

In This Chapter

- "I can't find Windows!"
- "I can't find Word!"
- "I lost my files!"
- "Where did my document go?"
- "Where am I now?"
- "It's not printing!"
- "Oops! I deleted my document!"

"There I was, minding my own business, when all of a sudden — for no apparent reason — Word *fill-in-the-blank*. Where is my baseball bat?"

It happens all too often. And it happens to everyone. "It worked just great when I did this yesterday. Why doesn't it work today?" Who knows? Retrace your steps. Check the grounds for signs of racoons. But in the end, turn to this chapter for some quick solutions.

"I Can't Find Windows!"

Nothing so induces the sensation that you just accidentally stepped out of the shower to find the crew from *60 Minutes* in your bathroom than returning to your computer and seeing . . . *nothing!* Uh-oh. Looks like Windows saw the Baskin-Robbins a few blocks back and didn't bother to tell you it was on an ice cream hunt. But where did it really go?

First things first. If the screen is blank, try pressing the Enter key. A screen-saver type of program may have taken over your computer's brain, and you need to wake it up.

If — peril of perils — you see the DOS prompt on the screen, don't think that your PC has gone retro-1988. Instead, type **EXIT** at the DOS prompt and press Enter. This command may turn the trick for you.

Some joker in the office may have told your computer to start in the "DOS mode" instead of Windows. (Yes, it can happen.) If so, try typing **WIN** at the DOS prompt now.

If this remedy *still* doesn't help, reset your computer. Press and hold the Ctrl and Alt keys and press the Delete key. Release all three keys. Your computer resets. When your computer is done restarting itself, start over yourself.

"I Can't Find the Taskbar!"

The taskbar is that grey strip along the bottom of the Windows screen (though it could be on the top or sides, it mostly lives on the bottom). One of the most annoying things that can happen in Windows is that the taskbar decides — all on its own — to play hide-and-seek. Here is how you can olly-olly-oxen-free it:

1. **Press Ctrl+Esc.**

   The Ctrl+Esc key combination pops up the Start menu.

2. **Press Alt+Space.**

   Pressing Alt+Space (the spacebar) pops up a shortcut menu for the taskbar.

3. **Press S.**

   This step chooses the Size command, which resizes the taskbar.

4. **Press the up-arrow key.**

   Keep pressing it until you see the taskbar.

   If this doesn't work, there's an outside chance the taskbar may be on the right or left side of your screen. If so, try pressing the left-or right-arrow key on the keyboard a few times.

5. **Press the Esc key.**

   This action returns you to normal Windows mode from taskbar-resize mode.

Your taskbar should now be visible.

"I Can't Find Word!"

Sometimes Word takes a vacation. Where did it go? It all depends on how you lost it.

If you just started your computer, started Windows, and can't find Word, you have a few options. The first is to press Ctrl+Esc to pop up the Start thing's menu. Then look for Word, which should be right on the main Programs menu. If not, try looking in a Word or WinWord submenu. Chances are, if Word was there yesterday, it should be there today.

If you were just using Word and now . . . it's gone! . . . several things may have happened. Most commonly, you probably switched away from Word by pressing Alt+Esc or Alt+Tab. To get back into Word, look for Word's button on the taskbar, as shown in Figure 32-1. When you find the button, click it to return to Word.

Figure 32-1: Word lurks on the taskbar.

If you still can't find Word, or the taskbar has more buttons on it than the clown parade at the circus, take these steps:

1. **Press Alt+Tab.**

   Press and hold the Alt key, and then tap the Tab key. Release both keys. This action switches you to the next program running in Windows.

2. **If you found Word, you're done!**
3. **Keep repeating Steps 1 and 2.**

   Hopefully, you'll eventually find Word.

- If none of these steps works, you probably accidentally quit Word, which has been known to happen in the easy-to-use (and goof-up) Windows environment. Just restart Word as discussed in Chapter 1.
- Word does not self-destruct. If you used your computer and Word yesterday, Word is still on your computer today. It just may be hidden or out of reach. Under no circumstances should you reinstall Word unless your guru directs you to do so.

- If all else fails, check your wallet for missing credit cards and then call the airlines. Remember, even in the summer months, Word can find great skiing bargains south of the equator.

"I Lost My Files!"

Sometimes Windows has a hard time bolting files down on a disk. Because the disk is constantly spinning, I assume that centrifugal force flings the files outward, plastering them to the inside walls of your disk drive like gum under a school desk. That's the mental picture I get. Whatever the case, you can find a lost file quite easily. Doing so just takes time — a putty knife is optional.

If you're in Word, finding files can be done with the handy Find File command. Chapter 20 covers this feature in detail in the section "Finding Files in Word."

If the Find File command doesn't help you locate your file, you need to use the Windows File Finder program. Follow these steps:

1. **Activate the File Finder.**

   The File Finder is located on the Start thing's main menu. Click the Start button or press Ctrl+Esc. Then choose Find⇨Files or Folders. The Find: All Files dialog box appears, looking a lot like Figure 32-2.

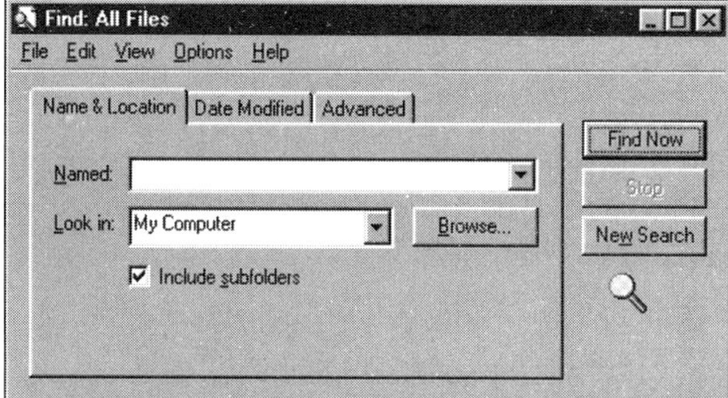

Figure 32-2: The Find: All Files dialog box.

2. **Select My Computer from the Look in drop-down list box.**

   Click the down-arrow by the Look in box and choose My Computer from the list. Doing so directs Windows to look all over your computer, in every disk drive, on every hill, in every mountain and village, for the file in question.

3. **Make sure that a check mark is in the Include subfolders box.**

   Never mind the reason, just do it.

4. **Click the mouse in the Named box.**

   Type some semblance of the file's name. For example:

   ```
   LETTER
   ```

   Now that's pretty dumb, but typing **LETTER** causes Windows to find every file named **LETTER** or containing the word **LETTER** all over your computer.

   You can type all or part of a filename; Windows finds the closest matches. For LETTER, Word would find everything from LETTER1 to LETTER TO THE EDITOR to LETTERHEAD.

5. **Click Find Now.**

   Windows busily looks everywhere for your file. An entertaining magnifying glass icon amuses you while you wait.

6. **Eventually (and hopefully), files are found.**

   Windows lists its results in a new hangy-on thing at the bottom of the Find: Files named letter dialog box (see Figure 32-3). Scroll through the list to hunt down the file you're looking for.

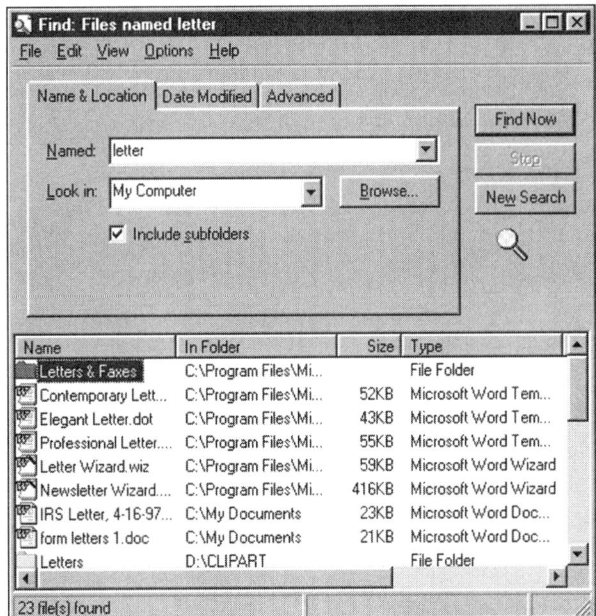

Figure 32-3: The results of a successful search.

If no matching file can be found, you see the message `0file(s) found` appear in the bottom of the Find: Files named letter dialog box. Try again using another name (or check to see if the file was deleted; see the section "Oops! I Deleted My Document!" later in this chapter).

7. **To begin editing the file in Word, double-click its name.**

   This opens the file, starting Word and loading the document for editing.

- If you aren't sure of the characters in a filename, substitute the * (asterisk). For example, T*S would locate all files from TIPS to TABLE OF CONTENTS.
- If you double-click a found file and it doesn't open Word, what you found probably wasn't a Word document. Try again.
- All Word documents have a Word icon by their name.
- If the file isn't found, consider that you may have saved the file under a different name.
- To return to your adventures in word processing, click the Microsoft Word button on the taskbar.

"Where Did My Document Go?"

"Whoa! What's the blank screen doing there? Wasn't I already five pages into this report on human fungus?"

Never fear, documents slide away. Try moving the cursor up and down a few pages: Press the PgUp or PgDn keys. What may have happened is that the next page in your document is blank, and you're only seeing the blank part on your screen. Fiddling with the cursor keys should get you re-oriented.

Another trick: Look in the Window menu to see whether you accidentally switched windows.

Finally, as a last resort, press Ctrl+Z just in case you deleted everything.

"Where Am I Now?"

If the keys appear to be too close together, or your fingers suddenly swell, you may find yourself accidentally pressing the wrong cursor keys and, lo, you're somewhere else in your document. But where?

Rather than use your brain to figure things out, press Shift+F5. Shift+F5 is the Go Back command, and pressing it moves you to the previous cursor position and resets your document as you remember it.

"It's Not Printing!"

Golly, the printer can be a dopey device. You tell Word to print, and the printer just sits there — deaf as a post! "Doe, dee, doe," it says. "Aren't you glad you paid twice as much money for a laser printer? Yuk! Yuk! Yuk!"

Believe it or not, the printer is not being stupid. Now stop banging your head on the table; it's not you either. Some connections are probably just loose. Check the printer's first. Make sure that the printer is on. Make sure that it is online. You then need to check for paper to print on. Then confirm that the printer cable is still connected. Only after these steps should you phone the local computer store about free pickup of loony bin merchandise. (It does happen.)

- If a large picture or drawing has been inserted into your document, it will make the computer and printer think harder before the printer starts to print. Have patience.
- Do not try printing again; don't try pressing harder on the keys. When the printer doesn't work, it doesn't work. Fixing this problem requires more attention than telepathy.
- If you keep pressing the Print command, each print order just keeps stacking up one behind the other and when you do finally get the printer to respond, it will spend the next 72 hours printing out your report on the mating habits of Monarch butterflies. You really don't want that, do you?
- Refer to Chapter 9 for additional information about printing.

- Make sure that the computer and printer are off — and unplugged — before you plug in a printer cable.
- The printer probably needs to be connected to the computer before the two are simultaneously turned on so that they can *recognize* each other.

"Oops! I Deleted My Document!"

Deleting files is necessary, just like stepping on cockroaches. But what if you found out a cockroach was really a reincarnation of your Aunt Mildred? Wouldn't you want her back? The same thing holds true with files. Sometimes you may accidentally delete a file. If you do, follow these steps to reincarnate your file:

1. **Minimize everything.**

   You need to shrink down all the windows on the desktop so that you can see the desktop.

The easiest way to minimize everything is to right-click the mouse on the taskbar, preferably a blank part of the taskbar (and if you can't find a blank part, right-click the far right side of the taskbar, where the time is displayed). Choose Minimize All Windows from the shortcut menu that pops up.

2. **Open the Recycle Bin icon.**

The Recycle Bin contains all the files you've recently deleted because, sneaky-sneaky, Windows doesn't delete anything. Just like a cat prowling for a fish bone, you're about to dig through Windows' own dumpster to look for your lunch, er, lost file.

Open the Recycle Bin by double-clicking it with the mouse. Doing so displays the Recycle Bin window, which looks like any other old My Computer window.

3. **Click the Date Deleted heading.**

Doing so sorts all the files in the order they were deleted, most recently deleted first. (If it doesn't, click it again.)

4. **Look for your file in the list.**

5. **When you find your file, click it once to highlight it.**

This selects the file.

6. **Choose File⇨Restore**

Ahhh! Ahhh! (Song of angels rejoicing.) Your file is restored, put right back on disk, and in its old, comfy folder, just as it was before you accidentally murdered it.

7. **Close the Recycle Bin window.**

Click its X Close button.

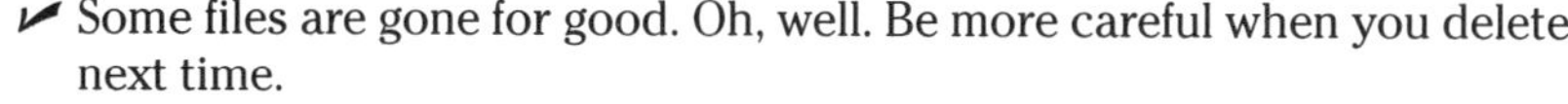

- Some files are gone for good. Oh, well. Be more careful when you delete next time.
- You cannot use the Undelete command on a network drive. Contact your network guru and explain the problem. Try not to refer to anything as "dumb" or "asinine."

Part VII

The Part of Tens

"THAT'S RIGHT, MS. BINGAMAN, HE'S COLLECTING A ROYALTY FROM EVERYONE ON EARTH, AND THERE'S NOTHING WE CAN DO ABOUT IT."

In this part . . .

Don't you just love trivia? And what's the best type of trivia? Lists! For example, "Ten ways to start living healthy," or "Ten tools you should always have in your home," or "Ten other things to blame the smell on when you know darn well what it is." This book deals with Word, so this part of the book is devoted to interesting lists of ten about Word.

Most of the chapters in this part contain ten items. Some chapters contain more, others contain less. After all, if I were as thorough as I could be in Chapter 36, "Ten Features You Don't Use but Paid For Anyway," this book would be as fat as those other books on Word.

Chapter 33

The Ten Commandments of Word

In This Chapter

- Thou shalt not use spaces.
- Thou shalt not press Enter at the end of each line.
- Thou shalt not neglect thy keyboard.
- Thou shalt not reset or turn off thine PC until thou quittest Word and Windows.
- Thou shalt not manually number thy pages.
- Thou shalt not use the Enter key to start a new page.
- Thou shalt not quit without saving first.
- Thou shalt not press OK too quickly.
- Thou shalt not forget to turn on thy printer.
- Thou shalt not forget to back up thy work.

When Mel Brooks played Moses in *History of the World,* he walked reverently down the mountain holding three tablets. "I thank you, Lord, for these, thy 15 commandments," he said, just before he broke one of the tablets. "Make that ten."

This chapter contains the ten (not 15) commandments of Word. It's a bunch of do's and don'ts, most of which are covered elsewhere in this book, especially way back in Part I (the contents of which have probably spilled out of your left ear by now — so listen closely to the recap).

I. Thou shalt not use spaces.

Generally speaking, you should never find more than one space anywhere in a Word document. Yeah, I know, most of us former touch-typists typed two spaces at the end of a sentence. With a word processor, that's unnecessary, so wean yourself from the habit.

Any time you have more than one space in a row in your document, you should probably be using the Tab key instead. Use the spacebar to separate words and to end a sentence. If you align lists of information, use the Tab key. If you want to organize information into rows and columns, use the Table command (see Chapter 14).

II. Thou shalt not press Enter at the end of each line.

Word automatically wraps your text down to the next line as you approach the right margin. You have no need to press Enter, except when want you to start a new paragraph. (Of course, if your paragraph is only a line long, that's okay.)

III. Thou shalt not neglect thy keyboard.

Word is Windows, and Windows is mousy. You can get a lot done with the mouse, but some things are faster with the keyboard. For example, I routinely switch documents with Ctrl+F6. And stabbing the Ctrl+S key to quickly save a document or Ctrl+P to print works better than fumbling for the mouse. You don't have to learn all the keyboard commands, but knowing those few outlined in this book helps a lot.

At various spots throughout this book (and in Word), I show you places to assign shortcut keys to certain Word commands or functions, such as assigning a shortcut key to a style (Chapter 15) or an oddball character (Chapter 26). Use them!

IV. Thou shalt not reset or turn off thy PC until thou quittest Word and Windows.

Always exit properly from Word and especially from Windows. Only shut off or reset your computer when you see the "It's now okey dokey to turn off this PC" type of prompt on-screen — never when you're running Word or have Windows active. Believeth me, if ye do, ye are asking for mucho trouble, yea, verily, woe.

V. Thou shalt not manually number thy pages.

Word has an automatic page numbering command. Refer to Chapter 13 in the section "Where to stick the page number?"

VI. Thou shalt not use the Enter key to start a new page.

Sure, it works: Press the Enter key a couple of dozen times, and you are on a new page. But that's not the proper way, and you mess up your new page if you go back and re-edit text. Besides, pressing Ctrl+Enter is quicker. Doing so inserts a *hard page break* into your document. Refer to Chapter 13, in the section "Starting a new page (a "hard page" break)," for the details.

VII. Thou shalt not quit without saving first.

Save your document to disk before you quit. Shift+F12 is the key combo to remember. Or Ctrl+S is the one you don't even have to remember because it's so sensible. If only all of life — no, forget life — if only all of Word were so sensible.

VIII. Thou shalt not click OK too quickly.

Word has many Yes/No/OK-type questions. If you click OK without thinking about it (or press Enter accidentally), you could be deleting text, deleting files, or performing a bad Replace operation without knowing it. Always read your screen before you click OK.

Some dialog boxes have a Close button instead of OK. These buttons are typically used when you make some choice or reset some option, but you don't want to continue with the command. For example, you can change printers in the Print dialog box and then click the Close button to continue without printing.

IX. Thou shalt not forget to turn on thy printer.

The biggest printing problem anyone has is telling Word to print something when the printer isn't on. Verify that your printer is on, healthy, and ready to print before you tell Word to print something.

X. Thou shalt not forget to back up thy work.

Keeping emergency copies of your important documents is vital. Computers are shaky houses of cards, which can collapse at any sneeze or hiccup. Always make a safety copy of your files at the end of the day or as you work.

Chapter 34
Ten Cool Tricks

In This Chapter

- Adding an envelope button to the standard toolbar
- Bullets and numbering
- The AutoSummarize command
- Draft view
- Select all
- Inserting the date
- Sorting
- Automatic saves
- Fast saves
- Inserting cool characters

Determining what's a cool trick (and what's not) is purely subjective. I'm sure that people who formerly numbered their pages manually think Word's Page Numbers command is a cool trick. I think AutoCorrect is a great trick. And I'm certain some two-fingered typist out there thinks the on-the-fly spell checker is keen. Now if the boys and girls in the Word labs could only come up with a handy tool that lets you take back something you said aloud, we'd all truly be blessed.

This chapter explains some of the neater Word tricks — mostly obscure stuff that I may not have mentioned elsewhere in this book. Some are simple and straightforward; some take a little longer for the human mind to grasp.

Adding an Envelope Button to the Standard Toolbar

Here's something really nerdy you can try: adding an Envelope button to the Standard toolbar. This task isn't something you'll be doing every day in Word, but if you print many envelopes, an Envelope button can come in handy. In fact, you can use these steps to add just about any special command to the Standard toolbar.

Here are the instructions — way too terse for the main part of this book — for adding the envelope button to the standard toolbar:

1. **Choose Tools⇨Customize.**
2. **Click the Commands tab in the Customize dialog box.**
3. **Choose Tools from the Categories list.**

   Click it once with your mouse to select it. This displays commands found in the Tools menu over in the Commands list side of the dialog box.
4. **Locate the Envelopes and Labels command from the Commands list.**

5. **Drag the Envelope icon from the Commands list and drop it onto the Standard toolbar.**

   The mouse changes to a weird plus-insertion thing that tells you approximately where the Envelope button will be "dropped" onto the toolbar. I put mine between the Print and Print Preview buttons on the left side.
6. **Click Close.**

   You're done.

Word may ask if you want to save the changes to the NORMAL.DOT file when you quit Word. Click Yes or OK to make that change.

You can add any command to the toolbar. Just choose the proper menu and command item from the preceding Steps 3 and 4.

By the way, with the Customize dialog box open, you can move any button around on the toolbar by using your mouse. To remove a button from the toolbar, just drag it down into the writing part of Word's window, and it's gone.

Bullets and Numbering

Often, you need to drive home several points, and nothing brings that home like putting bullets in your text. No, these aren't the lead-propelled things used to kill tourists and innocent bystanders. Bullets are typographical dingbats, like this:

- Bang!
- Bang!
- Bang!

To apply bullets to your text, highlight the paragraphs you want to shoot and choose Format⇨Bullets and Numbering. You don't need to dawdle in the dialog box; just double-click the type of bullets you want and your highlighted text is all shot up, nice and neat. (You can also click the Bulleted List button on the Formatting toolbar.)

You can also apply numbers to your paragraphs. When you see the Bullets and Numbering dialog box, click the Numbered tab to bring that panel forward and then click OK. (Or click the Numbered List button on the Formatting toolbar.)

AutoSummarize

In the category of "how the heck did they do that?" comes the AutoSummarize tool. Just like buying those prehighlighted used text books in college, this tool takes any document and immediately fishes out all the relevant points, highlighting them on the screen. I have no idea how this tool works, but it's pretty keen — for Word, that is.

To AutoSummarize your document, choose the Tools⇨AutoSummarize command. In a few minutes (longer if the computer is unplugged), the AutoSummarize dialog box appears. Click OK. (You can peruse the options in the AutoSummarize dialog box on your own, if you like; clicking the OK button generally does what you want it to do.)

Splat! Your document then appears on the screen with relevant parts highlighted in yellow. Also visible is an AutoSummarize floating palette, which I have yet to figure out.

To return to normal editing mode, click the Close button on the AutoSummarize palette. Your document returns to normal.

No, it's the AutoSummarize tool that makes it bright and sunny outside.

Draft View

No. That says *Draft View,* not *daft* view. Some people . . .

Word demands a lot of its owner. If you have a file with many graphics or a variety of different fonts, a slower computer can take forever to display a page of text. You can avoid this delay by switching on the ugly Draft view for your document:

1. **Choose Tools⇨Options.**
2. **Locate the View panel and bring it forward.**
3. **Put a check mark in the Draft Font box, in the upper-left corner of the panel.**
4. **Click OK.**

There is a problem here, however. Because no graphics appear and because you can't see the different fonts, you may as well be using WordPerfect 5.1. Yech! Buy more memory; buy a better machine; sell your dog; anything but that!

Repeat the preceding steps to remove the check mark and rid yourself of Draft view. (But keep in mind that Draft view does pep things up on slower computers.)

Draft view works only from Normal view. This option is not available from Page Layout view. Also, you must show proper ID before ordering a Draft view in some parts of Wyoming.

Select All

There are times when you will want to block the whole shooting match; highlight everything from top to bottom, beginning to end; select the entire document. When you want to do so, click the mouse three times in your document's left margin. Click, Click, Zowie! There it is.

Oh, and you can hold down the Ctrl key and press the 5 key on the number keypad. Zap, Zowie! There you go.

Oh, and you also can press F8 (the Extended Text key) five times. Zap, Zap, Zap, Zap, Zowie! There you go again.

Oh, and the Edit⇨Select All command does the same thing. Press Ctrl+A. Zowie!

Inserting the Date

Word's date command is named Date and Time and hangs under the Insert menu. Selecting this option displays a dialog box full of date and time formats, one of which you're bound to favor. Click OK to insert the current date, time, or both.

Sorting

Sorting is one of Word's better tricks. Once you understand it, you go looking for places to use it. You can use the Sorting command to arrange text alphabetically or numerically. You can sort paragraphs, table rows, and columns in cell tables and tables created by using tabs.

Always save your document before sorting.

Sorting is not that difficult; all you have to do is save your document before sorting, highlight the stuff you want to sort — after you save your document first — and then select the text you want to sort. Save again. Then choose Table⇨Sort. Oh, did I mention that you first should save your file? Then mess around in the dialog box and decide how you want the information in that file you saved to be sorted, though clicking OK usually sorts in alphabetical order.

Why all this concern with safety? Well, sorting takes a bunch of memory, and the machine could hang or crash. Or you may just decide that you don't like the way the sorted document looks a split second after you hit the spacebar or type a letter — no more Undo command. You have to go back to square one.

Automatic Save

When the Auto Save feature is active, your document is periodically saved to disk. This isn't the same as pressing Ctrl+S to save your document. Instead, Word makes a secret backup copy every so often. In the event of a crash, you can recover your work from the backup copy — even if you never saved the document to disk.

To turn on Auto Save, choose Tools⇨Options. Click the Save tab to bring that panel up front. Click the Save AutoRecover info box to put a check mark in that box if one isn't already in place. Then enter the backup interval in the minutes text box. For example, I type **10** to have Word back up my documents every ten minutes. If the power is unstable at your home or office, enter **5**, **3**, **2**, or even **1** minute as the backup interval. Press Enter to return to your document.

With Automatic Save, you won't recover all your document in case of a mishap, but you get most of it back.

Fast Saves

Fast Saves is one of those ideas that sounds real good . . . until you use it. The idea is to avoid having to save everything every time. "Why not just save the changes? This option makes things go oh so much faster," the folks at Microsoft said. "Because," retorted a Word Dummy, "you can't give a Fast-Saved file to other people and expect them to be able to read it on their computers."

If Word only saves your changes to disk, what's someone else going to make of such a file? What if Tolstoy only changed a character's name in Chapter 43? He would have turned in a disk to his publisher with a Chapter 43 file that contained only the single word *Ludmilla*. That just doesn't work.

My advice is to disable Fast Saves. Choose Tools⇨Options. Then click the Save panel by clicking its tab. If the Allow fast saves box is checked, click it. Make it empty. Click OK to return your document. Heck, saving is something the computer can *take time* with, as far as I'm concerned.

Cool Characters

You can use the Insert⇨Symbol command to stick odd and wonderful characters into your document. Quite a few Windows fonts have a few weird and wonderful characters in them. The Symbol font is full of neat stuff; the Wingdings font has all sorts of fun doodads; even the normal font, Times New Roman, has several cool characters in it.

You can insert any of these funky characters into your document at your whim. Simply put the toothpick cursor where you want the symbol to appear, choose Insert⇨Symbol, point at the cool character you want inserted, and click your mouse.

Refer to Chapter 26 for more information.

Chapter 35

Ten Weird Things You Probably Don't Know About

In This Chapter

- Paste Special
- The Style Gallery
- The Language command
- The Customize command
- Using the Options dialog box
- Inserting fields
- WordPerfect Help
- Mousy shortcuts
- Constructing a Master Document
- The unbreakable space and hyphen characters

Welcome to the bizarre. No one could say that better than Rod Serling. If good old Rod were still with us, I'm certain he'd love using Word to help him concoct more wonderful and, yes, bizarre stories. He'd probably enjoy using the strange and macabre features discussed in this chapter. No, none of this is secret. None of it is cool. It's all weird, strange, not-really-necessary, and somewhat bizarre.

Paste Special

Paste is paste, right? Well, not according to Windows. You can't just paste anything anymore. I mean, it's so, well, *kindergarten*. To help assist you with more daunting paste tactics, the folks at Microsoft have come up with the Edit⇨Paste Special command. Choosing it brings up a Paste Special dialog box, which enables you to paste something into your document in several ways.

The paste methods all depend on what you just copied. You can paste in text as "Unformatted text," which I do all the time because I don't like copying stinky formatting between documents. You can also experiment with *linking* items, which is the *OLE* stuff Microsoft is so big on with Windows. Strange stuff. Worthy of playing with, but definitely too weird to go anywhere but in this chapter.

The Style Gallery

The Style Gallery is a fun place to play. Basically, the Style Gallery is a workshop where you can experiment with applying various Word styles to your document. To do so, choose Format⇨Style Gallery. A humongous Style Gallery dialog box appears, with a list of styles on the left and a preview of how they affect your document on the right. It's kind of fun to poke around with different styles and see how they tweak your work.

If the results in the Style Gallery dialog box don't impress you, consider clicking the Example button. That way you see a preview of a sample document rather than your own text.

More style madness can be found lurking in Chapter 15.

The Language Command

The Tools⇨Language⇨Set Language command menu allows you to mark a block and tag it as being written in another language, say Norwegian Bokmål. There's only one reason to do this: When Word is spell-checking and comes across a foreign word, the program uses the appropriate language's dictionary instead of attempting to decipher the word as English.

A better purpose behind the Language command is to format some text as *no proofing*. In other words, you tell Word not to spell check that text. For example, I have a style I use for typing instructions to my editor or to the production department. That style has the Language set to no proofing; otherwise, Word would stop and try to spell check my rude comments and, really, why would I want to bother myself with that nonsense?

- Catalan is spoken in Catalonia. I wonder how many Word users live there?
- No, dude, there is no Surfer language. Bummer.

The Customize Command

The Tools⇨Customize command is an odd place to not only waste mountains of time but also feel that you have ultimate control over Word's fate. This command tears at the heart of the very fabric that is Word. By using the various controls in the Customize dialog box, you can actually change the way Word looks — for the better, for good.

The three panels in the Customize dialog box let you change Word's toolbars, commands, and general options. Hey, this stuff is real, and it's not for the faint of heart. You can build your own toolbar, add or remove menu items, and assign your own keyboard shortcuts. The whole program is up for grabs! I don't recommend messing with anything here. Wait a few months. Get comfy with Word. Then slash away and make the program your own!

Using the Options Dialog Box

Choosing the Tools⇨Options command accesses the Options dialog box. What you get in this dialog box is ten — count 'em, ten — panels of various things Word does. The settings in the panels control how Word behaves.

The Options dialog box doesn't really contain any hints or secrets. In fact, you've probably been here a few times if you clicked any Options buttons in the various Word dialog boxes — no big deal, just weird.

Inserting Fields

A field looks like text in your document. It smells like text. And it prints like text. But it's not text. Instead, it's a special marker — a fill-in-the-blanks thing that Word knows to complete at some later time. For example, typing the date in your document just slaps some words on the page. But sticking a date *field* in your document means that the field always displays the current date, no matter what the current date is.

You insert fields into your document by using the Insert⇨Field command. The Field dialog box displays a list of field categories and then individual types of fields. For example, the Date and Time category lists several types of date fields: the date the document was created, saved to disk, printed, the current date, and so on. An Options button allows you to further customize the field.

When you select them, fields appear like selected text but with a hazy gray background. Unlike real text, you must select and delete the entire field all at once. (Remember, fields are not text.)

WordPerfect Help

I suppose that I could go on and on about how the title of this section wastes a perfectly good word; anyone who uses WordPerfect needs help as a matter of definition. Anyway, the folks at Microsoft seem to think that WordPerfect users can be saved from the multicolored loony bin.

If you are a born-again Word convert from WordPerfect, you can find a special section of Word designed just to unconfuse you and put you back on the path of productive and sane word processing. Choose Help⇨WordPerfect Help to find out how the big boys do it. Doing so lets you grow accustomed to Word's commands as your contorted WordPerfect function key fingers discover how to grow straight again.

Mousy Shortcuts

Here are some interesting things you can do with the mouse:

- Double-click any toolbar to change it into a floating palette of tools. You can always double-click the floating palette's title to switch it back into a toolbar.
- Double-click the ruler to see the Page Setup dialog box.
- Double-click *in* the ruler to see the Tabs dialog box.
- Click the right mouse button over your document to see a quick pop-up menu with several editing and formatting commands on it.
- Click the right mouse button over a toolbar to display the Toolbars menu.
- Double-click the mouse on the three-letter acronyms in boxes on the Status bar to switch those items on or off.
- Double-click elsewhere on the status bar to bring up the Go To dialog box.

Constructing a Master Document

How big should your document be? Technically speaking, Word can handle a document probably as big as you could write it. Practically speaking, you don't want things to get too big. Word starts acting weirder than normal with big documents.

But how big is big? Here's my advice:

Keep your documents at chapter size.

Each chapter in this book is a document unto itself. This chapter is called CHAPTER 35 on disk. That's the way most writers work — a chapter is a document. The only drawback to this method is that it makes printing everything a pain. And if you dare to take advantage of Word's indexing and table of contents commands (I don't), they just don't work in separate documents.

The solution to the problem is to create what Word calls a Master Document. That's just another Word document, but it contains information about other documents and kind of links them all together. You still work with each chapter as its own document. But the whole shooting match can be printed, indexed, given a table-of-contents, and otherwise manipulated through the Master Document.

Yes, the concept is novel. Unfortunately, wrestling with it in Word is not fun.

To create a Master Document, start with a new document in Word. Choose File⇨New. Then choose View⇨Master Document. This changes the display and adds the Outline/Master Document toolbar. The buttons on the far right of the toolbar are used to add documents to the Master Document. (Hover the mouse over a button to see its function balloon display.)

Alas, that's all the help I can give you here; working with a Master Document involves a full tutorial.

The Unbreakables

The two weird keys on your keyboard are the spacebar and the hyphen. Both keys produce characters on the screen, but not normal characters. The space. What is that? Space! Outer space? And the hyphen isn't really a character at all. The hyphen is used to split text — to hyphenate words — between two lines. Indeed, both the space and the hyphen *break* your text between two lines. This result doesn't create a problem — unless you don't want the line to break in two.

There are times when you want to be sure that a space was not interrupted by something as mundane as the end of a line. For example, suppose that you work for the firm of Bandini, Lambert, and Locke and, by golly, Mr. Locke doesn't like to be left on a line by himself. If so, insert a nonbreaking (*hard*) space between each name to make sure that they're always together.

To prevent the space character from breaking a line, press Ctrl+Shift+spacebar.

The hyphen key, which also is the minus key, works to hyphenate a long word at the end of a line. But, sometimes, you may not want the hyphen to split a word. For example, you may not want a phone number split between two lines. Inserting a hard hyphen prevents text from splitting between two lines.

To prevent the hyphen character from breaking a line, press Ctrl+Shift+- (hyphen).

A scary weird thing you should avoid at all costs

Over the years of using Word, I've discovered one of the most annoying commands in the history of word processing. It's the terrifying menu item remover, something you may stumble over accidentally someday. (I hope you don't.)

If you press Ctrl+Alt+- (hyphen) in Word, the mouse pointer changes to a thick, horizontal line. That line is the menu item removal cursor. Just choose any menu item and — thwoop! — it's gone, deleted, zapped, dead. And there's no way to get that menu item back, either. Deadly! Scary! Not even Rod Serling could dream up something that bizarre.

If you do accidentally press Ctrl+Alt+-, quickly press the Esc key to cancel that mode. Yikes! What kind of sick mind thought up that trick, huh?

Chapter 36

Ten Features You Don't Use but Paid For Anyway

In This Chapter

- Drawing a table
- Table of contents
- Hyphenation
- Index
- Cross-reference
- Math
- Macros
- The Address Book
- Send stuff
- Random statistics

Word comes with many more features than you can ever use. Word definitely offers more than those listed here and probably several dozen that I've never heard of. Some people writing those massive complete Word tomes have been known to disappear into a room and not emerge for months — or years! Indeed, I seriously doubt if anyone who knows everything about Word has kept their sanity.

This chapter lists ten of the more interesting features that you bought when you paid for Word. (I'm not even bothering to mention some of the things that Windows lets you do with Word, such as embed sounds and other cute, but useless, things.) You probably didn't know that these goodies existed. That's okay — they're a bit technical to work with. This chapter covers each one briefly, but don't expect to find out how to use any of the paid-for-but-forgotten features.

Drawing a table (the new-fangled way)

Chapter 14 tells you everything you need to know about tables. But it doesn't tell you how to use the new Table Drawing tool. Sure, you might find this method of creating a table easier, but to me it's very redundant, which is to say, overly repetitive.

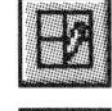

Click the Tables and Borders button on the standard toolbar and a floating palette doojobbie appears. If you then click on the Table Drawing tool, you can sketch out a nifty table in your document.

The table you create with the Table Drawing tool has only one cell (reminiscent of the old "frame" feature in Word). To create more cells, click the Split Cells button then enter the new number of rows and columns in the Split Cells dialog box.

Honestly, I see no advantage to this method over the method described in Chapter 14. This feature earns a big Why Bother award from the Word For Windows For Dummies Hall of Infamy.

Table of contents

It used to be that figuring out a table of contents could make a grown human of the masculine persuasion cry. (The task has never had the same effect on my wife, but, after childbirth, I guess not much is daunting.) Who, in their right mind, would want to go to the front of a document, type all those names, and then all of those dots, and then figure out what page what should be on? (And there's not even a coach standing by reminding you to breathe.)

Word, man, that's who! If you have been careful with your styles (see Chapter 15 to find out about styles), inserting a table of contents is a sure bet. Well, almost. Choose Insert⇨Index and Tables and then click on the Table of Contents tab. Word looks through your entire document and takes everything that has been tagged with a style of Heading (followed by some number), determines what page it is on, and builds the table of contents for you.

Sounds like fun? Yeah, but it's complex to set up. If you didn't follow the proper steps when you created your document, you may as well do it the old-fashioned way, weeping bitterly and all that.

Hyphenation

Hyphenation is an automatic feature that splits long words at the end of a line to make the text fit better on the page. Most people leave it off because hyphenation tends to slow down the pace at which people read. However, if you want to hyphenate a document, choose Tools⇨Language⇨Hyphenation. Continuously jab the F1 key when you need Help.

Index

This feature is interesting but complicated to use. The Insert⇨Index and Tables command (click the Index tab) marks a spot in a document to include in an index. For example, you can choose that command to mark a word and tag it for inclusion as an index entry. Then, using other commands too complicated to mention here, you can have Word generate an automatic index at the end of the document. This feature is a handy thing to have, but it takes time to understand, and you often don't need a full index for a five-page letter to Mom.

Cross-reference

The Insert⇨Cross-reference command allows you to insert a "Refer to Chapter 99, Section Z" type of thing into your document. This feature works because you've taken the Krell brain booster and now have an IQ that can only be expressed in scientific notation. Fortunately, you may have also used the Heading style to mark text in your document that you want to cross-reference. Using the Heading style means that the Insert⇨Cross-reference command works and sticks a "Refer to Chapter 99, Section Z" type of thing in your document — complete with an updated reference to that page should you overhaul your document.

Math

Did it ever dawn upon the Word people that math and English are two separate subjects for a reason? The math and English parts of the SAT scores are separate. Math and English are always taught as separate courses. So who needs a math function in a word processor? I don't know. Even if you did, it's still easier to calculate the numbers by using your desk calculator and typing them manually.

To use the Math command, you must first place your data in a table. Then highlight the row or column that you want computed. Choose Table⇨Formula. Word suggests a formula type, or you can tell Word what you want done with the numbers. On second thought, I guess this woulda been kinda handy during algebra class. Anyway, Word puts the answer wherever you left the insertion pointer.

Macros

A *macro* is a little program that someone has written to do some neat thing in Word. A whole special programming language is devoted to macros; therefore, writing macros is a job for the truly advanced or insane.

A macro is basically a shortcut. You can create a macro that automatically records something in your document, a set of commands, or anything that you normally have to repeat over and over. Macros automate the process. In Word, macros do more and comprise an actual programming language you can use to extend Word's abilities. This is heady, technical stuff, getting harder to grok with each version of Word. In fact, detailed books are devoted to the subject. If your name is Bill Gates, I'd buy one to check it out.

Address Book

Lurking around various Word dialog boxes, you find a cutesy little button with a drop-down arrow by it. Lo, it's the Address Book button, containing a link to your e-mail address book, the one you never bothered setting up when Windows insisted on installing its own mail system.

Mail is a bother. I told Windows not to install it on my PC and it did anyway. So when I press the Address Book button, my computer instantly, and most efficiently, wastes about four minutes of my time (during which I stew and repeatedly press the Cancel button). Don't bother with this button unless you really have an address book and really know how it works.

Various Send To commands

Lurking in the File menu is the curious Send To submenu, where you find interesting e-mail and faxing commands: Supposedly something there lets you use Word as your e-mail editor and then instantly send your document to someone else on your network or on the Internet. Sounds great, works terribly. Ditto for the Fax command, which is so painful it makes working a digital thermostat seem like fun.

Fear has prevented me from ever choosing an option in the File⇨Send To submenu. I haven't any idea what the things in there do, nor do I want to know.

Random statistics

This feature is something that you never use because it is a very unpopular thing. Besides that, it is a royal pain in the digit. Word tracks all sorts of statistics about your document. To see them, choose File⇨Properties. Yoikles! That's just more information than I care to know about at any given time. Silly stuff.

Chapter 37

Ten Shortcut Keys Worth Remembering

In This Chapter

- Strange, WordPerfect-esque function keys
- The document keys: New, Open, Save, Print
- The kindergarten keys: Cut, Copy, Paste
- The Undo-Redo keys
- Text formatting keys
- Font formatting keys
- Francis Scott Keys
- Paragraph formatting keys

This is sacrilege! You are forbidden — *forbidden* — to use the keyboard in Windows! Shame on you! Seriously, you can do lots of interesting things with the keyboard, things that can be done quite rapidly and without breaking off any nails. Although Word has a whole armada of key combinations, only a handful are worth knowing. This chapter contains the best, a shade more than ten, but those I feel you'll grow fond of as time passes.

Besides, the guy who invented the mouse doesn't even profit from it. He's an academic, so it's the intellectual property (or whatever that lame excuse is called) of Stanford University. But now he's on late-night TV where he gets to tell people how for 20 years people thought the mouse was an impractical and eccentric tool that would never take off for real computer use. He encourages the ingenious among us to invent and not be discouraged. He says he doesn't even mind not profiting from the mouse because his whole point was to fill a need in the computer industry — because the creation is the thing. Kinda gives you warm fuzzies, huh?

Strange, WordPerfect-esque Function Keys

Thank goodness this program isn't WordPerfect. Those folks have lots of function keys, all of them required just to work the program. In Word, using the function keys is optional . . . so why bother? Actually, there are five function keys that you may want to become friendly with. No handy mnemonic here. You just have to get used to them; fortunately you only have to remember five of them.

F1, the Office Assistant key

In any Windows program, pressing F1 displays helpful information. In Word, the F1 key summons your office assistant which, they suppose, is better than help. Whatever. At least the computer doesn't reach out and touch you with electricity.

Shift+F3, the Switch Case key

To change the case of your text between all caps, lowercase, and mixed case, mark the text as a block and then press Shift+F3 until the text looks the way you like.

The F4 Repeat Command key

If you're applying formatting to a number of paragraphs or various text or just doing the same command over and over, press the F4 key. This key directs Word to pull a do-over and work the same command again. A common use for this key may be pasting in symbols. If you're using the Insert⇨Symbol command to poof up your document a bit, just press F4 to repeat the insert.

The Shift+F4 Repeat Find key

Find a bit of text. Great! Want to find it again? Shift+F4 makes Word look without your having to visit the Find dialog box again.

Shift+F5, the "Take me back to where I was" key

It's easy to get lost in Word. If you just pressed Ctrl+End for no apparent reason and suddenly find yourself at the end of your document, press Shift+F5 to get back to where you once were. This key is a big time-saver.

The Document Keys

You can do four things with documents, and you can use four handy — and mnemonic! — key combinations to do them:

Ctrl+N, New

Ctrl+O, Open

Ctrl+S, Save

Ctrl+P, Print

The only one missing here is a Close command. Don't bother with Ctrl+C; it's used to Copy text. Drat! We need a larger alphabet. The Close command is Ctrl+W, probably for "Would you please close this window?"

Save! Save! Save! Always save your document. Get in the habit of reaching up and pressing Ctrl+S often as you work.

The Kindergarten Keys: Cut, Copy, Paste

When you're working with blocks, three shortcut keys come in most handy:

Ctrl+X, Cut

Ctrl+C, Copy

Ctrl+V, Paste

To use these keys, first highlight a block of text. Then press Ctrl+X to cut the block or Ctrl+C to copy. Move the toothpick cursor to where you want the block pasted and press Ctrl+V. Refer to Chapter 6 for more information on playing with blocks.

The Undo-Redo Keys

The Ctrl+Z key is Word's Undo key. Undo will undo just about anything Word can do and undo what was done before that, too.

If you need to redo something — that is, un-undo — you can press Ctrl+Y.

Text-Formatting Shortcut Keys

You can use these four shortcut keys — either as you type or on a marked block of text — to affect that text's character formatting:

Ctrl+B, Bold

Ctrl+I, Italics

Ctrl+U, Underline

Ctrl+spacebar, Normal

Type Ctrl+B when you want unbolded text made bold. Or, if the text is already bold and you mark it as a block, Ctrl+B unbolds the block. The same holds true with Ctrl+I (italics).

The Ctrl+spacebar key returns text to normal. So if you mark a block of text that has all sorts of crazy, mixed-up formatting, press Ctrl+spacebar for an instant sea of sanity. Pressing Ctrl+spacebar as you're entering text can be used to instantly switch off whatever formatting you're currently using.

Font Formatting Keys

Forget the Font dialog box. If you have enough spare memory cells after all that alcohol in college (or from the Mail Merge chapter), you can use these key combinations to ease text formatting:

Ctrl+Shift+F, Font

Ctrl+Shift+P, Point Size

Ctrl+Shift+S, Style

Ctrl+Shift+>, Make text bigger

Ctrl+Shift+<, Make text smaller

The Ctrl+Shift+F, Ctrl+Shift+P, and Ctrl+Shift+S key combos work to highlight the list boxes on the Formatting toolbar. Type the font name, point size, or style that you want. This method of selection seems like quite a bit of work, but it can be quick if you get the hang of it.

The Ctrl+Shift+> and Ctrl+Shift+< nonsense makes no sense. But sometimes it's fun to mess with the text size of a selected block by using those key combinations. It's much more graphical than trying to mentally figure numbers in a dialog box.

Paragraph Formatting Keys

Select a paragraph as a block and then use one of the following key combinations to format it:

Ctrl+L, Left justify

Ctrl+R, Right justify

Ctrl+E, Center

Ctrl+J, Justify

Ctrl+1, Single space

Ctrl+2, Double space

Ctrl+5, 1½ space

The only oddball here is Ctrl+E to center a paragraph. Ack! Never mind. Just use the buttons on the Formatting toolbar. I actually used Ctrl+2 to double space a document the other day, which is why I'm listing it here.

Chapter 38

Ten Things Worth Remembering

In This Chapter

- Don't be afraid of your keyboard
- Have a supply of diskettes ready
- Keep printer paper, toner, and supplies handy
- Keep references handy
- Keep your files organized
- Remember the Ctrl+Z key!
- Save your document often!
- Use AutoText for often-typed stuff
- Use clever, memorable filenames and subdirectories
- Don't take it all too seriously

There's nothing like finishing a book with a few heartening words of good advice. As a Word user, you need this kind of encouragement and motivation. Word can be an unforgiving, but not necessarily evil, place to work. This book shows you that having a lot of fun with Word and still getting your work done is also possible. To help send you on your way, here are a few things worth remembering.

Don't Be Afraid of Your Keyboard

Try to avoid pressing Enter repeatedly to start a new page, using the spacebar when the Tab key will do better, or manually numbering your pages. You can use a handy Word command to do just about anything, and you'll never remember the commands if you're afraid to try them.

Have a Supply of Diskettes Ready

You need diskettes to use your computer, even if you have a hard drive! You need diskettes for backup purposes and for exchanging files with other PCs running Word, such as between home and the office.

Keep one or two boxes of diskettes available. Always buy the proper size diskette for your PC, either 5¼- or 3½-inch disks. Make sure that you buy the proper capacity as well, which is usually the high-capacity or high-density diskettes. And format those diskettes!

Keep Printer Paper, Toner, and Supplies Handy

When you buy paper, buy a box. When you buy a toner cartridge or printer ribbon, buy two or three. Also keep a good stock of pens, paper, staples, paper clips, and all the other office supplies (including diskettes) handy.

Keep References Handy

Word is a writing tool. As such, you need to be familiar with and obey the grammatical rules of your language. If that language just happens to be English, you have a big job ahead of you. Even though they're an electronic part of Word, I recommend that you keep a dictionary and a thesaurus handy. Strunk and White's *The Elements of Style* is also a great book for finding out where the apostrophes and commas go. If you lack these books, visit the reference section of your local bookstore and plan on paying about $50 to stock up on quality references.

Keep Your Files Organized

Use folders on your hard drive for storing your document files. Keep related documents together in the same subdirectory. You may need someone else's help to set up an organizational system. Refer to Chapters 18 and 20 for additional information.

Remember the Ctrl+Z Key!

The Ctrl+Z key is your undo key. If you're typing away in Word, press it to undelete any text you may have mistakenly deleted. This command works for individual letters, sentences, paragraphs, pages, and large chunks of missing text.

Save Your Document Often!

Save your document to disk as soon as you get a few meaningful words down on the screen. Then save every so often after that. Even if you're using the Auto Save feature (discussed in Chapter 34), continue to manually save your document to disk: Ctrl+S.

Use AutoText for Often-Typed Stuff

To quickly insert things that you type over and over, like your name and address, use an AutoText entry. Type your entry once and then define it as a glossary entry under the Edit menu. Then use the shortcut key to zap it in whenever you need it. See Chapter 26 for more about AutoText.

Use Clever, Memorable Filenames

A file named LETTER is certainly descriptive, but what does it tell you? A file named LETTER TO MOM is even more descriptive but still lacking some information. A file LETTER TO MOM, APRIL 23 is even better. Or if you want to be brief, try 4-23 MOM LETTER. You get the idea here: Use creative and informative filenames.

Don't Take It All Too Seriously

Computers are really about having fun. Too many people panic too quickly when they use a computer. Don't let it get to you! And please, please, don't reinstall Word to fix a minor problem. Anything that goes wrong has a solution. If the solution is not in this book, consult with your guru. Someone is bound to help you out.

Index

• A •

• B •

• C •

• D •

• G •

• H •

• I •

• K •

• N •

• O •

• Q •

• R •

• S •

• T •

IDG BOOKS WORLDWIDE BOOK REGISTRATION

We want to hear from you!

Visit **http://my2cents.dummies.com** to register this book and tell us how you liked it!

- Get entered in our monthly prize giveaway.
- Give us feedback about this book — tell us what you like best, what you like least, or maybe what you'd like to ask the author and us to change!
- Let us know any other *...For Dummies* topics that interest you.

Your feedback helps us determine what books to publish, tells us what coverage to add as we revise our books, and lets us know whether we're meeting your needs as a *...For Dummies* reader. You're our most valuable resource, and what you have to say is important to us!

Not on the Web yet? It's easy to get started with *Dummies 101®: The Internet For Windows® 95* or *The Internet For Dummies®*, 4th Edition, at local retailers everywhere.

Or let us know what you think by sending us a letter at the following address:

...For Dummies Book Registration
Dummies Press
7260 Shadeland Station, Suite 100
Indianapolis, IN 46256
Fax 317-596-5498